Many Paths, One Destination

Love, Peace, Compassion, Tolerance, and Understanding Through World Religions

Ram Ramakrishnan

Many Paths, One Destination: Love, Peace, Compassion, Tolerance, and Understanding Through World Religions

Published by Wheatmark®
610 East Delano Street, Suite 104
Tucson, Arizona 85705 U.S.A.
www.wheatmark.com

International Standard Book Number: 978-1-60494-148-7
Library of Congress Control Number: 2008931707

"No one can understand mankind without understanding the faiths of humanity. Sometimes naïve, sometimes penetratingly noble, sometimes crude, sometimes subtle, sometimes cruel, sometimes suffused by an overpowering gentleness and love, sometimes world-affirming, sometimes negating the world, sometimes inward-looking, sometimes universalistic and missionary minded, sometimes shallow, and often profound—religion has permeated human life since early and obscure times."

—Ninian Smart

Dedicated To

My mother, my father-in-law, Mr. Dayabhai, and Mr. Srinivasan.

With great respect, profound humility, and sincere love, I dedicate this book to my beloved mother, my loving father-in-law, and my two very good friends, Mr. Dayabhai Patel and Mr. Srinivasan. These noble souls are responsible for creating my abiding interest in religion, the scriptures, and holy places and for guiding me to the spiritual path.

As a young boy, my mother put the seed of spiritualism in my innocent and pure mind. She explained to me the need to pray, to be honest, to respect elders, and to reach out to the poor and the aged. She taught me that strong faith in God and sincere prayers would enable me to overcome all problems and achieve success in life.

After my marriage, I came to know my father-in-law. He was a Sanskrit scholar and a leading lawyer, well versed in all the Hindu scriptures. He used to deliver lectures on the Bhagavad Gita. He was such a noble, kind, and loving and compassionate soul. Two years after marriage, I fell seriously sick. I lost my job and was under treatment for several months. It was at this critical stage in my life that my father-in-law came to my rescue. He used to console me and cheer me by reading the Bhagavad Gita and explaining the meaning of the various verses. He taught me that everything in life, whether good or bad, is due to one's karma and that one should not be discouraged by temporary setbacks in life, such as illness or loss of job. The months I spent with him were the best part of my life; he opened my eyes to the power of faith and prayers.

This book of mine is the result of the suggestions made by good friends Mr. C. V. Srinivasan of Chennai, and Mr. Dayabhai Patel of Mumbai. Mr. Dayabhai Patel was an industrialist who believed in the power of prayers. He was my very good friend, spiritual guide, and "guru." We used to visit the Aurobindo Ashram in Pondicherry and spend time reading the works of Sri Aurobindo and practicing meditation. We discussed the basic teachings of various religions and the underlying unity of all religions. Mr. Dayabhai suggested that I write a book on the essence of all religions and distribute such a book to educational institutions, religious associations, old-age homes, hospitals, and the like. The idea was to propagate the central theme of all religions, namely peace, love, tolerance, compassion, and understanding. Unfortunately, Dayabhai passed away while I was writing this book, and he could not see his dream come true. I have great pleasure in dedicating this book to his loving memory.

Lastly, I am grateful to my good friend Mr. C.V. Srinivasan for his great help and encouragement in writing this book. Mr. Srinivasan lived opposite my apartment in Chennai, and we used to meet almost daily and discuss the various aspects of the Bhagavad Gita and other scriptures. Mr. Srinvasan was an erudite scholar, well versed in all the Hindu scriptures as well as in the basic teachings of other religions. Mr. Srinvasan wanted me to write a book on the essential teachings of all the major religions of the world and convey their message of peace, love, and compassion. This humble book of mine is the result of his tremendous guidance.

Contents

Foreword

It was in the late seventies that I met Mr. Ramakrishnan for the first time, even though we both had been working for the oil industry in Mumbai for several years. He was then in charge of supplies and logistics of lubricants in Burmah Shell (now Bharat Petroleum), and I was employed in a similar capacity in ESSO (now HPC). We met on numerous occasions, primarily to review and deal with some problems of the industry, often one on one and sometimes in industry meetings with representatives from other oil companies and from the Ministry of Petroleum, G.O.I. Differences of opinion and disagreements that arose during our animated discussions would promptly melt away to everyone's satisfaction. Over a period of time, Ram and I came to know each other better, and our personal relationship took a happy turn, for nobody can hold a grudge against Ram, who is such a fine gentleman, ever caring and considerate, and always gracious and pleasant.

Ram's excellent qualities seeped through his delightful book of verse that he wrote to celebrate his seventy summers, giving free rein to the feelings of his heart. Ten years later, at eighty plus, with his keen intellect, compassion, and benevolence, he has studied the various religions of the world to discover the similarity in the undercurrents of thought and teachings that run through them. We have dire need for such rational thinking, for in the world today, "the clear stream of reason has lost its way" in religious fanaticism and mindless bigotry. Ram's book will be a breath of fresh air that will restore goodwill and peace among men. No more will he have "reason to lament what man has made of man" or ask with Wilfred Owen, "Was it for this the clay grew tall?"

I am overwhelmed and profoundly touched by his request for a foreword. My family joins me in wishing him, his gracious lady, and all his children and grandchildren the very best in life, good health, good cheer, and God's bountiful blessings.

V. S. Moni

When I was asked to introduce Ram Nathan Ramakrishnan in his book, I thought it an unusual request. After all, I had met him in a doctor's office—I was the doctor and he the patient. Why would I be an appropriate person to write about this accomplished man? Then, however, I remembered our interactions over the years. He and I have talked about politics, yoga, previous jobs, people we'd met in our lives, his children and family—at the same time addressing his health care needs, which, frankly, were quite minimal due to his vegetarian diet, his practice of yoga, and his general positive outlook toward life. I noticed in Ram an ease, a spirituality, a charm that my fellow physicians in the practice commented on as well. "How come that skinny Indian guy is so happy all the time?" Well I have no specific answer other than advising to read his writing and try to derive from it what makes this man a pleasure to get to know.

Robert Salomon, MD

When Ramakrishnan, affectionately and popularly known as "RR," asked me to write an introduction to his forthcoming book, I was at my wits' end. I had no idea what subject matter was covered by his book. So, I wrote to RR requesting him to send me a brief note on his book. RR promptly sent me a comprehensive note detailing all the book's main points. Reading his note took my breath away when I noticed the Herculean task he had undertaken: highlighting the essence of all the major and minor religions of the world, as well as the lives and achievements of all the prophets and religious founders. RR also mentioned that he has taken the best from all the religions and avoided any controversial issue. I understand that RR took a few years to compile this very interesting, educational, and highly inspirational book.

I had the joy of working with Ramakrishnan in Burmah-Shell, India (owned by the Royal Dutch and Shell Petroleum Co. Ltd., London) for more than three decades. We have been very close friends for nearly forty-five years. RR was both my colleague and mentor in so many ways. He was a great admirer of Mahatma Gandhi, Nelson Mandela, Desmond Tutu, and Mother Teresa. His views on religion, politics, and family life are balanced and tempered with understanding.

Though born in a highly religious Brahmin family, RR took great interest in understanding the teachings of other religions. RR was involved and very helpful in several ways with my work of over twenty years with the Missionaries of Charity. He actively participated in the social work of several Christian and other religious organizations and also helped in raising funds for many noble and worthy causes.

Ramakrishnan's book is coming at the most opportune moment of our times, when we are witnessing a world torn apart by religious bigotry, hatred, prejudice, mayhem, and murder. May the message of peace, love, compassion, tolerance, and understanding conveyed by RR in his book be carried far and wide into every nook and corner of the world. I sincerely wish my good old friend RR success and his loving family the very best.

L. R. D. Morias

Preface

I was told that I was born during the early hours of the morning on July 12, 1926, in a village near the coastal town of Cochin, in South India. Two major incidents marked my birth, both of which greatly influenced the course of my life, my faith, my perception, my attitude, and my outlook. The first was a devastating flood on the day of my birth that stopped all traffic and communication. All activities came to a standstill. I was told that my mother developed pneumonia on the second day after my birth, and a day later, I followed suit. My grandfather had to literally swim to the doctor's house and fetch him in a boat. My mother recovered after a week, but my condition became worse. I was told that the doctor gave up all hope for my survival. When sickness strikes any Hindu home, it is the usual custom to light an oil lamp near the Hindu idols in the home and pray around the clock for the patient's speedy recovery. My mother used to tell me how she and her mother spent sleepless nights for a week, praying to God for my recovery. She said God spared my life in answer to their prayers. Till her death, my mother used to repeat again and again the story about my miraculous escape from death due to God's grace, telling me that infinite faith in God and sincere prayers can help one overcome all life's trials and tribulations. Thus, at a very young age, the seed of spiritualism was sown in my innocent and fertile mind. In the years that followed, this tiny seed grew into a mighty tree.

The second major incident was the spontaneous and sincere help from all our neighbors. Since the flood dislocated all traffic, our neighbors volunteered to procure medicines and other daily necessities. We were Hindu, but our house was surrounded by the homes of Christians and Muslims, who offered prayers for us in the local church and mosque. My grandfather used to tell me about this incredible show of love, kindness, and compassion from people who were of entirely different faiths.

The religious ideas of parents and grandparents, the place of birth, the surroundings, the community in which one lives, and one's schooling all play a vital part in molding one's character and religious belief. My grandparents and parents were very religious. My grandfather used to tell my siblings and me the stories from the Hindu epics and teach us Sanskrit prayers. My mother used to visit the local temples every day, taking us with her, and these trips gave us an insight into our traditions and religious beliefs.

Most of our neighbors were Christians and Muslims. As young children, we used to visit the village's churches and mosques and actively participate in their various festivals. In fact, all the non-Hindus used to join in all the Hindu festivals, and vice versa. There was an old and historical synagogue in Cochin that I used to visit with my Jewish friends.

The place where I was born was a standing monument to religious coexistence. Temples, churches, and mosques existed close to one another, and there was understanding, friendliness, and tolerance among people of different faiths.

As a student, I was eager to learn more about religions other than Hinduism, and I gained some knowledge of the Bible and the Qur'an. During my long career in Burmah-Shell India, I had to travel all over India, which gave me an opportunity to see various holy places. I visited Hindu holy places like Benares (now Varanasi), Hardwar, Rishikesh, Badrinath, and Kedarnath. I saw the Golden Temple of the Sikhs at Amritsar, the Jama Masjid in Delhi, the Buddhist holy place of Bodh Gaya, and the Jain temple in Calcutta, among others. Visiting all these broadened my vision and opened my heart to the eternal truth in other religions. I became deeply interested in all the world religions and the teachings of great religious leaders. The Bhagavad Gita, the jewel of India's spiritual wisdom, touched every nerve in my body, and I felt transported to a different world. Similarly, the teachings of Buddha, Mahavir, and Guru Nanak touched my heart. From my Parsi friends, I got some knowledge of Zoroaster and his teachings. My Muslim and Christian friends introduced me to the Bible and the Qur'an. I was thrilled and excited, like a boy entering Disneyland.

The steady advancement of human societies brought about many distinct changes in religion, as in all other things. As time passed, religion came to be seen as a system of belief and practice that gave meaning to or allowed acceptance of anything that transcended the natural or the known. Humans' original belief in many gods ultimately was replaced in many cultures by the belief in a Supreme Being.

As in the remote past, religion still provides answers to many timeless questions that have confronted humanity. How, why, by whom, and for what purpose was the universe created? What is the ultimate meaning of life? Why is birth inevitably followed by death? What happens to a person upon death, and does the human soul continue to exist after death? And if so, in what form? Why is there so much pain, sorrow, and suffering in this world, and why is there so much evil?

All the major religions of the world provide their followers with concrete and clearly stated ethical codes. They offer a set of moral instructions, clearly defining virtue and evil as well as what should be avoided and what is required to achieve goodness. Some of the moral imperatives are kindness, compassion, tolerance, and love towards others. All the world religions hold before man the ideal of perfection, which is termed variously as Brahman, Allah, Jesus Christ, Ahura Mazda, Tao, and so on. The religions stress moral purification and spiritual striving as the means for realizing the ideal. Even a brief survey of the essential points of the various world religions reveal this underlying unity of purpose, compassion, kindness, goodness, love, and harmony. Let us examine some of the major and minor world religions.

Let us take Hinduism. Hinduism is a way of life. All schools of Hinduism believe, in some form or other, in the Atman, the potential divinity of man; in Brahman, or the Supreme Spirit; in the ideal of self-realization; and in the path of yoga, leading to direct spiritual experience and realization of the Self. Hinduism holds the view that all religions are paths that lead to the one Eternal Truth. All souls will attain salvation in due course; world brotherhood can be based only upon the Divine Principle but not upon any personality. Hindus refer to their faith as Sanathana Dharma, which means eternal law or order.

Christianity accepts both the Old and New Testaments and emphasizes the necessity of a mediator, of Christ, the son of God.

Islam is a product of many influences, including Judaism and Christianity. It is the religion of submission to God and accepts Muhammad as the last of all prophets of God. Muhammad's living faith in God and in his own mission filled his followers with a tremendous vitality as well as faith. The revelations that Muhammad received from God are collected in the Holy Qur'an.

Judaism revolves around the worship of one God, Jehovah, who revealed his will to the prophets. He demands moral conduct from his worshippers. There is none beside him; therefore, man should keep his statutes.

Zoroaster, the great reformer of the ancient Persian religion, gave the ancient religion with many gods a monotheistic turn. Ahura Mazda, the Supreme Being, the author of the universe and its destinies, always wills what is good but it is opposed by Ahriman, the evil spirit. According to Zoroaster, life is an eternal struggle between the forces of good and evil. Zoroaster believed in the ultimate triumph of good. He stressed good thought, good speech, and good deed, which lead to this triumph.

Guru Nanak, the founder of Sikhism, stressed that God is one, God is love, and God is unity. According to him, "The same God resides in the temple and in the mosque and outside as well. All human beings are equal in the eyes of God. They are born and they die in the same way. Devotion to God and service to mankind, irrespective of caste, creed, or color, is the fundamental duty of every human being."

According to the Buddha, Truth is the highest reality, and this Truth he called Nirvana, or unconditional freedom. Truth, or Nirvana, is to be realized by right understanding, right thought, right speech, right action, right livelihood, right effort, right mindfulness, and right concentration.

Mahavir, the Jain prophet and founder of Jainism, stressed simplicity, nonviolence, non-attachment, austerity and compassion for all. The soul is the begetter of both happiness and sorrow. It is its own friend when it treads the path of righteousness and its own enemy when it treads the forbidden path.

To Lao Tze, the founder of Taoism, there is one Real Thing, who is called "Tao," but the word is a substitute for "the name, which cannot be named." Tao is the source of all things, omnipotent, through non-assertion. Tao also implied the inner order of the universe. "Alone It stands, and It changes not. Around It moves; and It suffers not. Even if one has a little knowledge, he can walk in the ways of the Great Supreme."

Confucius, great humanist and founder of Confucianism, based his humanism on moral life and conduct. He declared, "The higher type of man makes a sense of duty the groundwork of his character, blends with it in action the sense of harmonious proportions, manifests it in a sense of unselfishness, perfects it by the addition of sincerity and truth. When offered an opportunity of gain, he thinks only of his duty."

Similarly, all religions in some form or other promise joy, peace, felicity, beatitude, and bliss to their followers. Thus, Zoroastrianism holds that holiness, the best of all good, is also happiness. The man with perfect holiness is perfectly happy.

According to Judaism, being in the presence of the Lord fills one with everlasting joy.

Christianity declares that in the kingdom of God, there is righteousness, peace, and joy in the Holy Spirit.

According to Islam, the believer in God who desires union with God and the spiritual path attains real and lasting happiness.

Buddhism states that he who practices charity, tranquility, and friendship to all beings attains the state of abiding happiness.

Sikhism declares that whosoever searches for happiness everlasting and eternal should seek it in the all-pervading Spirit.

Lord Mahavir, the founder of Jainism, says that he who studies the scriptures with devotion and without any desire for personal praise and honor but for purging of his karmic pollution will have the benefit of scriptural knowledge, which is conducive to everlasting happiness.

Lao Tze, the founder of Taoism, says that the man who speaks, thinks, and practices what is good is blessed. Being in accord with the Supreme Reality, or Tao, he attains the abiding happiness of Tao.

Confucius advised man to be completely virtuous so that he may enjoy all happiness.

In Hinduism, the scriptures state, "That one Supreme Ruler, the Self of all beings, who makes his form manifest—those wise men who perceive him as existing in their souls, to them belong eternal happiness and to no one else. The yogi (one who practices yoga) who has become perfectly tranquil and has quieted his passions, who is free from all impurities, attains with ease everlasting happiness and the infinite bliss of communion with the Supreme Spirit."

From the foregoing it will be evident that all the religions of the world, without any exception, focus on peace, harmony, happiness, and supreme blessedness, and they assure bliss to their followers. Religious harmony, peace, love, and compassion have been the central theme of all the religions. The life and teachings of the illumined souls in each religious tradition point out the way to the Supreme Being by loving one's neighbors and developing virtues such as kindness, tolerance, compassion, and love for all.

Religion has, unfortunately, sown the seeds of hatred as well as love. In the words of Charles Caleb Colton, a well known English cleric, writer and collector, "Men will wrangle for religion, write for it, fight for it, die for it; anything but live for it. Where true religion has prevented one crime, false religions have afforded a pretext for a thousand." Jonathan Swift said, "We have just enough religion to make us hate, but not enough to make us love one another." Blaise Pascal stated, "Men will never do evil so completely and cheerfully as when they do from religious conviction."

How true, considering the acts of violence that we see all around us. Mahatma Gandhi, the apostle of peace and nonviolence who believed in the unity of all religions and who advocated tolerance and love towards the followers of all religions, observed,

> I believe in the Bible as I believe in the Gita. I regard all the great faiths of the world as equally true with my own. If in my innermost heart I have the suspicion that my own religion is the truest and that the other religions are less true, then although I may have a certain kind of fellowship with the others, it is an extremely different kind from that required in the international fellowships. Our attitude towards the others ought to be absolutely frank and sincere. Our prayers for others ought never to be: God, give them the light that

> Thou has given me, but give them all the light and truth they need for their highest development.

Sri Ramakrishna, the great Hindu saint and philosopher who in his own life practiced the various religions and tested them, declared, "You may say there are many errors and superstitions in another religion. I should say: 'Suppose there are.' Every religion has error. Everyone thinks that his watch alone gives the correct time. It is enough to have yearning for God. He sees the longing of our heart and the yearning of our soul."

Another famous historian, Arnold Toynbee, said, "The true purpose of higher religion is to radiate the spiritual counsels and truths that are its essence into as many souls as it can reach, in order that each of these souls may be enabled thereby to fulfill the true end of Man. Man's true end is to glorify God and to enjoy him for ever."

A comparative study of all the religions of the world has revealed new facts and challenges to the exclusive claims of any particular religion to be the sole custodian of Truth.

The purpose of any religion is to make its followers religious and to inculcate in them the spirit of service, love for neighbors, kindness, humility, compassion, and tolerance. The study of religion reveals that an important aspect of it is a longing for values in life, a belief that life is not purposeless and meaningless. The search for meaning leads to faith in a Supreme Power greater than the human and, finally, to a universal or superhuman mind that has the desire and will to maintain the highest values for human life. So religion satisfies a basic human need, such as food is needed to satisfy our hunger. To ensure a healthy and happy life, we should eat wholesome and nutritious food in moderation. In the same way, we require wholesome spiritual food to maintain our spiritual health. This aspect is correctly brought out in the Bible, which tells us, "Not by bread alone does man live, but by every expression of Jehovah's mouth."

Religions of the world should create a harmonious environment in which everyone can practice his or her faith and become good a citizen. History tells us how great nations were partitioned into two nations due to discord, prejudice, and mutual suspicion between the followers of two major world religions. Religious intolerance has fueled disputes as well as full-scale wars between peoples and nations time and time again, from the Crusades of the medieval period to the current bloodshed in the Middle East, Northern Ireland, Africa, and Asia. The reason for all this man-made suffering is a total lack of knowledge of religions other than our own and the consequent prejudice, misunderstanding, wrong judgment, hatred, and bigotry. The feeling and attitude that, "My religion is the only true religion, which takes you to heaven, while everyone else is going to hell" is the major reason for all the conflicts we see today in all parts of the world.

For peaceful coexistence, better understanding, and the development of a secular outlook, it is imperative that we know something about religions other than our own. Such knowledge is essential for a true understanding of our own religion as well as for an understanding of people of other lands and faiths.

With the vast and rapid improvement in transportation and communication and the tremendous strides in modern science and information technology, our exposure to the external world has increased considerably. No nation, people, culture, or religion can remain in isolation, and the increasing volume of our contacts with other nations and races make it vital for us to understand their ways of thinking, their culture, and their religious beliefs and practices. In this regard, nothing is more important than knowledge of the religion through which each people's basic ideals and convictions are expressed. Religion is thus one of the most powerful and dominant forces in human life. Therefore, to understand and fully know our neighbors, we should learn and understand something of the world's religions.

Since all the religions were founded by great men, a study of each founder's life and teachings will be helpful. A religion is the expression of a social movement, and it bears the imprint of many personalities as well as the impress of the life of a whole group through many generations. When we consider men whose ideas and ways of life are radically different from ours, we are likely to develop prejudice. With a prejudiced mind, it is impossible to understand and appreciate others' ideas and ways of life. We must, therefore, firmly refuse to think of the founders of religions other than our own as heathens. Our loyalty to our faith, and belief should not make us look down on other religions or seek flaws in them or their founders or make us blind to the religions' merits.

Religions made rapid strides during the period around 800 BC to AD 650. The world witnessed the arrival of great men who founded many great religions that are still followed today, men including Buddha and the Upanishadic seers and sages in India, Jesus Christ in Palestine, Muhammad in Arabia, prophets in Israel, Zoroaster in Persia, Confucius and Lao Tze in China, et cetera. All the great religions of the world have come from Asia. Judaism, Christianity, and Islam are closely related and came from the extreme western parts of the continent, where the Semitic people first lived. Hinduism, Buddhism, Jainism, and Sikhism came from India. Confucianism and Taoism came from China, and the Shinto religion came from Japan. These great world religions have held the belief of millions of people around the world and have ever remained vital, vibrant, and dynamic.

The faiths taught by all the great religious leaders have many teachings in common, such as loving one's neighbors, kindness to all living beings, compassion, humility, helping the needy, tolerance, forgiveness, shunning evil, and developing goodness. Most people have recognized a spiritual presence and divine power that we call God. These people are of the firm belief that a relationship between man and God is essential for man's welfare, peace, and prosperity. They are also convinced that this relationship depends very much on the way man thinks and behaves. The moral codes, written and unwritten, that are an important part of every faith are based on this conviction. These faiths also share other features, such as sacred scriptures, a systematized theology for relating the faith's teachings to man's life, a priesthood or ministry, ritual and prayer techniques, symbols, and pilgrimage.

There are also profound differences among the faiths, especially between those of the East and the West. The stark monotheism of Judaism confronts the system of countless gods and goddesses in the traditional Hindu pantheon. In the Western world, the idea of God is a personal one; it is a father figure loving and watching over his creation, of which mankind is held to be the most important part. The Buddhist, on the other hand, may believe in an impersonal God, who remains aloof from human scrambling. The Western believer may cherish the concept of an individual soul that will endure for all eternity, while the Easterner may see his soul merging ultimately with a single universal soul, just as the dewdrop eventually reaches the sea.

Of course, there are about as many ideas of God as there are people. Then there are millions of people who profess neither religion nor any belief in a God. They are atheists. Others, agnostics, believe that God is unknown and probably unknowable. However, that obviously does not mean that such people lack principles or ethics, any more than professing religious faith means a person does have them. If, however, one accepts the concept of religion as devotion to some principle—strict fidelity or faithfulness; consciousness, piety—then most people, including the atheists and agnostics, do have some form of religious devotion in their lives.

The many similarities and differences in the cultures of the world make an interesting, educational, and absorbing study. Nowhere are the differences more interesting and the similarities more important than in the field of religion. "God is one," said a Hindu saint, but God is worshipped in different ages and climes under different names and aspects. Sri Ramakrishna, the philosopher saint from India, realized God by following the path of Hinduism and also through the disciplines of Christianity and Islam. According to Ramakrishna, all religions of the world lead to the same God. Various are the paths that take men to the house of the Lord.

Ignorance is the root cause of all sorrows and sufferings. Ignorance breeds prejudice, hatred, fear, and misunderstanding. We see all around us much violence, hatred, and fear and much bloodshed all committed in the name of religion. With a bit of understanding of religions other than ours, and with a little bit of tolerance and compassion, we can create a better world of peace, harmony, and happiness. It is possible for people to remain good Hindus, good Muslims, good Christians, good Jews, good Buddhists, et cetera. and yet be united by the bonds of love, brotherhood, kindness, and compassion espoused by all the religions of the world. The wisdom of the teachings of the world's great religions should make us better citizens.

The purpose of this book is to present the great teachings of the world's religions as an invitation to all men and women to marvel at, learn from, and feel the sweet strangeness and magnetic attraction of the great and glorious religions of the world. In studying any religion, we have to follow the basic rule of comparing only equal with equal. For thousands of years, we have had the habit of comparing our own religion in its ideal form with the actual manifestation of other religions. In fact, the nature and structure of what we call religion differs dramatically from culture to culture, place to place, and time to time. Some Christians pose the question, "Is Buddhism, which does not recognize God, really be a religion?" Such a question seeks to impose the Western concept of God upon a different theology that begins and ends with a deep, inspired understanding of "nothingness," Nirvana. We should also refuse to compare our present-day faith with ancient religious practice. Religions develop and undergo changes from time to time.

This book aims to describe the most important aspects of the world's major as well as minor religions: their founders, their roots, their beliefs and practices. This is rather a difficult task, since some religions have evolved over millennia and continue to be practiced, while some others have more or less faded away. My main concern has been with living religions. Attempts to categorize religions are inadequate because a study of any group of religions will reveal that there are more differences than similarities between them. But in order to provide a reasonable and accessible framework, this book has been divided into three broad categories of contemporary faiths. These are the Abrahamic faiths, the Vedic faiths, and other major and minor traditions. The Abrahamic faiths include Judaism, Christianity, and Islam. These have been called the prophetic traditions because one of their distinctive features is the role of the prophets, who were sent to recall the people to their respective role in God's plan and God's creation. The Vedic traditions include Hinduism, Buddhism, and Jainism, and they are linked by a common root in the Vedic culture of ancient India and by a belief that all existence is cyclical. A universe arises, exists, declines, and fades, to be replaced by other universe, just as every being in this universe passes through many existences, a process called reincarnation.

Apart from these two major strands of religious traditions, there are several other faiths that have developed in individual ways. Some of these include indigenous religions, such as Taoism in China and Shintoism in Japan, which have evolved complex rituals and written texts. Others, such as Sikhism and to a certain extent Bahaism and Sufism, have been influenced by elements of Vedic and Abrahamic faiths.

This book is designed as an introduction to the teachings, beliefs, and practices of the world's major and minor religious traditions. The chapters on the major faiths look at history, each religion's founder, and the religion's basic beliefs, scriptures, places of worship, lifestyles, rituals, and festivals.

In general, I have tried to give an objective account of each faith from the point of view of its adherents, without making any claim regarding the truth of the faith's teachings. I have reviewed several publications and reference books about different religions and made an honest attempt to distil the essence of each religion.

Because I was born and brought up as a Hindu Brahmin, it has been a strange and wonderful experience for me to read the Bible, the Qur'an, the great books on Sufism, Bahaism, Sikhism, and others, to try to understand them and assimilate the teachings of all the faiths. Confronted by the vastness of the subjects, the rich variety of teachings, and the staggering power of religion on humanity, I felt, as Isaac Newton said, "like a boy playing on the seashore ... finding a prettier shell or a smoother pebble, whilst the great ocean of truth lay all undiscovered around me." All the religions of the world are pure rivers of spirituality that flow and merge into the mighty ocean of Truth. One must dive deep into this great ocean of Truth if one wants to see the purest, priceless gems of wisdom and knowledge.

A dispassionate, devoted, and sincere study of other religions should strengthen religious vitality. It should open our hearts and souls to the great eternal truths that each of the world's religions has to offer. It should instill in the minds of the reader respect for all the religions of the world and generate love, understanding, tolerance, kindness, and compassion for the followers of all religions other than our own. Such a mental awakening will usher in a world of peace, hope, love, and harmony. It is my sincere hope and humble prayer that the reader of this book will set a personal example by spreading the message of love, tolerance, understanding, and peace expounded in all the religions to his family and friends, his neighbors, society, country, and the world at large. I would like to end my preface with the following soul-stirring messages of Swami Vivekananda and Saint Francis of Assisi.

Swami Vivekananda said:

> If there is ever to be a universal religion, it must be one which will have no location in place or time; which will be infinite, like the God it will preach, and whose sun will shine upon the followers of

Krishna and of Christ, on saints and sinners alike; which will not be Brahamanic or Buddhistic, or Mohammedan, but the sum total of all these, and still have infinite space for development; which in its catholicity will embrace in its infinite arms, and find a place for every human being. It will be a religion which will have no place for persecution or intolerance in its polity, which will recognize divinity in every man and woman, and whose whole scope, whose whole force, will be centered in aiding humanity to realize its own true, divine nature. The Christian is not to become a Hindu or a Buddhist, nor a Hindu or a Buddhist to become a Christian. But each must assimilate the spirit of the others and yet preserve his individuality and grow according to his own law of growth.

Help not Fight, Assimilation and not Destruction, Harmony and Peace and not Dissension.

Saint Francis of Assisi said:

Make me an instrument of your peace.
Where there is hatred, let me sow love,
Where there is injury, pardon,
Where there is doubt, faith,
Where there is despair, hope,
Where there is darkness, light and
Where there is sadness, joy.
O Divine Master,
Grant that I may not so much
Seek to be consoled as to console;
To be understood as to understand;
To be loved as to love,
For it in giving that we receive
It is in pardoning that we are pardoned and,
It is in dying that we are born to eternal life.

Origin of Religion

The origin of religion is as old as the origin of mankind. According to archaeologists and anthropologists, there has never existed any people, anywhere, at any time, in all the world, who were not in some way or in some sense religious. Besides its antiquity, religion has existed in many varieties. Thus the headhunters in Borneo, the Eskimos in the Arctic, the nomads in the Sahara desert, the urban dwellers in the great cities of the world, and others had their god or gods and their ways of worship. It is interesting to note the diversity in religion over time.

When we think of the origin of religion, the question that comes to mind is the source of all religions. We might wonder where religion began, and how. There are many theories. For thousands of years, people more or less accepted the religious tradition into which they were born and brought up. Almost all of them were satisfied with the explanations given to them by their fathers and forefathers, and they believed that their religion was the truth. Further, due to poor communication and limited travel, people were not aware of other religions.

The picture changed during the nineteenth century. With the theory of evolution sweeping through intellectual circles and the advent of scientific inquiry, people began to question established systems, including religion. Looking for possible clues within existing religion, scholars turned their attention to the remains of early civilizations and to the remote corners of the world, where people still lived in primitive societies. They tried to apply to these the methods of psychology, anthropology, sociology, etc., with a view to find out how and why religion began.

The earliest theory was propounded by an English anthropologist named Edward Tylor. He developed the concept of animism in the late 19th century. According to Tylor, experiences such as dreams, visions, and hallucinations caused primitive peoples to conclude that the body is inhabited by a soul, "anima" in Latin. Since people frequently dreamed of their deceased loved ones, they thought that a soul continued to live after death and that on leaving the body, the soul dwelt in nature. In the end, the dead and the objects the souls were said to inhabit came to be worshipped as gods. According to Tylor, thus was religion born.

Another anthropologist, R. R. Marett, proposed a refined version of animism in 1909. After studying the beliefs Pacific islanders and the natives of Africa and America, Marett came to the conclusion that primitive peoples, instead of having the notion of a personal soul, believed there was an impersonal power or supernatural power that animated everything. That belief evoked emotions of fear and awe in man, which became the basis for his primitive religion. According to Marett, religion was mainly man's emotional response to the unknown supernatural power.

The next theory on the origin of religion was put forth by James Frazer. According to Frazer, man first tried to control his own life and his environment by imitating the happenings in nature. Thus, man thought he could invoke rain simply by sprinkling water on the ground, accompanied by thunder-like drumbeats. Similarly, he thought that he could cause harm to his enemy by sticking pins in an effigy. These practices led to the use of rituals, spells, and magic. When man found that they did not work as expected, he then turned his attention to placating the supernatural powers and beseeching their help. The rituals and incantations became sacrifices and prayers, and thus religion began. In other words, according to Frazer, religion is a "propitiation or conciliation of powers superior to man. (The Golden Bough, by James George Frazer, Robert Fraser)".

The noted psychoanalyst Sigmund Freud attributed religion to fear of a father figure. According to Freud, the earliest religion grew out of what he called a father-figure neurosis. He theorized that in primitive society, the father dominated the clan. The sons, who both feared and admired their father, rebelled and killed the father. To acquire the father's power, Freud claimed, "these cannibalistic savages ate their victim." Later, out of remorse, they invented rites and rituals to atone for their action. According to Freud's theory, the father figure became God, the rites and rituals became the earliest religion, and the eating of the slain became the tradition of communion practiced in many religions.

Religion can be classified under three basic categories, namely polytheistic, pantheistic, and monotheistic. Let us examine these three categories.

Polytheism is a belief in many gods. It is thought to have originated with Hinduism in about 2500 BC. Hindu beliefs are recorded in the scripture Bhagavad Gita, which states that many gods were subjected to a supreme Brahman. Polytheism was also the religion of many other ancient cultures, including Assyria, Babylonia, Egypt, Greece, and Rome. The ancient polytheistic belief systems viewed gods as being in control of all natural forces and events, such as rainfall, harvests, and fertility. Further, polytheistic cultures believed in sacrifices to appease gods. Thus, the Canaanites sacrificed to the male god, Baal, and his female counterpart, Ashteroth. Baal controlled the rain and the harvest, while Ashteroth controlled fertility and reproduction. The Greeks and Romans developed polytheism into a highly structured pantheon of gods and goddesses.

Pantheism is a belief that all is God. It prevailed in many cultures. The belief that the universe itself was divine was typified in the animist beliefs of Confucianism and Taoism, in the African and American Indian cultures, and in the later Egyptian religion under the pharaohs. Pantheistic beliefs are also finding resurgence among the various New Age movements. Since, in pantheism, God is everything and everything is God, nature is also part of God. Humans must be in harmony with nature, nurture it, and be nurtured by it. Humans are no different than any other animal. We must live in harmony with animals, understand them, learn from them, and focus on the relationship between mankind and the elements of nature.

Monotheism is a belief in one god. It is the foundation of the Judeo-Christian-Muslim line of religions, which began with a man named Abraham in about 2000 BC. From this point in history, God began revealing himself to the world through the nation of Israel. The Jewish scriptures record the journey of the Israelites from slavery in Egypt to the Promised Land in Canaan under the leadership of Moses. During a period of about fifteen hundred years, God revealed what became the Old Testament of the Bible, relating the history of Israel through the character and laws of God.

During the period of the Roman Empire, Jesus Christ was born in Bethlehem as the long-awaited Messiah. The ministry of Jesus Christ ended in about 32 AD, with his crucifixion and resurrection. After Christ's ascension into heaven, the Christian church grew in his name, and the New Testament was written.

About six hundred years later, Muhammad began preaching in Mecca. Muhammad believed he was the ultimate prophet of God, and his teachings became the precepts of Islam, as recorded in the Holy Qur'an.

Acknowledgments

At seventy, when I decided to write my first book of poems, I was enthusiastic, hopeful, and confident with the will to succeed. I finished the book in a couple of months, and I was thrilled and exuberant when the first copy was printed. At eighty, when I decided to write a book on the teachings, beliefs, and practices of various religions, I was doubtful and a bit nervous, because I was having lot of physical problems due to aging. Further, the subject was vast and complex, and the entire project looked formidable and almost impossible. It looked like a dream. Thanks to the tremendous support from my family, friends, and well-wishers, that dream became a reality. Unlike my first book, which took only few months, my second book took a couple of years.

I want to thank my three daughters, Raji, Shanti, and Geeta, for their understanding and encouragement. I could relax under the shade of their love, kindness, and tender care and work in a peaceful and congenial atmosphere. They cheered me up whenever I felt discouraged due to illness and other physical discomforts, and they enabled me to complete the book. I am deeply grateful to them.

I want to express my deepest gratitude to Chandru, Govi, and Geeta. Due to my ignorance of computing, I ran into innumerable problems with the computer almost every day. On all such occasions, they cheerfully came to my rescue, putting their important work aside and helping me correct the errors. I would have never completed my work without their tireless efforts, active help, guidance, and infinite patience.

I will be failing in my duty if I did not mention the tremendous moral and physical help rendered by my wife, Savitri. She was a source of enthusiasm, energy, hope, and confidence, and her active participation enabled me to complete this book. Many times while I was writing the manuscript, I felt a sense of gloom and helplessness due to illness and physical discomforts. At times, I even thought of giving up the project. It was during such critical moments that my wife cheered me with words of encouragement. In addition, she typed most of my manuscript. I am eternally indebted to her.

I am grateful to many of my Hindu, Christian, Muslim, Sikh, Jewish, and Parsi friends for their help and guidance. They supplied me with many publications and reference books on various faiths. I am deeply indebted to them for their sincere and timely help.

Born and brought up as a Hindu Brahmin, I found it an exciting and unique experience to read and understand the quintessence of all the major and minor religions of the world. I have taken all precautions to avoid any controversial matters or hurt the feelings of the followers of different faiths.

Since I had to go through several reference books and make my own inferences and interpretations, some errors of judgment are likely. I would ask the reader's indulgence on these.

Lastly, I want to thank God for giving me the life, strength, confidence, and faith to complete this book. Many times during the writing of this book, I felt that my work would end as a posthumous one. God has been merciful, and only by his grace was the book completed. I always remember my beloved mother's advice: anything is possible if one has abundant faith in God.

Ram Ramakrishnan

Chapter 1

Religions of the World

What Is Religion?

Religion is defined as the expression of man's belief in and veneration for a superhuman power recognized as the creator, sustainer, and governor of the universe. It is the spiritual or emotional attitude of one who recognizes with conviction the existence of a superhuman power. Religion can be termed as the bond between man and God. A person is said to be religious when he or she adheres to a religion both in belief and practice. A religious person can further be classified as devout, saintly, pious, or sanctimonious. "Devout" connotes inward faith and outward sincere observance of ritual and reverence. "Saintly" implies an exceptional quality of spiritual and religious integrity. "Pious" suggests a godly and reverential observance of religion. "Sanctimonious" connotes a pretense of piety or righteousness.

It is interesting to note how religion has been described by some of the world religions themselves. Let us examine some of these descriptions.

According to Hinduism, "Even the highest theism is only a sort of glorified anthropomorphism or concept of God as a human being with human attributes, but we cannot do without it."

According to Christianity, "Religion is not a proposition, but a system. It is a rite, a culture, a philosophy, a role of duty, all at once."

Islam states, "Religion is a candle inside a multicolored lantern. Everyone looks through a particular color, but the lantern is always there."

Judaism says that, "Every religion must go back to the fundamental problem of optimism and pessimism, a problem whether existence has a meaning and whether there is a world order which makes for the good."

According to Buddhism, "Buddhist religion is not a system of dogmas or a church building, but a way of life for people, who are molded according to Buddhist discipline. Buddhism is pervasive, but formless."

According to atheism, "Religion is the opium of society."

Religion has always been a central component of human culture, though its form and practice have changed through time. In ancient times, people lived in a world they could not comprehend or explain. For them, the world consisted of an environment controlled by vague and mysterious powers, which they attributed to a vast array of gods. Artifacts dating to a period before recorded history show that religion of the distant past more or less reflected this world of ours, consisting of several rituals devised to propitiate gods or to influence events under the control of gods.

We have seen how religion has been described by the world religions. Let us now examine how the concept of God has been viewed by different religions. God is defined as the perfect, omnipotent, omniscient originator and ruler of the universe, the principal object of faith and worship in monotheistic religions. God is visualized as a being of supernatural power or attributes, believed in and worshipped by people. God has also been defined as Existence, Knowledge, Bliss, Infinite Mind, Spirit, Eternal Truth, Life, and Love. Let us now examine the views of different religions on the concept of God, including some key quotes from the major texts of each religion.

Christianity

In the Bible, God is described at various times as omnipresent, omniscient, the Immanent, the Glorious, the Creator, the Comforter, the Eternal, et cetera.

- "God knows all things." (John 3:20)
- "With God nothing shall be impossible." (Luke 1:37)
- "The kingdom of God is within you." (Luke 17:21)
- "The heavens declare the glory of God and the firmament shows his handiwork." (Psalm 19:1)
- "Every good gift and every perfect gift is from above." (James 1:17)

Hinduism

The Upanishads describe the glory of God. According to the Upanishads, God is the Creator, the Sustainer, the Eternal, the Enjoyer, the Comforter. He is Omnipotent, Omniscient, Infinite Love, etc.

- "I am the source of all creation, everything in the world moves about because of Me; thus the wise full of wisdom worship Me." (The Bhagavad Gita)
- "God is that unique One, who assumes without any self-interest many

forms, first creates the universe and then in the end withdraws it unto Himself. (Upanishads) "He pervades all things. He is radiant, incorporeal, invulnerable, pure, and untouched by evil. He is the seer, wise, above things, and self-reliant. The Supreme Person alone is all this cosmos. He is the power of action, power of penance, power of creation and immortality." (Upanishads)

Islam

- "God has not created anything better than reason, for anything more perfect or more beautiful than reason; the benefits which God gives are on its account; and understanding is by it, and God's wrath is caused by it and by it are the reward and punishment."
- "Verily, God is mild, and is fond of mildness, and He gives to the mild what He does not give to the harsh and withhold from the unlawful and begging."
- "Whoever loves to meet God, God loves to meet him."
- "Verily, God is pure and loves the pure, is clean and loves the clean, is beneficent and loves the beneficent, is generous and loves the generous."

Sikhism

- "God is one, but He has innumerable forms. He is the Creator of all and He Himself takes the human form."
- "He is without any kind of fear. He has no enemy and He is beyond death and He is free from rebirths."
- "There is only One Being, who is the Creator and the uncaused Cause of all. He has created the whole universe through ever-active will which is diffused throughout."
- "All things are manifestations of His will, but his will is beyond description. By his will is matter quickened into life. By his will are men's joys and sorrows ordained and by his will the pious obtain salvation."

Zoroastrianism

- "Ahura Mazda is the Lord of life and wisdom, light and the truth."
- "When you go into darkness, take Ahura Mazda's hand in your hand. That will be better than light and safer than a known way. If one acts according to Ahura Mazda's commandments, one need not be afraid of any mortal, however mighty and powerful he may be. Sun, moon, and stars give light, but Ahura Mazda is the light that lights them to light the world."

Judaism

- "Hear, Israel: The Lord is our God, the Lord is one." (Torah (Deuteronomy 6:4))
- "God is unity. He is a single, whole, complete indivisible entity. The Lord is our God, the Lord alone. God is the creator of everything. God is omnipresent, omniscient, and eternal."

Sufism

- "O Thou Whose face is the object of my adoration, Whose beauty is my sanctuary, Whose habitation is my goal, Whose praise is my hope, Whose providence is my companion, Whose love is the cause of my being, Whose mention is my solace, Whose nearness is my desire, Whose presence is my dearest wish and highest aspiration, I entreat Thee not to withhold from me the things Thou didst ordain for the chosen ones among Thy servants. Supply me, then with the good of this world and of the next. Thou truly art the King of all men. There is no God but Thee, the Ever-Giving, the Most Generous."

Religion is not the goal, but only a path by which a devotee or an aspirant attains enlightenment or ultimate perfection. Over history, many people have asked, "Why are there so many different religions in the world?" This is because different religions are necessary to suit different human minds at different levels of knowledge, understanding, and evolution. All the religions of the world are working for the welfare and happiness of mankind. Each religion takes up a part of the universal Truth and exerts its entire force in embodying it.

It can be safely assumed that the greatly sought-for Universal Religion has always been in existence. It runs through all the world religions in the form of God Consciousness. The Universal Truth is the thread that binds and holds together the precious gems of the different faiths. Religion should, therefore, emphasize harmony and not dissent, love and not hatred, peace and not strife, friendship and not enmity, and compassion and not cruelty. Different religions are like different rivers, all flowing and ultimately merging into the vast ocean of Truth. Each river has a distinct name till such time as it reaches the ocean; once the rivers merge into the ocean, they lose their different names and identities and become part and parcel of one great ocean.

Water is called by different names by different people in different languages in different countries. Some call it water, some call it aqua, some call it pani, etc. Similarly, the One Supreme Being is invoked by some as God, by some as Christ, by some as Allah, by some as Jehovah, by some as Krishna, by some as Ahura Mazda, by some as Tao, and by some as Brahman. Different world religions are but different paths all leading to God.

The Hindu sages and spiritual leaders looked upon all the different religions as different paths leading to the same Godhead and God Consciousness. They taught people that the followers of different religions are only fellow travelers. The great saint Sri Ramakrishna followed many religious paths, namely Hinduism, Christianity, and Islam, and attained Godhead. He proved by his own life and experience the eternal truth of all religions and from his spiritual experience stated the universal spirit of all the world religions as follows:

> Truth is One, only it is called by different names: all people are seeking the same Truth: the variance is due to climate, temperament, and name. I had to practice each religion for a time—Hinduism, Islam, and Christianity. Furthermore, I followed the paths of the Saktas, Vaishnavas, and Vedantists. I realize that there is only one God towards whom all are traveling: but the paths are different. Everyone is going towards God. They will realize Him if they have sincerity and longing of heart. Religion is the experience of the eternal relationship between the eternal soul and eternal God. All the different religions of the world are paths leading to the same goal of spiritual experience or enlightenment or realization. The various religions are like radii leading to the same center. God is the center of all religions of the world and each one of us is moving towards Him along one the radii. At the center where all the radii meet, all the differences disappear. Till such time we reach there, there will be differences.

Harmony of all religions is a positive force that generates the power to grow in one's faith and at the same time accept, understand, and assimilate the faiths of others. The different religions of the world are neither contradictory nor antagonistic to each other. They are all various phases of one eternal religion and one eternal truth. One must respect all religions and try to accept them all.

The faiths taught by all the great religious leaders have many things in common such as loving one's neighbor, kindness to all beings, compassion, helping the sick, the poor and the neglected, facing the joys and sorrows with equanimity, tolerance, forgiveness, shunning evil etc. All people have recognized a spiritual presence and divine power that we call God. They are of firm belief that there is a relationship between man and God, which is essential for the welfare, peace, harmony and happiness of mankind.

Further, all the religions of the world have almost identical views on several aspects of life, including prayers and their efficacy; kindness and mercy;

faith and devotion. A few examples of prayers on peace will clearly illustrate the similar viewpoints of all the world religions.

In Hinduism, the invocating prayer for universal peace is a conventional practice when starting a spiritual book. Thus, a hymn to the Supreme Being begins, "May peace—physical, mental, and spiritual—be on us forever." Another Hindu prayer says, "May the Divine bring the world peace. May the holy prayers and invocations of peace-liturgies bring peace, harmony, and happiness everywhere."

In Islam, the prayer is, "O God, you are peace. From you peace comes and to you peace returns."

A Christian prayer says, "You, Lord, give true peace to those who depend on you, because they trust you. In the tender compassion of our God, the dawn of heaven will break upon us to shine on those who live in darkness under the shadow of death and to guide us into the ways of peace."

A Jain prayer says, "Lead me from hate to love and from war to peace."

A Zoroastrian prayer says, "Let us have peace on earth. Let us have peace born of fellow-feeling."

A Buddhist prayer says, "There is no ill like the body and no bliss greater than peace."

A Baha'i teaching says, "When love is realized and spiritual bonds unite the hearts of people, the human race will be uplifted. The world will grow spiritual and the happiness and peace of mankind will increase."

A Sikh prayer says, "They alone are in peace and attain the state of bliss, who lean on the true name."

The above prayers illustrate the similar viewpoints world religions hold on a very important aspect of human life: world peace.

Religious harmony and essential unity have been the core and central theme of all the religions of the world. All religions hold before man and woman the ideal of perfection, which is known as God, Allah, Christ, Krishna, Ahura Mazda, Tao, et cetera. In order to realize this ideal, all the religions of the world emphasize the imperative for moral perfection and sincere spiritual striving. The basic tenets and teachings of different religions clearly illustrate this underlying unity of purpose. Let us examine all the major and minor religions of the world in this regard.

Hinduism—Hinduism holds the view that all the religions are different paths to the Eternal Truth. Hindus refer to their faith as Sanadhana Dharma, which means eternal law or order. Hinduism is a whole complex of beliefs and institutions that have appeared from the time when their ancient and sacred scriptures, the Vedas, were composed until now. All the schools of Hinduism believe in the Atman, the potential divinity of man; in Brahman, or Supreme Being; in the ideal of self-realization; and in the paths of yoga leading to direct personal spiritual experience.

Christianity—Christianity accepts both the Old and the New Testament of the Bible and emphasizes the need for a mediator, Christ, the son of God. Some of the Ten Commandments reveal that the basic teachings of Christianity emphasize loving one's neighbor and loving the Lord with all one's heart and soul. They also emphasize world peace, purity of heart, mercy, and compassion. In the Sermon on the Mount, Christ told his followers, "Blessed are the poor in spirit; for theirs is the kingdom of heaven. Blessed are the meek; for they shall inherit the earth. Blessed are the merciful; for they shall obtain mercy. Blessed are the peacemakers; for they shall be called the children of God."

Islam—Islam is the religion of submission to God. The holy book the Qur'an, says, "Your God is one God. There is no God but He, the Compassionate, the Merciful. All on the earth pass away, but the face of the Lord shall abide, resplendent with majesty and glory. Call upon your lord with lowliness and in secret. Call on Him with fear and longing desire. Verily, the mercy of God is nigh unto the righteous." Islam lays great stress on charity, helping the poor and the needy, loving one's neighbor and fellow beings. According to the teachings of Islam, "All God's creatures are His family; and he is the most beloved of God, who tries to do most good to God's creatures. Love your fellow beings first."

Judaism—Judaism believes in the worship of one God, Jehovah, who revealed his will to the prophets. Judaism demands moral conduct from its followers. It instructs that "thou shall love the Lord with all thy heart and with all thy soul and with all thy might." Judaism holds the view that man is made in the image of God and has direct access to God. The Ten Commandments for worship and conduct instruct, "You shall have no other God besides Me. You shall not swear falsely by the name of the Lord. Honor your father and mother. You shall not murder. You shall not commit adultery. You shall not steal."

Buddhism—Buddhism is a religion of universal as well as individual peace, tolerance, kindness to all living beings, compassion, nonviolence, and love. According to Buddhism, Truth is the highest reality and this Truth—called Nirvana—can be attained through right understanding, right thought, right speech, right action, right livelihood, right effort, and right mindfulness. Lord Buddha said, "My doctrine is pure and it makes no discrimination between noble and ignoble, rich and poor. My doctrine is like water, which cleanses all without any distinction. My doctrine is like the heavens, for there is ample room for the reception of all, for men and women, boys and girls, powerful and lowly. The robe of mine is sublime forbearance and patience. The abode of mine is charity and love to all beings. The pulpit of mine is the comprehension of the good law in its abstract meaning as well as in its particular application."

Jainism—Jainism is a religion of ahimsa, or nonviolence, nonabsolutism, and nonpossession. Lord Mahavir, the founder of Jainism, said, "The essential nature of any substance is Dharma. Right faith, right knowledge, and right conduct constitute the Dharma. Other characteristics of Dharma are supreme forgiveness, supreme humility, supreme straightforwardness, supreme truthfulness, supreme purity, supreme self-restraint, supreme austerity, supreme renunciation, supreme detachment, and supreme continence." I forgive all living beings. May all living beings forgive me. I cherish friendliness towards all and harbor enmity towards none. Not to kill any living being is the quintessence of all wisdom. Treat others with care, respect, and compassion, as you treat yourself.

Zoroastrianism—Zarathustra, the founder of Zoroastriansim,gave humanity the priceless touchstone of the holy triad of righteous thoughts, righteous words, and righteous deeds.

Sikhism—Sikhism believes in one God, who is timeless and without form. The world and the universe are a reflection of God, who created them and directs them. The teachings of Sikhism emphasize equality, service, truthfulness, brotherhood, honest living, love, peace, and protection of the weak against injustice. Guru Nanak said, "Practice truth, contentment, and love, and the worship of God's Name shall be your treasure. Banish sin from your mind and the true one will bestow truth on you. Let contentment be your earrings, and endeavor for the Divine and respect for the higher self be your wallet. And constant meditation on him be your ashes. The highest religion is to rise to universal brotherhood."

Bahaism—Bahaism believes in the oneness of God, the soul's immortality, and the evolution of mankind—biological, spiritual, and social. Baha'i faith lays great stress on the brotherhood of man and equality of women. The Baha'is see their mission as the spiritual conquest of the planet. Bahaism believes in universal peace, praying at least once a day, service to humanity, and participation in community projects. The Baha'is abstain from participation in politics and believe in absolute obedience to the laws of the country in which they live.

Taoism—According to Taoism, there is one Real Thing, who is called Tao. The harmony and orderliness perceived in the world are manifestations of Tao, a sort of divine will. In other words, instead of believing in a creator God, who controls the universe, Taoists believe in a providence, a will of heaven—or simply heaven itself—as the cause of everything. Taoism believes that there is a natural and correct way to do everything and that everything and everyone has its proper place and its proper function. If people were willing to seek out the way, or Tao, and follow it, everything would be harmonious, peaceful, and effective.

The basic idea of Taoism is that everything will come out right if people sit back, do nothing, and let nature take its course. The essence of Taoism is peace, harmony, and living with nature.

Confucianism—The core of Confucianism is to teach rules of conduct and morals and to restore peace and order in society. According to Confucius, everyone from the emperor to the common man must learn what role he or she was expected to play in society and live accordingly. He declared, "The higher type of man makes a sense of duty the groundwork of his or her character, blends with it in action the sense of harmonious proportion, manifests it in a sense of unselfishness, perfects it by the addition of sincerity and truth." Confucianism places much emphasis on healthy family ties, on being industrious, and on education, peace, understanding, kindness, and compassion.

If we look into the scriptures, sacred texts, and teachings of all the religions of the world, we will find considerable similarity of thought and unity of purpose, as well as common threads between their various scriptures. Let us examine a few cases, beginning with the Holy Bible and the Upanishads of Hinduism. Let us see what the Bible and the Upanishads say about God, prayer, faith, etc.

God the Creator

The Bible states the following: "O Lord! How manifold are thy works! In wisdom has thou made them all." (Psalm 104:24)

"You are worthy, our Lord and God, to receive glory and honor and power, because you made all things. Everything existed and was made, because you wanted it." (Revelation 4:11)

The Upanishads says, "From him are born life, mind, and all the senses and also space, air, light, water, and the earth, which supports all." (Mundaka Upanishad)

"Infinite-Existence-Knowledge-Bliss is the basic Reality." (Vedanta)

Faith

The Bible says, "It is by faith we understand that the whole world was made by God's command so that what we see was made by something hat cannot be seen." (Hebrews 11: 3)

"Without faith no one can please God. Anyone who comes to God must believe that He is real and He rewards those who really find Him." (Hebrews 11:6)

The Upanishads say, "Nothing is impossible to the man of faith."

The Bhagavad Gita says, "I consider them to be the best yogis who, endowed with supreme faith and ever united through meditation with Me, worship Me with the mind centered on me."

There are many points of similarity in the scriptures of different religions. The essence of all the religions of the world as reflected in the life and teachings of their great spiritual leaders is the same: leading the sincere followers towards purity, harmony, love, peace, and perfection. In this connection, the following words of Mahatma Gandhi, the apostle of peace, are relevant. He said, "I believe in the Bible as I believe in the Gita. I regard all the great faiths of the world as equally true with my own."

All the religions of the world clearly bring out the central theme, namely, peace, love, compassion, understanding and harmony.

Love, Peace, Compassion, Tolerance, and Understanding Through World Religions

There are many religions in the world, each proclaiming its own image. All the minor and major religions of the world have many tenets in common, such as love, peace, compassion, tolerance, understanding, kindness to all beings, charity, and happiness in life. The essence of all religions is to achieve a sense of brotherhood, a good heart, respect for others, and universal love. All the religions of the world have love as their central theme and improving the conduct of their followers as their objective. All the religions teach us to be honest, unselfish, kind, and compassionate; to help the poor and the sick, to love our neighbor, and to lead a spiritual life.

Religion is basically an individual experience, namely, a happy, healthy and beautiful way of living one's life in peace and harmony. All human beings want happiness, and all the religions direct the way to achieve real and lasting happiness. They point out that all material things—such as wealth, power, and status—are impermanent. Real and permanent happiness comes only when the mind is made pure and directed towards God. All religions emphasize the importance of leading a spiritual life. For reviving our spiritual life, we must stress the central and essential theme of all religions. We need the ideal of self-realization. And along with this, we should also absorb all that is good and great in each religion. By understanding the basic and central elements of all the religions, we can definitely make our lives richer, fuller, and happier. What are the essential good and noble elements in all the religions?

- Love
- Peace
- Compassion
- Tolerance
- Understanding

Let us examine the above five elements, which are the vital themes in all religions. The essence of all the religions of the world is love. According to Bahaism, "Love is the secret of God's holy dispensation. It is the manifestation of the All-Merciful, the fountain of spiritual outpourings. Love is Heaven's kindly light, the Holy Spirits eternal breath that enhances and enlivens the human soul. Love is the cause of God's revelation to humanity, the vital bond inherent in accordance with the divine creation. Love is the only means and source that will ensure intense happiness in this as well as in the next world. Love is the light that illumines and guided us in darkness. It is the link that unites God with man and assures the progress of all illumined souls. The religion of God is the cause of love."

According to Hindu scriptures, the surest and easiest way to realize God is through divine love. Divine love is the way of pure devotion. Love is a powerful force and of all the types of love, love for God is the most powerful and most profound. According to a Hindu saint, "Divine love knows no bargaining and does not expect anything in return. It is spontaneous and is based on sacrifice."

Zoroaster, the founder of Zoroastrianism, wanted his followers to have hearts full of love. He said, "Just as fire in the censer consumes the sandalwood, let the fire burn within you and consume your heart with love for Ahura Mazda. Every place, whether tavern or temple, is the abode of God."

According to Christianity, love is God and God is love. The Bible says, "We all know the love that God has for us and we trust that love. Those who live in love, live in God." The Lord our God has, therefore, given love a very prominent as well as a dominant place on the scale of ethical values. Regarding the two commandments to love God and our fellow men, Jesus said, "The foremost is love." There is no other commandment greater than this.

Love is central in God's own nature, and he wants it to be central in man. Scriptures say that God loves all of us with all his heart. He longs for us to love him with all our power with all our heart and soul. Love is the self-imparting quality in the nature of God that moves him to seek the highest good of his creatures, in whom he seeks to awaken responsive love. Love is thus the basis of our knowledge of and understanding with God. According to John 4:8, "The one who does not love, does not know God." Love is not mere sentiment, but it is an activity. Love means willing sacrifice. Pure love is unselfish and outgoing.

Love occupies pride of place in Islam, as well. According to Islam, "Whoever loves to meet God, God loves to meet him. Verily God is pure and loves the pure, is clean and loves the clean, is beneficent and loves beneficent, is generous and loves the generous. Prophet Muhammad said, "Do you love your Creator? Love your fellow beings first.""O Lord, grant to me the love of you, grant me that I love those that love you; grant that I may do the deeds that win your love; make your love dearer to me than self, family, or wealth."

Sufism is basically a religion of love, a fact beautifully brought out by the Sufi poet Rumi. He said, "When I come to love, I am ashamed of all that I have ever said about love." According to Sufism, love permeates all aspects of love. Love is the core of all religions, and all religions glorify love of God. Man's love can be classified under two types: first, true love—or love for God—and second, love for everything else. Love for God involves strictly obeying God's commandments and leading a truly spiritual life. Love is the water of life, and one should drink it to the heart's content. Without the sweet life of love, living will be nothing but a burden. Love is the elixir of life and it will deliver you from death. Love is the be all and end all of life. A life devoid of love will be a total waste. Love is like the sun radiating warmth and joy. A heart without love is nothing but a piece of stone. To love is to see good and beautiful in all God's creation and in everything in this world."

Guru Nanak, founder of Sikhism, preached love. He wanted his followers to practice love by serving the poor, the sick, and the aged. He said, "Practice truth, contentment, and love and then the worship of God's Name shall be your treasure."

All the religions of the world extol the practice of love and repeat that the surest way to reach God is through love. Love brings peace, understanding, harmony, and happiness in the lives of the people. The seed of pure love sprouts easily in the pure hearts, which are freed from anger, hatred, jealous, greed, and lust.

Peace

Next to love, peace is the most important theme in all the world's religions. All the prophets, saints, and sages are unanimous in their declaration that peace is the key to happiness, prosperity, and growth of the individual, society, and nation. Without exception, all the religions stress again and again that universal peace is vital for the survival of humanity.

Let us now examine what the great prophets have said about universal peace. Of all the religious leaders and prophets, Baha U'llah, the founder of

Bahaism stands like a colossus in his great vision of world peace and universal brotherhood. In his various writings, Baha U'llah spoke of what he called Great World Peace, which he said would mitigate people's sorrows and sufferings. According to him, when all humanity embraces the Revelation of God and, through it, ensures the Great World Peace, there will be more peace and harmony on earth. In order to usher in a Great World Peace, Baha U'llah recommended the adoption of several steps.

According to his vision, a time will come when the need for holding a vast and all-embracing assemblage of men and women will be universally recognized and realized. All the world leaders must attend and make a firm and unanimous resolution for the sake of peace. In the unlikely event of any future war between two nations, all others should unite to restore peace between those nations. With wars eliminated, the world's resources could be utilized for improving the standard of living. Further, Baha U'llah said that the day is not far off when all peoples of the world will adopt one universal language as well as a common script. In Baha U'llah's vision of the Great World Peace, there will be perfect understanding, love, and goodwill among the people of the world, ensuring lasting peace and harmony.

The essence of Christianity is peace, and Jesus was an apostle of peace. In his Sermon on the Mount, Jesus said, "Blessed are the peacemakers, for they shall be called the children of God." Saint Francis, in his famous Peace Prayer, said, "Lord, make me an instrument of your peace. Where there is hatred, let me sow love."

All the Hindu scriptures begin and end with an invocation to peace, as illustrated by the following lines from the Upanishads: "May the world attain peace, may all beings be freed from dangers, may all beings realize what is good, may all beings be actuated by noble thoughts, may all beings be happy everywhere. Om, peace, peace, peace."

Zoroaster said, "Sublime peace in the inner world of man is happiness."

Buddha was an apostle of peace. He preached and practiced peace. He said, "There is no fire like lust, no crime like hatred, no ill like the body, and no bliss greater than peace."

Guru Nanak said, "The Lord's name is the ocean of peace."

Compassion

All religions stress the need for everyone to develop compassion. In fact, the founders of all the major and minor religions, as well as the scriptures, emphasize the vital importance of compassion. Confucius, the great Chinese philosopher and teacher, summed up compassion thus: "Do not do to others as you would not have done to you." He wanted his pupils to listen to themselves. They had to look into their own hearts, discover what gave them pain, and then vigorously refrain from inflicting that suffering upon other people.

When we think of compassion, we think of Buddha, who preached compassion throughout his lifetime. He advised his followers to undertake meditation and send out thought of compassion, benevolence, and sympathy to the four corners of the world. He wanted everyone to show compassion to all living beings.

Jesus preached compassion and advised his followers to love even their enemies. According to Jesus, if someone struck you on the face, you must turn the other cheek, rather than retaliate.

Judaism also laid great importance on compassion. When Rabbi Hillel, the great Jewish rabbi, was asked to sum up the whole of Jewish teachings, he replied, "That which is hateful to you, do not do to your neighbor."

The essence of Islam is compassion. According to the Qur'an, it is wrong to build up a private fortune at the expense of the poor; one should share his wealth to create a just and fair society, where the poor and the vulnerable are treated with respect.

All the Hindu scriptures are full of praise for the virtue of compassion. According to Hindu sages, practicing compassion, love, and renunciation of worldly desires will take one closer to God.

All world religions are unanimous on the primacy of compassion, a discipline preached by all the prophets and sages. They knew that greed and selfishness were the root cause of all human suffering and misery. When people gave up those vices and practiced compassion instead, they found happiness and harmony. Compassion is reaching out to people. The practice of compassion has to be consistent. It is not selective. This explains why Jesus wanted his followers to love even their enemies.

Compassion should come naturally, but for some, compassion has to be taught. The ancient Greeks had a novel way of teaching compassion: they staged tragedies written by famous Greek playwrights. Suffering and sorrow came alive onstage, and as spectators watched, they wept in sympathy and compassion. It was a course in empathy.

We have seen in our own lifetime how Mother Teresa, the apostle of compassion, brought hope, joy, and peace to millions in the slums of Calcutta, in India. Like a river in flood, infinite compassion flowed out of the noble heart of Mother Teresa to the poor, sick, neglected and downtrodden. She reached out to them and helped them with kind words and deeds. Her infinite compassion transformed the lives of millions.

The history of all the religions represent the eternal struggle between the evil forces of hatred and selfishness and the mitigating virtue of compassion. We have seen how religious-inspired hatred has caused unimaginable suffering misery around the world, from the Middle East to Africa, Asia, and other places. The atrocities committed in the name of religion would not have taken place if people were properly educated in the virtue of compassion.

On compassion, the following words of Buddha are relevant: "I look for no recompense—not even to be reborn in heaven—but I seek the welfare of men to bring back those that have gone astray, to enlighten those that live in the night of terror, to banish all pain and suffering from the world. Not for the sake of my own well-being I practice universal benevolence, but I love benevolence because it is my desire to contribute to the happiness of living beings. All beings long for happiness; therefore extend your compassion to all."

Tolerance

Tolerance is the capacity for or the practice of allowing or respecting the nature, beliefs, or behavior of others. All the religions of the world want their followers to practice tolerance. In a world with so many different faiths, religious practices, diverse customs and cultures, it is essential for everyone to practice tolerance. Within a family, one should be tolerant of the views, beliefs, and practices of other members of the family. If every human being could practice a little tolerance, there would be harmony in the world.

Baha U'llah, the founder of Bahaism, wanted his followers to practice tolerance. The Baha'is view all religions as coming from God and call upon followers to join all other religions in the essential purpose of religion: establishing unity, peace, harmony, understanding, and love among mankind. The Baha'is are advised to show tolerance for other religions and develop a spirit of understanding for the followers of all other religions.

Guru Nanak was a strong advocate of tolerance. He said, "God is one, God is love, God is unity. The same God resides in the temple and in the mosque and outside as well. All human beings are equal in the eyes of God. Devotion to God and service to mankind, irrespective of caste, creed, or color, is the duty of everyone."

In today's world, we witness much senseless violence, killing, and bloodshed, all in the name of religion. Religious fanatics devoid of tolerance have caused untold sorrow and misery for millions of innocent men, women, and children around the world. The need of the hour is for people of different faiths to propagate the fundamental truths of all religions—love, peace, compassion, tolerance, and understanding. Leaders of all religions should instill in their followers the imperative need to practice tolerance in their lives, which would go a long way to eliminate prejudice, hatred, and misunderstanding and to create a more loving climate. In this connection, the soul-stirring words of Baha U'llah are so very relevant today. He said, "Each person should show forbearance, kindness, compassion, and love to one another. One should also display a spirit of extreme kindness, compassion, understanding, love, and goodwill to those who are incapable of fully grasping the truth or who are striving to understand it. The duty of every man is to attain that share of grace which God passes forth for him."

Baha U'llah's writings praise the great contributions that organized religions have brought to humanity. His writings are generous in their appreciation of the positive contributions of priests and clergymen of all faiths. At the same time, Baha U'llah severely condemned the barriers that organized religions have erected between humanity and the Revelation of God. Dogmas and prejudices have been imposed on a Divine Power, whose sole objective has been spiritual and moral. Instead of creating love, understanding, and unity, religions have caused hatred, sorrow, and suffering. The consequence has been the worldwide disputes, misunderstanding, prejudice, and misconception into which religions have fallen.. Further, organized religions have themselves become the cause of hatred and conflict among the peoples of the world.

Understanding

All the religions of the world have stressed the importance of correct understanding and interpretation. Hindu scriptures state the need for everyone to develop correct understanding. In the Bhagavad Gita, the Lord says that by knowledge alone will one have correct understanding. The first step in acquiring knowledge is eradicating ignorance, which clouds the vision and understanding. By meditation, one will develop a pure heart—and in a pure heart freed from all negative elements, knowledge will shine.

Buddha taught the Eightfold Path, which enabled one to develop right understanding, free from superstition and delusion.

Lord Mahavir wanted his followers to develop right thoughts and practice right deeds so as to develop correct understanding.

Islam gives pride of place to knowledge and correct understanding. Prophet Muhammad said, "He who leave home in search of knowledge walks in the path of God. Acquire knowledge. It enables its possessor to distinguish right from wrong; it lights the way to Heaven; it is our friend in the desert, our society in solitude, our companion when friendless; it guides us to happiness; it sustains us in misery; it is an ornament among friends and an armor against enemies."

Zoroaster taught his followers to develop understanding. According to Zoroaster, all righteous words and righteous actions spring from correct understanding. He said, "Knowledge is man's highest acquisition. It is priceless. It is unfailing and lifelong friend, his surest and safest guide in life."

The late John Paul II explained the importance of correct understanding during his historic visit to the Holy Land in the year 2000. He offered the following advice to the Palestinians and Israelis: "It is the duty of believers—Jews, Christians, and Muslims—to seek every means to promote understanding and mutual trust in favor of peace for a land that God wanted holy."

We have seen how the present generation has strayed far away from the teachings of the prophets and saints. It is a great tragedy that humanity has failed to grasp the essential and central theme of all the world religions. In this connection, let us see what the great prophet Baha U'llah said.

> Only men of peace and wedded to peace can bring about unity, understanding, and harmony. There should be a crusade for peace by men of moral integrity, courage, and strong will. As a famous philosopher said, "First keep peace within yourself, then you can bring peace to others. Each one of us should become an agent of peace. We should ask God to give us the gift of his peace. We should ask God to give us the strength to forgive and love. Once our hearts are free from prejudice, mistrust, anger, greed, and misunderstanding, we are fit for waging peace in the world.

According to Baha U'llah, religious fanaticism and hatred are a menacing fire that will ultimately devour and destroy the entire world. The violence and consequent sufferings thus generated cannot be easily quelled. Further, he said, "Those whom God will hold responsible for this great tragedy are humanity's religious leaders. Their attempts to make the Word of God a purely private preserve and its exposition to further advance their own personal interests have been the greatest single handicap against which the advancement of civilization has struggled."

In fact, according to Baha U'llah, many religious leaders have not hesitated to raise their own hands against the messengers of God. Religious leaders have hindered their people from attaining the shores of eternal salvation, since they hold power and authority in their hands. Some for the lust of power, authority, and leadership and some others through lack of understanding and knowledge have been the main cause for the deprivation of the people.

Baha U'llah feels that organized religions can contribute to happiness, peace, understanding, and universal love, when their leaders are imbued with the spirit of self-sacrifice and a love of humanity, together with compassion and understanding.

All religions are unanimous in their enthusiasm for love, peace, compassion, tolerance, and understanding. They are also unanimous in their objective of serving humanity and encouraging inner peace—and through that, a peaceful human community. All religions agree upon the need to control the undisciplined mind and free it from all negative and impure thoughts. The religions teach and guide us to a spiritual state that is peaceful and disciplined, ethical and wise. It would, therefore, benefit humanity to sincerely try to understand and implement the sacred precepts of goodness taught by all the religions of the world.

CHAPTER 2

Christianity

INTRODUCTION TO CHRISTIANITY

Christianity, stemming out of Judaism and developing primarily in the West, has become the largest religion of the world, and except for Islam, it is the youngest major world religion. Approximately one in every three persons on earth is identified as a practicing Christian. A religion practiced by so many people naturally encompasses a wide variety of beliefs and practices. In general, Christians share a common belief in the uniqueness of Jesus of Nazareth as a truly divine and truly human incarnate son of God, who is the savior of mankind.

Christianity is a religion founded on the teachings of Jesus Christ. A Christian is one professing belief in Jesus Christ or following the religion based on the teachings of Jesus Christ. Christians believe in one God who created the universe and created human beings to have a special relationship with him. Through human willfulness, exemplified in the story of Adam and Eve, this relationship was broken. God showed his love for humanity by sending his son, Jesus, to bring humanity back to a personal relationship with God.

Christians take their name from the title given to Jesus: the Christ, meaning the "anointed one of God." After three years of teaching, Jesus was executed by crucifixion but was brought back to life again, showing God's power over death and suffering and demonstrating that death is not an end. Christians believe that they are called to be like Christ.

Jesus died on the cross, the normal method of execution in the Roman Empire at that time. It was a shameful and painful death, but Christians believe that through Jesus's resurrection, God showed his power over shame, pain, suffering, and death.

The teachings of Jesus Christ are so very noble, liberal, simple, and universal because he was an incarnation of God.

In his dealings with his followers and with the public in general, Jesus manifested great love and compassion. While preaching the message of God's kingdom, he personally practiced love, humility, and compassion. Thus, in the final hours of his life, he could say to his disciples, "I am giving you a new commandment, that you love one another. Just as I have loved you, that you also love one another. By this all will know that you are my disciples, if you have love among yourselves" (John 13:34, 35). Therefore, the essence of Christianity in principle is based on self-sacrificing love. In practice, this means a Christian should love even his enemies.

Christians number more than two billion worldwide. The largest branch or denomination of Christianity is Catholicism, with over nine hundred million followers. Other major branches are Orthodox and Protestants. Christians believe in justification by faith—that through their belief in Jesus as the son of God, and in his death and resurrection, they can have a relationship with God, whose forgiveness was given once and for all through the death of Jesus Christ.

Christians believe in the Trinity—that is, in God as Father, Son, and Holy Spirit. Christians believe in one God who took form on earth as Jesus Christ and who, through the work of the Holy Spirit, is present today and evident in the works of believers.

There are hundreds of Christian pilgrimage sites around the world. Israel is important because of its links with Jesus. Rome is the seat of the Pope, the spiritual leader of Catholics.

The Bible, the holy scripture of Christianity, consists of the Old Testament, written in Hebrew, and the New Testament, written in Greek, which contains the accounts of the life and teachings of Jesus Christ and letters from early Christians.

Christians regard the Bible as God's written message to mankind. In addition to it being a historical record of Jesus's life and miracles, the Bible reveals God's personality, great love, compassion, and truth, as well as how one can have a relationship with God.

Christianity

Of all the great religions of the world, Christianity is the most widespread, and it has the largest number of followers. More than two thousand years of history have brought an astounding diversity to this great religion. From the majestic and grand pontifical High Mass at Saint Peter's in Rome to the plain, simple Quaker meeting, from the historical and famous Saint

Paul's in London to the poor slums in Calcutta, where Mother Theresa lived and worked, one can see the power, glory, greatness, and beauty of Christianity. From this dazzling and wonderful complex, one can visualize the central strands that unite this great world religion and its three major divisions, namely Roman Catholicism, Eastern orthodox, and Protestantism.

Christianity is founded on concrete events and actual historical happenings. It revolves around the life of a simple Jewish carpenter who was born in a stable and did not have any college education. It is the story of a person who had no earthly possessions and who was executed as a criminal at the age of thirty-five. Nevertheless, his birthday is celebrated with great pomp, joy, and devotion throughout the world.

Jesus was a charismatic, ideal teacher and a wonder worker who stood in a tradition that stretched back to the beginnings of Hebrew history. The prophets and saints who comprised that tradition meditated between everyday wonder and the spirit world that enveloped it. From the spirit world, the prophets and saints drew power, which they used to help the poor and alleviate their pain. Jesus, who was oriented in the spirit world, utilized his spirit-derived powers for the benefit of the people, for the alleviation of their suffering and pain, and for bringing a new social order.

Founder

Jesus is the founder of the religion known as Christianity. Most Christians view him as the son of God. The Julian and Gregorian calendars are dated from the year of the birth of Jesus Christ. According to historical records and scholars, it is believed that Jesus was born about 3 BC and died about AD 30. He was born and raised as a Jew and later he became a rabbi and teacher. According to Christian scripture, he was the Messiah awaited by the Jews. Jesus Christ took up preaching and practiced healing at the age of thirty. Few years later, he was sentenced to death in Jerusalem, where he was executed by crucifixion. The scripture says that he soon rose from the dead.

Scripture

The chief scripture is the Bible. The Christian Bible consists of the thirty-nine books of the Hebrew scriptures, called by many the Old Testament, and the twenty-seven books of the Christian Greek scriptures, often called the New Testament. Thus, the Bible is a miniature library of sixty-six books written by some forty men in the course of six hundred years.

The Greek Scriptures include four Gospels, or accounts of the life of Jesus Christ and the good news that he preached. Two of these were written by contemporary followers of Christ, Matthew and John. The other two were written by the early believers Mark and Luke. The Gospels are followed by the Acts of Apostles, an account of the early Christian missionary activity complied by Luke. Next are fourteen letters from the Apostle Paul to various individual Christians and congregations, followed by letters from James, Peter, John, and Jude. The final book is Revelation, written by John.

That so many persons of diverse backgrounds and living in different times and cultures could produce such a harmonious book is strong proof that the Bible is not simply the product of human intelligence but is inspired by God. The Bible itself states, "All scripture is inspired of God." Thus, the scriptures were written under the influence of God's Holy Spirit, or active force.

Beliefs

These beliefs are key to the Christian faith:

- The Bible is the word of God. It is a complete and final revelation of God.
- There is one God and only one God. He is personal and knowable. He manifests himself in three persons: the Father, the Son, and the Holy Spirit.
- Jesus Christ is God manifested in the flesh, born of a virgin, without sin, and the chosen Messiah who will one day set up his kingdom on earth.
- Jesus Christ died on the cross for our sins, was buried, rose again from the dead, ascended back to heaven, and will one day return to this earth.
- All persons are sinners, guilty before God, deserving of judgment, and in need of a savior, Jesus Christ our Lord.
- Salvation from sin, death, and hell is by God's grace, based on the work of Jesus Christ alone. It is received by faith apart from any human performance or merit.
- Eternal life is a gift of God, and nothing can separate the believer from the love of God.
- Unbelievers face eternal punishment. Believers face eternal life.
- All believers should attend a local church for mutual edification, encouragement, evangelism, service, and worship

Practice

Most Christian denominations observe the rite of baptism, administered to children and to newly converted members, and the Eucharist, or Communion, in which members partake of bread and wine in commemoration of Jesus. Christians are organized into congregations and gather for worship in churches. Most denominations have designated Sunday as the day for special observance, prayer, and worship. In most Christian denominations, men and women observe monogamy, and divorce is very much discouraged. There are many different standards of personal conduct, ranging from the ascetic to the celebratory.

Schools and Sects

There are two historic divisions in Christianity. In AD 1054, the Eastern (or Orthodox) Church and the Western (or Roman) Church separated. Then, in the 1500s, reformers including Martin Luther and John Calvin broke from the Roman Church to form a number of separate denominations that together are called Protestant. The Orthodox churches remain dominant in Greece, the Soviet Union, and in parts of Eastern Europe. The Roman Church, known today as the Roman Catholic or simply the Catholic Church, predominates in southern Europe and in Latin America. Protestant churches are predominant in northern Europe (including Great Britain), North America, and Australia. Both Catholic and Protestant churches have conducted industrious missionary programs in Africa and Asia and share influence in these regions. In addition to the three main groups of Christians, there are many small denominations and sects that do not fit comfortably into any of the three.

History

At the time of his death, Jesus had only a small handful of devoted followers. Within a century, they had spread the teachings of Jesus to all parts of the Roman Empire. There were communities of worshippers in Greece, Asia Minor, Palestine, and the Roman Empire. Christians were cruelly persecuted by the Roman state, and the followers of Christ were driven underground. By AD 300, however, Christians attained recognition as well as influence. In 313, Emperor Constantine decreed tolerance for Christianity and was reportedly baptized on his deathbed. By the turn of the century, Christianity became the official religion of the Roman Empire itself.

This event marked the beginning of a new militant phase. Missionaries were sent to all parts of Europe to establish churches, and Christianity triumphed throughout Europe, from Ireland to Poland. After dividing from the Eastern churches, the Western churches became a major preserver and extender of learning at home. Abroad, it tried to dislodge by crusade the Muslim Turks, who had control of the Holy Land. A long period of religious strife began with the Reformation after 1517. Religious wars pervaded Europe, causing untold suffering. Further, European exploration and conquests were spreading Christianity to the Americas and to Asia. Roman Catholics and Protestants proselytized wherever they were predominant.

From the mid 1800s to the mid 1900s, the Western churches (Catholic and Protestant) carried out many missionary programs in Africa and East Asia, which contributed to the growth of vigorous and independent churches there.

Jesus Christ

It is believed that Jesus was born around 3 BC, to Joseph and Mary, in Bethlehem of Judea, during the reign of King Herod. After Joseph married Mary, an angel appeared before him in a dream and said to him, "[Mary] will bring forth a son, and you will call him Jesus. Jesus shall save his people from their sins."

When Jesus was born, some wise men saw his star in the East, and they wanted to see Jesus and worship him. They approached King Herod and asked him about the whereabouts of Jesus, who was born king of the Jews, telling the king they wished to worship Jesus. On hearing this news, King Herod feared possible loss of his kingship and ordered the massacre of all the newborn males in his kingdom so as to ensure his safety from a future enemy.

Divine dispensation saved Jesus. To escape the wrath of Herod, Joseph fled with his son to Egypt. Jesus returned to Galilee and then to Nazareth after the death of Herod. John the Baptist, a major religious preacher, baptized Jesus at the River Jordan. As soon as he was baptized, Jesus saw the Spirit of God descending like a dove and lighting upon him, and a heavenly voice said, "You are my Son, the beloved. I have approved you."

Complete details on Jesus's life and spiritual practices are not known, but available records indicate that after being baptized, Jesus was not seen for about forty days. Afterward, Satan tried to tempt Jesus in many ways, but as Jesus was ever conscious of his divine mission, Satan's attempts failed.

From that time onward, Jesus began to preach. One by one, the twelve famous disciples joined Jesus as he went from village to village, spreading his new Gospel, healing the sick, alleviating suffering, consoling the sorrowful, and even bringing the dead back to life. He never accepted any material rewards and did not look for wealth. Jesus said that there is more happiness in giving than in receiving. He also taught his disciples how to preach.

Jesus taught by using simple logic and parables—or illustrations from everyday life—which appealed to the heart and the mind of the people. His famous Sermon on the Mount, discussed below, is an outstanding example of his brilliant teaching methods. In his dealings with his followers and with the public in general, Jesus displayed great love, understanding, kindness, and compassion. While preaching the message of God's kingdom, Jesus also personally practiced love, compassion, and humility. In the final hours of his life, Jesus said to his disciples, "I am giving you a new commandment that you love one on another just as I have loved you. By this all will know that you are my disciples, if you have love among yourselves." (John 13:34–31) As Jesus indicated, the essence of Christianity in practice is self-sacrificing love based on principles. In practice, this means a Christian should love even his enemies although he may hate the enemies' evil works.

Hundreds of thousands gathered around Jesus wherever he went. They showered their great love and affection on him and hailed him as the King of the Jews. This spontaneous adulation aroused hatred and envy in vested interests. They accused Jesus unjustly and falsely of blasphemy. They conducted a farcical trial and, finally, sentenced him to death by crucifixion. Even at the time of his crucifixion, Jesus exhibited only love and compassion. As he hung on the cross, he prayed to God, saying, "Oh Lord, forgive them, for they know not what they do."

Jesus was an ideal preacher, a true friend and guide of mankind, and a repository of all virtue and goodness. His patience and meekness in suffering and his poverty have sanctified the homes of the poor. His tenderness and love for his followers, the downtrodden, the sick, and the poor fill the earth with innumerable works of tenderness, benevolence, and sympathy.

Jesus Christ was a liberal in his teachings and never forced anything on others against their will. In this connection, Jesus said, "I am not come to destroy, but to fulfill." Christ further said that when one's heart is pure, one will see God. No church, no priest, nothing at all could keep a pure heart from seeing God. The teachings of Jesus Christ are liberal and universal because he was an incarnation of God. Christ lived in God, loved in God, taught in God, suffered in God so that we too might live and love, suffer and teach as he did.

What Jesus taught was far from an ethic or philosophy. He pointed to God as the source of salvation when he said, "For God loved the world so much that he gave his only begotten son, in order that everyone exercising faith in him might not be destroyed, but have everlasting life." For God sent forth his son into the world, not for him to judge the world but for the world to be saved through him.

May the great teachings of Jesus Christ enrich, ennoble, and enlighten mankind.

The Holy Bible

The word Bible comes from the Greek word "biblia," which means "books." The plural is of great significance, since the Bible is a collection of books written by different men over a vast period of time. Further, the books of the Bible were written in widely different cultural and historic situations and in a rich variety of styles and languages. This collection has come to be regarded by Christians as a single holy unit, "the Bible." It consists of the Old Testament and the New Testament.

The Old Testament

There are two unequal parts to the Bible, and the first, which is far larger and is called by Christians the Old Testament, is simply the Hebrew scriptures of Judaism. The scriptures present the history and religious thoughts of the people of God through the time when Jesus came as the Jews' Messiah.

By and large, Christians have always considered themselves as the legitimate heirs to the religion of ancient Israel. Consequently, they accept the books of the Hebrew Bible as fully canonical, or part of Scripture. Without them, the specifically Christian scriptures could hardly be understood.

A number of Jewish works, known as the Apocrypha, are included in Roman Catholic editions of the Old Testament. Protestant Bibles do not, however, include these works, which Judaism did not accept as canonical. Sometimes, however, they are printed after the Old Testament as a separate section.

The New Testament

The Christian books of the Bible known as the New Testament comprise twenty-seven writings by Christians of the first century AD. Though most of the writers were of Jewish origin, the books are in Greek, which was the common language of the Roman Empire.

They consist of four Gospels, which relate from different points of view the life and teachings of Jesus Christ, together with the Acts of the Apostles, which is the continuation of the Gospel of Luke, telling the story of the first thirty years of the Christian church. There are thirteen letters by Paul, the great missionary leader, to churches and individuals; eight other letters by early Christian leaders; and the Revelation of John, a visionary work.

The New Testament writings, while produced within a relatively short period compared with the many centuries taken to complete the Old Testament, are mixed in style and content. Christians consider the Old and New Testaments as a unity, often referred to as the "Word of God." All followers of Christ have spoken of the Bible as "inspired," meaning that it is not merely great literature or that it brings spiritual enlightenment, but that it comes directly from God. Christians believe that what the authors wrote in their own language and in their historical setting was directed by God.

All Christians accept the Bible as an authority, both in guiding their actions and in forming their beliefs. However, there is disagreement on this. A goal of the Protestant Reformation (considered to have begun in 1517) was to restore the Bible to a place of authority above the pronouncements of the leaders of the church. Within Protestant Christianity, the Enlightenment of the eighteenth century led to a new confidence in human reason as the final guide to truth. Consequently, the Bible came to be considered a record of human development only and not a divine revelation.

At present, while evangelical Christianity accepts the Bible as its supreme authority, liberal Protestantism questions the place of the Bible as the supreme authority. In Roman Catholicism, there has been great resurgence of interest in the Bible.

The Sermon on the Mount

The Sermon on the Mount is an outstanding example of the teachings of Jesus. Included in the sermon is Jesus's model prayer, in which he gives a very vivid and clear picture of Christian priorities by giving the sanctification of God top priority. It takes readers to great spiritual heights and puts faith in their hearts.

> Blessed are those who feel poor in spiritual things, for the kingdom of heaven belongs to them. Blessed are the mourners, for they will be comforted. Blessed are the lowly in mind, for they will possess the land.
>
> Blessed are those who hunger and thirst for being and doing right, for they will be completely satisfied. Blessed are those who show mercy, for they will have mercy shown them. Blessed are the pure in heart, for they will see God. Blessed are the peacemakers, for they will be called God's sons.
>
> Blessed are those who suffer persecution for being and doing right, for the kingdom of heaven belongs to them.
>
> Blessed are you when people abuse you and persecute you, and keep on falsely telling all sorts of evil against you for my sake. Keep on rejoicing and leaping for ecstasy; for your reward will be rich in heaven; for this is the way they persecuted the prophets who lived

before you. You are the salt of the earth. But if salt loses its strength, what can make it salt again. It is good for nothing but to be thrown away and trodden under foot.

You are the light of the world. A city that is built upon a hill cannot be hidden. People do not light a lamp and put it under a peek-measure but on a lamp stand, and it gives light to all that are in the house. Let your light shine before people in such a way that they may see your good deeds and praise your father in heaven.

Do not suppose that I have come to set aside the law of the prophets. I have not come to set them aside but to fill them up to the brim. For I solemnly say to you, heaven and earth would soon pass away than the dotting of an "I" or crossing of a "T" from the law, until it all becomes in force. Whoever, therefore, breaks one of the least of these commands and teaches others to do so, will be ranked as least in the kingdom of heaven, but whoever practices them and teaches others to do so, will be ranked as great in the kingdom of heaven. For I tell you that unless your righteousness far surpasses that of the scribes and Pharisees, you will never get into the kingdom of heaven at all.

You have heard that it was said to the men of old, "You must not murder and whoever murders will have to answer to the court." But I say to you, everyone who harbors malice against his brother will have to answer to the court, and whoever speaks contemptuously to his brother will have to answer to the supreme court, and whoever says to his brother "you cursed fool" will have to pay the penalty in the pit of torture, So if, in the very act of presenting your gift at the altar, you remember that your brother has something against you, leave the gift right there at the altar, and first go and make peace with your brother and then come back and present your gift."

Mathew 5:2–24

God and His Attributes

The most important requirement for living in reality is to believe in God. Infinite belief and blind trust should be the first affirmation of the Apostles' Creed. As one draws closer to God, one is awed by his greatness and majesty. How can one know God? All of us can know God by our faith and by reason, by constantly thinking of him, speaking about him, and by worshipping him. Knowledge of God is the most important knowledge, since God is our ultimate end, our destiny, and our happiness. A life devoid of knowledge of God is empty and will be like a rudderless boat.

Let us examine some of God's attributes. God is infinite, and, consequently, he cannot be defined. God is righteous, wise, merciful, loving, and compassionate. We can know the nature of God by faith and prayer and, best of all, by loving him, doing his will, and obeying his commandments. We can also know something of God's nature from ourselves, from our deepest desires. God is our source of ultimate joy, and God is the one whose presence will give us infinite ecstasy, peace, and fulfillment. God is an ocean of infinite beauty, a light of infinite understanding, and a heart full of mercy, kindness, compassion, and love.

God is self-sufficient. God does not require any advice or aid from man to run his world. For man, God is a necessity, but man is not necessary to God.

God is omnipotent. He is all-powerful. He, who created everything from nothing, can do anything. Vast oceans are but a drop in the hand of the Infinite. Mighty mountains are like specks of dust in God's hand. His fingers are so far-reaching in their span that they encompass the heavens. He is the mighty God, and his works declare the glory of his name.

God is omniscient. God needs no assistance from any external source. His wisdom is inexhaustible, and he needs to consult no one. His knowledge is unlimited, and he knows all and foresees everything. He always knows what his next move will be, and his wisdom is unknowable.

God is love. His infinite love reaches out to all living beings. Self-giving love is what God really is. It is this self-giving love that motivates everything that God does—namely his creation, his redemption, and his care over our lives.

God is sovereign. He is transcendent. God sees all and controls the entire universe.

God is eternal. He transcends all time and space. He is everlasting and moves through eternity with unhurried tread, for he is "the high and exalted One who lives forever, whose name is holy." (Isaiah 57:15)

God is one. God is unique; there is only one God. God is perfect and righteous. He is both just and merciful.

The Bible says:

> "The Lord God is like a sun and shield; The Lord gives us kindness and honor. He does not hold back anything good from those whose lives are innocent" (Psalm 84:11).

> "Then the Lord said to Moses, 'I will do what you ask, because I know you very well, and I am pleased with you.' Then Moses said, 'Now please show me your glory.' The Lord answered, 'I will cause

> all my goodness to pass in front of you, and I will announce my name, the Lord, so you can hear it. I will show kindness to anyone to whom I want to show kindness, and I will show mercy to anyone to whom I want to show mercy'" (Exodus 33:17–19).

Joy

Joy is a condition or feeling of extreme pleasure or happiness. It is a mental condition of manifestation of delight and gladness upon achieving one's objective or attaining success or securing an object of one's desire. Joy is infectious; the joyous person spreads joy all around him. In the context of religion, real joy comes from loving God, the joy that comes from prayer and worship.

Joy is of two kinds, namely real and fleeting. We should understand the difference between the joy that is fleeting and superficial and the joy that is real and abiding, permanent and everlasting. Fleeting joy comes from material things, which are transient and ephemeral. If we want to experience real and lasting joy, we should shy away from all sensual pleasures that money can by and instead turn our attention to God. When a person turns his attention from the temporary joy that arises from material things and concentrates exclusively on God, he can immediately feel the difference. The mind previously bruised and battered by the disappointments and sorrows of life is now filled with lasting peace and real joy.

Real joy is the joy of giving. We should utilize any wealth we earned legitimately to help the poor, the sick, the aged, and the dispossessed. As Mother Theresa said, "One should go on giving more and more till it hurts." We can actually see the joy emanating from the faces of the poor and the sick when we reach out to them, touch their hearts, and lend them a helping hand. Wiping tears from the eyes of the suffering and bringing out a smile is the real joy of life. Money cannot buy such pure joy. There is so much suffering and sadness around us, but by showing compassion, we not only bring some joy into the lives of others, but we create real joy and inner bliss in our own hearts.

Good thoughts, good words, and good deeds produce real joy. While a mind filled with evil thoughts often causes others to suffer, good thoughts make the mind pure, and a pure mind exudes pure joy. By returning good words for abuses, by returning good deeds for evil, and by remaining calm against all provocations, we can attain peace and perfect joy.

Another source of great and lasting joy is forgiveness, the readiness to forget and forgive. We should all strive to follow Jesus's example when he said, "Oh Father, forgive them, for they know not what they do." When people cause us hurt and suffering—whether deliberately or unknowingly—often, our immediate response is one of anger coupled with a desire for revenge. Such an attitude will only aggravate the situation, so, instead, we should readily forgive and forget. Where there was previously anger and hatred, there will now be peace, understanding, love, and joy.

The real joy is the joy of living. We should begin each day with a prayer of thanks to God for another day of joyous life. Similarly, before going to bed, we should thank God for filling our day with joy. If we open and close each day with grateful thanks to God for all his blessings, God will bless our heart with indescribable, lasting joy. Jesus taught us how to pray. He said, "Our Father who is in heaven, hallowed be your name. Your kingdom come, your will be done on earth, as it is in heaven. Give us this day our daily bread and forgives us our debts as we forgive our debtors. And lead us not into temptation but deliver us from evil; for yours is the kingdom, and the power, and glory forever." Such a prayer will transform our lives and give us perfect peace and lasting inner joy.

Let us now examine what some saints have said about real joy.

> "Like Jesus, we belong to the world living not for ourselves but for others. The joy of the Lord is our strength." —Mother Teresa

> "I do not envy those who have never known any pain, physical or spiritual; because I strongly suspect that only those who have suffered great pain are able to know equally great joy." —Madeline L Engle

> "The safest remedy against the thousand snares and evils of the enemy is spiritual joy." Saint Francis

Peace

Almost all the religions of the world preach peace, love, and compassion as central themes, as reflected in the lives of their great mystics and prophets. This holds true in Christianity as well; its essence is peace, and the teachings of Jesus fully emphasize the need for peace.

Peace in its wider sense is the absence of hostilities like war. Viewed from the point of view of an individual's life, peace means freedom from quarrels and disagreements. Peace entails harmonious relationships and having understanding and compassion for others.

Jesus was known as the prince of peace. In the Sermon on the Mount, he said, "Blessed are the peacemakers, for they shall be called the children of God."

Saint Francis was another noble soul who had a deep faith in God and who devoted himself to following Jesus's example and practicing peace. Saint Francis's famous prayer demonstrates his deep and sincere commitment to peace.

Lord, make me an instrument of your peace;
Where there is hatred, let me sow love;
Where there is injury, pardon;
Where there is doubt, faith;
Where there is despair, hope;
Where there is darkness, light;
Where there is sadness, joy.
O Divine Master,
grant that I may not so much seek to
Be consoled as to console;
To be understood as to understand;
To be loved as to love;
For it is in giving that we receive,
It is in pardoning that we are pardoned,
It is in dying that we are born to eternal life.

Mother Teresa is another example of a great saint wedded to peace. She spent her entire life promoting peace and harmony. Working in the poorest and dirtiest slums, she carried the message of peace and brought hope and joy to the lives of millions of people. She fought against intolerance, prejudice, and hatred and was a crusader for peace.

We are witnessing in the world today the lack of peace: the fight between the haves and the have-nots, terrorism and bloodshed in the name of religion, brutal killings and suffering in all parts of the world. All of this is due to our total lack of commitment to peace. Only those wedded to peace can bring about unity, understanding, and harmony. There should be a crusade for peace by people of moral integrity, courage, and strong will.

As a famous philosopher, Thomas Kempis, said, "First keep peace within yourself, then you can bring peace to others." Each one of us should become an agent of peace by asking God to give us the gift of his peace, to give us the strength to forgive and love. Once our hearts are free from prejudice, mistrust, anger, and misunderstanding, we will be able to wage peace in the world. We should conscientiously practice goodness, purity, and nonviolence, irrespective of what others do to us. By responding to evil with good, by showing kindness and love in the face of hatred and anger, we can create a climate of peace and understanding. When we are surrounded by hot tempers and hurt feelings, we should pray to God to give us his peace.

When we calm our heart and breathe slowly as we pray, our heart will be filled within an inner calm that will allow us to be an instrument of God's peace in the world.

The Bible stresses the importance of peace. It tells us that God gives strength and confidence to people through his blessings of peace.

Love

The central theme of Jesus's teachings is love. In fact, God himself is love. For humans, love is the highest expression of goodness.

Love is God, and God is love. We all know the love that God has for us, and we trust that love; those who live in love, live in God. The Lord has given love a prominent as well as dominant place on the scale of ethical values. Love is central in God's own nature, and he wants it to be central in man. Scripture emphasizes that God loves all of us with all his heart, and he longs for us to love him with all our power, with all our heart and soul.

Love is the self-imparting quality in the nature of God that moves him to seek the highest good of his creatures, in whom he seeks to awaken responsive love. Love is basic to our knowledge of and intimacy with God. According to the disciple John, "The one who does not love does not know God, for God is love." (John 4:8) Love is not mere sentiment, but it is an activity. Love means willing sacrifices. Pure love is unselfish and outgoing. God's love moved him to sacrificial action: he sent his one and only son into the world that we might live through him. God's love compels him to seek the lost and recover the wanderers.

Genuine love for God is much more than a pleasant stirring of the emotions. It involves the whole strength of our moral natures. The flame of our love for God and our fellow men should be fed by fuel provided by our mind. The apostle Paul said, "I shall pray with the spirit, and I shall pray with the mind also." Our love for and worship of God must be sincere, true, pure. We should love and worship God with zeal.

Jesus Christ sets his own love before us as a model. "A new commandment I give to you that you love one another. Even as I have loved you, that you also love one another. By this all will know that you are my disciples, if you have love among yourselves."

In the Bible it is said, "God is love. Those who live in love live in God, and God lives in them." (John 4:16) The essence of Christianity in practice is self-sacrificing love based on principle. In practice this means that a Christian should love even his enemies, although he may hate their evil deeds. What a different world this would be if everyone actually practiced that form of love. If only humanity practiced what Jesus preached about love, this world of ours would be a better, safer, and happier place.

Prayer

The urge to live a peaceful and harmonious life, the desire to free the mind from all the stresses and strains of life, the burning desire to soar high and discover a divine existence—all these can be achieved through prayer. Thus, prayer can be defined as the most direct path to God for spiritual seekers. Prayer opens up humble and honest self-examination and produces a perfect alignment of one's relationship to the world and to God. The word "prayer" has been very much misunderstood and has come to denote some sort of beggary resorted to by the emotionally dependent. This is not true prayer. It is only preying upon God.

What is prayer? It is not an activity, but a way of being. Prayer is less a function and more a disposition. The catechism of the Catholic Church describes prayer as "a vital and personal relationship with the living God." Prayer means standing before God and raising up our mind and heart to him with reverent attention and devotion. Prayer is the sincere offer of the whole of ourselves in the Holy Spirit to the Father through Jesus Christ. Prayer engages and expresses our relationship with God. The essence of prayer is communication, our communication with God.

Prayer is talking directly to God. Great mystics are in a state of perpetual prayer. To them, God is much more real than the external world. Others pray to God, accepting his existence on faith. During personal misfortunes, failures, tragedies, and disappointments, something is stirred up in the human heart, faith in a Supreme Being or Supreme Power is born, and prayer follows. Prayer is thus the deepest impulse of the soul of man. Prayer by its very nature is something private—a soul speaking to the Soul.

Prayer takes five basic forms. These are adoration, petition, intercession, thanksgiving, and praise.

Adoration is the means to, and the expression of, the love of God—a love that finds its consummation in the intuitive knowledge of the Godhead, which is the fruit of contemplation. It is to these higher forms of communion with God that some philosophers refer whenever they use the word "prayer."

Adoration exalts the greatness of God, the creator and sustainer, in the spirit of humility and homage.

The prayer of petition acknowledges our dependence on God, the Father, especially as it prompts us to turn back to him in a spirit of repentance and contrition, asking for forgiveness. Through the prayer of intercession, we entrust ourselves to God's mercy, especially by placing before the Father the concerns and worries of others in need. The prayer of thanksgiving gives voice to the gratitude that befits every mature and honest person, especially as it calls to mind the redeeming deeds of Jesus that save us and make us free. The prayer of praise "lauds God for his own sake and gives him glory, quite beyond what he does, but simply because he is." (2639)

All the five different forms of prayer help us to love God—love him for his mercy, kindness, compassion, and assistance in our lives. They enable us to love God for his presence and his blessings, for his redemptive tenderness. They help us love God for himself.

Regarding prayer, Jesus said, "When you pray, do not pray like the hypocrite; for they love to pray standing in the synagogues and in the corners of the streets, that they be seen by others. Verily, they have their reward." Instead, he said, "Enter your closet, shut the door, and pray to your Father in secret; and your Father who sees you in secret shall reward you openly."

Faith

Faith is a confident belief in the truth, value, or trustworthiness of a person, idea, or thing. In the context of religion, it is a firm and unshakeable belief and trust in God and in the doctrine conveyed in the scriptures or other religious works. All the world religions stress the importance of faith and the power of faith in the lives of its followers. Prayer presupposes faith. In fact, prayer is an exercise of one's faith.

The mental makeup of a person is such that his heart naturally longs for a sanctuary, for satisfaction, for an abiding home. As a child has infinite faith and confidence about his or her mother's competence, a forlorn soul has faith and conviction about the omnipotence of God and longs for his help.

A person who prays generally has, among other things, faith in a religion, in scriptures, in an omnipotent superpower, in a sense of his own helplessness, and in a longing for a stable refuge. Faith is a quality much extolled in holy books. Faith is an intense, deep, strong trust in God and the conviction that God and God alone can help one face and overcome all the problems of life. The great sages, saints, and religious leaders who moved the world spiritually were all imbued with tremendous faith. As the saying goes, faith can move mountains.

Nothing is impossible to a man of abundant faith. Faith in oneself, together with devotion to the ideal and sincere effort to serve the ideal—all these put together is faith. Doubt, vagueness of purpose, and slovenly execution are the traits of a person lacking faith, whereas a person of faith is sincere, dedicated, and earnest in all his actions. All the great religious leaders of the world religions have demonstrated the power of faith. Their faith was so strong and powerful that they could convey their faith to millions of their followers.

Faith leads us to our ideal or our God. God is the source of energy, and when we attune our mind to God, we get energized. We then become endowed with indomitable courage, enthusiasm, hope, and optimism. When another person comes into contact with such a person, he or she in turn absorbs these qualities. This explains how ordinary men and women have become saints.

Faith is the answer to fear, worry, and insecurity. Deep down, we are all worried or afraid of something, such as suffering or dying—and people sin because of fear. Faith removes all fear, just as light destroys darkness. God has shined his light into the world, and it has removed all darkness. This light is Jesus Christ.

On faith, Jesus said, "Because your faith is too small, I tell you the truth. If your faith is as big as a mustard seed, you can say to the mountain, 'Move from here to there' and it will move. All things are possible for you." By this Jesus meant that with faith, anything is possible.

Forgiveness and Forgiving

One of the strongest themes in Jesus's teaching is forgiveness, a strong pillar of Christianity. Christians are called on to forgive enemies, both Christian and non-Christian, an act intended to benefit both parties. In many cases, forgiveness may win over the other person and restore a friendly relationship. However, even when it does not, forgiveness is very important.

Forgiveness is the noble trait of forgetting and excusing the fault or the offence of others. It is the magnanimous act of pardoning the person who has caused harm, removing anger or the spirit of vengeance. It requires both mental strength and large-heartedness to readily forget the faults of others, especially when one has deliberately caused suffering and pain. The petty-minded person tends to retaliate, while the magnanimous person readily forgives. The famous words of Jesus Christ should inspire humanity to practice forgiveness: "Oh Father, forgive them, for they know not what they do."

Christianity teaches us to get along with each other and to forgive each other. If someone does wrong to us or causes hurt or offense, we should forgive that person, because God will then forgive us. In fact, the essence of Christianity is forgiveness, illustrated by Jesus's words: "Yes, if you forgive other people for the things they do wrong, then your Father in heaven will also forgive you for the things you do wrong. But if you don't forgive the wrong things people do to you, then your Father in heaven will not forgive the wrong things you do." (Matthew 6:14-15)

The following lines from the Bible glorify forgiveness:

> "Happy is the person whose sins are forgiven and whose wrongs are pardoned. Happy is the person whom the Lord does not consider guilty and in whom there is nothing false". (Psalm 32:1-2 NCV)

> "Get along with each other, and forgive each other. If someone does wrong to you, forgive that person because the Lord forgave you." (Colossians 3 v 13-17)

Forgiveness of Sins

All around the world, Christians repeat the following familiar words of worship: "I believe in the forgiveness of sins. I acknowledge one baptism for the remission of sins." Jesus frequently said, "Thy sins are forgiven thee," a phrase that consistently accompanied the exercise of his healing powers. On one occasion, Jesus pointed to the healing of a palsy-stricken man as a sign that he had a right to declare to a man that his sins were forgiven.

Jesus says, "Hearken, again, that I may tell you the word in truth of what type is the mystery of baptism, which remitteth sins. When a man receiveth the mysteries of the baptism, those mysteries become a mighty fire, exceedingly fierce, wise, which burneth up all sins, they enter the soul occultly and devour all the sins which the spiritual counterfeit hath implanted in it." And Jesus adds, "This is the way in which the mysteries of the baptism remit sins and every inequity." (Esoteric Christianity, by Annie Wood Besant)

The concept of forgiveness of sins appears in almost all religions, and human nature responds strongly to the concept of sins being forgiven: we notice that people suffer remorse for wrongdoing, and when they free themselves from the shackles of this remorse, they go forward with a glad heart. They feel as though a big burden has been lifted from them. The sense of sin disappears, and with it the gnawing pain. There is a sense of inner peace, joy, freedom as a result of the forgiveness of sins.

The concept of forgiveness of sins in Christianity has a parallel in the Hindu scripture the Bhagavad Gita, where the God speaks as follows: "Even if the most sinful worship me with undivided heart, he too must be accounted righteous, for he has rightly resolved."

This sense of forgiveness is the feeling that fills the heart with profound joy when the will is turned to harmony with the Divine, when—the soul having opened its windows—the sunshine of love and light and bliss pours in, and when the heart feels oneness with the whole. This is the noble truth that gives vitality to even the crudest presentation of the forgiveness of sins, an inspiration to pure and spiritual living.

On the forgiveness of sins, Jesus said, "For if you forgive men their trespasses, your heavenly Father will also forgive you. But if you do not forgive them their trespasses, neither will your father forgive your trespasses."

Words of Wisdom

Every good action and every perfect gift is from God. These good gifts come down from the Creator of the sun, moon and stars, who does not change like their shifting shadows. God decided to give us life through the word of truth so we might be the most important of all things he made.

Some people are like the land that gets plenty of rain. The land produces a good crop for those who work it and it receives God's blessings. Other people are like land that grows thorns and weeds and is worthless. It is in danger of being cursed by God and will be destroyed by fire.

But if any of you needs wisdom, you should ask God for it. He is generous and enjoys giving to all people, so he will give you wisdom. But when you ask God you must believe and not doubt. Anyone who doubts is like a wave in the sea, blown up and down by the wind.

I was hungry, and you gave me food. I was thirsty, and you gave me something to drink. I was alone and away from home, and you invited me into your house. I was without clothes, and you gave me something to wear. 1 was sick and you care of me. I was in prison, and you visited me. Then the good people will answer, "Lord, when did we see you hungry and give you food or thirsty and gave you something to drink? When did we see you alone and way from home and invite you into our house? When did we see you without clothes and give you something to wear? When did we see you sick or in prison and care for you?" Then the King will answer, "I tell you the truth, anything you did for even the least of my people here, you also did for me."

God is fair; he will not forget the work you did and the love you showed for him by helping his people. And he will remember that you are still helping them. We want each of you to go on with the same hard work all your lives so you will surely get what you hope for. We do not want you to become lazy. Be like those who through faith and patience will receive what God has promised.

Love the Lord your God and always obey his orders, rules, laws and commands. Remember my words with your whole being. Write them down and tie them to your hands as a sign, tie them on your foreheads to remind you. Teach them well to your children, talking about them when you sit at home and walk along the road, when you lie down and when you get up.

Let us come near to God with a sincere heart and a sure faith, because we have been made free from a guilty conscience, and our bodies have been washed with pure water. Let us hold firmly to the hope that we have confessed, because we can trust God to do what he promised. Let us think about each other and help each other to show love and do good deeds. You should not stay away from the church meetings, as some are doing, but you should meet together and encourage each other. Do this even more as you see the day coming.

Live a life of love just as Christ loved us and gave himself for us as a sweet-smelling offering and sacrifice to God. Speak to each other with psalms, hymns, and spiritual songs, singing and making music in your hearts to the Lord. Always give thanks to God the father for everything, in the name of our Lord Jesus Christ.

Do not do wrong to repay a wrong, and do not insult to repay an insult. But repay with a blessing, because you yourselves were called to do this so that you might receive a blessing. The Scripture says, "A person must do these things to enjoy life and have many happy days. He must not say evil things, and he must not tell lies."

But I say to you, love your enemies. Pray for those who hurt you.

God's Love

The essence of Christianity is love. The teachings of Jesus are all about love. In fact, Jesus dying on the cross is the ultimate expression of His love for all humanity. Love is the greatest of all things stated in the Bible and given below are what the Bible says about God's love.

> "But God showed his great love for us in this way. Christ died for us while we were sinners"- Romans 5: 8

> "This is what real love is: It is not our love for God; it is God's love for us in sending his Son to be the way to take away our sins. Dear friends, if God loved us that much we also should love each other. No one has ever seen God, but if we love each other, God lives in us, and his love is made perfect in us".- 1 John 4:10-12

> "And so we know the love that God has for us, and we trust that love. God is love. Those who live in love live in God, and God lives in them. We love God because God first loved us". - 1 John 4:16, 19

"Love the Lord you Rod with all your heart, all your soul, all your mind, and all your strength. The second command is this: "Love your neighbor as you love yourself". There are no commands more important than these". – Mark 12:30

"Dear friends, we should love each other, because love comes from God. Everyone who loves has become God's child and knows God. Whoever does not love does not know God, because God is love". – 1 John 4:7-8

"The Lord shows his true love every day. At night I have a song, and I pray to my living God". – Psalm 42:8

"So these three things continue forever: faith, hope and love. And the greatest of these is love". – 1 Corinthians 13:13

"I love those who love me, and those who seek me find me". – Proverbs 8:17

Love Your Neighbor

Jesus wants us to love our neighbor. He commanded us first to "Love the Lord your God with all your heart, all your soul, all your mind and all your strength." The second commandment is, "Love your neighbor as you love yourself." There are no commandments more important than these. According to Jesus Christ, good neighborly relations ensured peace, understanding, and harmony. If each one of us took good care of the needs of our neighbors, it would result in the improvement of many ills and problems of society.

When Jesus spoke of loving our neighbor as we love ourselves, he did not mean just one neighbor; he meant that we should reach out to all those who need our assistance—such us the sick and the poor, the depraved and the deprived. Jesus wants each of us to find time in the midst of our busy daily schedule to give a helping hand to all those who are badly in need of it.

We should not remain indifferent to the suffering and sorrow all around us. All of us should follow the example of the Good Samaritan, who dismounted immediately and rushed to help the person lying on the road. Robbers not only robbed the man but also beat him on the road from Jerusalem to Jericho. The Good Samaritan attended to the wounds of the injured person, took him home, and spent his time, energy, and money in assisting the helpless victim. More than anything, the Good Samaritan offered his kindness and compassion with love. This is what Jesus wants everyone to do. By offering help to a needy person, we will be spreading the message of God's love and compassion for us.

Mother Theresa was a saintly soul who followed the commandment of Jesus to love all human beings by devoting her life to the poor, downtrodden, and weaker sections of society with dedication, deep faith, and great energy. Mother Theresa was able to provide shelters for the homeless and hospitals to look after the sick. Further, she personally attended and nursed the sick. For Mother Theresa, Jesus's words—"As you did it to the least of one of these my brethren, you did it to me"—were a lifelong commitment.

According to the teachings of Jesus, all of us should endeavor to reach out and help the disadvantaged. All of us should involve our family and our friends in this noble effort. Those who do not have the time to spare should make monetary contribution to charitable organizations involved in assisting the weaker sections of society. Let us remember the words of Jesus: "Those who know my commands and obey them are the ones who love me, and my Father will love those who love me. I will love them and will show myself to them."

Parable of the Prodigal Son

A parable is a simple story illustrating a moral or religious lesson. It is perhaps the best and easiest method to convey a great truth. Jesus Christ taught his followers and the general public through his famous, simple, and entertaining parables. The parable of the prodigal son is a good example.

> Jesus said: "A certain man had two sons. And the youngest of them said to his father, "Father, give me my share of the property." So the father divided the property between his two sons. A few days later, the younger son cashed in all and left home for a distant country and there he squandered all his property by wild and riotous living. When he had all that he had, there arose a mighty famine in that land and he started to be in want. So he went and hired himself out to a citizen of that country, who sent him to his fields to feed the hogs. And he would have been glad to fill up his belly on the pods that the hogs were eating. And nobody would give him anything to eat. Then he came to his senses and said, "How many of my father's hired men have more food than they can eat, and here I am starving myself to death. I will start and go back to my father and tell him, 'Father, I have sinned against heaven, and before you and I am no more worthy to be called your son; make me as one of your hired servants.'"

So he started and went to his father. While he was still far away, his father saw him and he felt sorry for him. He ran and put his arms around his son and kissed him, because he was so very happy to see his son. And the son told his father, "Father, I have sinned against heaven and against you. I don't deserve to be called your son anymore. Make me one of your hired men."

"Quick," the father said to his servants, "bring out a robe, the best, and put it on him; put a ring on his finger and shoes on his feet. And bring the fattened calf, kill it, and let us all celebrate. For, this son was dead, and is live again. He was lost and is found again." And they started to celebrate.

Now his elder son was in the field; and as he came and drew near to the house, he heard music and dancing. So he called one of the servants and asked him as to what was going on in the house. And the servant told him that his younger brother has returned, and your father has killed the fattened calf, because he got back his son safe and sound.

This made the elder son angry and he would not go inside the house. So his father came out and begged his elder son to come in and join the celebration. But he answered his father, "All these years, I have been working as a slave for you and I have never disobeyed your orders. And yet you never gave me even a little goat to celebrate with my friends. But as soon as this son of yours comes back, who devoured your property and wasted everything on prostitutes, you killed the fattened calf for him."

So the father said to him, "Son, you are always with me, and all that I have is yours. But it was right that we should all make merry and celebrate, for this your brother was dead, and is alive again and was lost and is found again."

All have sinned and are not good enough for God's glory, and all need to make right with God by his grace, which is free gift. They need to be made free from sin through Jesus Christ. God gave him as a way to forgive sin through faith in the blood of Jesus's death. This showed that God always does what is right and fair, as in the past when he was patient and did not punish people for their sins. And God gave Jesus to show today that he does what is right. God did this so he could judge rightly and so he could make right any person who his faith in Jesus.(Romans 3:23–26).

The Good Samaritan

Jesus was the very embodiment of love and mercy. All his teachings stressed the importance of kindness and compassion and the need to reach out to the poor, the sick, and the needy. Through his famous and effective parables, Jesus conveyed his message of love and kindness and related his desire for his followers and believers to follow his teachings.

Jesus told followers the following parable of the Good Samaritan. Then an expert in the Law came forward in order to test Jesus. "Teacher," he asked, "what do I do to get everlasting life?" "What is written in the Law?" Jesus asked him. "What do you read there?" "Love the Lord, your God with all your heart and with all your life and with all your strength and with all your mind and love your neighbor as yourself," he answered. Jesus told him that he was right and he advised him "to do that and you will live." But the expert in the law wanted to justify himself and so he asked Jesus "and who is my neighbor?"

Jesus then went into the matter and told him the following,

> "A man was going from Jerusalem to Jericho. During the journey, he unfortunately fell into the hands of some robbers. They stripped him, struck him blow after blow, removed all the valuables and went away, leaving the poor man half dead. Just at that moment, a priest happened to go along that road, but when he saw the person lying half dead on the road, he quietly passed by on the other side. Similarly a Levite, who came to that place, also looked at the person lying on the road, and he too passed by on the other side.
>
> "Then a Samaritan who was traveling came that way and when he saw the person lying on the road totally helpless, he felt deep sorrow and sympathy for that unfortunate person. He quickly dismounted and went to the man lying on the road and bandaged his wounds pouring on oil and wine. Then he put him on his own animal, took him to a nearby inn and took care of him. The next day he went to the innkeeper and gave him some money and told him, 'Take care of him, and if you spent anything else on him, I will repay you when I come back.' Which of those three, do you think, was a neighbor to the man who had fallen into the hands of robbers?" "The one who was kind enough to help him," he said. Then Jesus told him to go and do what the good Samaritan did.

The parable of Good Samaritan illustrates what kindness, compassion, and charity are all about. It also clearly shows how some people are sometime indifferent to the suffering of others. Kindness is a God-given gift, and whoever practices it will be doubly blessed by God. Little acts of kindness produce great joy, and blessed is the person who shows kindness to all God's creation. Regarding kindness and charity, the following words from the Bible are relevant: "If you want to be perfect, go and sell what you have, give to the poor, and come and follow me. And you will have treasure in heaven."

Opening Our Heart to God

In deep prayer, we can open our heart to God, and daily prayer is the only way to foster intimacy with God. In fact, our fellowship with God should become the most important and enduring relationship with God. God is full of love for us, and he will take the initiative to draw nearer to us. We must endeavor to communicate with him and open our heart to him, and the surest and most effective way is through prayer. We should attune our mind with the Lord through prayer and constant remembrance of God. Once we open our heart to God, all our worries, fears, and tensions are washed away, and our mind is filled with peace, harmony, and joy.

All of us have learned from an early age to define prayer as lifting our heart and soul to God. In prayer we have also experienced inner peace and happiness. Prayer teaches us that God is far beyond our normal experience in life, and prayer entails some discipline as well as sincere and dedicated efforts on our part. Prayer is not mere repeating of words, but a sincere effort to free the mind from the dead weight of worldly life. Sincerity is an essential element of proper prayer.

Prayer can be defined as an opening of the heart and soul to God. Such a definition appears apt, because the idea of opening one's heart highlights receptivity and responsiveness. Further, to open oneself to another implies that the other remains the dominant partner. Prayer is a dialogue, and thus there are two parties: the one who speaks and the other who listens. In prayer, the dialogue is between us and God, and since God is the Lord, he alone can initiate the encounter. Hence, what we say in prayer will depend on what God does or says first.

Prayer involves sincerity as well as humility. In the words of William Law, "To pretend to devotion without great humility and renunciation of all worldly tempers is to pretend to impossibilities. He that would be devout must first be humble, have a full sense of his own miseries and wants and the vanity of the world, and then his soul will be full of desire after God. A proud, or vain, or worldly-minded may use a manual of prayers, but he cannot be devout, because devotion is the application of a humble heart to God as its only happiness."

Teresa of Avila said, "The most important thing in prayer is not to think much but to love much. The goal of our prayer is the encounter with God in love. And love consists not in the extent of our happiness, but in the firmness of our resolve to try to please God in everything."

The Bible says:

> "Serve only the Lord your God. Respect him, keep his commands, and obey him, Serve him and be loyal to him."
>
> "Shout to the Lord, all the earth. Serve the Lord with joy; come before him singing."
>
> "If you worship the Lord your God, I will bless your bread and your water. I will take away sickness from you."

Christian Healing

Healing is an important aspect of Christianity. When one thinks of Christian teachings on the subject, one is reminded of Mother Theresa, who dedicated her life to healing the sick, the poor, and the downtrodden. Her life is a shining example of the essence of Christian teaching, namely healing. Preach the gospel and heal the sick have been the mottos of all Christian churches.

According to historical records, in 1944, William Temple founded the Churches' Council for Health and Healing to foster cooperation between doctors and clergy by bringing the work of healing into the regular work of the churches. This event had great significance, since the Roman Catholic Church subsequently restored the sacrament of anointing with oil as a sacrament of healing. There has also been greater consultation, coordination, and working together among the healing profession.

The pastoral and sacramental ministry of the church reminds the sick of God's power to heal—both within their innermost being and through those treating them. The stress is on God's power to heal, and these words express the mind of the church on Christian healing. It is Jesus Christ setting free all the forces on health on every level—body, mind, spirit, emotions, and bioenergy. Christians believe that Jesus is the source and inspiration as well as the agent of this healing.

Further, the two Gospel sacraments of baptism and the Eucharist contain within them the essence of Christian healing. Baptism declares a new birth. It speaks of a life redirected from brokenness and disease towards integration and wholeness. In the Eucharist, Jesus is present to heal in his "timeless potency."

There are also a number of other specific means of bringing Christian healing to those in need. Anointing with oil is a sacramental means of healing grace. The service includes prayer with the laying-on of hands, following Jesus's example of blessing and healing. The minister makes the sign of the cross on the forehead and sometimes on the palms or the affected part of the body. The laying-on of hands can also be administered separately, often during times of prayer.

Another form of Christian healing is the confession of sins before a priest or before other fellow Christians.

Counseling is also often used to help administer healing. Many Christians are trained counselors and do invaluable work in the area of healing. Some Christians have done pioneering work in the medical profession and with others connected to the medical profession.

Healing meetings have been a regular feature of the newer charismatic movement of Christianity. Many churches now have a special part of the regular service dedicated to prayer for the healing of people present. Many claim that it is God's will that all people should be healed as part of the salvation Christ won for Christians. Some others see this as lying in the future, when the entire creation is to be remade without sin, suffering, and death. Christian healing is a declaration of God's kingdom here and now.

No discussion of Christian healing would be complete without reference to the Christian movement of hospice care. This great and noble humanitarian movement has brought immense hope, relief, and peace to many seriously ill people around the world by offering them personalized, special care in the context of Christian love and compassion. Hospice care brings mental peace and relief not only to the sick, but also to the members of their family.

Hard Work Brings Prosperity

One very important truth the Bible teaches is that to succeed in life, we should work hard, with dedication and sincerity. Besides working hard, we should be honest in all our dealings. It is the wise person who utilizes his time judiciously, whereas a foolish person idles away his time. Hard work not only brings prosperity, but also leadership. The foolish person, on the other hand, leads a lazy life, which will make him a slave. Let us examine what the Holy Bible has to say regarding hard work and prosperity.

> "To learn, you must want to be taught. To refuse reproof is stupid. A good man's mind is filled with honest thoughts; an evil man's mind is crammed with lies."

"It is better to get your hands dirty and eat than to be too proud to work and starve."

"Hard work means prosperity; only a fool idles away his time. Telling the truth gives a man great satisfaction, and hard work returns many blessings to him."

"A fool thinks he needs no advice, but a wise man listens to others. A fool is quick tempered; a wise man stays cool when insulted."

"A good man is known by his truthfulness, a false man by deceit and lies."

"Truth stands the test of time; lies are soon exposed."

"Deceit fills hearts that are plotting for evil. Joy fills hearts that are planning for good."

"No real harm befalls the good, but there is constant trouble for the wicked."

"God delights in those who keep their promises and abhors those who don't."

"A wise man doesn't display his knowledge, but a fool displays his foolishness."

"Work hard and become a leader; be lazy and never succeed."

"The good man asks advice from friend; the wicked plunge ahead—and fall."

"A lazy man won't even dress the game he gets while hunting, but the diligent man makes good use of everything he finds."

"Those who work hard make a profit, but those who only talk will be poor."

"Remember this: The person who plants a little will have a small harvest, but the person who plants a lot will have a big harvest."

"A lazy person will end up poor, but a hard worker will become rich. Those who gather crops on time are wise, but those who sleep through the harvest are a disgrace."

"If someone is lazy, the roof will begin to fall. If he doesn't fix it, the house will leak. Hard workers will become leaders, but those who are lazy will be slaves."

> "A wise person does the right thing at the right time. There is right time and a right way for everything, yet people often have many troubles. They do not know what the future holds, and no one can tell them what will happen."

> "The Lord sees everything you do, and he watches where you go."

Show Me the Right Path

The Bible shows the devotee the right path to follow in his or her spiritual journey. The first and foremost requirement is faith. The Lord will come to the help of those who have faith in God and trust him. As the scripture says, "Anyone who trusts in him will never be disappointed." The following lines from the Bible show the way to the right path.

> "To you, O Lord, I pray. Don't fail me Lord, for I am trusting you. Don't let my enemies succeed. Don't give them victory over me. None who have faith in God will ever be disgraced for trusting him. But all who harm the innocent shall be defeated."

> "I wait for the Lord to help me, and I trust his word."

> "Wait for the Lord's help. Be strong and brave, and wait for the Lord's help."

> "Show me the path where I should go. O Lord, point out the right road for me to walk. Lead me; teach me, for you are the God who gives me salvation. I have no hope except in you. Overlook my youthful sins, O Lord. Look at me instead through eyes of mercy and forgiveness, through eyes of everlasting love and kindness."

> "Let us live in a right way, like people who belong to the day. We should not have wild parties or get drunk. There should be no sexual sins of any kind, no fighting or jealousy. But clothe yourselves with the Lord Jesus Christ and forget about satisfying your sinful self."

> "The Lord is good and glad to teach the proper path to all those who go astray; he will teach the ways that are right and best to those who humbly turn to him. And when they obey him, every path he guides us on is fragrant with his loving-kindness and his truth."

> "But Lord, my sins! How many they are. Oh, pardon them for the honor of your name."

"Where is the man who fears the Lord? God will teach him how to choose the best."

"Let us hold firmly to the hope that we have confessed, because we can trust God to do what he promised."

"We shall live within God's circle of blessings and his children shall inherit the earth."

"I find rest in God; only he gives me hope."

"Yes, my dear children, live in him so that when Christ comes back, we can live without fear and not be ashamed in his presence."

"So our hope is in the Lord. He is our help, our shield to protect us."

"Friendship with God is reserved for those who reverence him. With them alone he shares the secrets of his promises."

"We all share in Christ if we keep till the end the sure faith we had in the beginning."

"They will run and not need rest; they will walk and not become tired. My eyes are ever looking to the Lord for help, for he alone can rescue me. Come, Lord, and show me your mercy, for I am helpless, overwhelmed, in deep distress, my problems go from bad to worse. Oh, save me from them all."

Rich and Poor

According to the Bible, it is better to be poor, honest, and humble than to be rich, proud, and dishonest. In this connection, Jesus said, "If you want to be perfect, go and sell what you have, give to the poor, and come and follow me. And you will have treasure in Heaven." By helping the poor, we become happy, while those who oppress the poor will end up in poverty. Let us now examine what the Bible says about the rich and the poor.

"Better be poor and honest than rich and dishonest."

"Better be pure and humble than proud and rich."

"A wealthy man has many 'friends'; the poor man has none left."

"A poor man's own brothers turn away from him in embarrassment; how much more his friends. He calls after them, but they are gone."

"When you help the poor, you are lending to the Lord—and he pays wonderful interest on your loan."

"Just as the rich rule the poor, so the borrower is servant to the lender."

"It is easier for a camel to go through the eye of a needle than for a rich man to enter the kingdom of God. Truly, a rich man shall hardly enter the kingdom of heaven."

"When you have a feast, call the poor, the maimed, the lame, the blind and you shall be blessed, for they cannot recompense; for you shall be recompensed at the resurrection of the just."

"The rich and the poor are alike before the Lord who made them all."

"Happy is the generous person, the one who feeds the poor."

"He who gains by oppressing the poor or by bribing the rich shall end in poverty."

"Don't rob the poor and sick. For the Lord is their defender. If you injure them, he will punish you."

"When dining with a rich man, be on your guard and don't stuff yourself, though it all tastes so good, for he is trying to bribe you, and no good is going to come of his invitation."

"Don't weary yourself trying to get rich. Why waste your time? For riches can disappear as though they had the wings of a bird."

"Whosoever exalts himself shall be abased; and he that humbles himself shall be exalted."

"The rich man thinks of his wealth as an impregnable defense, a high wall of safety, What a dreamer!"

"Rich men are conceited, but their real poverty is evident to the poor."

"Trying to get quick rich is evil and leads to poverty."

"Respecting the Lord and not being proud will bring you wealth, honor, and life."

"If you give to the poor, your needs will be supplied. But a curse upon those who close their eyes to poverty."

"I will provide for their needs before they ask, and I will help them while they are still asking for help."

Moral Principles

Moral principles find a pride of place in the Bible. In order to follow God's commandments, people should be honest, upright, generous, kind and compassionate and should reach out to the poor, sick, and the aged. God will love such people and will always come to their help. Let us examine what the Bible says about moral principles.

"The Lord hates cheating and delights in honesty."

"Proud men end in shame, but the meek becomes wise."

"Blessed are the meek; for they shall inherit the earth."

"A good man is guided by his honesty; the evil man is destroyed by his dishonesty."

"A good man out of his good treasure of his heart brings forth that which is good; and an evil man out of the evil treasure of his heart brings forth that which is evil."

"The upright is directed by their honesty; the wicked shall fall beneath their load of sins."

"The good man's goodness delivers him; the evil man's treachery is his undoing."

"God rescues good men from dangers while letting the wicked fall into it. Evil words destroy. Godly skills rebuild."

"The whole city celebrates a good man's success—and also a godless man's death."

"The good influence of godly citizens causes a city to prosper; but the moral decay of the wicked drives it downhill."

"Those who give one of these little ones a cup of cold water because they are my followers will truly get their reward."

"Whoever does not care for his own relatives, especially his own family members, has turned against the faith and is worse than someone who does not believe in God."

"Your own soul is nourished when you are kind; it is destroyed when you are cruel."

"The evil man gets rich for a moment, but the good man's reward lasts forever."

"The good man finds life, the evil man death."

"He that is faithful in that, which is least, is faithful also in much; and he that is unjust in the least is unjust also in much."

"You can be sure that the evil man will not go unpunished forever. And you can also be very sure that God will rescue the children of the godly."

"You are the salt of the earth. But if the salt loses its salty taste, it cannot be made salty again. It is good for nothing, except to be thrown out and walked on."

"The good man can look forward to happiness, while the wicked can expect only wrath."

"If you search for good you will find God's favor, if you search for evil you will find his curse."

Miracles of Christ

A miracle is an event that appears unexplainable by the laws of nature and, consequently, is considered something supernatural. In theological terms, a miracle can be called an act of God. During his life, Jesus Christ performed many miracles. These miracles reveal the divine powers of Jesus, his concern for the sick and the poor, his love for all human beings, his kindness and compassion. Below, we will examine some of the miracles performed by Jesus Christ.

One of the greatest miracles was bringing his friend Lazarus back to life. Setting out for Lazarus's home, Jesus said to his disciples, "Lazarus our friend has gone to rest, but I am going there to awaken him from sleep." When Jesus arrived at Bethany and Martha, Lazarus's sister came out to meet him. He said to her, "Your brother will rise." And Jesus went to the cave where Lazarus was entombed and called him forth alive in the sight of his sisters and neighbors. Accordingly, the crowd that was with him when he called Lazarus out of the memorial tomb and raised up from the dead kept bearing witness. They had seen the miracle themselves.

At another time, after sending away a great number of people, Jesus and his disciples began a journey by ship. Suddenly, a great storm arose, and large waves began to pound the ship. Jesus was fast asleep, when his disciples woke him and said, "Master, carest thou not that we perish?" Jesus arose and rebuked the wind and said to the sea, "Peace, be still." The wind ceased completely, and there was perfect calm.

Once, one of the rulers of the synagogue, Jairus, came to see Jesus. Jairus fell at the feet of Jesus and told him, "My little daughter is at the point of death. I pray to thee to come and lay thy hands on her so that she may be healed and live." Jesus went with him. A large crowd followed him in a throng. One woman, who was seriously sick and had spent all the money she had, wanted to see Jesus. She came along with the crowd and touched Jesus's garment, feeling that if she could touch but his clothes, she would be whole. Immediately after she touched Jesus's clothes, she was healed of her plague. Jesus asked who had touched his clothes. Filled with fear and trembling, the woman came forward and fell down before him and told him the truth. Jesus told the woman, "Daughter, thy faith has made thee whole. Go in peace and be whole of thy plague."

When Jesus spoke thus, there came from the ruler of the synagogue's house some commotion. And someone in the house said, "Thy daughter is dead. Why trouble the Master any further?" As soon as Jesus heard these words, he told the ruler of the synagogue, "Be not afraid, only believe." He then entered the room where the damsel was lying and took the damsel by the hand and said to her, "Damsel, I say unto thee, arise." And immediately the damsel arose and walked away as if getting up from a dream. All were wonder struck at this miracle of the Lord.

At another time, Jesus took his disciples to a desert place for rest. But the people somehow knew where Jesus was and as usual flocked there to see and hear their Lord. And as Jesus came out and saw so many people, he was moved by love and compassion for them and he began to teach them many things. And when the day was now far spent, his disciples were worried as to how they could feed such a large crowd. They wanted to send them away. But Jesus told them to give them something to eat. Jesus asked them how many loaves have they got. They replied that they have five loaves and two fishes. And Jesus commanded them to make all sit down by companies upon the grass. And the crowd sat down in ranks, by hundreds and by fifties. And when Jesus had taken the five loaves and the two fishes, he looked up to heaven, and blessed, and broke the loaves and gave them to his disciples to set before them; and the two fishes divided among them all. And the entire crowd ate and they were filled.

There are many other miracles that Jesus performed out of love and compassion for humanity.

Miracles of Saints

We have seen the miracles performed by Jesus Christ. Like Jesus, his followers also performed many miracles. The saints, who themselves performed miracles, fulfilled Jesus's prediction that his disciples would perform greater miracles than his own. The miracles of the saints are illuminating, since they are the windows to the divine and the supernatural. The miracles attributed to saints demonstrate what can happen when human beings are touched by God. Let us examine some of the miracles performed by saints.

Saint Martin de Porres single-handedly transformed his monastery into a service center for the sick, the poor, and the needy, distributing food and clothing to hundreds of people. Martin used herbal medicines, poultices, and other natural remedies to heal the sick. Many miracles happened through Martin's prayer or touch. Once, the saint visited a woman who was very sick and on whom the doctors had given up. Martin assured the sick woman that she would be healed. When he prayed for her, the Lord revealed to him that the woman would be saved. As predicted, the woman was returned to good health.

Saint Theresa Margaret was another saint who healed the sick. In the convent where Saint Theresa lived, Sister Mary Victoria was suffering from a chronic toothache. It so moved Theresa Margaret that she leaned over Mary Victoria and kissed her cheek; whereupon, the woman was freed from the acute pain that had plagued her.

When Theresa Margaret died on March 7, 1770, for fifteen days her body lay exposed without showing any sign of decay or decomposition. This miracle attracted thousands. One day, the convent carpenter took a violet from the saint's bier and touched it to the face of a woman nearby, who was immediately cured of a disfiguring skin disease. Another workman took a flower and touched his son's arms, which had been almost crippled by inflamed joints. The boy was immediately cured.

Saint Catherine of Siena cared for the sick and healed many plague victims when she prayed for or touched them. Once, on a visit to Pisa, Catherine found herself in a very serious medical condition, so weak she could not move. Her friend Raymond of Capua and other friends who had accompanied Catherine sought a remedy to strengthen her. They searched for some Vernaccia, a wine that, when applied to a sick person's temples and wrists, would bring immediate relief and energy. They asked a wine dealer, who always stocked Vernaccia, to give them a decanter. He replied that he would have given a barrel if he had stock but that his barrel was totally empty. To prove his point, he pulled the spigot from the barrel. To the amazement of all, wine gushed out of the empty barrel. News of this great miracle spread throughout Pisa.

Saint Elizabeth of Hungary was the daughter of the country's king. She gave everything to the poor and also built a hospital to take care of all the poor and sick. On one occasion, when Elizabeth was praying at a church near the hospital, she saw a blind man feeling his way about the building. When she asked the blind man why he was wandering around the church, he replied that he wanted to meet "the lady" who helped the poor. Elizabeth then asked him whether he would like to see the church. The blind man replied that he would love to, but he was born blind. Elizabeth then knelt and prayed, and as she did so, the blind man was restored his sight. News of this miracle also spread like wildfire.

Once, Elizabeth, out of compassion for the sick, put a leper in the bed that she and her husband shared. On hearing this, her husband was enraged. He rushed to the bed and pulled back the blanket. And what a wonder he saw. Instead of seeing a leper, he had a vision of the crucified Christ lying on the bed.

There are many other saints who performed miracles, including saint Clare of Assisi, Saint Dominic, Saint Teresa of Avila, Saint Francis of Assisi, Saint Anthony of Padua, Saint Vincent Ferrer, and Saint Joan of Arc.

Love Your Enemies

The central theme of the teachings of Jesus is love. Jesus wanted everyone to love each other, because love comes from God. He further said that whoever does not love, does not love God, since God is love. He exhorted his followers to love even their enemies. His immortal advice to humanity is given below.

> "Look, all of you, love your enemies. Do good to those who hate you. Pray for the happiness of those who curse you; implore God's blessings on those who hurt you."
>
> "If someone slaps you on one cheek, let him slap the other too. If someone demands your coat, give him your shirt besides. Give what you have to anyone who asks for it; and when things are taken away from you, don't worry about getting them back."
>
> "Treat others as you want them to treat you."
>
> "Do you think you deserve credit for merely loving those who love you? Even the godless do that. And if you do good only to those who do you good—is that so wonderful? Even sinners do that much. And if you lend money only to those, who can repay you,

what good is that? Even the most wicked will lend to them own kind for full returns."

"Love your enemies. Do good to them. Lend to them. And don't be concerned about the fact that they won't repay. Then your reward from heaven will be very great, and you will truly be acting as son of God; for He is kind to the unthankful and to those who are wicked."

"A tree from good stock does not produce scrub fruit nor do trees from poor stock produce choice fruit. A tree is identified by the kind of fruit it produces. Figs never grow on thorns or grapes on bramble bushes."

"A good man produces good deeds from a good heart. An evil man produces evil deeds from his hidden wickedness. Whatever is in the heart overflows into speech."

"Don't judge and you will not be judged. Don't condemn and you will not be condemned. Forgive and you will be forgiven. Give and it will be given you. A good measure, pressed together, shaken down, and running over will be put into your lap. You see, the measure you use will be used for you. He pictured it to them this way. 'Can a blind man lead another blind man? Won't they both fall into a ditch? A pupil is not above his teacher. But anyone who is well trained will be like his teacher.'"

"And why do you look at the speck in your brother's eye and don't notice the log in your own eye? How can you say to your brother, 'Brother, let me take the speck out of your eye, as long as you don't see the log on your own eye. Then you will see clearly enough to take the speck out of your brother's eye.'"

The Bible says, "Love your neighbor and love even your enemies." Jesus said, "You have heard that it has been said, love thy neighbor and hate your enemy. But I say, love your enemies, bless them that curse you, and pray for them who despitefully use you and persecute you."

"Do not do wrong to repay a wrong, and do not insult to repay an insult. But repay with a blessing, because you yourselves were called to do this so that you might receive a blessing. The Scripture says, 'A person must do these things to enjoy life and have many happy says. He must not say evil things and he must not tell lies.'"

"But I say to you, love your enemies. Pray for those who hurt you."

"Do not evil deflect you, but defeat evil by doing good. It has been said that to understand all is to forgive all. If you really understand a person, you will see him correctly and not blame-worthy. Your enmity will then instantly cease. You will then be treating everyone with love and everyone reciprocating your love and you will be living in a world of love, free from any ill-feeling or enmity for anyone."

Chapter 3

Islam

Introduction to Islam

Islam means "Peace" or "submission," and a Muslim is "one who submits to God." The literal meaning of Islam is peace; surrender of one's will, namely losing oneself for the sake of God and surrendering one's own pleasure for the pleasure of God. The message of Islam was revealed by the angel Gabriel to the Holy Prophet Muhammad fourteen hundred years ago and was preserved in the sacred text of Islam, the Holy Qur'an. The Holy Qur'an carries a divine guarantee of safeguard from interpolation, and it claims that it combines the best features of the earlier scriptures.

The prime message of Islam is the Unity of God—that the Creator of the world is One, and he alone is worthy of worship. Muhammad is his messenger and servant, and the follower of this belief is called a Muslim. Islam also believes in God's angels, previously revealed books of God, all the prophets from Adam to Jesus, the Day of Judgment, and, indeed, the Decree of God. A Muslim has five main duties to perform in the course of his or her life. These include bearing witness to the Unity of God and Muhammad as his messenger; observing the prescribed prayer rituals; payment of zakah; keeping the fasts of Ramadan; and performing a pilgrimage to Mecca.

Islam believes that each person is born pure. The Holy Qur'an says that God has given human beings a choice between good and evil and instructs them to seek God's pleasure through faith, prayer, and charity. Islam believes that God created mankind in his image, and by imbuing the attributes of God on a human level, mankind can attain nearness to God. Islam's main instruction is to worship God and to treat all God's creation with kindness and compassion. Islam clearly states the rights of orphans, the needy, and parents in old age, and it even safeguarded women's rights some fourteen hundred years ago, when the rest of the world was in darkness about emancipation. Islamic teachings encompass every imaginable situation, and its rules and principles are truly universal and have stood the test of time.

In Islam, virtue does not connote forsaking the bounties of nature that are lawful. On the contrary, one is encouraged to lead a healthy, active life, with the qualities of kindness, chastity, honesty, mercy, courage, patience, and politeness. In short, Islam has a perfect and complete code for the guidance of individuals and communities alike. As the entire message of Islam is derived from the Holy Qur'an and the Sunnah and Hadith (the traditions and practices of the Holy Prophet), it is immutable in the face of change in time and place

Islam teaches that the path to spiritual development is open to all. Any individual who searches for the One Creator can seek nearness to God through sincere and earnest worship. This positive message for humanity fills hearts with hope and courage.

Islam

Founder

Muhammad, who is seen as a special prophet of the One God, is the founder of Islam. Muhammad was born in Mecca about AD 570 and died in 632 in the nearby city of Medina.

Scripture

At the core of Islam lies the Holy Qur'an, said to have been revealed to Muhammad by the angel Gabriel. The Qur'an (whose original language was Arabic) is considered to be the word of God, directly transmitted to the Prophet Muhammad. The Qur'an is the principal inspiration and refuge for all Muslims. It represents the supreme embodiment of the sacred beliefs of Islam and is the Muslim's main reference for all spiritual matters and the daily requirements for day-to-day living.

The Hadith, or Sunnah, "the deeds, utterances, and silent approval of the Prophet fixed during the second century in the form of written Hadiths. A Hadith, therefore, is a record of an action or sayings of the Prophet." The term can also be applied to the actions and sayings of any of Muhammad's companions or their successors. In a Hadith, only the meaning is viewed as inspired, not the words themselves.

The Sharia, or canon of laws based on principles of the Qur'an, regulates the entire life of a Muslim in the religious, political, and social senses. All man's acts are classified under five legal categories. These are as follows:

1. What is considered as absolute duty, involving reward for acting and punishment for failing to act;
2. Commendable or meritorious actions involving a reward, but no punishment for omission;
3. Permissible actions, which are legally indifferent;
4. Reprehensible actions, which are disapproved, but not punishable; and
5. Forbidden actions, the doing of which calls for severe punishment.

Beliefs

Muhammad began preaching about AD 610 and established Islam as a powerful new force before his death in 632. His teachings were based in part on those of Judaism and Christianity. In agreement with those religions, Muhammad recognized one God. He acknowledged Hebrew history and its religious teachers and recognized Jesus as a prophet. However, Muhammad's was an entirely distinct new revelation. His teachings are contained in the Islamic holy book, the Qur'an.

The Six Pillars of Belief

All Muslims are guided by the six pillars of belief. They are as follows:

1. Belief in one God, Allah;
2. Belief in angels;
3. Belief in the divine books: Torah, Gospel, Psalms, Scrolls of Abraham, and the Qur'an;
4. Belief in many prophets, but one message. Adam was the first prophet. Others have included Abraham, Moses, Jesus, and "the Seal of the Prophets," Muhammad;
5. Belief in the last day, when all the dead will be raised from their graves; and
6. Belief in destiny, its good and its bad. Nothing happens that God has not decreed.

Practice

Every Muslim has five main religious duties, which are called the five pillars of Islam, as follows.

1. Repetition of the creed (*Shahada*): "No God but Allah; Muhammad is the messenger of Allah." Every Muslim should profess faith in a statement that may be translated, "There is only one God, and Muhammad is his prophet."
2. Prayer (Salah): All Muslims should pray towards Mecca five times a day. In Islamic countries, criers from tall minarets call the times of prayer.
3. Charity (Zakah): Every Muslim is obliged to give to charity a percentage of his or her income and of the value of some property. The followers of the faith should give alms for the support of the faith and of the poor.
4. Fasting (Sawm): Every Muslim should observe a solemn fast during Ramadan, the ninth month in the Islamic calendar.
5. Pilgrimage (Hajj): Once in his or her lifetime, every Muslim must make a pilgrimage to Mecca. The only exemptions are those who are sick and poor.

Devout Muslims maintain strict rules of conduct. Women are expected to dress modestly and to cover their faces in public. The sale and consumption of alcohol is forbidden to all. As in Orthodox Judaism, eating pork is forbidden. Muslim places of worship are called mosques. The principal weekly worship is on Friday at midday.

Schools and Sects

The largest division in Islam is between the Sunnites (often called the orthodox Muslims) and the Shiites. Most Shiites live in Iran and Iraq. The original cause of the break between the Sunnites and the Shiites was a disagreement regarding the transfer of power from Muhammad to his descendents. Today, the Shiites follow somewhat different rituals from those of the Sunnites and recognize additional holy days and holy places.

History

From its earliest days, Islam has been an aggressive faith. During its first hundred years, Muslim leaders established an empire that stretched from Europe to Asia. In AD 732, a Muslim army tried to conquer Europe but did not succeed, and Muslims were overthrown in Spain. Muslim leaders often permitted practice of other religions in the territories they captured, though usually many people in the conquered lands accepted Islam and became Muslims.

During the Middle Ages, Christian countries made several attacks on

Muslim states in order to free the Christian holy lands. These attacks were called the Crusades. In spite of such attacks, the Middle East remained predominantly Muslim.

In 1453, the Ottoman Turks conquered the Christian capital of Constantinople, and the city's name was changed to Istanbul. The Turks, who were trying to push into Europe, were finally defeated in Vienna in 1683. From 1700 to the mid 1900s, many Islamic nations fell under the control of European powers, who introduced modern technologies and businesses. After the Second World War, politicians with modern views fought with Muslim traditionalists in many Muslim countries. Beginning in the 1970, Muslim traditionalists in Iran began a powerful counteroffensive and overthrew the Shah of Iran, who was major ally of Western powers and the USA.

The Qur'an

The Qur'an is the most sacred book in Islam. It is considered a perfect revelation from God, a faithful reproduction of an original engraved on a tablet in heaven that has existed for all eternity. The Qur'an is, therefore, treated with the utmost respect and is touched only after ceremonial cleansing. The sacred text is usually carefully wrapped in silk or an ornate cloth and it placed in an elevated position, such as above a door in a home. Many devout Muslims memorize the entire book, in its original Arabic; such people are called the "hafiz." All over the world, Muslims quote the first chapter of the Qur'an over and over again during the five daily prayer times.

The word "Qur'an" comes from the Arabic word meaning "to recite," reflecting the belief that most of the book consists of the words of Allah that Muhammad was commanded to proclaim. The Qur'an contains 114 chapters, or "suras." These chapters are arranged not chronologically or even by subject, but according to their length, the longest near the beginning and the shortest at the end. They are a composite of verses written at various stages of Muhammad's life. All the chapters, or suras, begin with the words, "In the name of God, the Merciful, the Compassionate."

The suras are divided into verses, called "ayat." The word ayat also means "miracle." When Muhammad was asked for an authenticating wonder to prove his role as a prophet, he simply referred to the verses of the Qur'an; they were his miracle.

According to Islamic tradition, many of the Qur'an's sections can be placed either in Muhammad's time in Mecca, before the emigration of AD 622, or in the time he spent at Medina, afterwards. The Medina passages are particularly important, as they reflect a change in Muhammad's role from prophet or spiritual preacher to military leader. He felt that military leadership would help unite all warring factions.

The Qur'an contains several different sorts of writing. For one, Muhammad records the experiences of early prophets, mostly from the Old Testament, who were often models for his own experiences. There are also frequent proclamations of imminent judgment and of sensuous enticements in heaven, as well as detailed descriptions of the pain and sufferings of the damned in hell. There is strict emphasis on monotheism throughout the text.

Legislative sections for the Muslim community as well as the laws governing family relations, relations with other members of the community, and inheritances are also included. In addition, there are some references to the historical war between the Greeks and the Persians, which took place around AD 614.

In the earlier parts of the Qur'an, Muhammad expressed friendship towards the Jews and Christians, who were referred to as "people of the book." Further, the Qur'an acknowledges many Jewish and Christian writings, such as the Torah, the Psalms of David, and the Gospel of Jesus, as revelations from God. Subsequently, when the Jewish and Christian people would not accept Muhammad as a prophet, the attitude of the Qur'an towards Jews and Christians underwent a change. Muhammad charged the Jews with corrupting their scriptures. He said, "They have perverted the words." He leveled the same charges against the Christians.

The angel Gabriel is credited with revealing the Qur'an to Muhammad. Gabriel proclaimed it was only a part of the text, even though Muhammad claimed that the whole Qur'an existed complete in heaven. Islamic tradition holds that the Qur'an was originally written on palm leaves, on shoulder bones of camels, and on stones.

After the death of Muhammad, Islamic tradition states that the first caliph (a title given to the successors of Muhammad), Abu Bakr, ordered Muhammad's former secretary to collect and arrange the writings. This work was undertaken in cooperation with others, and finally an authorized revision of the text was established by the caliph Uthman. Other versions in existence were ordered to be destroyed. Thus, although there are many sects, all Muslims use the same Qur'an, which can be traced back to the original version.

The Founder

Muhammad was born in Mecca in AD 570. At the time of his birth, Arabia was in a state of political, social, and religious unrest. The wandering inhabitants of Arabia were idolaters who worshipped stars and stones and fetishes. Several Jewish colonies came into existence in the area consequent to the destruction of Jerusalem. The chief of these sects were Nestorians and the Iriyans, among others, and many other forms of religious practices were also in vogue.

Many people in Arabia felt the urgent need for some sort of moral reform before the arrival of Muhammad, and there was great expectation regarding the emergence of an Arabian messiah who would found a new religion. Thus, the conditions were ripe for a great social and religious revolution. It was at this critical time that Muhammad appeared on the Arabian horizon.

At the time of Muhammad's birth, Mecca was a prosperous trading and religious center for the entire Arab world. Early in life, Muhammad lost his parents and experienced the misery and helplessness of an orphan. At the same time, he also learned what it meant to be surrounded by a community wider than immediate family. He was at first looked after by his grandparents and later by his uncle. At the age of twenty-five, Muhammad obtained employment as a caravan driver for a rich widow named Khadija. He did his work so well that Khadija offered him her hand in marriage. Muhammad was now rich, and he became a respected and influential citizen of Mecca.

Although he had attained wealth and influence, Muhammad was not satisfied with all the material comforts and security. Early on, he had shown a love for solitude. Many questions oppressed him, and he became very restless. This restlessness drove him 'round in circles, and before long he came to a severe crisis in his life. He began to withdraw from business dealings, family members, as well as friends and sought the solitude of the desert. It was in this period that a momentous event occurred that changed his life and affected the whole world.

It is believed that during the events of the fateful night in Muhammad's life, Muhammad was spending his time alone on Mount Hira, when archangel Gabriel appeared before Muhammad. When the angel asked Muhammad to read a piece of material, Muhammad had to reply that he could not read. When commanded by Gabriel to read this yet again, Muhammad is said to have felt like he awoke from his sleep and felt like the words were written in his heart.

From that incident, Muhammad was certain that he had been called upon to be the prophet of the one God. He returned to Mecca and began to preach. On the busy street corners, Muhammad preached about the resurrection of the dead and God's judgment. "God will judge you according to your actions," he called to the local traders, challenging them to submit their lives to God. He urged all to practice love towards the poor and the needy, to the slaves and the foreigners. His language and words had a unique power, something gripping about them. People who heard him thought that Muhammad was possessed. Some thought that he was dangerous, a revolutionary. They also immediately recognized that Muhammad was directing his preaching against the polytheism of the town. Since Mecca was the destination of Muslim pilgrims, which was the city's most important source of income, the traders felt threatened, and, consequently, their opposition grew. They became increasingly aggressive and forced Muhammad and his small group of followers to flee and live in a ghetto. During this period, his wife died, and immediately thereafter he also lost his uncle, who had earlier protected him. Muhammad left Mecca.

Like Abraham, who left his ancestral land to form the Jewish nation, Muhammad left the town of his father and family, destined for Medina. The year AD 622, the year of Muhammad's journey, or Hijra, marks the start of the Islamic calendar. From this time on, Islam was no longer just a religion, but also a distinct political power. In Medina, the community of believers became a virtual state, with Muhammad as its religious and political leader. There, the social and religious practices of Islam were developed.

Muhammad expected that the Jews who lived in the town would recognize him as God's prophet; however, they did not, and their attitude disappointed Muhammad. The Jews were driven out, and the Jewish clans were destroyed. Later, Muhammad raised an army of nomadic Arab tribes and began armed raids on Mecca, and, in 630, they easily took Mecca. Surrounded by cheering and jubilant followers, Muhammad rode on a camel to the center of the pilgrimage, the Kaba. Mecca was immediately cleared of all images and symbols of pagan belief. Muhammad announced the end of idolatry and the beginning of the new age of the one God. There was no opposition; by and large, the announcements of Muhammad were accepted. Mecca thus became the focal point and the place of the new state of God.

Two years later, Muhammad again left the train of pilgrims to the Kaba. In front of all the people present, Muhammad declared the last message of God: "Today, I have completed my religion for you, and I have fulfilled the extent of my favor towards you. It is my will that Islam be your religion. I have completed my mission. I have left you the Book of Allah and clear commandments. If you keep them, you will never go wrong." The same year, Muhammad died.

Origin of Islam

Like Judaism and Christianity, Islam had its origin in the Middle East. It was not a totally new monotheistic religion that sprang up in isolation; belief in one God had been flourishing for many centuries. In fact, knowledge of Judaism, Christianity, and Zoroastrianism had been brought to Mecca in Arabia by foreign caravan traders. Further, Christian, Zoroastrian, and Jewish tribes lived in Arabia.

In the sixth century, Mecca was beginning to emerge as a prosperous and leading commercial center with vast resources of new wealth. Then there was a growing division between the rich and the poor, challenging the traditional systems of Arab tribal values and social security. This was the time and social environment in which the Prophet Muhammad preached his message of the Qur'an, which formed the basis for the religion we now know as Islam—urging all to return to the worship of the one true God and calling for a socially just society.

Muslims believe that God sent revelations first to Moses, in the form of the Hebrew scripture, the Torah; then to Jesus, in the form of the Gospels; and finally to Muhammad, through the Islamic scripture, the Qur'an. Like the biblical prophets who came before him, Muhammad was a religious reformer. Muhammad said that he did not bring a new message for a new God but called people back to the one true God and to a way of life they had either forgotten or deviated from. Because it is not a new revelation, the Qur'an itself contains many references to stories and figures from the Old and New Testaments of the Bible, including Adam and Eve, Abraham and Moses, David and Solomon, and Jesus and Mary.

Islam and the worship of Allah—the Arabic word for God—was a return in the midst of a polytheistic society to the forgotten past, to the faith of the first monotheist, Abraham. To Muhammad, most of his contemporaries in Mecca, with its tribal polytheism, lived in ignorance of the one true God and his will, as revealed to the prophets Adam, Abraham, Moses, and Jesus. The revelation that Muhammad received led him to believe that Jews and Christians had, over time, distorted God's original message to Moses and, later, to Jesus. Thus, the Torah and the Gospels were seen by Muslims as a continuation of original revelation and later human additions, such as the elevation of Jesus from prophet to the son of God.

The revelations that Muhammad received were calls to religious and social reforms. They emphasized social justice and concern for the rights of women, widows, the poor, and the orphaned; they corrected the distortions to God's revelation in Judaism and Christianity and warned that many had strayed from the message of God and his prophets. They called upon all to return to what the Qur'an refers to as the straight path of Islam, or the path of God, revealed one final time to Muhammad, who was the last, or "seal," of the prophets.

Islam—What It Means

The word "Islam" is derived from the Arabic root "SLM," which means peace, purity, submission, and obedience. From the religious point of view, Islam means total submission and obedience to the will of God. Only by submission to God's commands and obedience to his will can one achieve lasting peace and purity. Muslims do not believe that Islam was founded by Muhammad. According to Islamic teachings, the original founder of Islam was none other than God himself, and the religion dates to the time of Adam. Islam has existed in one form or another all the time. Thus, the true name of the religion is Islam. Those who follow this religion are Muslims.

Unlike people of other religions—including Jews, Hindus, and Muslims—who worship their leaders, Muslims do not worship Muhammad. The Muslims worship God alone. For Muslims, Muhammad was only a mortal commissioned by God to spread his message, teach the Word of God, and lead an exemplary life. Muhammad stands in history as the ideal and best model for man in piety, purity, and perfection. He is living proof of what man can be and what he can accomplish in the realm of excellence, leadership, and virtue.

Though Islam entails submission to the will of God and obedience to his law, it does not involve in any way the loss of individual freedom or surrender to fatalism. Islam describes God as the "Most Merciful and Gracious" and as the "Most Loving." He is concerned with the welfare of human beings and as full of wisdom and care for all his creatures. His will, therefore, is a will of benevolence, mercy, and goodness, and his laws are in the best interest of mankind. Thus, submission to the will of God does not take away man's freedom. On the contrary, it gives freedom of a high degree, in abundant measure: it frees the mind from superstitions and fills it with truth, besides freeing the soul from sin and wrongdoing. It fills the soul with purity and goodness and removes vanity, greed, envy, fear, and insecurity.

Submission to the good will of God and obedience to his beneficial law is the best safeguard of peace, purity, and harmony. It enables man to make peace between himself and his fellow beings and between the human community and God. According to Islam, all things in the world and all phenomena are created by God and administered by God. Consequently, the entire physical world should be obedient to God and submissive to his laws. Man is, fortunately, blessed with intelligence and the power of making choices; because he possesses these qualities, he is invited to submit to the will of God and obey God's commands.

The will of God is defined by the Qur'an as good and compassionate, and his law is defined as the most just, beneficent, and equitable. Any human being who submits and obeys is, therefore a Muslim. It is in this context that the Qur'an cites Abraham and all authentic prophets and gives all true religions one and the same title: Islam. Hence, Muslims are not followers of Muhammad exclusively; they are also followers of Abraham, Moses, Jesus, and God's other messengers.

Lastly, the word "Allah" in Islam means "the one and only eternal God, creator of the universe, Lord of all lords, and King of all kings." The only unforgivable sin in Islam is the belief in any deity other than God.

The Five Pillars of Islam

As mentioned earlier, there are five very important basic practices in Islam, called the five pillars of Islam. They include bearing witness, prayer, fasting, charity, and pilgrimage. These religious practices are rooted in the teachings of the Qur'an.

The first pillar is bearing witness. The first words that are recited into the ears of an infant are, "I bear witness that there is no God but God, and I bear witness that Muhammad is a servant and a messenger of God." The recitation of these words is essential and also a sufficient condition for becoming a Muslim. When we accept God, we accept God as the greatest influence in our life. Similarly, when we acknowledge Muhammad as God's messenger, we promise to follow his teachings, since they came from God. Witnessing represents both the beginning of Islam and Islamic spirituality.

The second pillar is daily prayer. All Muslims respond to the call to prayer five times a day. They answer to the following exhortation:

> God is greater, God is greater
> I bear witness that there is no God but God
> I bear witness that Muhammad is God's messenger...

Daily prayers are said just before sunrise, just after noon, in later afternoon, after sunset, and after dark. Prayers begin by facing Mecca.

The third pillar is fasting. During the holy month of Ramadan, all Muslims fast every day, from before dawn to sunset, by abstaining from drinking, eating, smoking, and quarreling. The purpose of fasting is to make us aware of the conflicting forces of our lower and higher natures. Further, by fasting, we strengthen our will. Fasting purifies the mind. For the Sufis, fasting is a spiritual discipline for inner purification and outer asceticism. The Prophet Muhammad made the following statement on the first day of Ramadan: "Holy Ramadan, the best of all months, is here today. God, Most High, has made it obligatory to fast during the days of this month and make it voluntary to pass the night in prayer."

The fourth pillar is charity. All Muslim households donate one-fortieth of their wealth to the poor at the end of Ramadan. This annual charity is considered to purify one's wealth. It reminds believers that all things come from God and all things belong to God; the owners of wealth are only custodians of whatever has come to them.

The fifth pillar is pilgrimage. All Muslims are expected to make a pilgrimage to Mecca once in their lifetime, if they are in sound health and if they can afford it. The Kaba, the shrine in the heart of Mecca, is the holiest of holy sites in Islam. Faithful Muslims from all over the world enter into a profound devotional and spiritual state as they circle the Kaba, as part of the pilgrimage ritual. The annual pilgrimage to Mecca, usually takes place during the 12th month of the Islamic calendar, and is a metaphor for the journey of life. According to the Qur'an, all things come from God and all things return to God. Similarly, the pilgrimage and the journey of life lead to God.

Thus, the five pillars of Islam are the core of the faith, to be observed by faithful Muslims with great devotion.

Basic Beliefs

Islam is firmly anchored in two fundamental concepts: expressing faith, called Iman, and doing the right thing, called Ihsan.

The most important prerequisite for becoming a Muslim is to perform the Shahadah, or open testimony that "There is no God but God." This testimony is then accompanied by a second important pronouncement: "And Muhammad is the messenger of God." By uttering the first part of the Shahadah, one becomes a Muslim, submissive to God and his will. By pronouncing the second part, one becomes an adherent of the religion of Islam, acknowledging his dependence on God and his solidarity with his fellow believers.

By a careful combination of will and design, Muhammad succeeded in reducing the essence of the doctrine to the believer's level of understanding. This was essential for all the followers to understand and follow his teachings. He inculcated his followers with the strong will to abide by the ordinance and injunction of Allah. Muhammad preached total submission to Allah.

The term "Al-Islam" signifies complete submission to the will of God. In the Qur'an it is decreed, "Lo, the religion of Allah is Al-Islam; Surrender to his will and guidance.

The most important and vital point in Islamic doctrine is the emphasis on Allah's absolute oneness. Allah in his essence is one, as he is in his attributes and acts. He is the almighty, judge of the universe. He knows, sees, and hears everything. He is the Creator of heaven and earth, of life and death. His knowledge is perfect and his power irresistible. All these qualities are manifest in his creation.

The principal element of worship in Islam involves belief in one God, his angels, scriptures, the messengers, and the Day of Judgment. Recognition of God is the supreme manifestation of faith. The majority of Muslim theology is concerned with Allah as the one real God.

The role of God as creator is greatly emphasized in the Qur'an, which says, "He hath created the heavens and earth with truth. His verily is all creation and commandment. Blessed be Allah, the Lord of the Worlds."

Further, the text also emphasizes Allah's omniscience: "He is the Knower of the invisible and the visible, the Great, the High Exalted."

The sovereignty of Allah is related to his omnipotence, and both are conceived in equal terms. The Qur'an says, "Say, O Allah! Owner of Sovereignty. Thou giveth sovereignty unto whom thou will and thou withdraweth sovereignty from those whom thou will."

His attributes, suggested in the Qur'an, distinguish him from his creatures. The Qur'an says, "Allah's are the fairest names. Invoke him by them." Theologians have stated that Allah has ninety-nine beautiful names, all of which are repeated by Muslims with great fervor and devotion. Allah's omnipotence is mitigated and tempered with justice, because Allah is equitable.

God rewards as well as punishes. He is also just, all-merciful, and compassionate. God is gentle, and he loves gentleness. Whoever loves to meet God, God loves to meet him. God's kindness towards his creatures is more than a mother's towards her babe.

Basic Practices and Customs

These are the profession of faith, or Shahada; worship, or Salah; alms-giving, or Zakah; fasting, or Sawm; and pilgrimage, or Hajj. These five practices are strictly regulated by the Islamic laws, though the practices vary between the Sunnis and the Shiites. The exact time for observance of the annual practices, particularly the fast during the month of Ramadan and the pilgrimage to Mecca, are determined by the Islamic lunar year established by Muhammad during his last year of life.

The essence of being a Muslim is to recite with sincerity and devotion the fundamental Islamic creed, called Shahada. This is very important for every follower of the faith. Shahada consists in reciting the two statements, "There is no God but God" and "Muhammad is the messenger of God." The performance of Salah is another essential practice for all Muslims, who are expected to pray five times a day facing Mecca. Similarly, Friday worship is enjoined on all Muslims, a practice instituted by Muhammad.

Alms-giving, or Zakah, is the sharing of one's wealth with the poor and the needy. The Qur'an stresses the importance of sharing wealth. Since everything belongs to God, it is but natural that the rich should share their wealth with the poor.

Fasting, or Sawm, during the month of Ramadan is another important practice in Islam. If someone is sick or is taking a journey, he may break his fast for those days, but should make them up later. Muslims are permitted to eat and drink during the night.

The last practice is the great pilgrimage, or Hajj, to the sacred monuments in and around Mecca. Every Muslim is required to make this pilgrimage at least once in his lifetime, unless he is poor or he is not in a position to make this trip.

Muslims throughout the world observe other practices as well. The Qur'an stipulates regulations on matters pertaining to marriage, divorce, inheritance, and types of food. It makes prohibitions against gambling, intoxicating liquors, eating pork, etc. There are also specific customs involving wedding, funerals, and other ceremonies.

In Islam, men and women are considered and treated as equals, and Muslim women are required to observe the five pillars of Islam and other religious and moral duties. However, in some matters the Qur'an and the Islamic law place men above women. This is due to several social factors. For instance, it is the responsibility of the man to provide for the welfare of his family. Due to this, under the law a higher percentage of an inheritance usually goes to the male heir.

The Qur'an enjoins women to dress modestly and stipulates correct behavior for men and women. It does not explicitly require the veiling of women, and each Muslim country has its own norm in this regard. Some women cover themselves from head to toe, while others dress in the Western manner or simply cover their heads with scarves.

The Concept of Faith

Faith is the core of Islam. The Arabic word Iman, rendered in English, means "faith," or to know or believe, to be convinced beyond the least shadow of doubt. Faith is thus a firm belief arising out of knowledge and conviction. Those people who know and possess unshakeable belief in the Unity of God in his attributes, in his laws, in the Revealed Guidance and the Divine Code of Reward and Punishment are called the faithful. This faith leads a person to a life of total obedience and submission to the will of God. Without this faith, or Iman, no person can be a true Muslim. It is the very starting point without which no beginning can be made. The relation of Islam to faith is the same as of a tree to its seed: just as a tree cannot sprout without its seed, it is not possible for a man who has no faith to become a Muslim.

From the Islamic point of view, the people can be classified into four categories of belief.

1. Those who have firm faith, a faith that makes them wholeheartedly submit to God

2. Those who have faith, who believe in God, his law, and the Day of Judgment, but whose faith is not deep and strong enough to make them totally submit to God
3. Those who do not possess any faith at all
4. Those who neither posses faith nor do good deeds

The above classifications of mankind show that the real success and salvation of man depends entirely on faith.

Faith in Islam is a state of happiness acquired through good action and good deeds. The Holy Qur'an clearly states the required standards and measures which can build up a meaningful and firm faith. Thus the true faithful, according to the Qur'on are:

Those, who believe in God, His angels, His Books, His Messengers with Muhammad being the last of them, the Day of Final Judgment, the absolute knowledge and wisdom of God. The true believers always trust God and have unshakeable confidence and faith in Him.

Those, who observe their daily prayers regularly and who spend in the way of God of what He has given them in the form of wealth, health, knowledge and experience

Those, who are faithful pay, their religious taxes or alms or 'zakah' to the rightful individuals as well as institutions. They enjoin the right and good and combat the wrong and evil by all lawful means.

The true believers are those, who obey God and His Messenger Muhammad and experience increasing faith when reciting the Qur'an and possess humility of heart when God's name is mentioned.

Those who love God and His Messenger most and love their fellow men for the sake of God. They love their near and distant neighbors and display kindness and love to their guests. They only speak the truth and engage in good talk.

According to the teachings of the Qur'an, true faith has a decisive impact on every aspect of man's life, and none can be a true believer unless he loves for his fellow human beings what he loves for himself.

Fundamental Articles of Faith

The fundamental articles of faith in Islam, which a true and faithful follower believes are as follows.

One God

The true Muslim believes in one God, supreme and eternal, infinite and mighty, merciful and compassionate, creator and sustainer. He will have complete trust and faith in God, with submission to his will and reliance on his help. Faith ensures the dignity of man and saves him from fear, despair, guilt, and confusion.

All the Messengers

The faithful Muslim believes in all the messengers of God, who were great teachers and were chosen by God to teach mankind and deliver his divine message. The Holy Qur'an mentions the names of twenty-five messengers, and the Muslim accepts all of them as authorized messengers of God.

Revelations of God

The true Muslim believes in all the scriptures and revelations of God, which were the guiding light that revealed the right path of God. In the Qur'an, reference is made to the books of Abraham, Moses, David, and Jesus. However, long before the revelation of the Qur'an to Muhammad, some of these books and revelations got corrupted, forgotten, or neglected. The only authentic and complete book of God today is the Qur'an.

The Angels of God

All Muslims believe in the angels of God, who are spiritual beings with no physical desires or material needs of any kind. They spend all their time in the service of God. Belief in the angels originates from the Islamic principle that knowledge and truth are not confined, only sensory knowledge and perception.

The Day of Judgment

The true faithful believes in the Last Day, the Day of Judgment, when the dead will rise to stand for their final and fair trial. On the Day of Judgment, they will be brought forward, and people with good records will be generously rewarded, while those with bad records will be punished.

Knowledge of God

The true Muslim believes in the timeless knowledge of God and in his power to execute his plans. God is wise and loving, and whatever he does, he has a good motive and some meaning. A true Muslim should, therefore, accept with good faith all that God does, although he may not fully comprehend it.

Sublime Purpose of Life

Muslims believe that God's creation is meaningful, and therefore, life has a sublime purpose beyond the physical needs and material activities of man.

The purpose of life is to worship God. To worship God is to know him, to obey his commandments, and to enforce his law in every aspect of life.

Qur'an as the Word of God

The true Muslim believes that the Qur'an is the Word of God, revealed to Muhammad, in Arabic, by the angel Gabriel. Every letter in the Qur'an is the Word of God. The Qur'an is the first and most authentic source of Islam.

The other important aspect in the Qur'on that every person is born free from sin. When they reach the age of maturity, they are accountable for their deeds. People are not only free from sin until they commit sin, but they are also free to act according to their plans, for which they are responsible. A true Muslim believes that his salvation is through God's guidance. A Muslim should build his faith on well-grounded convictions. Islam demands sound convictions and is against blind imitation.

Righteousness

Islam places great importance on righteousness, as illustrated in the Holy Qur'an:

> It is not righteousness that you turn your faces in prayer towards east or west, but it is righteousness to believe in God and the Last Day, and the angels and the Holy Books and the Messengers; to spend your wealth—in spite of your love for it—for your kith and kin, for the orphans, for the poor and the needy, for the wayfarer, for those who ask, and for the ransoming of the slaves; to be steadfast in prayer and practice regular charity; to fulfill the contracts into which you have entered; and to be firm and patient in pain and adversity, and throughout all periods of panic. Such are the people of truth, the God-minded.

Righteousness should ensure strict compliance with all the salutary regulations and should make the love of God the prime and fundamental motive of life. Besides love of God, a righteous person should love his fellow brethren for the sake of God. As regards righteousness, there are four important elements, as follows.

1. One should have true and sincere faith. Faith is the firm belief and unshakeable trust in God and in the doctrines expressed in the scriptures and other sacred works. Faith is firm religious conviction. Faith is the core of Islam.

2. A righteous person should show it in his or her deeds of charity or alms-giving and kindness to other fellow beings, particularly to one's kith and kin, neighbors and travelers.
3. One should be a good citizen by supporting charitable institutions and various social organizations.
4. Righteousness should make a person steadfast and unshakeable in all trials and tribulations.

Thus, righteousness is not merely a matter of empty utterances but should be grounded on strong faith and constant practice. It should cover a person's thinking as well as all his actions and extend to his inner and outer life, to his individual and collective affairs. When the Islamic principle of righteousness is established, it will provide the individual with peace under all circumstances, since the guiding principle of righteous conduct is peace of mind. The individual and the society will have security on all levels. The nation will have strength and solidarity, and the international community will have peace, hope, and harmony.

Righteousness has great significance, since right conduct ensures belief in God, love for all human beings, steadfastness in prayers, practice of alms-giving, facing all circumstances with faith, keeping promises and contractual commitments. When people practice righteousness, life is enjoyable, purposeful, and peaceful. What could be more reassuring than the firm conviction and faith in the beneficent creator and investing in good, worthy, and noble causes? What could be more humane than reaching out to those who are poor, distressed, and in dire circumstances, alleviating the sorrow and sufferings of the exploited, and helping those who are helpless?

Righteousness ensures fulfillment of all commitments, preservation of a clear conscience, and the maintenance of integrity in all matters. Further, it is spiritually uplifting to do all this for the love of God.

Responsibilities and Duties

The Qur'on clearly describes the responsibilities and duties of Muslims and these are given below:

> "Charity is a duty unto every Muslim. He, who has not the means thereto, let him do a good deed or abstain from an evil one. That is his charity."

> "When you speak, speak the truth. Perform when you promise. Discharge your trust. Commit no fornication. Be chaste and have no

impure desires. Withhold your hand from striking and taking that which is unlawful and bad."

"The best of God's servants are those who, when seen, remind one of God and the worst of God's servants are those, who carry tales about to do mischief and separate friends and seek defects of the good. He who believes in one God and the life beyond, let him not injure his neighbors."

"Feed the hungry and visit the sick and free the captive, if he is unjustly confined. That person is most respectable and near God, who pardons, when he has in him in his power, him who would have injured him."

"Whoever desires the world and its riches should do so in a lawful manner, in order to withhold himself from begging, and for a livelihood for his family and for being kind to his neighbor."

"Whoever believes in God and the Hereafter must respect his guest; and whoever believes in God and the Hereafter must not trouble his neighbors."

"He is not of us, who is not affectionate to the little ones and does not respect the reputations of the world; and he is not of us, who does not order that which is lawful and prohibit that which is unlawful. The exercise of religious duties will not atone for the fault of an abusive tongue."

"That person is wise and sensible, who subdues his carnal desires and hopes for reward; and he is an ignorant man, who follows his lustful appetites and with all this asks for God's forgiveness."

"Gratitude is another important responsibility and duty, namely gratitude to one's parents and gratitude to God. The Prophet was asked as to whom one owed the greatest debt of gratitude, the Prophet replied, 'Your mother.' When asked, 'Who then,' he again said, 'Your mother.' When he was asked again, 'Who then,' he replied for a third time, 'Your mother.' When he was asked again for a fourth time, he replied, 'Your father.' The Prophet also taught that paradise is under the feet of the mother."

"Similarly, one should remember with gratitude all that one has received from one's father and ask oneself how best to express one's gratitude to him."

"Gratitude to God is another important factor. God is the ultimate source of life and all things come from God."

Freedom and Equality

Islam places great importance on freedom and equality. The question of freedom in respect to belief, worship, and conscience is of utmost importance in Islam. Similarly, the principle of equality or equity is another important element in the value system of Islam.

Islam attaches much importance to freedom: freedom for the individual, community, society, and nation. Islam teaches freedom, which it cherishes and wants to guarantee to all Muslims and non-Muslims. The Islamic concept of freedom applies to all voluntary activities of man in all walks of life. According to Islam, every man or woman is born free, free from subjugation, sin, inherited inferiority, and ancestral hindrance. This right of freedom is sacred as long as he does not deliberately violate the law of God or the rights of others. On the spiritual side, the main objective of Islam in respect to freedom is freeing the mind from superstitions and uncertainties. Freedom should liberate the soul from sin and corruption, the conscience from oppression and fear, and the body from disorder and degeneration.

In Islam, every individual is entitled to exercise his or her freedom of belief, worship, and conscience. The Qur'an says, "There need not be any compulsion in religion. Truth stands out clear from error. Whoever rejects evil and believes in God has grasped the strongest bonds that can never break. And God knows and hears all things." The above illustrates that it is meaningless to use force in religion; religion depends upon faith, will, sincerity, devotion, and commitment.

The Islamic concept of freedom is an article of faith, a solemn command from the Supreme Creator. It is built on the following principles. First, man's conscience is subject to God only. Second, every human being is responsible for his deeds. Third, God has delegated to man the responsibility to decide for himself, and last, man is provided with spiritual guidance and endowed with rational qualities to make correct choices. According to the teachings of Islam, all human beings are equal in the sight of God. Certainly, there are differences in abilities, potential, wealth, and so on. But none of these can establish a status of superiority of one person or race to another. The only distinction God recognizes is the distinction in piety and goodness, and the only criterion God applies is the criterion of spiritual excellence, devotion, and goodness.

The differences of race, color, or social status are purely accidental and do not in any way affect the real stature of man in the eyes of God. The value of equality is not simply a matter of constitutional rights, but an article of faith, which a Muslim takes very seriously and to which he or she should adhere sincerely and strictly. The foundations of this Islamic value of equality are firmly and deeply rooted in the structure of Islam. Equality stems from the following basic principles: "All mankind is created by One and the same Eternal God. Everyone belongs to the human race and shares equally in the common parentage of Adam and Eve. God is just, fair, and kind to all his creatures, and he is not partial to any race, age, or religion. The entire universe is his dominion, and all people are his creatures. All people are born equal, in as much as none brings any possession with them, and they die without taking back any worldly belongings. God judges every individual on the basis of his or her own merits and according to his or her own deeds. Lastly, God has conferred on man a title of honor and dignity."

Justice, Brotherhood, and Peace

Justice, brotherhood, and peace are considered the most fundamental elements in the value system of Islam. Of these, the pride of place goes to justice, a concept derived from one of the attributes of God, who is called the Just. According to the Qur'an, "God commands justice, the doing of good, and giving to kindred, and he forbids all indecent deeds and evil and rebellion; he instructs you that you may receive admonition."

In Islam, the concept of justice is so comprehensive that it covers every aspect of human virtue and human behavior. Since justice is an attribute of Allah, it is imperative for all the followers of the faith to act justly in all situations, even when doing so is detrimental to their own interests or to those who are dear to them. Further, followers have to be just with those whose opinions differ, and they should not let their feelings towards others prevent them from acting justly. This is clearly stated in the Qur'an and the Sunnah: "O you who believe! Stand out firmly for Allah, as witnesses to fair dealing, and let not the hatred of others to you make you swerve to wrong and depart from justice. Be just; that is next to piety; and fear Allah, for Allah is well acquainted with all that you do. And when you judge between people, judge with justice. Allah commands justice."

Another important element in the value system of Islam is human brotherhood. This value is connected to freedom and equality. Human brotherhood in Islam is based on an unshakeable belief in the oneness and universality of God, the unity of mankind, the unity of religion, and the medium of worship. For the Muslim, God is one, eternal, and universal. He is the Creator of all human beings. He is the provider and sustainer of all human beings, the judge of all human beings, and the lord of all human beings. Social status, racial origin, and other issues are insignificant to him. For him, all men are equal and brothers of one another.

The Muslims believe in the unity of mankind. The source of creation is God himself. The original parentage is that of Adam and Eve, and every human being belongs to this parentage. Muslims believe in the unity of God's religion, which means that God does not confine his religion to any particular nation, race, or age. It also means that there can be no contradictions or differences in the religion of God.

The concept of peace is the core of Islam. The Arabic words for "peace" and "Islam" are derived from the same root and so may be considered synonymous. One of God's names is "Peace." The concluding words of the daily prayers of every Muslim are words of peace. The greetings of the Muslims, when they return to God, is peace. The daily salutations among the Muslims are also expressions of peace. Heaven in Islam is the abode of peace.

It will be noticed that the fundamental and dominant theme of peace is in Islam. The individual who approaches God through Islam has to be at peace with God, with himself, and with other fellow human beings. Men of good faith and principles, by their deeds, try to make a better world, where there will be human dignity, justice, brotherhood, and equality. And in such a world, there will be peace and harmony.

For all the followers of faith, heaven in Islam means an abode of peace.

Morality

Islam has specific and comprehensive views on morality. The concept of morality in Islam revolves around certain basic beliefs, principles, and regulations. Some of the beliefs and principles concerning morality are given below.

1. God is the creator, sustainer, and the source of goodness, truth, justice, mercy, and beauty. Man's responsibility is to God, and his highest aim and goal in life should be the pleasure of his creator.
2. Man is a responsible, dignified, and honest agent of God on earth. God has put everything in the heavens and the earth in the service of humanity.
3. God is all-merciful, just, and wise, and he does not expect anything impossible from man, nor does he hold him responsible or accountable for anything beyond his power. God also does not forbid man from enjoying all the good things of life.
4. In the sight of God, it is the intention behind any action or behavior that makes such an action morally good or bad.

5. Moderation, equality, knowledge, practicality, and balance are the guarantees of integrity and sound morality.

The regulations and principles of morality in Islam are many and comprehensive. Morality in Islam mainly deals with the relationship between man and God and man and his fellow human beings and other creatures of the universe. A Muslim should guard his thoughts, words, and deeds as well as his feelings and intentions. His aim in life should be to champion what is right and to fight what is evil. His goal in life should be truth, virtue, humility, courtesy, and compassion.

Basically, the relationship of Muslim to God is one of total obedience, complete trust, peace, and steadfastness. In his relationship with others, a Muslim should display kindness and compassion for the young, old, and the sick. He should reach out to the needy and show sympathy for the grieved and the depressed. He should have patience with the misguided and tolerance for the ignorant and the helpless. A Muslim must respect the legitimate rights of others as much as he does his own.

The moral principles of Islam are positive commitments that must be fulfilled. Similarly, those commitments that are negative must be avoided. Irrespective of whether they are positive or negative, they are mainly designed to build in the person a sound body, mind, and soul, as well as a strong personality and a healthy body. These are the essential requirements for the welfare and prosperity of mankind. In order to help man to achieve these, Islam has laid down the following regulations:

1. To bear witness to the oneness of God and Muhammad as his messenger;
2. To observe the daily prayers with devotion and sincerity;
3. To ensure that the religious tax known as charity or alms-giving is properly paid, when due;
4. To strictly follow fasting in the holy month of Ramadan; and
5. To make a pilgrimage to the holy city of Mecca at least once in a lifetime, provided one is in a fit condition financially and physically and without any insurmountable hindrances.

The range of morality in Islam is so inclusive and integrated that it combines faith in God, religious rites, spiritual observances, social conduct, and good behavior.

Personal Conduct

"Wealth and children are the real ornaments of the life of the world. But the good deeds which last are better in thy Lord's sight for rewards and better in respect of life."

"Shun much suspicion, for some suspicion is a crime. And do not spy and backbite one another. Would any one of you love to eat the flesh of his dead brother? You abhor that, so abhor the other. And keep your duty to God. God is Relenting, Beneficent and Merciful. No man is a true believer unless he desires for his brother what he desires for himself."

"We have created man and woman and have made you tribes and nations that you may know one another. The noblest of you is the best in conduct in the sight of God. God is All-Embracing, All-Knowing, All-Forgiving, and Merciful."

"No man is true in the truest sense of the word but he who is true in word, in deed, and in thought. It is one's own conduct which will lead one to reward or punishment, as if you had been destined therefore."

"One should deal gently with the people, and be never harsh, cheer them and condemn them not. When you speak, only speak the truth; perform what and when you promise, discharge your commitment and trust, have no evil thoughts and impure desires, withhold your hands from striking and from coveting other's property and taking that is bad and unlawful."

"He who is a true believer in one God and the life beyond, should not injure his neighbors. The best of God's servants are those, who when seen, remind one of God. One should feed the hungry and visit the sick. One should help any person who is oppressed, whether Muslim or non-Muslim."

"Man is a state of loss, except those who believe and do good works, and urge strongly one another to truth and exhort one another to endurance. Remember and speak well of your dead, and refrain from speaking ill of them."

"The likeness of those who spend their wealth for God in God's way is like likeness of a grain, which grows seven years and in every year a hundred grains. God gives increase many times to whom He will. God is All-Embracing and All-Knowing."

"The wealth you invest in lending money for interest so that it should grow at the cost of other people's wealth, does not grow in the sight of God. But the wealth that we give in charity, seeking God's face is multiplied several fold."

"Let not your wealth and your children distract you from remembrance of God. Those who do so, they are the losers. Those who believe, seek courage in patience and prayer, for God is with those who are patient and persevering. It is unworthy of a believer to injure people's reputation. It is also unworthy to curse another and abuse anyone. One should be thankful to God in prosperity and resign to his will in his adversity."

Service to Humanity

Islam gives much importance to serving humanity through charity, feeding the hungry, caring for one's parents, respecting women, helping fellow beings, reaching out to those who are suffering and in want.

"He is true who protects his brother both present and past. One should discharge one's responsibilities to his family, friends, relatives, and neighbors."

"To gladden the heart of the weary, to lessen if not remove the sufferings of the afflicted, has its own reward. In the day of trouble, the memory of the action comes like a rush of the torrent, and removes all our troubles, besides lessening our burden."

"One should help his fellow creatures when they are badly in need of help. A person who rushes to assist his fellow beings in the hour of need and who helps those who are oppressed, him will God help in the day of travail."

"Service to humanity brings a lot of happiness and a feeling of fulfillment. Some of the actions which bring this real happiness are to feed the hungry, to help those who are suffering, to remove the sorrow of the sorrowful, and to remove the wrong and injustice inflicted on people. He who tries sincerely to remove the want of his brother, whether he be successful or not, God will forgive his sins."

"All God's creatures are one's family. He is the most beloved of God, who tries his utmost to do most good to God's creatures. The best of men is he from whom good accrues to humanity."

> "Whoever is kind and compassionate to his creatures, God is kind and compassionate to him. One should, therefore, be kind to all fellow beings on earth, whether good or bad; and be kind to the bad, is to withhold him from badness, so that those who are in heaven may be kind to you."

> "Visit the sick, comfort his grief and pain, and console him with kind words such as, 'You will get well and live long.' Whoever visits a sick person, an angel calls from heaven, 'Be happy in the world, and happy be your walking, and take you a habitation in paradise. By loving your fellow creatures, you love your Creator."

> "Someone said to the Prophet, 'Pray to God against the idolaters and curse them.' The Prophet replied, 'I have been sent to show mercy and have not been sent to curse.'"

> "Verily my heart is veiled with melancholy and sadness for my followers and verily I ask pardon of God one hundred times a day."

> "O Lord, grant to me the love of You; grant that I love those that love You; grant that I may do the deeds that win Your love; make Your love dearer to me than self, family, or wealth."

Moral Obligations

Moral obligations are given great importance in Islam. Obligations in Islam are of two types: moral and ceremonial. The moral obligations relate to the concept of right doing, called Ihsan, which relates to man's relations with man and with God.

Personal morality emphasizes selflessness as a form of gratitude towards God. This gratitude constitutes an element of love for Allah, which is a fundamental article of Muslim faith. Next comes total obedience to Allah and his messenger Muhammad.

Caring for the destitute, the orphaned, the poor, and the dispossessed are integral parts of Islamic belief. Qur'anic teachings instruct all followers to "Show kindness unto parents, and unto kindred, and orphans and the needy and unto the neighbor." This includes sharing wealth. Thus, giving alms and charity are part of the moral obligations.

For women, chastity and restraint are decreed. Women are enjoined to be decent and modest, revealing their charms only to their husbands and near relatives. Men should treat their wives with kindness and gentleness, justness and consideration. Women should be shown respect, since they are the mothers, aunts, and grandmothers.

The other decrees are that the faithful be honest in their dealings with others and true to their promises and commitments. They should be loyal, humble, and peace-loving. Social obligations in Islam place duty before right. Duties in Islam are incumbent on all the faithful, irrespective of their standing and status in society.

Another important obligation is justice, which ensures fraternity and equality. To be beneficent is another duty, one that obligates the faithful to act rightly at all times. While Islam does not place any constraint in respect to making wealth, vulgar display of wealth and ostentation are frowned upon. Similarly, Islam prohibits taking interest on money loaned. Usury is condemned in Islam.

Another article of faith is respect for a fellow believer's welfare in society. Islam lays great importance on building understanding and fraternity between followers of the faith. Qur'anic teachings stress the need for creating solidarity between individuals and the society at large.

Personal morality is considered as important as social morality. Mercy is another important article of faith, one of the highly stressed injunctions of Islam, In fact, right doing rests on showing mercy, which is regarded as an essential characteristic of God.

Prayer and Worship

Prayer is any act of communion with God, including praise, confession, thanksgiving, or petition. It is a specially worded form used for addressing God. Worship is reverent love and allegiance accorded to God, and a set of ceremonious prayers or other religious forms by which this love is expressed. Thus, prayer and worship go hand in hand.

Prayer is the most direct path to God for all spiritual seekers. It purifies the mind and can lift one to great contemplative height or transform a person's character. The highest form of prayer culminates in union with God.

The Prophet Muhammad summed up the importance and significance of prayer in the following words: "The key to paradise is prayer, and the key to prayer is ablution. One must pray to God with absolute faith in the morning and evening and utilize the day on one's avocation."

According to the prophet Muhammad, "In prayers, all other thoughts should be set aside., but those of God; in conversation, no word to be uttered which may afterwards be repented of; do not covet from others or have any hopes from them."

"O Lord! Keep me alive a poor man, and let me die poor; and raise amongst the poor. Do not turn the poor away, without giving them, if but half a date."

"Seek for my satisfaction in that of the poor and needy."

"Say your prayers standing; but if you are not able, do it sitting; and if not sitting, on your sides."

"Let none of you long for death because of a certain injury which has befallen him; and if he must need do it let him say, O God; let me live so long as life is better for me, and let me die when death is better for me."

"Nothing keeps away the decree of God except prayer, and nothing increases the life of a man except goodness, and man is only denied the provisions of life because of sins upon which he falls."

"There is polish for everything that takes away rust; and the polish for the heart is the remembrance of God."

"O God, grant to me the love of You; grant that I love those that love You. Grant that I may do the deeds that win Your love; make Your love dearer to me than self, family, or wealth."

"In the name of Allah, the Beneficent, the Merciful, Praise be to Allah, Lord of the Worlds, the Beneficent, the Merciful, Owner of the Day of Judgment, Thee alone we worship; Thee alone we ask for help. Show us the straight path, the path of those whom Thou hast favored. Not the path of those who earn Thine anger nor of those who go astray."

"Adore God as you would if you saw Him; for, if you see Him not, He sees you."

God

"Glorified is God and exalted above what they say; The seven heavens and the earth praise Him. There is not a thing that does not proclaim His praise. He is ever Merciful and All-Forgiving."

"God it is who created the seven heavens and the earth and seated Himself upon the throne. He directed the affairs from the Heaven unto the earth. In the name of God, the Beneficent, the Benevolent, the Merciful; Praise to the God, Lord of the Worlds, the Merciful, the Beneficent, Master of the Day of Judgment. Thee alone we worship and ask for help. Show us the straight path, the path of those whom Thou hast favored."

"Everything in the heavens and the earth Glorifies God. He is the Mighty, He is the Wise and He is the Sovereign of the heavens and the earth; He is the First and the Last and the Outward and the Inward. He is the Knower of all things."

"God is the Light of the heavens and the earth. The likeness of His Light is as a niche wherein is a lamp. The lamp is in a glass and the glass is like a brilliant star. God guides unto the light whom He Will. God is the Knower of all Things."

"He is the God and there is no other God but He. He is the Knower of the Visible and the Invisible. He is Merciful and He is Beneficent."

"He is God and there is no other God but He. He is the Sovereign Lord, the Holy One, Peace, and Keeper of Faith. He is the Guardian, the Majestic, the Compeller, and the Superb."

"He is God, the Creator, the Shaper out of nothing; the Fashioner. His names are the most beautiful. All that in the heavens and the earth glorify Him. He is the Mighty and the Wise."

"God is gracious to him, who earns his living by his own labor and not by begging. God's kindness towards His creatures is more than a mother's towards her babe. Adore God as you would if you saw Him; for, if you see Him not, He sees you."

"'O Prophet of God,' said one of his disciples, 'I have heard so many things from you, and I fear that I may forget their end and aim; so tell me that may contain everything.' The Prophet said, 'Fear God according to what you know and act accordingly.'"

"When one of you sees another, who is superior to him in point of wealth and creation, let him look to him who is below him. That is more proper that you hold not in contempt the favor of God towards you."

"Whoso will remain abstemious, God will keep him abstemious and whoso will keep himself independent, God will keep him independent; and whoso will be steadfast, God will keep him steadfast, and no one is granted a better thing than that. God has not created anything better than reason, or anything more perfect or more beautiful than reason; the benefits which God gives are on its account; and understanding is by it, and God's wrath is caused by it, and by it are rewards and punishments."

Sayings of Muhammad

"There are only two types of persons you should envy; the man to whom God has given wealth and the power to spend it all in the cause of truth; and the man to whom God has given wisdom and who judges by it and teaches it."

"The person who goes in search of knowledge is on active service for God until he returns. It is the duty of every Muslim, male and female, to seek knowledge. He dies not who gives life to learning. Whoso honors the learned, honors me."

"Those who lead the prayer act on your behalf, if their prayers are correct, they will benefit you. If their prayers are defective, it is they and not you who will be held responsible and the prayers will still benefit you. The prayer performed in company is twenty-seven times better than prayer performed alone."

"The value of an action depends on the intention. Everyone will be rewarded in accordance with the goal which he set himself. If he emigrated for the sake of God and His messenger, his emigration will be counted to him for God and His messenger. If he emigrated in order to gain something in this world, or find himself a wife, his emigration will be counted to him for the goal he set himself."

"There are three things which, when you possess them, make you taste the sweetness of faith. First, to love God and His messenger more than all other things. Secondly, to love others solely for God's sake. Lastly, to detest the thought of lapsing into unbelief as much as the thought of being thrown into hell."

"Three things are characteristic of a hypocrite; when he speaks, he lies; when he makes a promise, he fails to keep it; and when you put your trust in him, be betrays you."

"Each night, when the night is two-thirds spent, our blessed and exalted Lord descends to the nether heaven and says, 'If anyone invokes Me, I will answer his prayer. If anyone asks Me for something, I will grant him it. If anyone seeks forgiveness, I will forgive him.'"

"The sun and moon are not eclipsed for anyone's birth nor for anyone's death. Solar and lunar eclipses are two of God's signs, so that when you see them, you should pray."

"Three things follow a dead person to the grave and two of them return while one remains with him. His family, his wealth, and his deeds follow him; his family return home with his wealth, but his deeds remain."

"Even if there were a valley full of gold, man would want two of them. Nothing but the dust of the grave will stop his mouth. Yet God will turn to those who repent."

"Spend generously and do not keep an account; God will keep an account for you. Put nothing to one side; God will put to one side for you."

"Wealth does not consist in the abundance of possessions. Wealth is wealth of the soul."

Death and Afterlife

Death, according to the Qur'an, is not so much as an end to life as it is a return to God. God is the creator of all things, and God, therefore, decrees when all things cease to be. Belief in an afterlife is an essential aspect of Islamic faith, and through this belief, Muslims affirm the presence of God and his divine justice. Death also explains the significance and purpose of this life, with all its trials and tribulations. According to the Qur'an, "Every soul shall face death and on the Day of Judgment only will receive full recompense."

Death is viewed as the decision of God to end the temporary existence of all human beings on earth. It is a change from one mode of life to another. Life on this earth is seen as fleeting and incomplete, so death is viewed as an important state. The physical body disintegrates and disappears as the soul, now liberated from all physical constraints, moves to a new different plane.

Islam teaches that man has a soul that goes on to a hereafter. The Qur'an states, "Allah receiveth men's souls at the time of their death, and that soul which dieth not in its sleep. He keepeth that soul for which He hath ordained death." According to the Qur'an, the soul can have one of two destinies, which can be either a heavenly garden of paradise or the punishment of a burning hell.

Muslims believe that a dead person's soul goes to the barzakh, or partition, the place or state in which people remain after death and before Judgment. There, the soul experiences what is termed the "chastisement of the tomb" if the person has been wicked or enjoys happiness if he has been faithful. But the faithful must also experience some torment because of whatever sins they committed while they lived. On the Judgment Day, each faces his eternal destiny, which ends that intermediate stage.

The righteous are promised heavenly gardens of paradise: "And as for those who believe and do good works, we shall make them enter Gardens underneath which rivers flow to dwell therein for ever."

It is Islamic custom to say prayers for the dead and wash the corpse before burial. The only exception is in the case of martyrs, who are buried in the state in which they died. In many regions, funeral processions for the dead are common, and verses are recited from the Qur'an at Islamic funerals. The death prayer is performed while standing, which means that one neither bows nor falls to one's knees. A Muslim in his deathbed still tries to recite the words of the creed, or shahada, while those surrounding the dying person try to help by chanting the shahada in loud voices. After death, the attendants pour water on the corpse, and after ritual cleaning the corpse is wrapped in three white cotton sheets. The service for the dead occurs as soon as the dead is covered in the burial shroud.

Islam does not have any specific death or funeral rites or ceremonies, because death represents only an intermediate stage before resurrection. Consequently, excessive expenses for the grave are prohibited.

Islam also prohibits turning burial places into pilgrim sites or prayer places, because of the danger of polytheism. The Prophet Muhammad himself warned of the danger even while he was dying, and several Hadiths warned of such customs as well.

Chapter 4

Judaism

An Introduction to Judaism

Judaism is one of the three Abrahamic faiths, in addition to Christianity and Islam, that recognize Abraham as a patriarch. Moses, Jesus, Mahler, Marx, Freud, and Einstein all have something in common. They are all Jews, and all of them have affected the history of mankind. The Bible itself is testimony to the significance of Jews over thousands of years.

Unlike other ancient religions and cultures, Judaism is rooted in history, not in mythology. Christianity, founded by Jesus, who was a Jew, has its roots in the Hebrew scriptures. And as any reading of the Qur'an will show, Islam also owes much to those scriptures.

Jews are a microscopic minority, representing only 0.2 percent of the human race, yet, Jewish influence in the social, political, and economic spheres has been quite great, much more than their numbers would indicate.

Jews believe in one God, who is the Creator and Lord of the universe. They believe that God has a special relationship—the Covenant—with the Jewish people, a relationship that has guided and will continue to guide Jewish people. The Bible says, "Obey my voice, and I will be your God, and you shall be my people; and walk in all the way that I command you, that it may be well with you."

The Law, written in the Jewish holy book the Torah, was said to have been given to Moses by God, on Mount Sinai and guides Jews on how to live in accordance with the Covenant. Jews look forward to the coming of the Messiah, a leader from God, who will bring a time of peace, fruitfulness, and security to the whole world. At this time, too, the dead will be brought back to life and judged by God.

The symbol of Judaism is the menorah. The menorah, a seven-branched candlestick, stood in the Temple of Jerusalem in ancient times, and its design is described in the Torah. The central branch is said to represent the Sabbath, the day when God rested after spending six days creating the world.

Israel is regarded as the historic Promised Land. The Western Wall in Jerusalem, an important place of prayer, is all that is left of the last Jewish temple there, destroyed in AD 70.

The Hebrew Bible consists of the Torah (the Five Books of Moses), the Prophets, and other writings, including the Psalms. The Torah contains laws and guidance and tells the early history of the Jewish people. It is written in Hebrew.

Judaism

Founder

There is no single religious leader who founded Judaism. In this respect, it differs from Christianity and Islam, which have single religious founders. Jewish people are descendants of an ancient Hebrew speaking Semitic race. Judaism developed amongst several wandering Semitic tribes, who were termed as Hebrews, Israelites and finally as Jews. About 4,000 years ago, their forefather Abraham emigrated from the city of Ur to Canaan, of which it has been said that God assigned the land to Abraham's offspring. In Genesis 14:13, Abraham is spoken of as Abraham, the Hebrew. Later, his name was changed to Abraham and Jews draw a line of descent from Abraham's son Issac and his grandson Jacob. Jacob's name was later changed to Israel. Israel had 12 sons and they were the founders of twelve tribes. The word "Jew" was derived from Judah, one of the sons of Israel.

The name "Jew" was applied to all Israelites. Over the millennia, the ancient Jewish religion has developed and grown into a world religion. Judaism is now practiced by millions around the world.

According to available records, in the year 1943 B.C., God chose Abraham as his special servant. Abraham proved his faithfulness by offering his son Issac as a sacrifice. This sacrifice never materialized and God made a solemn promise to the effect that he will bestow his blessings on Abraham and his descendents. Further, God said that since Abraham obeyed his command, He will make Abraham's descendents as numerous as the stars in Heaven. To carry out his promise to Abraham, God laid the foundation for a Jewish nation by establishing a covenant with the descendants of Abraham. God's covenant was established through Moses, the great Hebrew leader. Moses was singled out by God to lead the Jewish people from captivity to freedom. Moses thus became the prophet, judge, leader and guide of Jews.

The Law that Israel accepted consisted of the Ten Commandments and over 600 laws which formed the basis and guidance for the daily conduct of the Jews. The descendants of Abraham thus became a nation dedicated to the service of God and the Jewish religion took shape. Thus, the Israelites became God's chosen people to serve God's purpose.

Scriptures

The sacred Hebrew writings began with the Tanakh, a word that derives from the three divisions of the Jewish Bible in Hebrew: Torah (Law), Nevi'im (Prophets), and Kethuvim (Writings), using the first letter of each section, to form the word TaNaKh. These books were written in Hebrew. Jews believe that they were written under different and diminishing degrees of inspiration. Consequently, they were put in the following order of importance.

Torah—The Five Books of Moses, or the Pentateuch, the law, consisting of Genesis, Exodus, Leviticus, Numbers, and Deuteronomy. However, the term "Torah" may also be used to refer to the Jewish Bible as a whole, as well as to the oral law and the Talmud.

Nevi'im—The Prophets, covering from Joshua through the major prophets—Isaiah, Jeremiah, and Ezekiel—and then through the twelve minor prophets from Hosea to Malachi.

Kethuvim—The writings, consisting of the poetic works: Psalms, Proverbs, Job, the Song of Songs, and Lamentations. In addition, the Kethuvim includes Ruth, Ecclesiastes, Esther, Daniel, Ezra, Nehemiah, and First and Second Chronicles.

The Talmud—From the Gentile point of view, the Tanakh, or the Jewish Bible, is the most important of Jewish writings. However, the Jewish view is some what different. Many Jews would agree with Rabbi Adin Steinsaltz, who said, "If the Bible is the cornerstone of Judaism, then the Talmud is the central pillar, soaring up from the foundations and supporting the entire spiritual and intellectual edifice. No other work has had a comparable influence on the theory and practice of Jewish life." Orthodox Jews believe not only that God gave the written law, or Torah, to Moses at Mount Sinai, but also that God revealed to him specific explanations as to how to carry out that law, and that these were to be passed on by word of mouth. This was called the oral law. Thus, the Talmud is the written summary of that oral law, with later commentaries and explanations, compiled by rabbis from the second century AD into the Middle Ages.

The Talmud is usually divided into two main sections: the Mishnah and the Gemara. The Mishna is a collection of commentaries supplementing scriptural law, based on the explanations of rabbis called Tannaim (teachers).

It was put into written form in the late second and early third centuries AD. The Gemara (originally called the Talmud) is a collection of commentaries on the Mishnah by rabbis of a later period.

In addition to these two main divisions, the Talmud may also include commentaries on the Gemara by rabbis into the Middle Ages. Prominent among these were the rabbis Rashi, who made the difficult language of the Talmud far more understandable, and Rambam, who reorganized the Talmud into a concise version, thus making it accessible to all the followers of the faith

Beliefs

The early Jews, in contrast to neighboring peoples, worshipped one God, whom they recognized as the Creator of all things and the God of all. Among God's characteristics were both judgment and mercy. His covenant with Jews promised them his care and protection, and they were to follow his laws. During the time of the prophets, when the Jewish states had declined, the prophets told of the coming of a leader anointed by God—the messiah. The Jews still await the coming of the Messiah.

Jews worship in synagogues, often modest places of worship for a small congregation. Saturday, the seventh day of the week, is the day of Sabbath, a special day of rest, prayer, and worship. Worship consists of reading from the scriptures and chanting or singing of psalms or other songs of praise and prayer.

Schools and Sects

There are three main branches of modern Judaism. Orthodox Judaism is the most conservative branch, observing laws concerning clean and unclean foods, purification, and many other ancient rituals. One part of orthodoxy is the Hasidim, the fundamentalist sects that grew up in Eastern Europe in the 1700s and 1800s.

Reform Judaism, strong in the United States, is the most liberal of the three main branches. Reform Jews seek to follow the spirit of Judaism and are free to disregard part of the ancient rules of conduct and ritual. Reform places of worship are called temples. Some of the temples resemble Christian churches in their design and in their observances, which may include, for example, music from a pipe organ and choir.

Conservative Judaism seeks a middle road between Orthodox and Reform. It is the most recent of the three branches and is strong in the United States.

Historical Background

After the glorious and prosperous reign of David and Solomon, which was a period of wealth, power, and influence for Jews, the Jewish state disintegrated and was divided by dynastic feuds into a northern and southern kingdom. In the course of time, these kingdoms met with their doom and fell victims to neighboring power. In 587, the southern kingdom called Judah was captured by Babylonians, and many Jews were forcibly taken away as slaves to Babylon. The famous and beautiful temple built by Solomon at Jerusalem was completely destroyed.

After about fifty years, the Jews were freed from slavery, and the temple was rebuilt. Later, the entire region was captured by the Romans. The Jews revolted against Roman occupation, which resulted in severe reprisals. The Romans inflicted untold suffering on the Jews, and the second temple was also destroyed. During this period, the Jews were dispersed in all directions. They did not have a land of their own for over nineteen hundred years.

Judaism and the Jewish people survived in many parts of the world. They were subjected to many hardships and severe persecution. During this period, the Jews were dispersed in Palestine, Babylon, Spain, France, Germany, Poland, and Russia. In Europe, there was persecution of Jews and anti-Semitism was widespread. There were laws preventing Jews from owning land and engaging in certain types of business. There were times when mobs destroyed the homes and property of Jews. Later, Hitler and his Nazi party systematically eliminated most of the Jews from all the towns in Europe. Millions of Jews were killed in what was known as the Holocaust. This was the worst, most sorrowful and painful time for Jews in their history.

The Holocaust and the anti-Semitism in various parts of the world finally convinced Jews and their leaders of the imperative need for the establishment of a Jewish state, where Jews could follow their faith and live peacefully. After various political discussions and debates after World War II, Jews received the support of Britain and the United States for the creation of a Jewish state. In 1948, a new nation called Israel was created. Since it came into existence, Israel has been harassed and attacked by its neighbors, who had never agreed or reconciled to the creation of a Jewish state in the midst of a Muslim world.

Historic Judaism teaches that Jews are the chosen people through whom God has spoken to the world and revealed how to live in accordance with his laws. They are a nation in the sense that they form a distinct ethnic group. In addition to the ethnic identity, an observant Jew chooses to follow the laws given by God to Moses.

Abraham is said to have lived around 1900 BC, and he is regarded as the father of the Jewish people. The Jewish scriptures tell how God made a covenant or agreement with Moses that his descendants would be God's chosen people. The people's part in this covenant is to strictly abide by God's laws. At Mount Sinai, God called Moses to the top of the mountain and gave him the laws on slabs of stone. The best known of these are the Ten Commandments. Although many Jews live all over the world, the history of Judaism is rooted in the land of Israel, the land promised to Abraham in the Bible. This was the land to which God led the people on the journey out of Egypt.

The city of Jerusalem—the capitol city of David, Israel's greatest king—is specially important to all Jews. David's son Solomon built a great temple in Jerusalem that was destroyed many times and rebuilt many times. The temple was finally destroyed once and for all in AD 70. The site of the temple is a great place of pilgrimage for all the followers of Judaism and a place of celebration and prayer. The single remaining wall of this temple is referred to as the Wailing Wall.

The roots of the Jewish religion go back thousands of years, and other major religions are indebted to its scriptures to a greater or lesser degree. Christianity has its roots in the Hebrew scriptures. Similarly, any reading of the Qur'an will show that Islam also owes much to those scriptures. Further, Jewish religion provides an essential link in mankind's search for the true God. According to the Hebrew scriptures, Abraham, the forefather of Jews, was already worshipping the true God nearly four thousand years ago

Basic Teachings of Judaism

At the center of Jewish belief lies faith in God, who made the heaven and the earth and all that they contain. God took the Israelis out of their bondage and slavery in Egypt, revealed his divine teachings in the Torah, and finally took them into the Holy Land. The Jewish faith in God has greatly colored the Jew's view of his situation since the biblical period, and he hopes that one day the Messiah will come to usher in a time when all Jews will be gathered once again in the land of Israel. The concept that Israel is a people chosen by God is associated in Jewish consciousness with the revelation of the teachings of Moses as they wandered in the wilderness after the exodus from Egypt. An often repeated benediction of the liturgy says God "has chosen us from all the nations and given us his Torah."

Maimonides, the leader of the Egyptian Jewish community and its principal teacher and philosopher, propounded the thirteen fundamentals of Jewish belief that has come to be accepted as the official creed of Judaism.

The whole of the Torah was revealed to Moses by God, and the Torah will not be changed or supplanted by another revelation from God. The idea of prophetic revelation was seen as a basic element of Judaism in the past.

The messianic hope was vital in holding the Jewish people together throughout their many ordeals and sufferings. Judaism undoubtedly owes its survival, to a considerable extent, to the steadfast faith in a future messiah. But with the rise of modern Judaism, many Jews ended their passive waiting for the Messiah; many lost their patience and hope. They began to view the messianic message of Judaism as a liability and so reinterpreted the time spoken of in the Bible merely as a new age of prosperity and peace. Although there are many exceptions, contemporary Jews as a whole can hardly said to be waiting for a personal messiah.

Simply put, Judaism is the religion of a people. Judaism is a monotheistic religion. It states that God intervenes in the case of Jewish people. Although there are no creeds or dogmas accepted by all Jews, the confession of the oneness of God as expressed in the Shema, a prayer based on Deuteronomy, forms a central part of synagogue worship: "Hear, O Israel: The Lord our God, the lord is One."

What Jews Believe

It has been said that Judaism has no dogmas. This is more or less true. There have never been propositions drawn up by scholars, thinkers, and sages regarding the belief and purpose incumbent upon every Jew. This, however, does not mean that Judaism as a faith has no fundamental beliefs. Since the beliefs are defined by consensus among Jews, their formulation is bound to be flexible. Thus, some Jewish teachers stress one belief and others a different belief.

The search for the essence of Judaism has engaged the minds of many Jewish teachers and intellectuals. Some of them have tried to find the essence of Judaism in the Ten Commandments. Of these, only the first two commandments—namely, "I am the Lord thy God" and "Thou shall have no other gods"—have to do with belief. The rest are only rules of conduct.

It was not until the Middle Ages that an authoritative list of fundamental beliefs was drawn up, by the Egyptian Jewish sage Maimonides. Maimonides himself stressed these beliefs as extremely essential. The thirteen principles of faith drawn up by Maimonides won wide acceptance. There has been, however, some different interpretations of some of them.

The thirteen principles of faith are as follows:

1. Belief in the existence of God;
2. Belief in the unity of God;
3. Belief that God is incorporeal;
4. Belief that God is eternal;

5. Belief that God alone is to be worshipped;
6. Belief in prophecy;
7. Belief that Moses was the greatest of the prophets;
8. Belief that the Torah is from God;
9. Belief that the Torah is unchanging;
10. Belief that God knows the thoughts and deeds of man;
11. Belief that the righteous are rewarded and the wicked are punished;
12. Belief in the coming of the Messiah; and
13. Belief in the resurrection of the dead.

The principles formulated by Maimonides are concerned with three basic ideas. The first five fundamental beliefs are concerned with God and the nature of God. The next four principles of faith are mainly concerned with revelation. The last four principles of faith are concerned with the doctrine of divine providence.

The thirteen fundamental beliefs drawn up by Maimonides have been accepted by Jews. These beliefs play a crucial role in the day-to-day lives of the followers of the faith, and they form a central part of worship.

Human Existence

The most important determinant of people's outlook is their self-image. They were eager to understand human nature and human existence. They knew for certain that human life was limited. When compared with the majesty of the heavens, people were insignificant, and the powers of nature could crush them. Their earthly life was as brief as grass and as troubled as a sigh. At times, the Jews wondered why God should give people a second thought. A remarkable feature of their study of humankind was that without losing sight of human weakness, they saw its accompanying grandeur.

Moral weakness weighed more heavily on Jews than did physical weakness. In this connection, it is interesting to note a verse from the Jewish scriptures, often quoted among Jews: "I was born guilty, a sinner when my mother conceived me." It would not, however, be correct to judge from this verse that Jews considered human nature depraved or sex something evil. The verse, however, contributes something of importance to Jewish study of human nature and human existence, particularly its societies and customs. The word "sin" comes from a root meaning to miss the mark, and this people repeatedly do. Their missteps are not preordained, though, for Jews believe that people shape their destinies through their freely chosen decisions. As regards life and death, another interesting verse says, "I have set before you life and death. Therefore choose life." It is evident from this verse that people have the freedom to choose life and forge their destinies.

It follows from the Jewish concept of their God as a kind and loving God that people are God's beloved children. In one of the beautiful and tender metaphors of the Bible, the prophet Hosea describes how God yearns over people, as though they were toddling infants. Hosea says, "It was I, who taught Ephraim to walk. I took them up in my arm; I led them with cords of human kindness with bonds of love."

Justice

The teachings of prophets tell us that individuals are responsible not only for their face-to-face dealings, but for the social structures of their societies. Further, the future of any people depends to a great extent on the justice of its social order. In the biblical period, prophets were considered a special group of persons who spoke for God. A review of the prophetic movement shows it not to have been a single phenomenon. Moses stands in a separate class by himself, but the prophetic movement passed through three stages. In each of which Yahweh worked differently.

The first stage relates to prophetic guilds. Here, prophecy was a phenomenon, a form of collective and self-induced ecstasy. With the help of music and dancing, prophetic bands would work themselves into fever pitches of possession. The members of the band would lose their self-consciousness in divine intoxication. This ecstatic state of consciousness made the prophets assume that they were divinely inspired.

The second stage of the prophetic movement began with ethics. At this stage, the prophetic guilds launched individuals like Elijah, Elisha, and others. Since prophecy was still in its pre-writing stage, no writings are attributed to them. Divine visitations would come to them while they were alone, and Yahweh voiced his concerns through them.

The third stage of the prophetic movement began with the great writing prophets, including Hosea, Amos, Jeremiah, Isaiah, and others. They continued to be ecstatic, and the ethical note that the pre-writing prophets struck was retained, but with an addition. Whereas Elijah registered God's displeasure over an individual act, the writing prophets perceived Yahweh's disapproval of injustice that was implanted firmly in the social fabric. The writing prophets found themselves at a time that was full of inequities, special privileges, and injustice, in which they saw the threat to the international standing of the Jews. They heard Yahweh telling them that Israel's corruption would result in an attack by its neighbors.

According to the prophetic principle, the prerequisite of political stability and social order is social justice. It is natural that injustice will not endure. From the theological point of view, this means that God has high standards; divinity cannot and will not put up with exploitation, corruption, and injustice. The prophets of Israel were outstanding and brilliant persons and they spoke words that the world could never forget. The one thing common to all was the firm conviction that every human being is a child of God and therefore in possession of right, which everyone in this world, including kings, must honor and respect.

God's Revelation

The Jews firmly believed that they were able to find the meaning of life because the truths were revealed to them by God. Viewed from a theological angle, revelation means divine disclosure. Jews have recorded Yahweh's disclosures to them in the divine and holy book of the Torah and commentaries on it. According to traditions in Judaism, it was through actions that God revealed himself. The greatest of these actions was the Exodus, a decisive action in which God liberated an utterly disorganized, frustrated, and suffering enslaved people from the most fearful and mightiest power of the age. This incredible event bonded the Israelites as one nation and one people. It was also the first clear act by which Yahweh's character was revealed to them.

Jews all over the world were of the firm conviction that the incredible and impossible escape from the clutches of the dreaded and mighty Pharaoh was only due to the direct intervention by their God. Without God's direct help, they would have never succeeded in their efforts and survived as a nation. Thus, Jews were convinced that their liberation and subsequent freedom was a divine miracle. The biblical book of Exodus says, "I am the Eternal, your God who brought you out of the land of Egypt." (Exodus 20:2) Jews could clearly see God's personal intervention in every step of their memorable journey to freedom and becoming a nation.

Every Jew was convinced of God's help at every stage of their historical journey from bondage to freedom. They also believed that without God's active help, they would never have become a nation. Following the Exodus, every subsequent development and event fell into proper place. From the beginning, God had been guiding, leading, protecting, helping, and shaping his people for the great Exodus, which culminated in a nation for Israelites.

The Exodus revealed the nature of God to all Jews. It gave them unshakable faith in the existence of God, the unity of God, and God's concern for the welfare of his children. They were convinced that Yahweh was the most powerful, since he had been able to undo the mightiest power of the time. His action had shown Yahweh to be a god of goodness, compassion, and love, with deep concern for the welfare and happiness of his followers. This gratitude for God burst into a song: "Happy are you, O Israel, who is like you—a people saved by Yahweh." (Deut 33:29) Freedom came to them as a result of Yahweh's grace, kindness, goodness, and great love for them.

Further, the Exodus also revealed many other aspects of their God; it showed them a God who was deeply concerned with the welfare and happiness of his people. For Israelites, God had come to them in an historical event. They would no longer be party to cajoling the forces of nature. They would sincerely and honestly attend to the will of Yahweh and try to obey his commands. For the Israelites, the Exodus disclosed the power, goodness, love and concern for them. Just as he was good, Yahweh wanted his people to be good. Hence at Mount Sinai, the Ten Commandments were established as the Exodus's immediate corollary.

The Ten Commandments are a comprehensive set of directions and guidance for the daily conduct of the Jews. They address the holy and the mundane—the physical and moral requirements as well as the worship of God. During the Exodus, God promised them, "If you will obey Me faithfully and keep My covenant, you shall be to Me a kingdom of priests and a holy nation."

Hallowing Life

Judaism is a monotheistic religion in the strictest sense. It holds that God intervenes in human life, especially in relation to the Jews. In Judaism, worship involves several annual festivals and various customs, and rituals and traditions play a vital part in the lives of Jews. Judaism has no official creed, but ceremonies and rituals are major events; they are considered important and useful functions. For instance, a handshake creates friendship. Similarly, when death or disaster strikes, rituals come into play when people reach out to the bereaved. Rituals also give confidence and courage. The Bible says, "The Lord giveth and the Lord taketh away, blessed be the name of the Lord." Rituals can turn adverse events into celebrations.

In Judaism, the function of ritual is basically to hallow life. Jews see life as reflecting the source of all holiness, namely Yahweh. The route to this viewpoint is piety. The Talmud states that to eat or drink without first making a blessing over the meal is tantamount to robbing God of his property. In fact, Jewish laws sanction all the good things in life, such as eating, singing, dancing, marriage, children, family, and so on. The only condition is that they should be hallowed. The Talmud teaches that people should prepare the tables and then eat in the presence of the Lord. Further, it teaches that the people should drink and that they should use wine to consecrate the

Sabbath. It teaches that people should be contented and happy and that they should dance around the Torah.

One may ask the question as to how this sense of the sacred can withstand the dull routine and monotony of daily life. Jews' answer to this question is by binding life in tradition. Without proper care and attention, the human awareness of wonder and sense of the holy and the sacred will not be a steady flame. To steady the flame, we should tend to it with great care and devotion. The best way to do this is to immerse ourselves in a history that proclaims God's providential acts and infinite mercy in every generation.

Judaism, the most historically minded of all religions, finds holiness and history very much united. In tracing their roots into the distant past, Jews derive considerable strength, faith, courage, and hope from events in which God's acts were manifest. Jews find meaning in the Sabbath, the Passover feast and its symbols, the solemnity of the Day of Atonement, the scroll of the Torah. This meaning spans countless years in affirming God's goodness, caring, concern, and love for all his people.

God in Judaism

Let us examine the nature of God in Judaism. It is one of the few areas of abstract Jewish beliefs where there are a number of specific and clear-cut ideas in respect to which there is agreement. Some of these aspects are listed below.

God Is One

One of the fundamental expressions of Jewish faith, recited twice daily in prayer, is the Shema, which begins, "Hear, Israel: The Lord is our God. The Lord is One." This statement encompasses three different ideas. These are the following:

1. There is only one God. No other being participated in the work of creation.
2. God is a unity. He is a single, whole, complete indivisible entity. He cannot be divided into parts or described by attributes.
3. God is the only being to whom we should offer praise.

God Exists

The fact of God's existence is accepted without question. No proof is needed. The Torah begins by stating, "In the beginning, God created...." It does not tell who God is or how he was created. Judaism stresses the existence of God which is essential for the existence of the universe.

God Is the Creator of Everything

Everything in the universe was created by God and only by God. Judaism totally rejects the dualistic notion that evil was created by Satan or some other deity. All comes from God. As Isaiah said, "I am the Lord, and there is none else. I form the light and create darkness, I make peace and create evil. I am the Lord, that does all these things." (Is 45:6–7)

God Is Incorporeal

Judaism firmly maintains that God has no body. Any reference to God's body is simply a figure of speech, a means of making God's actions more comprehensible to beings living in a material world. Jews are forbidden to represent God in a physical form. That is considered idolatry.

God Is Neither Male Nor Female

This aspect follows directly from the fact that God has no physical body or form. Jews refer to God using the masculine term simply for the sake of convenience, since Hebrew has no neuter gender. Although Jews usually speak of God in masculine terms, there are instances when God is referred using feminine terms. The Shechinah, the manifestation of God's presence that fills the universe, is conceived of in feminine terms, and the word Shechinah is a feminine word.

God Is Omnipresent

God is in all places at all times. He fills the universe. He is always near to us to call upon when needed, and he sees all that we do. God is universal. He is not just the God of Jews; he is the God of all nations.

God Is Omnipotent

God can do anything since he is omnipotent. It is said that the only thing that is beyond his power is the fear of him; that is, we have free will, and he cannot compel us to do his will. This belief in God's omnipotence has been tested during the many persecutions of Jews, but Jews have always maintained that God has reason for allowing these things, even if people in their limited perception and understanding cannot see the reason.

God Is Omniscient

God knows all things, past, present, and future. He knows all the thoughts of people.

God Is Eternal

God transcends all time. He has no beginning and no end. He will always be there to fulfill his promises.

God Is Both Just and Merciful

Of the two names of God most commonly used in the scripture, one refers to his quality of justice and the other to his quality of mercy. Judaism also maintains that God's justice is tempered by mercy, the two qualities perfectly balanced.

Judaism—Significance of Moshiach or Messiah

Moshiach (or Messiah in English) means the "anointed one" in Hebrew. It is the most single and fundamental belief in Judaism, next to the Torah. It describes the purpose and direction of Judaism. Moshiach is a part of the thirteen principles of faith propounded by Maimonides.

According to modern scholars, the concept of Moshiach was introduced later in the history of Judaism. No mention is made in the Torah regarding the concept of Moshiach or Messiah. The traditional Judaism, however, maintains that the messianic idea has always been a part of Judaism. The Moshiach is not mentioned explicitly in the Torah since the Torah was written for the common man. The abstract concept of Moshiach and a distant spiritual, future reward was beyond the comprehension of ordinary people.

According to Judaism, the Moshiach will be a great political leader, descended from King David. He will be an authority in Jewish law, a charismatic leader inspiring others to follow his example. The Moshiach will also be a great military leader. He will be victorious in all battles and win battles for Israel. He will be a human being and not a God or demi God or a supernatural being.

As regards the timing of the arrival of the moshiach or when exactly he will come, there are a wide range of opinions among Jews. Some Jewish leaders and philosophers have opposed the idea of predicting the coming of the Moshiach. According to them, any error in such prediction would result in the loss of faith in Judaism itself. The general belief among Jews is that the Moshiach will come when he's most needed or at a most desirable time.

According to Jewish belief, the world after the arrival of the Moshiach will be characterized by peace and peaceful coexistence of all people. Intolerance, prejudice and hatred will cease to exist. There will be no murder, robbery or sin. All the Jewish people will return from their exile to their home in Israel.

Charity

Judaism places great importance on charity, which is a part of the daily life of Jews. Charity is considered a moral commandment in Judaism. If the poor asks us for help and we are unable to help him, we should try to soothe him with kind and loving words. The idea is that the poor asking for help should not feel humiliated. We must not rebuke the poor and should never get annoyed or angry with him. According to rabbinic teachings, we should be like a father to the poor man. We should be kind, compassionate, and loving and full of understanding.

Judaism has laid down certain norms for charity. In giving charity, there are eight degrees, which are as follows:

1. The highest and the most important degree is making a gift or giving a loan to a poor person, or taking him as a partner or securing him employment, which will enable him to become self-supporting. The idea is that the person in need of help should not lose his self-respect.
2. Another good charitable act is when the donor does not know the identity of the receiver and vice versa. This will avoid all possibility of embarrassment on either side and is considered a noble and good form of charity.
3. The next form is giving charity to the deserving poor whose identity is known though the recipient is unaware of the donor's identity.
4. The next form is the reverse: giving charity without knowledge of the receiver, although the receiver is aware of the donor's identity.
5. Another noble form of charity is to understand a poor man's need and make charity voluntarily, without being asked. This prevents the poor from any embarrassment in asking for help.
6. The next form of charity is to give only after being asked.
7. In certain cases, it may not be possible for one to give the poor the full help asked for. In such cases, the giver should give graciously, although what is given is inadequate.
8. The last type of charity is giving grudgingly.

The teachings of Judaism stipulate that venerable men of sound judgment should give charity before each prayer. In fact, they are to give charity first and only then begin the prayers.

Another important concept is that one should always press himself and undergo suffering rather than depend on charity from others for his existence. He should never become a burden on the community. In other words, charity is to be availed of only when absolutely necessary to tide one over a temporary difficulty.

Sometimes even a person who is learned, wise, and respected becomes poor due to circumstances beyond his control. In such cases, the person should engage himself with some trade rather than depend on the charity of others.

There have been instances of many sages and learned men who engaged themselves in various trades such as wood-chopping, gardening, or working with iron, steel and coal. They worked and did not ask the community for help, and when it was offered to them, they refused.

Love and Serve God

Serving God is an important aspect of Judaism. Rabbi Eliezer, the great Jewish philosopher and thinker, said, "You shall love the Lord with all your heart, with all your might and with all your soul." One should love God with devotion at all times. The essence of Judaism can be found in the Ten Commandments. The first two commandments—"I am the Lord thy God" and "Thou shall have no other Gods"—are the core of Jewish belief. The thirteen principles of faith drawn up by Maimonides deal with the nature of God and how to love and serve God.

Serving and loving God were part and parcel of Jewish life, since Jews firmly believed that they were able to find meaning in life because God revealed the truths to them. Jews believed they could secure freedom only due to direct intervention and involvement of God. Jews believed that their liberation was a divine miracle, and they saw God's helping hand in every stage of their momentous journey to freedom. Loving and serving God thus assumed great importance in Judaism.

How to serve God? The best way is to imitate his ways. We should be just and merciful as he is just and merciful. We should have absolute faith and devotion in God. The best way to serve God is to obey his commandments and to follow them in our day-to-day lives.

We should be constantly mindful of the glory of our creator. In whatever we do, we must be sincere, alert, and careful that it does not produce anything that could be a profanation of the glory of heaven. Every man must be careful not to indulge in anything that is improper for a man of his status. All the thoughts and actions of a person should be in glorification of God.

God is the source of joy and happiness. A major principle in the service of God is, therefore, joy. One should serve the Lord with joy. One should come into his presence with singing. According to Judaism, there are three basic elements in the service and love of God: joy, devotion, and enthusiasm. To love God is to passionately long for his nearness, praise him, and pursue his holiness, as one pursues something that he strongly desires. One's love and devotion should be sincere and pure. One should love God, not because God is good and kind to him or grants him wealth or success, but one should love God as naturally and as lovingly as a son loves his father. Neither hardship nor misfortune nor suffering should lessen one's love for God.

Another major principle in serving and loving God is ridding oneself of sadness as much as possible. Weeping in grief is very bad for a man or woman, since one should serve God in joy and happiness. Sadness is a great obstacle to the service of God.

Even if a person has sinned, he should not be sad, lest he neglect the service of God. He should, of course, be sad because of the sin, but he should then retire to rejoice in God

Love Your Neighbor

The Torah clearly states, "You shall love your neighbor as yourself; I am the Lord." These words sum up the attitude we should have about our neighbor. Whatever we consider hateful and bad, we should not do to our neighbor.

The phrase "I am the Lord" explains two important things. First and foremost, souls are all a part of God. Since the soul of one man and the soul of his neighbor are both parts of God, love for your neighbor as for yourself is meant literally. Secondly, if your love for the neighbor is the same as the love for yourself, then this is considered the same as love for God.

The practice of loving-kindness is essential for a pious and spiritual life. Loving-kindness is far superior to giving charity. Charity means giving away one's possessions, like wealth and property, while the practice of loving-kindness entails giving of oneself. Normally, charity is given only to those who are poor and who are in need of help, whereas loving-kindness may be shown to one and all, to both the rich and the poor. In addition, while charity can be given only to the living, loving-kindness can be shown both to the living as well as the dead.

Loving-kindness demands that we should never cause pain or suffering to any human being or to any other living being. We must be kind, merciful, and compassionate to all animals, for it has been written that a righteous person has regard for the life of his beast.

In every human being, there is a spark of the Divine Soul. The power of evil in a person darkens this flame and causes the flame to be extinguished. Brotherly love among all men and women rekindles the soul and brings it close to its source.

The concept of loving your neighbor in Judaism is similar to the commandment in Christianity that states "You shall love your neighbor as yourself." Since the souls of all beings are part of God, loving one's neighbor is equal to loving God. This same concept is extolled in many other religions.

Jewish Ritual

Jewish worship involves several annual festivals, rituals and various customs. Judaism expresses its beliefs and attitudes more through its ritual nexus rather than through abstract doctrines. Rabbinical Judaism is concerned with agricultural laws, benedictions, festivals, relationship between men and women, matters relating to civil and criminal law and damages, ritual purity and the temple ritual and its sacrifices. In the debates and formulation of these issues, the rabbis gave expression to the ethos of Judaism.

In the day-to-day life of a Jew, his life will be structured around several rituals, which shapes his approach to life, his relationship to God, his relation ship to his family and fellow beings and to the community and the world around him. They are the prime repository of his faith. There is a very wide gap between the traditional and the modernist Jew. It is not only the difference in doctrine which divide them, but the difference in the life-style, liturgy, festivals, rituals, laws regarding food, marriage and divorce procedure etc.

The Jewish ritual year is a lunar year of twelve months. The year begins in late September/early October with the New Year festival Rosh Ha-Shanah. For Jews this is a period of divine judgment in which the fate of the world in the coming year ahead is determined. Jews repent their sins, the ram's horn is blown in the synagogues summoning man and woman to an awareness of his or her failures and shortcomings; and the idea of God as the divine King is emphasized in the liturgy. For two days of the festival, Jews eat sweet food as a symbol of the good year to come. This festival is also a celebration to show that they are confident of God's love, kindness and mercy. The day after Rosh Ha-Shanah is a fast day for Jews, lasting from dawn to dusk. This is to commemorate a tragic event in Israel's past.

Ten days after the New Year is the day of Atonement. It is called Yom Kippur. This is a day of atonement, a solemn festival characterized by fasting and self-examination. It culminates the Ten days of Penitence that begin with Rosh Ha-Shanah, the Jewish New Year. Yom Kippur is a twenty-four hour fast and all food and drinks are completely forbidden. Most of the time is spent in prayers in the synagogue, seeking atonement from God for all the past sins. The central message of Yom Kippur is that God forgives the truly penitent sinner.

Five days later is the festival of tabernacles. This festival is called Sukkot or festival of Booths or Tabernacles or ingathering. It celebrates the harvest and end of the major part of the agricultural year. This festival is usually held in October. It is an eight-day festival and during this festival, Jews live in a little shack.

Two months later is Hanukkah. This festival of Dedication is held in December that commemorates the Maccabees' restoration of Jewish independence from Syro-Grecian domination and the rededication of the temple at Jerusalem in December 165 B.C.E. This festival is usually distinguished by the lighting of candles for eight days.

The next festival is Purim or festival of Lots. Celebrated in late February or early march, in commemoration of the deliverance of the Jews in Persia during the fifth century B.C.E. from Haman and his genocidal plot.

Another festival is Pesach or festival of Passover. Instituted to commemorate the deliverance of Israel from captivity in Egypt. It is the greatest and oldest of Jewish festivals. It usually falls at the end of March or beginning of April. Each Jewish family comes together to share the Passover meal or Seder. During the following seven days, no leaven may be eaten.

Dignity and Responsibilities of Man

Judaism has laid down norms regarding responsibilities of man. The guidelines enable Jews to lead a good and pious life. Great importance is given to the observance of the responsibilities, since the welfare of the people as well as the nation depend to a very great extent on citizens discharging their responsibilities.

God created man in his own image. This is the biblical doctrine of man. God loves justice and mercy. It is, therefore, the responsibility of man to be true to his divinely ordained character by practicing all the virtues. To be like God means to be his partner in creating a just order in the world. Man can rise to great heights and he can also sink to great depths, but he is not by nature sinful. There are, of course, many temptations to evil in this world, but the path of piety is not renunciation of the world. Man's task is to hallow life and raise his workaday to its highest estate so that all his actions reflect the divine unity of all being.

Man is very dear to God because he was created in the divine image. Man is especially dear to God, since he has been made aware that he was created in the image of God. It is, therefore, man's responsibility to think and act in such a manner that reflects his divinely ordained character.

God is omnipotent, and yet man is responsible for his actions. Everything is foreseen and yet man has his free will. Man knows that he has choices to make and that he is morally responsible for those choices. He also realizes that there is a God, who judges him and his actions and upon whom he cannot place responsibility for his own misdeeds.

Man is not responsible for only himself; his actions have a bearing on the lives of others. He is responsible for the well-being of all other men as well as to the society and the nation. Man's responsibility in life is piety and reverence not only before God, but before all other men.

Everything is foreseen by God, and he has given the freedom of choice to man. The world is judged with goodness, and all depends upon the preponderance of good over evil deeds. Just as the world is judged according to the preponderance of good or evil, man is also judged in the same way.

If man fulfills one commandment, he is truly blessed, for he has tipped the balance to the side of merit not only for himself, but for the whole world. If he commits one transgression, he tips the balance to the side of guilt for himself as well as for the world.

The world is made up of good and evil. One sinner can destroy much good. One sin of an individual destroys much good for himself and for the entire world. Since man is created in the image of God, it is man's responsibility to practice all the virtues—such as love, kindness, compassion, justice, and mercy—and be God's partner in creating a just order in the world. Since God has given man the gift of judgment and choices, it is up to him to carry out his responsibilities so as to create a just world order.

Rules of Conduct

The Ten Commandments in Judaism are concerned with religious belief, worship, and conduct. These commandments reveal the connection between correct conduct and the correct relationship with the Creator. The rules of conduct are to be followed by all followers of the faith. The rules of conduct specifically state the proper relationship between members of a family and one's relationship with other members of the community.

The commandments are as follows:

- One should honor one's father and mother.
- One should not steal.

- None should commit adultery.
- One should not murder.
- A person should not bear false witness against his neighbor.
- Lastly, it is stipulated that one should not covet one's neighbor's house or his wife.

These commandments for conduct enable Jews to lead a pious life and live as good citizens.

According to Judaism, the first and essential rule of conduct for man is imitation of God. Whatever his circumstances may be, a man should organize his life to conform to basic beliefs of Judaism, and that is the basic principle of his conduct. The rule tells man to live every moment of his life in the awareness that he is not alone, that God is ever present.

A person should devote to science, religion and moral living. A habit is master over all things; consequently, one should ensure the habit of moral living. Since it is very difficult to change a habit once formed, it is necessary to pursue good habits at all times.

Show respect to yourself, your family members, your neighbors, and your friends and relatives. Provide decent clothing to your children and other family members. Dressing shabbily reflects adversely on the head of the family. Reach out to the poor and others who are in need of help. Attend to the sick and render them all assistance. You can take fees for your services from the rich, but not from the poor. Help and heal the poor, and the Lord will requite you; thereby you will find favor and good understanding in the sight of God and man. Thus, you will win respect and honor from the high and low, and your good name and fame will spread far and wide.

Lend your books to those who are unable to purchase them. You should make it a rule to read the scriptures in your house every day.

Honor your friends and find opportunities to benefit from their wisdom. Listen to your father's advice and instructions. Similarly, do not forsake your mother's teaching.

Speak kindly and gently to everyone at all times. Be kind, compassionate, and loving to all. Never lose your patience and get annoyed or angry. Be humble, for the reward of humility is the fear of the Lord. Reverence results from humility. Humility reminds you before whom you should give account in the future: the King of Glory.

> "You shall walk after the Lord your God. The Lord your God is a consuming fire."

On Right and Wrong

Judaism places great importance on doing the right thing. In fact, there are specific rules for conduct, and all the followers of the faith are expected to adhere to these rules. The Ten Commandments for worship and conduct explain what is right and wrong.

According to some Jewish philosophers, there are people who while performing good and noble deeds have evil intentions in their hearts. They argue that such a man's deeds are at variance with his inner character, his lusts, his greed, and his psychological make-up. Although he does good, it really pains and hurts him. The desire and inner nature of the saintly man, on the other hand, are in full accord with his deeds. Such a man not only does good, but sincerely desires to do so. He takes pleasure in doing good deeds.

All these philosophers agree that the saintly man is far superior to the man who has to exercise self-control, since the latter really wants to do evil even though he does not then do it. His very desire to do evil is in itself an unwholesome trait of his character.

The superiority of the man who has no desire to do evil over the man who wants to do evil but controls himself is not in the deeds themselves, since both types of men do good. The difference between them is that the man who really wishes to do evil suffers from a severe fault of character. There is something unwholesome about him if he wants to do wrong, even though by exercising self-control, he never actually does it.

We can imagine the case of a man severely tempted to steal because of his acute poverty, but who struggles with himself not to do so. In many respects, such a person, who has the mental strength not to resort to stealing in spite of his poverty is greater than the person who enjoys a happy existence and never had any temptation to steal.

The difference, therefore, between doing the right thing and wrongdoing is basically one of character. The person who wants to do a wrong thing but refrains from doing it by exercising self-control lacks character.

On Truth and Falsehood

Truth and falsehood are two important aspects of character, the positive and the negative. Regarding truth and falsehood, the scriptures say, "You shall not steal, neither shall you deal falsely, nor lie to another."

We must know that the world exists because of truth. The world depends for its existence on three important things: justice, truth, and peace. These three characteristics are more or less interlinked. It will be seen that there is no need for justice, where there is peace. Similarly, where there is truth, there will be peace. Truth is thus a vital aspect for the maintenance and well-being of the world.

Falsehood, or a lie, is the opposite of truth. One should desist from uttering falsehoods; even comparatively harmless lies should be forbidden. Some people utter falsehoods whenever they relate events, without any gain to themselves and without causing any harm to others. Such people imagine that the telling of falsehoods is of some benefit to them. There are some people who take pleasure in telling untruths.

One school of thought holds that it is permissible to lie for the sake of keeping the peace. In other words, some deviation from truth is permitted if it brings peace to people at large.

Far worse are those who deny that they owe a debt, when in realty they do, or deny that something has been deposited with them, when in fact it has. Such scoundrels are guilty of falsehood, robbery, greed, and covetousness. Teachings of Judaism clearly and categorically state that one should not steal or deal falsely or lie to another.

When people get used to speaking falsely, it becomes their second nature. Such persons come to take pride in their lies. Evil results.

Happy, peaceful, and contented will be the man who keeps himself distant from falsehood and trains his mind and mouth to speak only truth and righteousness. If a person follows the path of truth, he will attain all his wishes in this world and the next. Such an honest person will teach his children in the way of truth and righteousness, and he will be saved from all troubles.

A person who is truthful in all his actions will find peace. H will be setting a good example to the younger generation. An honest person is an asset to the society as well as to the country.

Covenant

At the core of Judaism lies a covenant between God and the Jewish people. The term "covenant" signifies an agreement made between parties, which must be distinguished from related ideas like "testament" and "contract." A covenant is different from a testament in that a covenant involves a personal response from a second party in order to make it truly effective. A covenant is also different from a contract.

The covenant in Judaism is between God and man. The Jewish covenant generally has the following three elements:

1. A historical prologue describing the deeds of the maker of the treaty;
2. A list of obligations binding the lesser of the two parties; and
3. A list of rewards for fulfilling the obligations and punishments for transgression.

Jewish covenants are grounded in divinely ordained events. They contain a set of conditions and end with a list of blessings and punishments. The first covenant mentioned in the Jewish scripture is that between God and Noah, when God preserved Noah and his family during the flood. The covenant with Noah provided the basis for the subsequent covenant between God and Abraham, the great patriarch of Israel. In the covenant between God and Abraham, God promised to make Abraham the ancestor of a great nation and give him and his descendents the land of Israel.

After six hundred years, the covenant was reaffirmed and extended at Mount Sinai with all the people who came out of Egypt. This covenant recalled God's historical deliverance of them from slavery in Egypt and his promise that Israel would be his special possession among all nations. There were, of course, obligations, in the form of the Ten Commandments and people's acceptance of their responsibilities. This covenant was an expression of God's grace as well as his demands.

At Sinai, God entered into a covenant with the people of Israel. The Torah is the sacred writ of that covenant. It describes the story of how the Jewish forefathers were admitted into the covenant and how they struggled to construct their lives according to the Torah. It brought them into the presence of prophets, who were granted an immediate vision of the divine and brought God's message to the people, admonishing and rebuking them, comforting and consoling them and holding out hope, all in the spirit of the covenant.

As mentioned above, the covenant with Israel was not the first God made with his creatures. After a cataclysmic flood had destroyed the earth, God made a pact with Noah, and through him with all humanity. The Bible says, "I now establish My covenant with you and your offspring to come and with every living thing that is with you: birds, cattle and every wild beast as well. And I will maintain My covenant with you. This is the sign of the covenant that I set between Me and you, and every living creature with you for all ages to come. I have set my bow in the clouds, and it shall serve as a sign of the covenant between Me and the earth." (Gen 9: 9–13) All of nature and all of humanity stand under this covenant for eternity.

As a people standing under a divine covenant, Israel is unique. The covenant makes Jews one people linked to one God.

Path of Discernment

Discernment means to perceive differences, make distinction and discriminate. According to Judaism, God's promise that He will be with the Jews is the heart of all discernment. The story of Exodus clearly shows that there are certain qualities and experiences that serve as road markers on the path of discernment, particularly, peace, clarity, empowerment as well as conquest of fear and release of inner joy.

Shalom, or peace, is the opposite of agitation, tension, anxiety, and worry. Peace is the most essential factor in a seeker's spiritual path. We will find ourselves at peace not only when we are resting, but when we are absorbed in work that draws all our abilities, such as prayer or worship or meditation.

Clarity, purity, and simplicity go hand in hand. Clarity is hearing the music without any background noise. Over the course of our life, we have internalized many different voices. When we are faced with making a decision, we can hear the disapproving voices of a former teacher, the encouragement from our parents, or doubt of a friend. Which of these voices is our own deepest nature that directs us to our own good? We arrive at clarity not by silencing those inner voices, but by letting them talk themselves out. This practice gives us the perceptual distance to listen without any conflict or agitation. With patience, clarity arrives, and we can then begin to listen for our greatest good.

Another significant signpost in the spiritual path is the conquest of fear and an increase in trust. Fear blocks our perception, and noise obscures our capacity to appreciate. The main cause of fear is lack of understanding. We do not know, and we cannot understand, predict, or control. Discernment involves the acceptance of this uncertainty, acceptance of a species of darkness, a letting go of purely rational assurance. This is hinted at in the representation of God in the dark cloud surrounding the peak of Mount Sinai. Darkness need not be an occasion for fear; it can be a way of knowing God.

When we are whole, undivided, clear in our vision, and free from fear, we have strength and joy. The absence of fear and doubt makes us feel strong and ready to undertake any task. Along with a sense of power, freedom from fear and anxiety leads to a sense of tenderness for all living beings. This feeling of tenderness brings inner peace, and we then begins to perceive the world as it is.

When the mind is free of all fear and there is inner peace and clarity, we experience joy. Joy is greater than pleasure or happiness. It is a total experience of the self and a release from any sense of limit, control, or constraint.

Chapter 5

Sufism and Bahaism

An Introduction to Sufism

Sufísm is the mystical core of Islam. It at first appeared as a separate discipline within Islam, in the eight century, with the teachings of Hasan al Basri. According to Sufi scholars, Sufism can be described as the universal mystic dimension of all religions. For all the Sufis, Sufism is a tree, the roots of which are outward religious practices.

Sufism is the mystical dimension of Islam based on the esoteric, or inner meaning of its scripture, the Qur'an. Sufism's central doctrine is based on a verse of the Qur'an in which God says, "I created man and breathed My spirit into him." This "divine spark" placed into every individual, says the Sufi, must be nurtured and cherished. Furthermore, each individual spark or spirit separated from the Universal Spirit—God—desires to return and reunite with the Universal Spirit. This is confirmed by another verse in the Qur'an, which says, "From God we came, and to God shall we return." This returning is vital and central to the Sufi doctrine. The Sufi embarks on a spiritual journey known as the Sufi path, a path of devotion and love, which leads the devotee to none other than God himself.

The word "Sufi" is derived from the Arabic word "suf," meaning "wool." Garments woven from wool were generally worn by early mystics, who came to be known as Sufis. A Sufi is a mystic who strives towards intimate knowledge or communion with God through contemplation, meditation, and inner vision.

The Sufi firmly believes that each individual spirit desires union with the Universal Spirit after death. He believes that it is possible to experience God in this very life. Sufism teaches that the Sufi who seeks God must advance by slow stages along the path to God. The stages relate to repentance, followed by abstinence, renunciation, poverty, patience, and infinite trust in God. These stages constitute the ethical and ascetic disciplines of Sufism. Total commitment at each stage is vital in the spiritual progress of the Sufi.

Sufism's primary teaching is based on the Unity of God. Its main emphasis is on the oneness and uniqueness of God. The Sufi believes that God's earliest creation was the human intellect, which enables humans to discern and to choose between right and wrong and good and evil. This knowledge in Sufism is raised to a higher level, which arises from the heart rather than the mind.

The central doctrine of Sufism is love and divine love. According to Sufism, God's love is his supreme attribute. The Sufi believes in the doctrine and concepts of the fear of God and God's wrath on the Day of Judgment. The Sufi maintains that obedience to God's commands should ensue not out of fear of punishment or the desire for reward, but rather with sincere motive and the intention of attaining proximity to God.

The Sufi attests that God has created man with a mind, free will, and love, with the emphasis on love. Consequently, the Sufi path becomes a path of love, where the Sufi becomes the "lover" and God the "beloved." This love affair ends only with the ultimate union with the beloved. This love relationship between the Sufi and God is portrayed in Sufi poetry and literature.

History of Sufism

Islam like every religious tradition divided into Sunnis and Shiites, who differ in opinion about who should succeed Muhammad. There was another division: the division between the mystics of Islam, called Sufis, and the remaining majority of the faith. After Muhammad's death, many Muslims, who were very much attached to the spiritual teachings of the Qur'an, began to wear coarse woolen garments, from which the name Sufi emanated. It was a sort of protest against the silks and satins of sultans and caliphs.

Sufis were alarmed by the worldliness they saw as overtaking Islam, and they wanted to purify the faith from within. According to their thinking, external should yield to internal, matter to meaning. They proclaimed, "Love the pitcher less and the water more." These Sufis were convinced of the Qur'anic teaching that there is an inward as well as an outward side to the divine nature. For majority of Muslims, God's relatively obvious aspects were sufficient, but the Sufis wanted to plumb Allah's depths. They wanted to experience him now and in this very life itself, rather than wait until the afterlife. This necessitated special methods, and to effect them, Sufis gathered the gifted among them. These gifted Sufis were called sheikhs, or masters.

Later, these communities crystallized into orders, whose members were called "faqirs," meaning poor in the sense of poor to the world, while being rich in God. They constituted a special spiritual elite who aspired higher than other Muslims and who were willing to assume greater austerities and disciplines. They were not cloistered, and most of them got married and engaged themselves in normal occupations. They would then listen to the discourses of their masters for spiritual advancement. All the Sufis sincerely yearned for spiritual knowledge. They all wanted to be burned by God. This required getting very close to God, and for this purpose Sufis developed certain distinct traits and characteristics.

The first of these is the love of poetry. Sufi love of poetry is world renowned. For many Sufi writers, complex and deeply felt feelings and ideas found their most suitable expressions in poetry. Sufism has generated a large body of often very difficult writings concerning spiritual knowledge and mystical union with the divine presence.

Among the great poets are Ibn al-Arabi, Fared al-Din al Attar, and Ibn al-Farid. Jal al-Din al-Rumi is another outstanding Sufi poet, who produced a body of mystical poetry that is considered among the gems of medieval Islamic works.

Most of the Sufis conveyed their deep yearning for God in beautiful poems. According to them, God's love is at the core of the universe. They felt that not to steep oneself in that ocean of love and reflect it to others was to surrender life's beatitude. Further, love is never more evident and profound than when the object of the love is absent. Many Sufi poets dwelt at length on the pangs of separation in order to deepen their great love of God and draw closer to God.

The Sufi approach to the divine presence could be called ecstatic. At times, they are so engrossed in their ecstatic experience that they forget themselves and their surroundings. They lose consciousness of who they are, where they are, and what is happening to them. Sufis honor the ecstatic. Sufis also have a distinctive approach to intuitive discernment. According to Sufi masters, love and mysticism give great knowledge, ecstasy yields visionary knowledge, and intuitive mysticism brings mental knowledge.

What is Sufism?

Sufism can be described as the religion of the heart. A Sufi is one, who considers his heart as the shrine of God. He discovers God within his heart by removing the false self. The word Sufi means purity, wisdom and love. The meaning of Sufism is the selfless experiencing of Truth. The practice of Sufism lies in the sincere desire to know the Truth by means of love, service and devotion. According to the Sufi saint Ruwayn Ibn Ahmad, "Sufism consists in abandoning oneself to God in accordance with God's will." While Sufism did not exist prior to Islam, Sufi doctrine contains several elements that go beyond the teachings of Muhammad. The sacred knowledge of Sufi masters and saints was not written, but was passed on orally from generation to generation. Hence it is difficult to trace the history or evolution of Sufi doctrine.

Early Sufi Orders

According to historians, Quadiriyya is considered as the first major Sufi order to emerge. His sermons in Baghdad were very popular and attracted large crowds. His sons and followers laid the groundwork for the order. The reputation of Quadiriyya can be judged from the fact that many pilgrims still visit his tomb.

Towards the end of the eighth century AD, many austere Muslims, whose lies were consumed by great devotion and love for God decided to give up all material comforts and devote their entire lives exclusively to prayer. To proclaim their non-attachment to worldly matters and desires, they switched on to wearing wool. These people came to be known as Sufis. The name Sufi comes from "suf', the Arabic word for wool, or "saf", the Persian word for pure.

Fundamentals of Sufism

The genesis of Sufism emphasizes the esoteric doctrine of the Prophet as may be found in references in the Qur'an. Sufism is based on Islamic faith, which has six pillars, namely, God exists, God is one, there are angels, there are prophets, there is a day of restoration, and there is fate. Sufis regard their creator as their "Llah," or deity, and worship him alone and they believe that there is none other than he.

Sufis call the ideas of God the "essence of things". God is one, but his ideas are many. Ideas depend on God for their existence, but God exists independently.

Islam is the religious tradition taught by the Prophet Muhammad. The aim of Islam is harmony with God and attuning the individual will to God's will. Islam stresses honesty, charity, service, and other virtues, all of which form the foundation for the spiritual practices of Sufism. According to some Sufi saints, "Sufism without Islam is like a candle burning in the open without the protective lantern. Winds are likely to extinguish the candle, but if there is a protective lantern with protective glass, the candle will burn safely." Sufis believe that the great religions and mystical traditions of the world share the essential truth. Sufism proposes that all the great religions as well as their spiritual teachers were sent by one God. Further, what all the true teachers taught was nothing but truth. The Sufis accept and love them all because they believe there is one God and one message with many prophets.

Sufis believe that the differences among the world's religions are of human origin and that the truth of all religions is one and the same—namely, God. For Sufis, Prophet Muhammad is a role model to be studied, understood, and followed. Sufis also consider Jesus Christ to be one of the greatest prophets. They call Jesus the Spirit of God. Sufis also love and revere Moses. The perception of God as the Beloved is common to both Christianity and Sufism.

According to Sufi masters, all love is nothing other than the love for God, since everything in this world is God's reflection or His shadow. Love for God should be the sole aim of life. Love for God should permeate all his thoughts and actions. Love of God is the panacea for all human ills. With the heart overflowing with love of god, life will be fruitful and purposeful.

Sufism teaches that at each moment, man's actions should conform to the teachings of the Sufi masters. They should abandon themselves to God. One should not possess anything, nor should anything possess one. The essence of Sufism is the Truth. It is the selfless experiencing and actualization of the Truth.

The Lower Self

Every man and woman is made up of a higher self and a lower self, which can make or mar their life. The higher self is the divine and noble aspect that leads us in the spiritual path and enables us to become close to God. The lower self, on the other hand, leads us away from the spiritual path and thus away from God. It also prevents us from remembering God. Sufism is mainly concerned with the things that either help or harm people in their spiritual path. In each one of us, there is an element that can lead us away from the spiritual path. This element is called "nafs" in Sufism. It is an Arabic term that can be translated as ego or self.

In Sufism, nafs refers to anything that goads an individual to the wrong path, that invites a person to wrongdoing. This includes greed, selfishness, conceit, arrogance, anger, passion, and lust. These undesirable characteristics constitute the lower self, which deflects our efforts to reach God.

The lower self is not something created by the interaction of the body and soul. By themselves, the body and soul are pure. But when our soul becomes attached to our body, we forget our original soul-nature and become attached to this world and all worldly things, developing the characteristic of the lower self.

To progress on the spiritual path, we should always be on the alert, avoiding the pitfalls that lie in our way. We should struggle to do only the right things that are best for us. We should struggle even harder to avoid immoral and unethical actions. Why should we struggle? Because when we are convinced that our action is right and correct, our lower self tries to make us do the opposite. Even when we see everything clearly, our lower self makes us forget, and, inadvertently, we do the wrong thing. It is, therefore, imperative that if we aspire to progress in the spiritual path, we should always watch out for the lower self trying to change our correct course.

The lower self is always obsessed with gaining the good opinion of others. This results in increased acquisitiveness of material things and pride in them, as well as arrogance, contempt for others, lust for power, and self-glorification. The lower self avoids whatever others disapprove of, even though these things please God.

The lower self can be compared to a flame. While the flame is beautiful to watch, it has the hidden potential for great destruction. The lower self is so well-organized that it is difficult to get rid of it or overcome it without the help of God. Further, as the lower self prevents us from remembering God, it is all the more necessary to have God's help.

We should all, therefore, develop our higher self, since it leads us to God. We should constantly watch out to prevent the lower self from making us do the wrong thing. With God's help, we can overcome the evil intention of the lower nature. Through devotion, meditation, and prayers, we can eliminate our lower nature.

Virtues

Faith is belief and trust in and loyalty to God. While on the face of it, spiritual faith seems simple, it is rather difficult to practice. All of us seem to put our faith in doctors and lawyers when we have sickness or legal problems. Similarly, all of us put our faith in amassing wealth and in our intelligence. All of us seem to have faith in creation and not in our Creator.

It is rather strange but true that instead of putting our faith in God, we seem to put our faith in material things as well as human beings. Real security, safety, happiness, and health will come to us if only we put our complete faith in God. While wealth can give us temporary happiness, real peace and mental harmony will come only through total faith in God and God alone. God often tests our faith to enable us to understand ourselves better.

Humility is the quality of being humble, without pride, and with modesty. A humble person assumes his true measure and does not hide from the truth of that realization. According to Sufism, humility is achieved through awareness. Without humility, we tend to become arrogant, conceited, and vain. The more humble we become, the closer we are drawn to God.

Gratitude is the state of thankfulness. It is the noblest of all virtues, and it transforms an individual. It opens the heart and brings it closer to God. All of us receive many blessings from God, but we rarely feel gratitude. This is because we take these blessings for granted. We never pause even for a moment to express our gratitude to God for all the blessings of life, which he has freely given us. On the subject of gratitude, Prophet Muhammad said, "Gratitude for the abundance you have received is the best insurance that the abundance will continue."

To the followers of Sufism, poverty means lack of attachment to anything but air, food, and sleep. According to the teachings of Sufism, the heart filled with thoughts of material things has no place whatsoever for thoughts of God. A heart filled with worldly desires is actually empty, with much space for God to fill.

According to Sufi masters, all a person needs is food to satisfy hunger, a roof to cover the head, and clothes to cover the body. We should ask only for these essential things and nothing more. If we are to lead a spiritual life, all other things are superfluous and divert our focus from God.

In order to travel the spiritual path, the Sufi needs strength supplied by proper bodily nourishment. It has been said that whatever a Sufi eats gets transformed into spiritual qualities and light. However, the food of non-Sufis, since it but serves their own desires and fears, only strengthens their selfish attachments and takes them farther away from the truth.

Patience is another great virtue. It can be termed as a spiritual state. Patience is a real accomplishment, since it is difficult to attain. With patience, we can achieve anything in this world, and all difficult tasks become easy. Patience has the power to help us overcome all obstacles and difficulties. Our lives will be greatly enhanced spiritually by patience.

The Religion of Love

Sufism is basically a religion of love. This aspect was beautifully brought out by the famous poet Rumi, who wrote, "When I come to Love, I am ashamed of all that I have ever said about Love."

Love permeates all aspects of life. It is the core of all religions, and all religions glorify love of God. Man's love can be classified under two types: true love—or love for God—and love for everything else. Love for God involves strictly obeying his commandments and leading a truly spiritual life.

The important aspect of love has been beautifully brought out by Rumi and other Sufi poets and philosophers, and some of these are listed below.

One's life should be spent in cultivating love for God. Any time that passes without love of God will be a shame before God. A life devoid of love for God is absolutely nothing and a waste. Such a life is of no account. A life without love for God is meaningless and useless.

Love is the water of life and one should drink it to the heart's content. Without the sweet life of love, living will be nothing but a burden. Love is the elixir of life and it will deliver you from death.

Love is the bottomless ocean of life and everlasting life is the least of its gifts. Love is the elixir of life and it makes the earth into a mine of meanings. A lover's food is love for God.

Love squeezes water from rocks and love removes and cleans dust and rust from mirrors. Love is like a lion, without deception and trickery; not like a fox one moment or a leopard the next.

When love provides replenishment, the spirit is freed from this dark and narrow body. From the beginning, love is bewilderment. It stuns the intellect and dazzles the spirit.

Love is the be-all and end-all of life. A life devoid of love will be a total waste. If love's pulse does not beat within a man's heart, he is only an ass, even if he is Plato. If a head is not full of love, such a head is behind the tail.

The school is love, the teacher is God and we are all like students. Love removes all the angularities in a person and makes him a rounded personality.

The famous Sufi poet Rumi described love as follows: "Mount upon love, and do not think about the way. For the horse of love is steady and sure-footed. Though the path may be rough and uneven, it will take you to your destination in a single gallop."

Love is like the sun, radiating warmth and joy. The heart without love is nothing but a piece of stone. To love is to see good and beautiful in all God's creation and in everything in this world.

Love is like a seed. On a good heart, it will sprout and grow into a big and healthy tree. This tree will then blossom, giving sweet flowers and fruit. And a person who tastes that fruit will know what real and true love is.

Love is the panacea for all the ills of mankind. It makes bitter things sweet. Love will destroy all sufferings and pains.

Wisdom

Sufism lays great importance on cultivating wisdom. According to Sufi masters, humanity will benefit from those who are wise. By cultivating wisdom, Sufis can become useful and productive members of society. Like other world religions, Sufism wants its followers to cultivate wisdom and in that process contribute to the betterment of society.

Humility and self-awareness are two of the most important and essential prerequisites to wisdom. Many people like to think that they are very wise, a notion that makes them commit many foolish mistakes. Unless we are wise enough to dispassionately analyze our mistakes, we can never learn from them. By pretending to be wise, we are ignoring the reality of our weaknesses and deficiencies. False notions of wisdom lead us to the wrong path.

We should be humble, which can lead us to wisdom. Humility is the quality of being modest and devoid of any pride. Next comes self-awareness. We should be aware of ours limitations. These are the two initial steps for cultivating wisdom.

Action is another important component of wisdom. It is not enough to know something; a person should take prompt and correct action based on his or her knowledge. There is a saying among Sufis that "A donkey with a load of books in its back is still only a donkey." The moment we act on our knowledge, we attain wisdom.

The best way to cultivate wisdom is to listen attentively to the words of great teachers and Sufi masters. Listening to what they say, comprehending what they mean, and acting upon their words is the best way to attain wisdom. All the great teachers and masters convey to the younger generation through their speeches and books great words of ripe wisdom. By listening to these masters, we also become wise, and then our wisdom will be a source of guidance to others.

Knowledge is like rain. Although the source of rain is unlimited, rain falls only according to the season. We should guard our heart from thoughtlessness and protect our lower self from desires. We should also guard our intellect from ignorance, a great danger. Only knowledge can remove ignorance. The moment ignorance is eliminated, a person becomes really wise. Further, we should diligently cultivate the company of wise persons, which will help us acquire wisdom. It is the sacred duty of every man and woman to seek and acquire knowledge.

God created angels and blessed them with reason. He created animals and conferred passion upon them. When God created man, God blessed him both with passion and reason. Thus, in the case of a person, if his reason prevails over his passion, he is higher than an angel. If, however, his passion prevails over his reason, he is lower than an animal.

Another important method of acquiring wisdom is by questioning and listening. By listening to great masters and questioning them, we acquire wisdom. In fact, asking intelligent questions is half of the learning process. According to Sufi masters, those who possess knowledge and those who seek knowledge will be useful members of society who will benefit humanity.

Prayer

Prayer is an expression of our great love for God. It is the deepest impulse of the soul of man and is an integral part of all the religions. There are different types of prayers, such as inner and outer forms of prayers. There are prayers performed in absolute silence, and there are prayers that are either spoken or chanted or sung aloud in groups. Then there are formal prayers, prayers at specific times, and prayers inspired by the heart. The purpose behind real prayer is a deep and sincere longing for God and an earnest yearning for connection to the divine.

Many people pray for some sort of benefit for themselves or for others. Such people know prayer only as a form of petition, applied for securing a desired object. Prayer takes other forms, depending on the person who prays and the circumstances leading to the prayer. Prayer is adoration, an expression of one's love for God. Prayer is contemplation, a person's desire for union with God.

Everything in this world is in prayer. Every creation is worshipping God. Human beings, who have free will, have, however, the option to pray or not to pray. And for such people, real prayer does not come spontaneously. Prayer has to be achieved.

The greatest hurdle to prayer is distraction or lack of concentration. The mind has to be constantly focused in prayer, and this will pose the greatest challenge. There should be a burning desire to pray, and this desire, coupled with dedication, will ensure that the mind does not wander. Prayer is efficacious when the mind is solely fixed on God

According to Sufi saints and masters, prayer is an invitation to man from God, an invitation to the divine presence. Prayer connects the person praying to the one prayed to. Prayer can thus be described as an entrance to the presence of God.

The road to the divine presence, by which our prayers can reach God, is keeping our heart pure, by eliminating all negative thoughts. The mirror of our heart should be kept clear, clean, and polished by our unwavering faith, great devotion, and sincerity.

There are no limits to praying. We can pray as much as we want, depending on our capacity and ability. The prayers should come spontaneously, and there is no need to go to extremes. Prayer by its very nature is essentially private. It is the soul seeking God and trying to attain union with God. Those who sincerely practice daily prayer know its power and the sublime heights to which it can lift the mind. In prayer we can experience how a mind bruised by worries and tensions can within a moment of prayer be completely rejuvenated.

The benefit of prayer is that it relieves the mind of all worry and tension. Prayer creates peace and mental harmony. The Prophet taught the following prayer to his followers: "O God, grant me love of you, and to love those who love you and to love whatever brings me nearer to you."

Remembrance of God

One of the important and basic Sufi practices is opening one's heart in remembrance of God. According to Sufi masters, remembrance of God has four basic meanings. The first and foremost is the act of constantly and continuously striving to be mindful of God. Prayer to God is remembrance and unites the person making the prayer to his presence. Secondly, remembrance is the repetition of the divine names such as, "There is no God, but God." This constant repetition is the remembrance of the tongue. The third remembrance means the inner state, in which awareness of God overwhelms the devotee, and he or she is free from all worries and concerns of the world. This is the remembrance of the heart. The fourth and the last remembrance is a deep, abiding, and strong inner state in which prayer and mindfulness become constant. This is the remembrance of the soul.

Remembrance of God should fill the heart and soul of all the followers of the faith. Prayers and worship are the two most vital aspects in the remembrance of God. Once a devotee is fully engaged in prayers and by constant repetition of God's names, his or her heart and soul are automatically filled with remembrance of God and all other thoughts are eliminated.

In Sufism, there are various practices of remembrance of God. They include silent remembrance, in which the devotee meditates on God in silence. In silence remembrance, the devotee's heart is focused only on God. Then there are prayers, worship, and chanting of divine names of God. Then there is the practice of groups of devotes chanting together and singing together.

According to Sufi masters, it is believed that our souls were in the world for thousands of years. There, bathed in God's presence, our souls experienced the Divine deeply. Remembrance is recapturing a small part of that blessed divine state.

The Sufi saints have said that what you are is what you think. A person becomes according to his thoughts. Thus by constant practice of remembering God, a person will be in a constant state of remembrance of God. At this stage, the self of the person falls away. What remains is God.

All creation is calling upon God. The essence of everything is continuous remembrance of God and calling on God. The purpose of life, according to Sufi masters, is this constant remembrance of God through various practices such as prayers, worship, and the constant repetition of God's names. These practices create a mental state in which the devotee's heart is fully focused on God and all other worldly thoughts are totally removed. In this state, remembrance of God fills the heart and soul of the devotees.

Some Gems from Sufism

"If you have never trodden the path of love, go away and fall in love, then come back and see us." – Jami (Essential Sufism)

"If words emanate from the heart, they will enter the heart. If the words come from the tongue, they will not pass beyond the ears. Man may be idle, but the mind must be awake in the right way. When he awakes, he will have the means to profit from his wakefulness." (Al-Suhrawardi (Essential Sufism))

"A donkey with a load of holy books is still a donkey." - Traditional (Essential Sufism)

"I searched for God and found only myself. I searched for myself and found only God" – A Sufi proverb

"When you do things from your soul, you feel a river moving in you, a joy". – Rumi

"Enlightenment must come little by little, otherwise it would overwhelm." – Idries Shah

"God turns you from one feeling to another and teaches you by means of opposites, so that you will have two wings to fly; not one." – Mevlana Rumi

"If you try, everything you strive will come close to you, and you will reap the benefit. May God give you that help, that grace, that wisdom and His qualities. May He do what is good. f you believe in Him, He will never let you go. If you intend Him, He will come looking for you. If you call Him, He will call you. If you love Him, He will love you. If you search for Him, He will search for you. Know this. Amin. Amin." – M.R. Bawa Muhaiyaddeen

"Ordinary human love is capable of raising man to the experience of real love." – Hakim Jami

"Look to this day, for it is life, the very life of life. In its brief course lie all the verities and realities of your existence; the bliss of growth, the glory of action, the splendor of beauty. For yesterday is but a dream and tomorrow is only a vision. But today well lived makes every yesterday a dream of happiness and every tomorrow, a vision of hope. Look well, therefore to this day, such as the salutation of the dawn." – The Sufi, 1200BC

"Do not buy the enmity of one man for the love of a thousand men." – Essential Sufism.

Sufism—The Path of Islamic Mysticism

Mysticism is derived from the Greek root "myein," which means "to close the eyes." Mystics of all religions seek to uncover the same divine mystery that is hidden both within and without. According to a famous Sufi scholar, Sufism can be compared to a river that flows through many countries. Sometime, the river flows underground and then emerges somewhere else unexpectedly. Different countries give the river different names. But the river is the same river, wherever it flows.

The mystics are those who seek direct experience of God. They seek to know God. They dedicate their entire lives to traveling the path of God. For them, God is truth, and truth is God. God is their goal, and God is also their guide. According to the Qur'an, "All things return to Me." But the Sufis are impatient and they do not want to wait. They want union with God now itself, in this very life.

The practice of Sufism varies widely. The mystical practices of Sufism have developed for over a thousand years, and these have been based on the experiences of many Sufi masters. Further, these Sufi practices have adapted to the cultures, customs, and societies in which Sufism has been practiced.

The term "Sufi" has several root meanings in Arabic, including "purity" and "wool." All Sufis seek outer as well as inner purity. During early times, the Sufis wore rough and patched woolen clothes instead of fancy clothes. At the time of the Prophet, there was a group of very devoted Muslims who sat in a row in front of the house of the Prophet. They accompanied the Prophet wherever they could and it is said that this group received esoteric instructions from the Prophet. These were the first Sufis.

There are several terms for those who practiced Sufism. They are also called "dervishes," a Persian word related to "door." A dervish stands at the threshold between the material and spiritual worlds, constantly endeavoring to enter more fully the realm of spirituality.

Another term used for the Sufi is "fakir," from the Arabian root for "poverty." Poverty refers to the very simple lifestyle practiced by the Sufi. In the early times, many Sufis were wandering mendicants who depended on the charity of others for food as well as shelter. Another meaning that can be ascribed is inner purity, a lack of attachment to material possessions and wants. Fakir also means "dependent on," as in solely dependent on the power of the divine.

By and large, Sufis worship God and live a highly moral and ethical life, abiding by the teachings of their religion. For the mystics, outward practices are only a means towards unity with God, which is the only aim of their life.

Love, Harmony, and Beauty

The teachings of Sufi masters revolve around three aspects of human life: love, harmony, and beauty, words have profound influence on the human soul, since they are the very nature of life. Love is the nature of human life, beauty is the outcome of life, and harmony is the nature by which life accomplishes its objectives. When one reflects on life in this world, one can visualize that its objective is to express an ideal of love, harmony, and beauty. Love could not have manifested itself if there was no object to love. There should be something to love and to be loved. Further, what could love have done if there were no beauty? What is beauty and what has created beauty? It is only love that has created beauty. As famous masters have said, love is beauty and beauty is love. It is love that has made beauty. Whatever God has created in this world, he has made out of his infinite love. There is a famous Sufi saying: "Beloved ones of God, whatever God has created are His beloved ones."

Human beings have their own likes and dislikes. This explains why some people are liked and others are not. Some people are considered worthy of honor, while others are not. To God, however, all beings are alike. They are his creation, and he likes them all. God is love, and he has created all human beings out of his infinite love. How, then, could God be pleased if one has a hatred or prejudice against a fellow being? God created a human being in order to love him. God, the Father and Mother of all beings, is equally pleased with all his creatures.

God is the love and the manifestation of love at the same time. According to Hindu mythology, this concept is called Shiva and Shakti. The one part is love, and the other part is beauty. Love has created beauty so that it may be able to love God is love and that is why he is called the Creator. The lover alone has the power to create, and whatever he creates is for receiving his love.

The Prophet said, "God is beautiful and He loves beauty." Here the word "beautiful" does not refer to the form of God, since God is without any form. Consequently, it is not his personality that is beautiful, for God is beyond what in the ordinary sense of the word is called personality.

All things that men and women make are the work of their hands. They are what they create, and they are greater than their hands. Similar is the case with love. Love is greater than beauty because love creates the beauty that loves and is loved. By loving, love no doubt becomes limited—limited as beauty.

Love is very powerful and exerts tremendous influence on the life of human beings. persona person's life undergoes complete transformation after being melted in the fire of love. The fire of love will exalt a person to such an extent that his power will influence everything, even animals and birds. Burned in the fire of love, one becomes purified and one then becomes attractive to every soul.

A Sufi master said, "To a human soul, love means affection; to an animal soul, love means passion; to an angelic soul, love means glory and to a jinn soul, love means admiration. It will be thus seen that love, harmony and beauty appeal to the human soul, because they are the very nature of human life in this world and they are the means by which life accomplishes its goals."

An Introduction to Bahaism

The followers of Bahaism follow the teachings of Baha U'llah, the founder of that faith. Baha U'llah lived in Iran in the nineteenth century. He taught his followers that God provided successive revelations to humanity through a series of divine messengers to bring mankind to spiritualism and spiritual maturity. Each of these messengers, or prophets as they are called, has been the founder of one of the world's greatest religions, and Baha U'llah taught that he was the last of these.

The central message of his teaching was the unity of all people. Bahaism can be summed up in the words of Baha U'llah: "The earth is but one country and mankind its citizens." The followers of the Baha'i faith respected all other religions The Baha'i teachings are based on the principles of economic justice, world peace, equal rights and opportunities for women and men, and education for all people.

As a religion, Bahaism preached tolerance and love for the followers of different faiths. The essence of Bahaism was love for all beings, understanding, and world peace. Baha U'llah wanted all nations to live in peace and harmony and to break down all the traditional barriers of race, class, and creed.

The symbol of Bahaism is interlocking triangles. This interlocking of triangles represents the interdependence of all people in the world in one essential unity.

Baha U'llah preached love for mankind. He said, "Show forbearance and benevolence and love to one another. Illumine and hallow your hearts; let them not be profaned by the thorns of hate or the thistles of malice. You dwell in one world and have been created through the operation of one Will. Blessed are those, who mingle with all men in a spirit of utmost kindness and love."

Baha U'llah wanted his followers to beautify their tongues with truthfulness and adorn their souls with the ornament of honesty. He wanted everyone to be the trustees of God among his creatures and the emblem of his generosity.

There are five to six million Baha'is worldwide in more than 175 countries, with the largest concentration in Africa and the United States.

Baha'is meet in local assemblies, but their administrative and spiritual center is in Haifa, Israel. The two most holy places are the tomb of Baha U'llah and the shrine of the Bab (the founder of Bahaism), both in Israel.

Bahaism

Founder

Bahaism, or the Baha'i faith movement, originated in the 1860 as a faction within Babism. Babism was founded by Bab and was a messianic sect of Shia Islam that began in Iraq and Iran in 1844. The founder of the Baha'i faith or Bahaism is Baha U'llah, who claimed to be a new prophet and developed his religion through divine revelation.

The prophet Baha'i U'llah was born in Persia on November 12, 1817, to a wealthy and noble family that could trace its ancestry to the great dynasties of imperial Persia. Baha U'llah was offered a ministerial job in the government, which he declined. Instead, he chose to devote his energies to a range of philanthropies, and this earned him the title of "father of the poor." He then became one of the leading advocates of a movement that changed the course of his country's history.

The period in which Baha U'llah lived was very turbulent. It was a time of great unrest, political conflicts, and turmoil. In Europe and America, a group called the Templers believed that they had found in the Christian scriptures evidence to support their conviction that the return of Jesus Christ was imminent. Similar sentiments developed in the Middle East with the belief that the fulfillment of the prophecies in the Qur'an and Islamic traditions was at hand.

The greatest of the movement was, however, in Persia. There, in the city of Shiraz, a young merchant known as Bab was capturing the imagination and the minds of men and women with his teachings and new ideas. For more than nine years, from 1844 to 1953, all Persians were in a state of excitement and great hope aroused by a statement made by Bab that the day of God was at hand and that he was himself the One promised in the Islamic scriptures. He further declared that people would witness many revolutionary changes in all aspects of life. The human race was called by God to accept these changes by undertaking a transformation of its moral and spiritual values. Bab further declared that his mission was to keep humanity for the great event: coming of that universal messenger of God.

Bab's radical claims and statements created violent hostility, anger, and great prejudice among the entrenched and powerful Islamic clergy, who maintained that the process of divine revelation had ended with Prophet Muhammad. According to the Islamic clergy, any view to the contrary was blasphemy. Bab's claim was considered apostasy, which was punishable by death. The Muslim clergy denounced Bab as a renegade and traitor, and they sought support of the Persian authorities. Thousands of Bab's followers were put to death and Bab, was executed in public on July 9, 1850.

Baha U'llah, who rose to prominence because of his defense of Bab's cause, was arrested, chained, and taken to Teheran. He was spared the sentence of death because of his social standing and personal reputation. He was cast into a notorious dungeon with other criminals and thugs, and a heavy chain was clamped around his neck. During the time he was in the dungeon, attempts were made to poison him. Every day, prisoners were dragged out by the guards and summarily executed. It was under such critical circumstances, and faced with his own imminent execution, that Baha U'llah received the first intimation of his mission. One night in a dream, he heard these exalted words: "We shall render Thee victorious by Thyself and by Thy Pen. Grieve Thou not for that which has befallen Thee. Afraid Thou not, for Thou art in safety. Soon will God raise up the treasures of the earth-men who will aid Thee through Thyself and through Thy name, wherewith God hath revived the hearts of such as have recognized Him."

Finally, Baha U'llah was released from prison without any trial, and he was banished from his native land. All his wealth and properties were confiscated. Though some friends offered him protection and refuge in another land, Baha U'llah refused such offers. Instead, he chose to accept banishment to the neighboring country of Iraq. This was the beginning of forty years of exile, imprisonment, and persecution.

By 1863, Baha U'llah decided that the time had come to begin acquainting all those around him with the mission entrusted to him. His influence grew bigger and bigger. Fearing the acclaim and popular enthusiasm, the authorities moved Baha U'llah to Constantinople. Before his departure, he called together all those around him and confided to them his mission. Over the next few years, many of his friends and followers shared the news that the Bab's promise had been fulfilled and the day of God had dawned.

Baha U'llah's influence and reputation began to soar. The authorities got worried at this growing influence and decided to banish him to the fortress town of Akka. Baha U'llah and members of his family who were exiled with him were placed under house arrest. Here, they experienced great hardship and suffering. Baha U'llah died in the town of Bahjf on May 29, 1892, in his seventy- fifth year.

Scriptures

Bahia's scripture consists of Arabic and Persian writings of Bab, Baha U'llah, and Abd al-Baha. The first two represent revealed scripture, and the third represents commentary and an extension of the former two. The works of Bab composed over a period of six years fall into two distinct periods, with major shifts in his thought between the two. These works were written in Arabic and Persian. The writings of Baha U'llah are concerned with ethical issues, mysticism, and scriptural interpretation, besides formulation of laws, rituals, and the like. Abd al-Baha's works consist mainly of collected letters and lectures.

Beliefs

The essence of the Baha'i faith is the oneness of human kind. Its central message is that the day has come for the unification of humanity into a global family. Bahaism asserts that God has set in motion historical forces that are causing universal recognition that the entire universe is a unified, distinct species, and this will ultimately result in the emergence of a global civilization. An important teaching of the founder Baha U'llah is that God's greatest gift to humanity is reason. The belief of all the followers of Bahaism is that reason must be applied to all the phenomena of existence, including those which are spiritual, and the instrument to be used in this effort is the scientific method. According to the Baha'is, any religion that contradicts science or that is opposed to it is only ignorant, and ignorance is the opposite of knowledge

Other major Baha'i beliefs include the soul's immortality and the social, spiritual, and biological evolution of mankind. They reject the concept of angels. They also reject belief in the trinity and reincarnation.

According to Baha U'llah, the purpose of God in revealing his will was to effect a transformation in the character of humankind, to develop within those who respond the moral and spiritual qualities that are latent within human nature.

Bahaism as a Religion

The Baha'i faith is the youngest of the world's independent religions. From its humble beginnings in Iran during the mid nineteenth century, Bahaism has spread to almost all parts of the world. The Baha'i faith is an independent and distinct religion It is not a cult or reform movement or a sect within another faith. Bahaism is an independent religion on par with Islam, Christianity, Buddhism, and other world religions.

Baha U'llah's writings are in full praise of the great organized world religions,which have contributed to peace and harmony in the world. He condemned the artificial barriers that organized religions have created between humanity and the revelation of God by imposing dogmas and prejudices on a Divine Power. According to Baha U'llah, religions have caused hatred, sorrow and suffering, instead of creating peace, love, unity and understanding.

Further, Baha U'llah said, "Those whom God will hold responsible for this great tragedy are humanity's religious leaders." Their attempts to make the word of God a purely private preserve and its exposition to further advance their own personal interests have been the greatest single handicap against which the advancement of civilization has struggled. In fact, according to Baha U'llah, many of the religious leaders of world religions have not hesitated to raise their own hands against the Messengers of God. Baha U'llah further said leaders of religions have hindered their people from attaining the shores of eternal salvation, since they held the power and authority in their hands. Some for the lust of power, authority, and leadership and some others through lack of understanding and knowledge have been the main cause for the deprivation of the people. Thus if the heart of a man is corrupted, his limbs will also be automatically corrupted. If the root of a tree is corrupted, then its branches, its leaves, its flowers and fruits will also be corrupted.

The challenge to humanity is to recognize these pitfalls. All the peoples of the world, the believers and the nonbelievers, clergymen and laymen, leaders and followers of all faiths should recognize the dangers and consequences now being visited upon humanity as a result of universal competition of the religious impulse.

Baha U'llah felt that organized religions could contribute to happiness, peace, understanding, and universal love, if the clergymen and religious orders of all world religions were imbued with the spirit of self-sacrifice, love of humanity, love, compassion, and understanding. In this connection Baha U'llah stated, "Those divines, who are truly adorned with the ornament of knowledge, love and of noble character and integrity are verily as a head to the body of the world and as eyes to the nations."

The religious matrix of the Baha'i faith was Islam. Just as Christianity was born out of the messianic expectation of Judaism, Bahaism as a distinct faith arose from the eschatological tensions within Islam. The Baha'i faith is thus an entirely independent world religion

Vision of Baha U'llah

The vision of Baha U'llah captured the imagination, enthusiasm and loyalty of millions of people around the world. Baha U'llah claimed to be the messenger of God and his vision was to create understanding, love, harmony and unity among the followers of different faiths.

An important aspect of Baha u'llah's writings is that it totally forbids the aggressive proselytism through which many of the world religious messages were promulgated. The crux of the prophet's writings was am exposition of great ideas which had preoccupied religious thinkers and scholars, namely God, the role of Revelation in history, the importance of faith and the relationship of the different religious systems to one another. The writings of Baha u'llah states the prophet's own experience, of His response to the

Divine summons and His dialogue with the Spirit of God. The vision of the prophet is beautifully explained in the two major works of Baha u'llah, namely The Hidden Words and the Book of Certitudes. According to Baha u'llah, the main purpose of God in His Revelation is to effect a transformation in the character and integrity of human kind and to develop within those who respond to the moral and spiritual qualities that are latent within human nature. Each person who has recognized the Revelation has to share it with those who are seeking it.

Each person should show forbearance, kindness, compassion and love to one another. One should also display a spirit of extreme kindness, compassion, understanding, love and goodwill to those who are incapable of fully grasping the truth or who are striving to understand it. The duty of every man is to attain that share of grace, which God passes forth for him. Another outstanding advice given by the prophet to his followers is to behave and lead a life like good and noble citizens. They should behave towards the government of the country in which they live with loyalty and truthfulness. This is something unique and normally not found in many other world religions. This perhaps explains the tremendous growth of this comparatively new religion.

According to the teachings of Baha u'llah, the welfare of humanity, peace and security of the world cannot be achieved unless and until its fundamental unity is firmly established. Only a unified global community can provide security, lasting peace and a sense of belonging to the peoples of the world. In all the writings of the prophet, this theme of unity, understanding and love is highlighted, emphasized and repeated. Baha u'llah also advised his followers to associate with the followers of all other religions of the world in a spirit of understanding, love, kindness, friendship and fellowship. This will strengthen the bonds of love between different sections of the society, which will contribute to peace harmony and goodwill. According to the prophet," You are all the fruits of one tree and leave of one branch"

This glorious vision of Baha U'llah is indeed divine and truly noble.

A New World Faith

Bahaism is a new world faith, and, compared to other world religions, it is modern. The Baha'i faith originated in the last century, in Iran. It drew international attention and interest due to the persecution of its followers and the sufferings and humiliation suffered by its prophet, Baha'i U'llah.

Bahaism is one of the world's fastest growing and youngest religions, in terms of number of believers. It is an independent, distinct, and separate religion and is based on the teachings of the prophet Baha'i U'llah, its founder.

It is neither a cult nor an offshoot of any religion or any religious reform movement. From a very humble beginning, it has spread like wildfire to all parts of the world and has made a tremendous impact and created great enthusiasm and interest everywhere.

Baha'is believe that God's series of interventions in human history have been progressive and each revelation of God more complete than those that preceded it. Islam was the immediate historical predecessor to the Baha'i faith. Consequently, one can find many Qur'anic terms and concepts in the writings of Baha'i U'llah. Bahaism, however, is an independent religion and separate from Islam.

The central and vital aspect of Bahaism is the oneness of humanity and an emerging world order. The Baha'i faith covers a wide range of spiritual teachings, such as the unity of all religions, equality between men and women, economic and social justice, peace and harmony. The focus of the teachings of the prophet was on reason, which he termed as God's greatest gift to humanity. He firmly believed that the day had come for the final unification of humanity into a single and compact world family.

Another most important aspect of Bahaism is the acceptance, without any reservation, of the validity of all other world religions. This is unique to the new faith. The followers of the Baha'i faith believe that Abraham, Moses, Zoroaster, Jesus, the Buddha, and Muhammad are all messengers of God. Further, they also believe that all world religions are part and parcel of one Divine Plan. Basically, the essence of Bahaism is based on religious and ethical values such as universal peace and world harmony and world understanding.

Baha U'llah emphasized in all his writings that the historical forces set in motion by God will eventually bring about the recognition of the entire human race as a unified and distinct society, and this will result in world peace and world understanding.

Precepts and Beliefs

The followers of the Baha'i faith believe that God has revealed himself to mankind by means of divine manifestations and that these included Abraham, Moses, Krishna, Zoroaster, the Buddha, Jesus Christ, Muhammad, the Bab, and Baha U'llah. They also believe that all of the men are messengers of God and that all religions of the world are part of one Divine Plan. The followers of Bahaism further believe that these messengers of God were provided to guide humanity through an evolutionary process in which the appearance of the Bab initiated and set in motion a new age for mankind.

Baha'is declare that, to date, the message of Bab and Baha U'llah are the fullest revelation of God's will and that it is the primary God-given instrument that will ensure world unity, understanding, and world peace.

One of the important basic precepts of Bahaism is that all the great religions of the world are divine in their origin and that all their basic principles are in complete harmony. If there are some differences, they are only in the non-essential aspects of their doctrines.

Another major belief of Bahaism is the oneness of God, the immortality of the soul, and the social, spiritual and biological evolution of mankind. On the other hand, Baha'is reject the common concept of angels. They also reject the theories of the trinity, reincarnation, and man's fall from perfection and subsequent ransom through the blood of Jesus Christ.

The other major beliefs of Bahaism include the brotherhood of man and the equality of women. Men and women are treated equally. Baha'is practice monogamy, and this sets them apart from other religions. According to the teachings of the prophet, the followers are expected to pray at least once a day. They can pray any one of the three prayers revealed by Baha'i U'llah.

Baha'is undertake fasting from sunrise to sundown during the nineteen days of the Baha'i month of Ala.

In the Baha'i faith, there are not many set rituals. Further, it does not have any organized clergy like other religions.

Baha'is see themselves as having the mission of the spiritual conquest of the planet

The followers of the prophet Baha U'llah try to spread their faith and the teachings of their founder through participation in various community projects and informational meetings and campaigns. All Baha'is believe in total obedience to the laws of the country in which they live. They emphasize living as good, noble and honest citizens. They are not to get involved or participate in any politics, and they should strictly obey the laws of the land. This unique principle sets Bahaism apart from all other religions.

Baha'is prefer noncombatant duty in the armed forces, wherever possible, but there are not serious objections. The teachings of the prophet stress the need for all the religion's followers to set an example as good citizens by getting involved in all social activities that improve the welfare of the poor and the needy. They should be generous and practice kindness and compassion. They should reach out to their neighbors.

Another important aspect of Bahaism is upholding truth under all circumstances. Baha'is are expected to be strictly honest and straightforward in all their dealings.

Human Conduct

Bahaism has laid down norms for the conduct of its followers, in respect to each aspect of human conduct. Right conduct ensures discipline and self-control.

Bahaism stipulates daily prayer and meditation for individual discipline and self-control. The books of prayers have been published in several languages, and these books help the followers in their devotional lives. The followers of Bahaism should say prayers at least once every day. This is compulsory for all those who have attained the age of maturity. This obligatory prayer has three different forms, and the individual can choose whatever form he prefers for any given day.

Followers of Bahaism are strictly forbidden to consume alcohol and narcotic drugs. According to the teachings of the founder, alcohol and drugs cause great harm to an individual's physical and mental faculties. Since they hamper spiritual development, Baha'is are strictly forbidden to use them in any form. The only exception is for medical treatment. There are no other restrictions or prohibitions regarding food. Smoking tobacco is not forbidden, although it is condemned, since it is detrimental to health and well-being.

Bahaism places great stress and importance in the practice of fasting as a discipline for the soul. It has stipulated a nineteen-day period every year when adult followers of the faith fast from sunrise to sunset each day. Pregnant women, the sick, the elderly, and laborers involved in heavy manual labor are, however, exempted from the practice of fasting.

Besides the laws for every believer, Bahaism has laid down a number of social laws and principles. Thus, backbiting and criticism of others are condemned, since they are injurious to spiritual health and spiritual progress. Baha'is are also advised to be honest in all their actions and dealings.

Bahaism considers marriage as both a spiritual and social institution. Marriage affects not only the couple and their children, but also parents, grandparents, and grandchildren. Bahaism, therefore, places great emphasis on educating the couple so that they do not make any mistake in their relationship to each other. The Baha'i teachings enjoin chastity before marriage. Although divorce is allowed in the Baha'i faith, it is strongly discouraged.

Another important law of the faith is the requirement that followers should strictly abstain from involvement in political activity. This practice of total noninvolvement in politics is taught both in the belief and practice of Baha'i teachings. According to Baha U'llah, it is incumbent on all followers to display loyalty to the government of the country in which they practice their faith. They should observe and follow the laws of the land and be good citizens.

Economic Justice

Abdul Baha'i, a leading light of Bahaism, said, "When we see poverty causing starvation, it is a sure sign of tyranny." Great importance has been given to the subject of economic justice in Bahaism. The founder of the Baha'i faith wanted the unity of mankind based on economic justice. There is so much economic disparity between the rich and the poor in every part of the globe, as well as a grave imbalance in material conditions. A very small percentage of humanity has all the wealth, and this handful of people keeps very tight control over all the resources and means of production and distribution. In fact, this small minority literally holds the world's wealth in their hands while the majority of the world's population continue to live in abject poverty, extreme misery, and untold suffering. The economic imbalance exists both in industrialized as well as underdeveloped countries.

In spite of economic growth around the world, the gap between the rich and the poor has only increased, and it continues to widen each year. This has resulted in much poverty among a large population of the world, with all its concomitant evils and suffering. The existing system is ample proof that there is economic injustice in the world. The present system is unfair and unjust. It is incapable of ever restoring a fair and equitable balance.

Baha U'llah strongly asserted that economic injustice is a moral evil and should, therefore, be strongly condemned. Further, he enjoined the economic offenders of society to withdraw their hands from such manmade tyranny and suffering and said he pledged not to forgive any person's injustice. To eradicate such an offensive system, the founder of the Baha'i faith made some recommendations, which if implemented, will eradicate human suffering. Baha U'llah wanted cooperation to replace competition and to utilize the material and human resources for the long-term maximum good of all instead of the short-term profit of a handful of people. There should be a mechanism to control all the natural resources of the world, including their production and distribution. Unless and until such a system is put in motion, the existing glaring imbalance will continue, causing more misery and suffering for a majority of the peoples of the world.

Baha U'llah further suggested that both the workers and the owners in all enterprises should be engaged in a spirit of cooperation and understanding. The owners should willingly agree to share the profits of the enterprise with the workers. This would not only improve the profitability of the enterprise, but it would totally remove any conflict of interest. By such an arrangement, the economic imbalance, injustice, as well as exploitation of the poor can be eliminated. That the founder of the faith could conceive of such a pragmatic economic vision in his time shows the founder's abiding faith in economic justice. He deeply and sincerely felt that only by removing the economic imbalance and closing the gap between the rich and the poor can mankind live in peace and harmony.

Baha U'llah strongly felt that the poverty, suffering, and starvation existing in the world is entirely due to the greed of a few who monopolized all the material resources as well as the means of production and distribution. He sincerely desired a change of heart of those who were responsible for causing such widespread poverty. The Baha'i teachings envision a new economic order in the world based on a just and equitable distribution of goods and services in a spirit of cooperation, understanding, and goodwill.

Human Nature

The Baha'i concept of human nature is unique, since it highlights the importance of religion to human nature. Most of the peoples of the world simply carry on their lives without reflecting on life and its meaning for them. They are fully engrossed in all their routine activities that they have no time even to reflect on their lives. This is true of almost all the peoples in the world. Men and women marry, have children, become professionals, and run their business enterprise, without any knowledge whatsoever or understanding of the purpose of all their actions. In their lives of automation, they have no idea as to who they really are, or the purpose of their actions, or their destiny. They forget that only religion and spirituality can give meaning to their existence.

According to the teachings of Baha U'llah, only true religion and spirituality can give purpose and meaning to human existence. It is only in relation to God and the exact purpose which God has fixed for his creatures that human existence has any relevance or meaning. According to the Baha'i faith, the purpose of God in creating man or woman is to enable him or her to know and understand his creator and endeavor to attain his presence.

Life is a continuous process of spiritual discovery and growth. In the early stages of human life, a person undergoes a period of training and education. This enables him or her to obtain the spiritual tools for spiritual growth. And attaining physical maturity, he makes further progress and makes greater efforts. According to the Baha'i teachings, man's real nature is spiritual. Besides the physical body, every human being has a soul. This soul does not depend on the body, since it is a non-material entity. The body only serves as soul's vehicle in the world. The soul continues to exist even after the death of the physical world. The soul of the individual is the seat of his or her personality, self, and consciousness.

The basic purpose of human existence is the development of the soul. This development is towards God, and its objective is to know God and to develop love for him. The more one knows and understands God, the greater will be his love for him, and this will enable the person to develop a close communion with God. As we draw nearer to God, we become more and more spiritual and our actions will reflect more of the attributes and qualities of God.

Bahaism teaches that this capacity to reflect on the attributes of God is the soul's real nature. Man is created in the image of God, and the divine qualities are latent in the soul of man. This explains why the soul of an individual is the seat of his or her personality, his or her self and consciousness.

The words of Baha U'llah in this regard are pregnant with meaning. He said, "When I contemplate, O my God, the relationship that binds me to Thee, I feel to proclaim verily I am God. But when I consider my own self, I find it coarse than clay."

Some Spiritual Gems

The writings of the Baha U'llah unfolds a unifying vision of the nature and purpose of life and of the future of society. His writings on building a spiritual civilization are illuminating and inspiring. Some of the spiritual gems from his writing are given below:

It is incumbent upon everyone to observe God's holy commandments in as much as they are wellspring of life.

The purpose of religion should be to establish unity and concord among the people of the world and not to cause hatred, dissension and strife.

The word of God can be likened to a sapling, whose roots are implanted in the hearts of men. It is incumbent upon everyone to foster the growth with the water of wisdom and holy words, so that its roots are firmly fixed and the branches may spread as high as the heavens.

Through the power of good words and righteous actions, one can succeed in winning the hearts of people.

Everyone should strive so as to promote fellowship, kindliness and unity and ensure freedom, well-being, tranquility and advancements of all.

The tongue is a smoldering fire and excess of speech is a deadly poison. While the material fire consumes the body, the fire of the tongue devours both heart and soul.

The earth is but one country and mankind its citizens.

All the major religions come from one God.

All prejudices – racial, religious, national and international are destructive and these should be overcome by means of love, kindness and understanding.

The seeker must at all times put his trust in God, must renounce the people of the earth, must detach himself from the world of dust and cleave unto Him.

Beautify your tongue with truthfulness and adorn your souls with the ornament of honesty. Beware not to deal with anyone, who is treacherous. You must be the trustees of God among His creatures and the emblem of His generosity among His people.

Humility and Honesty

Humility and honesty are considered greatest and noblest of all virtues in Bahaism. The followers of the faith are expected to be scrupulously honest and humble. They should overlook the faults of others and look only for their virtues. In fact they should find out their own faults, if any, and should not take into account their virtues. In this connection, Baha U'llah said, "Let your life be an emanation of the Kingdom of Christ. He came not to be ministered, but to minister. In the religion of Bahaism, all are servants, brothers and sisters. If anyone feels a little better than that and a little superior to the rest, he or she is in a dangerous position. Unless he casts away such evil thoughts, he or she is not a fit instrument for the service of the kingdom."

A person who is happy and satisfied with himself or herself is the manifestation of evil, and the person, who is not contented with himself is the manifestation of goodness. Even if a person is endowed with many good and noble qualities, he or she should overlook them. He or she should strive to find out his or her own defects, weaknesses and imperfections. To blow one's own trumpet and praising one's own self is considered as a sign of arrogance, pride and selfishness.

All the followers of the faith are commanded to recognize and sincerely repent their sins. The practice of making confession to priests and others are strictly forbidden in Bahaism. According to Baha U'llah, "The sinner, when his heart is free from all save God, should seek forgiveness from God alone for God alone in all His great Mercy can forgive." Making a confession before men is not permitted, since such a confession leads to humiliation.

In Bahaism, great importance is attached to honesty and integrity. Honesty is considered the foundation of all virtues of mankind. Successes in life are possible only with observance of truthfulness in all one's words and deeds. Without honesty, there cannot be any progress in any field of human activity. Further, when one is firmly established in truthfulness, all other divine qualities will automatically accrue to that person. Honesty is the door that opens to peace and harmony to all in this universe. Honesty is the sign of glory from the presence of the Merciful One.

According to the teachings of Baha U'llah, whosoever has achieved truthfulness and honesty has attained all the treasures and affluence. Honesty is the door leading to security, understanding, and lasting peace of mankind. The stability of every action and affair depend on honesty. The world of honor, glory, greatness, and affluence are illumined by the brilliant light of honesty.

In the final analysis, a person is judged by the way he has led his life, namely by humility, honesty, and truthfulness. All the true followers should strictly follow the founder's commands in leading a life of purity, honesty, and humility.

On truthfulness and honesty, Baha U'llah said, "Honesty is the best garment for your temple. It is the most splendid crown for your heads. Truth and honesty are the foundation of all the virtues of humanity." Let the light of truth and honesty shine from your faces. Then everyone will know that your word is a word of trust and every action of yours is good and noble.

Prayer

One of the most important laws prescribed by the founder Baha U'llah for individual discipline is daily prayer. For all the followers of the Baha'i faith, daily prayer is a must. Besides the general injunction for daily prayer as well as meditation, Baha U'llah also ordained an obligatory prayer to be made by every Baha'i who has attained the age of maturity. Such obligatory prayer has three different forms, and the follower can choose whatever form he likes best. The important thing to remember is that whatever form a person chooses, he or she should make that prayer without fail every day.

The obligatory prayer is to be said between noon and sunset each day. An obligatory prayer reads like this: "O, my God, Thou has created me to know Thee and worship Thee. I testify to my powerlessness and to Thy might, to my poverty and to Thy wealth. There is no other God but Thee, the Help in Distress, the Self-Subsisting."

Prayers have tremendous powers. They awaken you and make you conscious of God. According to Baha U'llah, the prayer brings into action higher forces. The power that brings about answers to prayers is the unlimited, inexhaustible power of God. The part of prayer is only to exert the least force necessary to release the flow of divine bounty.

There are many types of prayers for specific purposes and for various times. The aspirant should understand the greatness of conception and the depth of spirituality embedded in the prayers. By making prayer a regular and important part of their day-to-day lives, one can comprehend the efficacy of prayers and realize their infinite power for good. Some of the prayers in the daily life of a Baha'i are as follows.

"O my God. Thou has created me to know Thee and to worship Thee. Unite the hearts of Thy servants and reveal to them Thy great purpose. May they follow Thy commandments and always abide in Thy Law. Help them in their efforts and grant them the necessary strength to serve Thee. Guide their steps by the light of knowledge and cheer their hearts by Thy love. Thou art their helper, guide and their Lord."

"O God. Thou art kind to all. Thou has provided for all, does shelter all and confers life upon all. Thou has endowed everyone with talents and faculties and all are drowned in the ocean of Thy mercy. O Kind Lord, unite all. Let all the religions agree and make the nations one. Let everyone see each other as members of one loving family and the entire universe as one home. May all live together as members of one family in peace and harmony."

"O God, gladden our hearts through the rich fragrance of Thy love. Brighten our eyes through the light of Thy guidance. Thou art Mighty and Powerful. Thou art forgiving and Thou overlook the shortcomings and failures of all mankind."

"O Thou Benevolent God, forgive our sins and overlook our faults. Provide us shelter and drown us in the ocean of Thy love. Heal us of all our sickness, sufferings and disease. Purify and sanctify us. Bless us with a portion of Thy divine holiness so that all our sorrows and sufferings will vanish and joy and happiness will prevail. Help us to change our despondency and helplessness into cheerfulness and trustfulness. Thou art Forgiver, Compassionate, Generous and Beloved."

Daily prayers make the followers conscious of God and enable them to lead good, noble, and spiritual lives. Prayers are a vital part of the daily lives of all the followers of the faith.

Future World Order

Baha U'llah was a man of vision. He had dreamt about the establishment of a World Order and a united human race. It was a glorious vision characteristic of a divine soul. Baha U'llah visualized a World Order that included the establishment of a world commonwealth in which all the nations of the world, all races, castes, creeds, classes, and colors are intimately and permanently united. In such a commonwealth of nations, the autonomy of all the member countries and the personal freedom of the individuals that compose them will be definitely and completely safeguarded. Baha U'llah further envisaged that such a commonwealth must consist of a world legislature whose members will act as the trustees of the entire mankind. The commonwealth will control and coordinate all the resources of the world for the common good of mankind and will enact rules and regulations so as to regulate the life, satisfy the human wants, and adjust the relationships of all the races and peoples of the world.

A world executive body, backed by an international peacekeeping force will carry out all the decisions made the world executive body and implement the laws enacted by the world legislature, besides safeguarding the unity of the commonwealth of nations. This great vision of Baha U'llah has no parallel in the world, and his vision has more or less materialized, with the establishment of the United Nations as well as the U.N. peacekeeping force.

In case of any disputes that may arise, a world tribunal will be created, which will adjudicate and deliver its final verdict. Such a verdict by the world tribunal will be binding on all the nations and the parties concerned. Baha U'llah also envisioned a world language, a world literature, a uniform and universal system of currency, a uniform universal legal system, and uniform weights and measures. According to Baha U'llah, these steps will ensure cooperation and understanding, and will facilitate meaningful and purposeful discussions between nations and races. National and international rivalries, border disputes, hatred, and intrigues will come to an end, thereby creating an atmosphere of peace and harmony. Racial animosities and prejudices will be replaced by racial unity and better understanding and cooperation. Further, distinction between classes will be obliterated.

Another major achievement will be the total elimination of religious fights, religious intolerance, and religious prejudices. All economic barriers and restrictions on the movement of people will be completely abolished. This will bridge the gap between rich and poor nations as well as between and developed and underdeveloped nations.

Baha U'llah envisioned the establishment of a World Order in a phased manner, and in gradual and slow stages. He also visualized an initial period of social breakdown, law and order problems, and widespread suffering. Out of this worldwide spiritual, physical,mental and social convulsion, humanity will eventually progress towards a World Order. Then there will be peace, understanding, righteousness, justice, and harmony upon the earth.

According to the vision of Baha U'llah—the creation of a World Order—the human race will become like one united family and this should bring about peace, prosperity, and plenty in the world. In such a World Order, people will come to recognize the will of God for humankind and will witness the establishment of God's kingdom on earth.

World Peace

Of all the religious leaders and prophets, Baha U'llah stands supreme in his great vision of world peace and universal brotherhood. In advocating a commonwealth of nations and world peace, Baha U'llah stands like a colossus. In his various writings to humanity, Baha U'llah urged the adoption of several steps towards achieving what he called the Great World Peace. He strongly felt that these steps would mitigate the sorrows and sufferings of people as well as the dislocation that he visualized lying ahead of the human race. He envisaged that until the entire humanity embraces the Revelation of God and through it ensures the emergence of the Great World Peace, there would not be peace and harmony on earth.

Advocating the cause of world peace, Baha U'llah said, "Regard the world as the human body, which though whole and perfect at its creation, has been afflicted through several reasons, with great disorders, disruptions and maladies. Not for one day did it gain ease. Its sickness became worse and more pronounced as it fell under the treatment of ignorant physicians, who were interested only in their personal welfare. All men have been created to carry forward an advancing civilization. It is unworthy of men to act like wild beasts. The virtues that befit his dignity are patience, kindness, compassion and loving-kindness towards all the peoples of the world of all faiths." Baha U'llah strongly recommended moderation in all matters. This will ensure understanding among people, besides creating peace, and harmony. Anything in excess will prove a source of evil and bring in its wake unnecessary troubles and tensions.

If the commonwealth of nations can prevent any war between member nations, then the nations of the world will not need to build up arms, except to maintain law and order within their territories. Such a step will stop the mad arms race among nations, which will disrupt the economy of the entire world. Further, by preventing wars between nations, the resources of the world can be better utilized for improving the standard of living of the peoples of the world.

According to the vision of Baha U'llah, the day is not far off when all the peoples of the world will have adopted one universal language as well as a common script. Such a step will usher in a world of peace and harmony. When such a step occurs, to whatever city a person may go, it shall be as if he or she were entering his or her own home. This earth will then be one country and the entire mankind will be its citizens.

Baha U'llah's vision of the Great World Peace, when implemented, will usher in a world where there will be perfect understanding among the peoples of the world, and such a world will ensure lasting peace and harmony.

Devotion and Love of God

Love is the secret of God's holy dispensation. It is the manifestation of the All-Merciful, the fountain of spiritual outpourings. Love is heaven's kindly light, the Holy Spirit's eternal breath that enhances and enlivens the human soul. Love is the cause of God's revelation to humanity, the vital bond inherent, in accordance with the divine creation. Love is the only means and source that will ensure intense happiness both in this as well as the next world. Love is the bright light that illumines and guides us in darkness. It is the living link that unites God with man and assures the progress of all illumined souls. The religion of God is the cause of love.

Love is the greatest and most powerful law that rules this mighty and heavenly cycle. It is the unique power that binds together all the diverse elements in this material world. Love is the supreme magnetic force that attracts, directs, and pulls the movements of the spheres in the celestial realms. Love reveals with unfailing and limitless power all the mysteries latent and inherent in this universe. Love is the spirit of life in the adorned body of mankind. It is the establisher of true civilization in this material, mortal world. Love sheds its brilliance of imperishable glory upon every race and nation.

Baha'is are required to develop sincere, whole-hearted, and complete devotion to God. According to Baha U'llah, the purpose of man's creation is that he may know God and have devotion and adoration for him. In this connection, he said, "The cause of creation of all beings has been love, as it is said in the well known tradition, "I was a hidden treasure and I loved to be known. Therefore, I created the creation in order to be known."

The sole aim of life for the followers of the faith is to be God's lover, to have God as his closest companion and the most intimate friend. And to love God means to love everything and everybody, for all are of God. The true Baha'i will be a perfect lover of God. He will love everyone sincerely and fervently, with a pure heart. He will not have any hatred for anyone. He will not despise or annoy anyone, for he will see the face of the Beloved in every face as well as God's traces everywhere. His love will be unlimited, beyond sect, nation, class, or race. According to Baha U'llah, love of one's country is an element of the faith of God.

Devotion to God implies severance from everything that is not of God. It means severance from all selfish and worldly desires. Severance does not mean indifference or passive resignation to evil conditions. A true follower of the Baha'i faith will not be callous or careless or apathetic or indifferent. He will find abundant joy in the path of God. Devotion to God involves implicit obedience to God and to his commandments. Devotion to God also implies a life of service to man's fellow creatures. He should reach out to all those who are in need of help. According to the teachings of Baha U'llah, if man turns his back on his fellow men, he will be turning his back upon God. To serve mankind and to minister to the needs of the people is real worship. In fact, service is prayer.

In this connection, Baha U'llah said, "The religion of God is the cause of love, but if it became a source of enmity and bloodshed, its absence is preferable to its existence, for it then becomes detrimental, satanic and obstacle to the human world."

CHAPTER 6

Zoroastrianism

INTRODUCTION TO ZOROASTRIANISM

Zoroastrianism is one of the oldest religions. It has a unique place in the history of religion, since it has made tremendous contributions to other faiths, particularly to Christianity, Judaism and Islam.

Zoroaster was the first religious leader to teach the doctrines of an individual judgment, heaven and hell, the future resurrection of the body, the general Last Judgment, and life everlasting for the reunited soul and body. These doctrines were to become familiar articles of faith to much of mankind, through borrowings by Judaism, Christianity, and Islam.

Zoroastrian is a very ancient religion. According to Zoroastrianism, the world is a combination of both good and evil. Creation cannot exist without the presence of both good and evil. In the beginning of creation, Ahura Mazda, the Supreme God created two spirits called Spenta Mainyu, the good spirit and the evil spirit. Creation is possible only when they both come together.

According to Zoroastrianism, Ahura Mazda, the Supreme God, charged Zarathustra with the task of inviting all human beings to choose between good and evil. Zoroastrianism is a highly ethical religion. Zarathustra taught that human beings are free to choose between right and wrong, truth and lie, light and darkness, and that their acts, words and thoughts would affect their lives after death. He was thus the first to promote a belief in two heavenly judgments; of the individual soul right after death and of all humankind after a general resurrection.

Zarathustra's ideas of heaven and hell, and the resurrection of the body profoundly influenced Judaism, Christianity and Islam.

The main sacred text, the Zoroastrian "Avesta" ("Book of the Law") is a fragmentary collection of sacred writings divided into liturgical works and hymns ascribed to Zarathustra; invocations and rituals to be used at festivals; hymns of praise; and spells against demons and elaborate procedures for purification. Complied over many centuries, the Avesta was not completed until Persia's Sassanid dynasty

Zarathustra's message to humanity can be classified under three headings, namely, mysticism, philosophy, and ethics and morals. Basically, they are belief in one supreme God, Ahura Mazda, immortality of the soul, and fire as the symbol of divinity; the significance of good and evil and the constant struggle between the forces of good and evil; and lastly, the holy triad of righteous thoughts, righteous words, and righteous deeds.

Zoroastrianism has all but disappeared in Persia after the Muslim invasion. Only a few hundred survive in remote villages in Iran. Over the centuries, many Zoroastrians sought religious freedom in India.

Zoroastrianism

Founder

Prophet Zarathustra, called Zoroaster, is the founder of Zoroastrianism. He is believed to have lived about 600 BC. Accurate details of Zarathustra's life, his parents, his nativity etc are not available since almost the entire religion, culture, literature of ancient Iran was totally destroyed when Alexander of Macedonia ransacked and burned down the imperial library in Persopolis. Further, whatever could be salvaged by the Parthians was systematically destroyed by the Arab invaders in the seventh century AD. Fortunately, there were several rock-cut inscriptions on inaccessible mountains and oral traditions carried on from generation to generation. The Arab and Greek vandals could not lay their hands on these and thus posterity could know from these two indestructible sources about Mazdayasna and its revival by Zoroaster. We know that in Mazdayasna, the ancient Iranian, possessed a treasure house of mysticism, philosophy, morals, and ethics.

Zarathustra' s birthplace is said to be Rae in north Iran. From Rae, he traveled the length and breadth of Iran and finally settled down in Balkh (now part of Afghanistan), where he propagated Mazdayasna under the patronage of king Vishtap. Zoroaster attained martyrdom there at the age of seventy-seven, while fighting in self-defense against the Tooranian hordes, who destroyed and desecrated the Fire Temple when he was praying. Zarathustra is credited with the performance of many miracles from his birth until death.

Beliefs

Considered the world's oldest surviving monotheistic religion, Zoroastrianism was established around 3500 years ago—before Christianity, Islam, and Jainism. Based on the teachings of prophet Zarathustra, Zoroastrianism was once the state religion of the then Persian empire. Zarathustra preached that there was only one God, Ahura Mazda. The term Ahura Mazda is commonly used in Avesta language for God, just as Allah is in Arabic and Jehovah in Hebrew. Ahu means the "living," "life," or "spirit," and Ra means to "give." Thus, Ahura Mazda means "Life Giver," the "Great Creator." Zarathustra's message to mankind can be classified under the following headings:

1. Mysticism—This consists of belief in Ahura Mazda, immortality of the soul, and fire as the symbol of divinity.
2. Philosophy—This consists in the significance of good and evil and life as an eternal struggle between the forces of good and evil.
3. Ethics and Morals—These consist of the holy triad of Hu'Mata, or righteous thoughts, Hu'Ukta, or righteous words, and Hu'Varshta, or righteous deeds.

Zarathustra gave humanity the priceless holy triad of Hu'Mata, Hu'Ukta, and Hu'Varshta to test the validity and veracity of any statement made by any personality or book, however sacred it may be. If any statement conforms with the holy triad, then it can be accepted wholeheartedly. If not, it should be summarily rejected.

Scriptures

The Zoroastrian scripture is the Avesta. Its contents were made over many centuries. The oldest part of Avesta was composed in Gathic Avesta, the language of the prophet Zarathustra. The part of Avesta in Gathic includes the seventeen hymns or psalms composed by Zarathustra. Zoroastrians consider their scripture to have great spiritual powers. From the scriptures came the liturgy and daily prayers of Zoroastrians.

The Avesta began as an oral document, memorized and recited by priests. In the days of Zarathustra, writing was unknown and the training of priests required feats of good memory. Only after four hundred years, scribes began to collect scattered pieces of Avesta. Through the fourth and fifth centuries, they collected volumes of materials and assembled the "Great Avesta."

The sacred scripture of the Avesta has six parts. They are as follows:

1. Yasna, sacrificc, worship. The main liturgical text includes the Gathas, the teachings of Zarathustra. The Gathas of83,000 words in the language of Avesta, to this day serves as the holy book of Zoroastrians. Its creed can be translated as " good thoughts, good deeds and good words."
2. Visperad, All the Lords" A liturgical text invoking saints and heavenly beings, used on Zoroastrian holy days.
3. Yashts- Hymns of praise to Zoroastrian saints and angels. The yashts praise many of the deities from Iranian religion, before the reform of Zarathustra.
4. Vendidad.- A priestly code dealing with rituals, regulations and purification.
5. Minor texts- Khordaavesta, Nyayesh,Gah, used as prayers and invocation by both priests and lay people.
6. Fragments of the lost Avesta-Prayers, invocations and blessings.
7. The Avesta is one of the world's oldest scripture. Its blend of ritual and inspiration contains all that the Zoroastrians need to follow their faith. It remains the basic guide to the "good religion" that Zoroastrians rely in their devotion and in their daily lives.

The Message of Zarathustra

According to Zoroastrian tradition, the coming of Zarathustra was predicted and foretold long before his birth. It was said that when he was born, there was a brilliant light like the blazing fire and a twilight irradiating from his house in all directions, as a sign of his divinity, greatness, and exaltation.

Zarathustra began to consider the question of righteousness and the conflict between good and evil even at very young age. He became a priest when he was thirty, and during one of his priestly duties, an angel appeared before him and asked him what was the most important thing in his life. Zarathustra's reply was that he wanted most of all to be righteous and pure and gain wisdom. The angel then took him into the presence of Ahura Mazda. Thus Zarathustra was ordained to be Ahura Mazda's prophet and received the gift of preaching directly from him.

The prophet Zarathustra was against all rituals and practices of the society at that time, against stealing and slaughtering cattle and terrorizing people. He denounced drunkenness, animal sacrifice, and the excesses of the old religion. In place of rituals, Zarathustra demanded that people should become righteous and pure and turn their hearts and minds to Ahura Mazda.

Zarathustra preached the concept of one supreme true God, Ahura

Mazda, who created all visible and invisible things and human life. Along with all the things of the earth, Ahura Mazda also created two opposing and conflicting forces. These are the Truth and Goodness and the destructive Lie. Zarathustra visualized a world of ethical goodness, in which people worked hard, raised families, engaged in agriculture, raised cattle, and helped the needy. They would develop good thoughts, good words, and good deeds. They would shun evil, do good to others, and thus create a peaceful, loving, and prosperous society. People would be judged according to how they had chosen to live their lives. It was left to people to choose Truth and Goodness over Lie.

According to Zarathustra, the world would finally come to an end in a fire, and during this time all the evil in the world would be destroyed, and the righteous people would be saved. The prophet also declared that women were equal with men in the eyes of Ahura Mazda and had the same hope of salvation.

What is Zoroastrianism?

Many concepts such as the notion of one God, heaven and hell, truth and lie, the dualism of good and evil and life everlasting can trace their roots to the religion founded by Zarathustra, who originated the concept one great and supreme God.

He explained the problem of evil in a world created by a good God through the notion of truth and Lie, which are present in the human heart. To the question as to how a good and loving God could permit evil and suffering in the world, Zarathustra said that evil and suffering are the work of Lie and that people should choose good over evil.

Zoroastrianism has many things in commotion with other religions and consequently exerted some influence over them. Like Judaism, Christianity and Islam, Zoroastrianism is monotheistic. Its followers believe in one supreme and great God. They believe in life after death, as well as in heaven and hell. Zoroastrianism has a strong code of ethics, which its followers are expected to follow in their daily lives. Like the Christians and Jews, Zoroastrians believe in the eventual arrival of a savior to lead the faithful into a perfect world.

Zoroastrianism also differs from other religions in some ways. Unlike Islam, it is not fatalistic. The evil in the world is not the will of God, but due to the flaws in the material world and within the human heart. Zoroastrianism differs from Christianity, whose believers are saved by faith in Jesus Christ and by God's grace than by their good deeds. Further, Zoroastrians do not believe in original sin. According to Zoroastrianism, people are born pure, but they are influenced by the evil around them. For Zoroastrians, it is the strict adherence to the teachings of Zarathustra that will ensure salvation and not faith. Zoroastrianism also differs from Hinduism in as much as there is no belief in reincarnation and the doctrine of the transmigration of the soul.

Though the smallest when compared to other world religions like Christianity, Islam, Hinduism, and Buddhism, Zoroastrianism has the power to be an enduring and lasting faith. Its creed of good thoughts, good words, and good deeds has great significance, relevance, and importance in today's world. Though the followers of Zoroastrianism today are comparatively few in numbers, its followers can be proud of a very great heritage that goes back thousands of years. They can also be proud of their great courage, zeal, and determination in carrying the torch of their beliefs through centuries of persecution, religious intolerance, great hardship, and suffering.

Basic Observances

Zoroastrians are expected to pray five times every day, at sunrise, noon, sunset, midnight, and dawn, in the presence of fire, the symbol of purity and righteousness. The prayer is made standing and while untying and tying the sacred cord called kusti. The sacred cord should be worn constantly. It goes three times round the waist and is knotted over the sacred shirt, the sedra. Before prayers, the Zoroastrians perform ritual ablutions. Faith considers cleanliness as part of godliness. According to Zoroastrianism, anything not clean is considered evil.

The ancient veneration of fire centered on the ever-burning hearth fire. The concept of sacred fire in Zoroastrian temples was instituted in the 4th century B.C. There are three types of sacred fire, called Atash Bahram, Atash Aduran, and Dadgah. Atash Bahrain (victorious fire) is consecrated with many rites and is kept blazing brightly. The second sacred fire, Atash Aduran (fire of fires), is simply installed and allowed at times to lie dormant. The Dadgah in an appointed place, which is a hearth fire, is placed in a consecrated building. Sacred fires are very much beloved to Zoroastrians, and devout parents take their children to the sacred fires at an early age.

Men and women have equal access to temples, and boys and girls have the same initiation into faith, which takes place between the ages of seven and nine. The occasion, called "Naojote," is an important family event. The child, who has already learned the kusti prayer, is bathed and given a consecrated liquid for inward cleaning, and then the sacred shirt is put on the child. The priest then performs the ceremony of investing him or her with the sacred kusti. Similarly, before marriage, the bride and the bridegroom undergo a ritual purification and put on new garments. During marriage, Avestan and Pahlavi words are spoken by the officiating priest in the presence of witnesses from the two families.

A birth is very much rejoiced and is considered a happy event. Ceremonies of death are very simple and have a double aim: to isolate the impurity of the dead body and to help the soul. The dead body is carried on an iron bier, and after prayers by priests, is then consigned to a stone tower called a dakhma, where the dead body is left to be eaten by vultures. Religious ceremonies are performed for the departed soul.

Zoroastrians have many holy days, which are celebrated with great joy. These include seven obligatory holy days designated by Zarathustra himself in honor of Ahura Mazda.

Basic Principles of Zoroastrianism

Zarathustra revealed his vision of the good religion in a series of psalms called Gathas. The Gathas are personal expressions of Zarathustra's belief in the one great and supreme God, Ahura Mazda, and Zarathustra's conversation with him. All Zoroastrian beliefs and rituals are based on the Gathas.

Zarathustra preached the existence of one supreme God, whose name is Ahura Mazda. Ahura Mazda means the wise Lord, and he is the creator of the universe and all the things in the universe, including mankind. Zarathustra taught that Ahura Mazda is all good and all wise. He is the father of truth and goodness. He is to be loved and respected, but never to be feared. He is the source of all happiness, peace, and love.

Zoroastrianism states that the twin spirits of Truth and Lie govern all human thought and activity. Ahura Mazda first created consciousness and a knowledge of perfect good, which is the spirit of Truth. But when he created the physical world, evil came into being in the form of ignorance and sin and violation of the natural order, which Zarathustra called the spirit of evil, or Lie. The struggle between these forces governs all aspects of human activity and thought.

Ahura Mazda does not order every aspect of human life. At the time of creation, he gave humanity the gift of free will. All followers of Zoroastrianism should think and reason for themselves. They have the complete freedom to choose good over evil. Free will and intellect give the followers of the faith the choice to do the will of Ahura Mazda and lead their lives according to Truth and Righteousness.

Most Zoroastrian devotions end with the prayer in Avestan, which is one of the three cardinal prayers that is spoken to concentrate the mind on righteousness. The prayer confirms that righteousness is good. It is happiness. Happiness comes to the person who is righteous.

Teachings of Zarathustra

Most Zoroastrian scriptures were destroyed during the invasion of Persia by Alexander, and subsequently by the Arabs. Fortunately, the Zoroastrian priests preserved some of the important sacred texts through oral tradition. The most important of these texts are known collectively as the Yasna, which contains seventy-two sections. The five Gathas, or stories of Zarathustra, are found among these sections. These five Gathas, especially the first one, called Ahunavaiti, contain most of the teachings of Zarathustra. The core of his teachings are given below:

The world is a combination of both good and evil. Life is an eternal struggle between the forces of good and evil. Creation cannot exist without the presence of both good and evil.

Ahura Mazda, the supreme God, created two spirits, namely the good spirit and the evil spirit. It is for the individual to use the reason and wisdom given by God to lead a good life with good thoughts, good deeds, and good words.

There is only one God, Ahura Mazda, and everything and everyone is part of it. Everything emanates from him, and everything dissolves in him in the end. He is formless, and he alone should be worshipped. He is to be loved and respected and not feared. Though he is formless, he has six aspects or emanations through which human beings are expected to approach him.

The purpose of life on earth is to live a rich and full life. People should take responsibility for their action or inaction.

All the thoughts should be inspired by Ahura Mazda, words dictated by him, and deeds guided by him.

The Principle of Zarathustra's teachings is called the Seven Am-Asha-Sepentas. Am-Asha-Sepentas means the Laws, based on ever-existing and everlasting Truth—or, in other words, the Eternal Law. These are:

1. Good Mind—One should make good use of the mind. The mind, the brain, should be used in a good way and each one to their maximum capacity.
2. Good Truth—The using of our mind in a good way and to its maximum results in good discoveries, good inventions, good knowledge, good understanding of the natural laws. These are the Good Truth.
3. Good Guidance—We should make use of the information, the truth,

and the discoveries to make life better. Life can be made better by making good rules, good products, good laws and giving good guidance and good services.

4. Lawful Desire—The result of lawful desire is Righteousness, a Righteous society, a paradise where people live in perfect harmony and understanding with each other and with nature. Where there is lawful desire, there will be no war, no pollution, no sickness, no lies, no thefts, and no fear.
5. Perfection—Perfection ensures Righteous society. In a righteous society, people will have a chance to advance mentally, physically and spiritually. The result will be perfection. There will be perfect doctors, perfect engineers, perfect musicians, perfect formers, perfect poets, perfect athletes, perfect priests, and perfection in all aspects and in all fields.
6. Immortality—Free from fear. Perfection will create a mental stage in human life where one is free from the fear of death, free from the fear of the unknown. One does not belong to the material world, but to a timeless, spaceless world where death has no meaning.
7. Ahura Mazda Wisdom in Existence—Having attained perfection and lost the sense of fear, the final stage is attained and one understands and becomes one with the Wisdom in Creation, the Universal Great Wisdom, the Power, the living Wisdom, the active, creative, expanding Force that keeps the universe in action and chain reaction, and the Creator of this Wisdom.

Just as the different beams of fire, when brought closer, merge into one another, all the individual souls merge with one another to form the universal soul.

Nothing is lost when death takes place. Death is not the end of life. Death does not mean the death of the soul. Soul is immortal and so is the Holy Spirit.

Just as gold has to be melted in a crucible before it can be freed of all its dross, so a person needs to be put in the large crucible of the world's rough and seductive ways before he or she can rightly consider himself or herself to be free of earthly dross.

Constructing a thousand shrines of worship is not better than making a single soul happy. If a person can make one independent-minded man his slave by showering love and kindness upon him, it is much better than freeing a thousand slaves from slavery.

The efficacy of prayer is indeed very great. It opens the gate of one's inner temple to let Ahura Mazda in. Prayer is the most potent means of fellowship between man and God.

All righteous thoughts, words, and deeds spring from knowledge and wisdom. Wisdom is the discerning exercise of knowledge. Neither deep learning nor profound knowledge is wisdom. It is the judicious use of knowledge that is wisdom.

Feeling and Imagination

Zoroastrianism lays great stress on the fineness of nature, which has tremendous impact on feeling and imagination. One should cultivate feeling and imagination. This enables one to develop that fineness of structure in the body, which renders it capable of the most delicate sensation and fineness of structure in the mind. This in turn makes it capable of the most delicate sympathies—in short, fineness of nature.

Imagination, far from being a false and deceptive faculty, is the most accurate and truthful faculty which the human mind possesses. Consequently, whenever we want to know what are real and underlying facts of any object or any case such as our religion, we should not go to a mathematician but to a poet, since a poet alone can go to flights of imagination. Poets alone can clearly see into the heart of things by their marvelous faculty of imagination.

It is far better to make a single soul happy than constructing a thousand shrines of worship. It does not mean that constructing a shrine of worship is not important. A shrine of worship will enable many souls to come and offer prayers. If one can make one independent-minded person one's slave by showering love, kindness and compassion on him, it is far better than freeing a thousand slaves from captivity.

In case you decide to shower rose petals upon someone you love, you must do it most gently and tenderly. This is because the heart within our bosom is more delicate and fragile than glass

You should continue to enjoy the joy of living. Let the joy of living fill your heart to overflowing. One should not lose the joy of living as one advances in age. Ageing is a natural fact of life. One should not allow the joy of life be destroyed or crushed by the burden of years. On the other hand, it should be one's sincere endeavor to carry on one's joyous life, unaffected by any external or internal matters.

If a person, however powerful or strong, realizes that there is someone more powerful and stronger than he, then that person will automatically refrain from persecuting and tyrannizing others who are weaker and less fortunate.

Ahura Mazda

Ahura Mazda means Life Giver, the Great Giver, the Great Creator. Ahura Mazda means God. He is the Lord of life, wisdom, light and the truth. One should have complete faith in Him. If one does everything according to the commands of Ahura Mazda, he can overcome all problems in life. He need not be afraid of any human being, however powerful and mighty he may be.

Ahura Mazda will guide His followers at all times. When one goes out into darkness, one should take Ahura Mazda's hands. Then his path will be brighter and safer, making it easy for the one to reach the destination. The sun, moon and the stars no doubt give light. But Ahura Mazda is the light of all lights. He is the Light that lights them to light the world.

Ahura Mazda wants His followers to develop good thoughts, good words and good deeds. Let your thoughts be inspired by Ahura Mazda, your words dictated by Him and your deeds guided by Him.

Mountains and oceans do not separate His followers from Ahura Mazda. Only evil thoughts and actions separate Him from man or woman. One need not scale the heights of heavens or travel along highway of the world to find Ahura Mazda. One can find Him with purity of mind and holiness of heart.

One should live with Him not only on fixed days of sacred feasts and holy festivals, but on all the days of the year. One should live in His blessed company throughout his lifetime. Ahura Mazda lives in the hearts of His followers.

During times of difficulties, chaos, strife and confusion, Ahura Mazda sends His special messenger to guide His followers and humanity to safety and along the path of divinity. He is rightly called the Great Giver and Life Saver. His body is light and His spirit, the truth.

Ahura Mazda does not like costly sacrifices and lavish gifts. He abhors them. He appreciates the sacrifices of a contrite heart and the gifts of persons of righteous thoughts, righteous words and righteous deeds.

Ahura Mazda is the refuge of the weak, weary and the wronged. All such persons who take refuge in Him will be saved and they will be blessed with happy lives. Ahura Mazda is merciful even to sinners who throw themselves upon His mercy.

Ahura Mazda means the Wise Lord. He is all good, all wise and all merciful. He is to be loved and respected by all. He is the eternal source of all happiness, mercy and love.

Fire

In Zoroastrianism, fire occupies an exalted and very important position. The followers of Zarathustra consider fire as the divine symbol of Ahura Mazda. Fire is not worshipped by Zoroastrians, and the sacred fire is not an object of worship.

One should contemplate the beams of fire with a pious and pure mind. Fire teaches many lessons to those who contemplate its beams with an inquiring mind. Fire soars only upwards and lifts the thought of the followers of Zarathustra far above the filth and dross of the material world. Fire purifies all the objects that it touches and itself remains pure. Gold, when it is put under fire, becomes pure. Nothing can pollute fire.

It will be noticed that fire is broad at the bottom and pointed at the top. Similarly, all differences and diversities at lower levels become resolved into unity and universality at the highest level, namely divinity.

Fire is latent everywhere. It can be easily produced by striking one piece of stick or stone against another. The response of fire is also very interesting. If you offer sandalwood and incense to the fire, it radiates fragrance all around. By the same token, the burning of a stinking corpse or carcass fouls the entire atmosphere with an offensive smell.

When different beams of fire are brought close to one another, they all merge into one big flame. In the same way, all individual souls merge with one another to constitute the universal soul.

Sun, which is a ball of fire, shines equally upon the good and the bad, pure and impure, clean and dirty. Its all-purifying, brilliant light cleanses all dirt and stench and all defiling and decaying matter.

The beams of fire are always moving in some direction. By ceaseless movement, the beams of fire remind us that activity is life and stagnation is death. Fire teaches us this great truth.

Fire is scrupulously impartial in all its dealings. It readily serves a sinner or a saint. It scorches everyone who comes in contact with it, whether he or she is a sinner, if it is carelessly handled.

The civilization of the world itself began only with the discovery of fire, and all the growth of humanity began with the advent of fire.

Fire is a symbol and reminder of Ahura Mazda. It captures the brilliance of the sun and various heavenly bodies. Fire is a symbol of power and strength. It means energy, the energy of truth. Fire represents purity.

When one turns one's face to the sun in yonder heaven or looks at the fire on the censer, it is you, Ahura Mazda, who is seen there. Zarathustra's message to humanity is, "Contemplate the beams of fire with a pious mind."

Death

Death is a fact of life. It is inevitable for everyone born in this world. We should not fear death, since it is natural process. We should not run away from death, for we can never die before the appointed time, and nothing can save us from death when the appointed time comes. This being the case, what is there for anyone to worry or fear about death?

Our present life is a prelude to a future life. It is a pilgrimage of sojourn to a higher life. We should count each day as a step forward towards the inevitable death. In fact, each and every day should be considered as if it was our last day on earth. We must lead our life fully prepared for death, so that we may meet our end with a calm face, peaceful attitude, and a smile on our face.

Knowing that death can come at any time, we should follow the commands of Zarathustra regarding the holy triad of righteous thoughts, righteous words, and righteous deeds. Following the teachings of Zarathustra in our daily life will give us the strength to face death.

Faith in life hereafter gives purpose and meaning to life here.

Nothing is lost when death takes place. Death is not the end to life. Death does not mean the death of the soul. Zarathustra's teachings stress the immortality of the soul. The soul is immortal, and so is the Holy Spirit.

On the day of Resurrection, everyone will be answerable to Ahura Mazda for his or her thoughts, words, and deeds.

We can never fully repay the debt of gratitude to our great ancestors. The best way to repay our great debt to them is by leading our life in such a manner that our living may be an honor to the departed.

The departed spirits are eager to know who amongst the living remember them and invoke them by their names and pray for their blessings.

We should lead a pure life and follow the teachings of Zarathustra, so that when finally the inevitable end comes, we will face it with peace and courage and without any fear.

Good and Evil

There is good existing side by side with evil. Where there is life, there is both good and evil. Life is an eternal struggle between the forces of good and evil; one cannot have only good. Zarathustra explained the problem of evil in a world created by a good God through the notion of Truth and Lie, which are present in the human heart. Regarding the question of why a good and loving God permits evil and suffering in the world, Zarathustra said that evil and suffering are the works of Lie.

Ahura Mazda created pairs of opposite characteristics in every walk of life in the entire creation. He is capable of exercising any one of the two features depending on what he thinks fit and fair to fulfill his eternal plan.

Ahura Mazda created human beings in his own image. He also bestowed on them the power to choose and exercise any of the opposite characteristics. In other words, it was left to every individual to choose between good and evil.

We should never be discouraged or dispirited if our efforts to achieve something are thwarted by the forces of reaction. Everything will depend on our sincere efforts and dedication. The greater the efforts, the greater the resistance.

Life is an eternal and continuous struggle between the forces of good and evil. According to the teachings of Zarathustra, there are two types of mankind, namely the righteous and the wicked. Or the good and the evil.

One should never wish bad or ill of others. A person who wishes ill of anyone achieves nothing worthwhile. No sooner does one does evil to someone, but one hundred evils will befall that person.

Just as gold has to be put in a crucible and melted before it can be freed of all its dross and thus purified, so too do we need to be put in the larger crucible of the world's rough and seductive ways before we can rightly consider ourselves to be free of all earthly dross and impurity.

We cannot call ourselves pure until we have faced and overcome all the evils and temptations that beset our path and turned to nobler channels the passions with which we are born.

We should seek the purity of a saint by casting away all unrighteous words, thoughts, and deeds. We should hold fast to the commands of Zarathustra and overcome evil with good.

An ineffable loveliness and charm come over the face of an earthly creature when its spirit is attuned to the highest, so that even a celestial being looks coarse and vulgar. Therefore, we should have conscience finer than the finest hair that would guide the mind and soul to completely abstain from evil and warn that crookedness never pays.

Love and Ecstasy

Just as the fire on the censer consumes sandalwood, let the fire burning within you consume your heart with infinite love for Ahura Mazda.

Every person, whether sober or intoxicated, is in search of the Beloved. Every place in the world, whether a tavern or temple, is the abode of love.

At the altar of love, only the good is sacrificed. Diseased and useless are not sacrificed at the altar of love. Are you a true lover? If so, you should not run away from being sacrificed. Only a carcass is not considered fit for sacrifice.

There is no point in telling the mysteries of love and ecstasy to an unbeliever. This is because a skeptic is so engrossed in worshipping his own self that he would rather prefer to die in ignorance of the existence of such qualities.

The finest and fairest, the gentlest and loveliest expression of speech is song. The Gathas are the sublime and divine songs of Zarathustra, who spoke not his speech, but sang his hymns.

Ahura Mazda is the first and foremost musician. His divine music pervades the entire universe, if only we have the ears to listen. The divine music can be heard in the silent whispers of the cool breeze, in the murmuring of the flowing water in the rivers and brooks, in the chirping of the birds and in the sincere outpourings of the thoughts of an ardent devotee.

The entire creation of Ahura Mazda itself is a song, so sweet, sublime, and divine.

May the songs of devotion pouring from my heart that glorify thee and magnify thee and reach thee, O Ahura Mazda.

The followers of Zarathustra are taught to love life and enjoy life's pleasures. The grass and trees, the wind and waves, the birds and beasts all sing, smile, and laugh. Let us join in that chorus of love and ecstasy.

Knowledge and Wisdom

The richest and most priceless treasure in the world is knowledge. It is man's highest acquisition. Knowledge is man's greatest friend, and it will never fail him. Wealth acquired over a period of time may suddenly disappear, whereas knowledge gained will always remain with you.

A person should give highest priority to acquiring knowledge. It is the sure passport to prosperity and happiness. Knowledge is unfailing and ever helpful. It is man's lifelong and trusted friend. It is the surest and safest guide in life.

Wisdom is the capacity to make use of one's knowledge. Whereas knowledge is direct perception and understanding, wisdom is the discerning exercise of knowledge. Neither deep learning nor profound knowledge is wisdom. Wisdom is the judicious use of knowledge.

Knowledge keeps a person young in body and mind. A person with good knowledge and wisdom is respected by one and all. One whose wisdom is clouded by intoxicating drugs and liquors will not have peace of mind or rest.

Time destroys everything in this world. Anything of brick and mortar made by man can be destroyed by time. But of all the great monumental and noble works, the outcome of knowledge and wisdom shall endure forever. All wisdom lies in temperance, tolerance, understanding, and charity.

One should pray to Ahura Mazda to give him or her the will to know and the will to learn. One should keep on learning all his or her lifetime. A person should gather information and instruction from anywhere and everywhere. Knowledge is so very vast and deep that one cannot master everything during one's lifetime.

Knowledge and wisdom enables one to develop the holy triad of righteous thoughts, righteous words, and righteous deeds. Life is a continuous struggle between the forces of good and evil. A person who has acquired knowledge and wisdom can overcome the forces of evil and lead a good life. The essence of Zoroastrianism is goodness, and all its followers are urged to choose goodness.

Knowledge and wisdom will enable one to have a good mind. From good mind good thoughts emanate, and good thoughts lead to good words and good deeds, so it is very important that everyone should sincerely endeavor to acquire knowledge and wisdom.

Rituals and Rites of Passage

Zoroastrianism has many rituals. These rituals may be traced to some of the Iranian religious customs in the time before Zarathustra. All the prescribed rituals are performed by priests in consecrated temples. These rituals can be witnessed only by members of the faith who are in a state of ritual purity. The basic rituals in Zoroastrianism consist of caring for the consecrated fire, performing the ritual known as the yasna, and purifying those who have come in contact with pollution. Priests also perform special rituals and prayers for those who request them.

All the rituals are memorized by the priests in the language of Avestan, which Zoroastrians believe is the most pleasing to the ears of Ahura Mazda. The traditional basic ritual is the yasna. In this ritual, priests extract juice from the haoma plant as an offering. The highest rituals can be performed only in the presence of consecrated fire.

For Zoroastrians, fire is the sacred symbol of Ahura Mazda. The rituals for purifying fire are performed 1128 times, a process that takes almost a year. The ceremony that accompanies the regular tending of fire five times a day is called Boi-Machi.

The Zoroastrian priesthood has traditionally been passed down through generations. The duties of a priest include reciting the liturgy in temples and in the homes of the followers, saying prayers for the dead, and performing weddings. Training for priesthood begins when the boys are in their mid teens. The prospective boys spend a period of nine days in retreat and undergo a purification ritual. The boys are dressed in white and ordained by a senior priest called a Mobed.

Zoroastrians join together during festivals and holy days. There are seven great Zoroastrian festivals each year, the greatest of which is called No Roz. The festival celebrates the creation of fire and Beneficent Immortal Asha Vahista, or Higher Truth. It is the most sacred and joyous of all Zoroastrian holy days.

Jashan is a ceremony for thanksgiving and memorializing. It is performed at any time that people want to express gratitude and happiness for any event, such as a wedding or house-warming. The ceremony is also an expression of happiness and gratitude for past blessings and joy for all good things in the present and future.

Nav Jote is a ceremony in which young people are initiated into Zoroastrianism. Marriage is another major ceremony, which begins with a benediction. Like all Zoroastrian ceremonies, marriage takes place in the presence of fire.

Death in Zoroastrianism represents the strongest form of ritual impurity. Zoroastrians have strict ritual associated with death and dying. Since the dead body represents a state of extreme pollution, it is disposed of in what is known as the tower of silence, where it is left to be devoured by vultures. The family offers prayers for the dead throughout the following year.

Zoroastrian Worship and Fire

In every Fire Temple, one can see a silver censer that holds the sacred fire. It is attended round the clock by a relay of priests called Athravans (the Avestan name for priests who look after the fire). The sacred fire is never allowed to be extinguished.

Prayers are said individually or in family groups. Prayers are made from the Avesta, the Zoroastrian scripture. The day is divided into five ritual periods, called gahs, which occur in the morning, at midday, in the afternoon, in the evening, and at night. At each of these periods, the Zoroastrians pause to repeat prayers.

The sacred fire is a symbol and reminder of Ahura Mazda. It captures the brilliance of the sun and other planets and heavenly bodies. Fire represents the power, might, and energy of Truth. Fire represents utmost purity and, in its purest form, it represents the highest truth. Priests perform all religious rituals and ceremonies in the presence of fire, which symbolizes the presence of Ahura Mazda. The sacred fires of Zoroastrianism are consecrated and contain fire from sixteen different sources, ritually combined by a series of purification rites. One part of a consecrated fire is fire struck by lightning, which comes directly from the Wise Lord and great God Ahura Mazda.

The sacred fires of Zoroastrianism are housed in Fire Temples, which have three grades. They are Atash Behram, Atash Adaran, and Atash Dadga. Of these three, Atash Behram is the highest grade of Fire Temple. It is also referred to as the Fire Cathedral and houses the holiest of consecrated fires. Most of the sacred Zoroastrian rituals are held in Atash Behram temples and these are performed by the high priests of Zoroastrianism. There are only ten Atash Behram temples in the world. Of these, eight are in India, and the remaining two are in Iran.

An Atash Adaran also houses consecrated fire. It differs from the Atash Behram in the number of rituals performed in establishing the temple and the number and type of ceremonies a priest must perform before entering the fire room.

The fire in an Atash Adaran is similar to a household fire. It is not specially consecrated, and no high rituals are held there.

Meditation in Zoroastrianism

Great importance is given to the concept of meditation in Zoroastrianism. A human being is a product of three functions: thoughts, words, and deeds. Zoroastrianism gives the first pride of place to thought or meditation, because humans think first. They then reveal their thoughts in words, either written or spoken, and finally they translate the words into actions. This sequence is always maintained in the immutable scheme of things.

When we say a person is incapable of thinking, what we mean is that that person is incapable of deep thinking or meditation. The words and deeds arising out of meditation will be of a higher and nobler quality than those arising from shallow thinking. Thus, speaking or writing or acting without meditation is considered irreligious and irresponsible, according to Mazdayasna.

According to Mazdayasna, meditation for the sake of meditation is of no value at all. Meditation should be always be a means of expression in words and deeds, and the quality of words and deeds will depend upon the quality of meditation.

Meditation should be positive. Positive meditation results in words and deeds of a higher and nobler quality. Negative thinking will lead to words that will injure the feelings and deeds and will debase the mind. Thus, Mazdayasna places great emphasis on positive thinking.

While meditating, the prophet Zarathustra exerted his utmost will to ward off evil thoughts. Only after fifteen years of struggle with evil thoughts, he felt that he had conquered evil passions and harmful emotions and proclaim to the world, "All righteous thoughts, righteous words and righteous deeds spring from knowledge and wisdom. Henceforth, the word meditation should be understood as meaning righteous meditation."

The seat or source of meditation is the mind, or "manas" in the Avestan language. Righteous meditation enables a person to perform righteous deeds for the good of the Creator and the glory of God. Zarathustra reveals the importance of righteous meditation in upholding the dignity of the individual.

Zarathustra prays to God, "Give us purity, which is the reward for righteous mind, that is meditation. Teach us the path of purity through righteous mind that is meditation." According to Zarathustra, the power to think is man's most precious and priceless right. It is also man's proudest privilege.

Willpower

Everyone should cultivate willpower. It should be firm and inflexible, based on truth and rectitude. Willpower enables one to overcome all the trials and tribulations of life. It leads to success and happiness.

When we fail to suppress the tumult of the senses and do not control and master our passions, the passions master us. Then we become a willful slave of our passion. With willpower, we can easily overcome all such temptations.

In life, we cannot escape hardships and misfortunes, sorrows and sufferings. These are part of life. To endure them patiently and bravely is to conquer them. That is the power of willpower.

Men and women can soar higher than angels. They can also sink lower than beasts. Success comes to those who can endure the most and who have developed willpower.

It takes honest efforts to make a good name, and it is equally difficult to retain the good name. Endurance, durability, patience, and confidence are the most powerful weapons in the battle of life. They are mightier than armed strength. They enable us to disarm and dislodge all misfortunes.

We should develop the courage and conviction to act according to our conscience. We should develop righteous thoughts, righteous words, and righteous actions.

It should be our honest endeavor to make a name for ourselves much greater than that made by our father for himself.

With willpower, we can achieve anything, and nothing will be beyond our reach. We have the spark of divinity within us. We can reach the greatest height of moral superiority.

We should think for ourselves and never through others. The power to think is the most precious gift and proudest privilege. We should not blame fate for failure caused by our own inadequacy and inefficiency.

Superstition is born of ignorance and fear. It thrives the most when reason is asleep. When emotions are uncontrolled by intellect, sentiment smothers judgment. The stars, planets, and constellations do not decide our fate.

Doubt with an enquiring spirit what you cannot honestly believe. Believe wholeheartedly what you cannot sincerely doubt. Let your faith be wedded to reason, and let it be based on conviction. Do not be superstitious, and do not believe in omens, portents, talismans, and lucky and unlucky numbers and days.

Life is a constant and continuous inquiry into the how, and why, and when, and where, and what, and who of existence. Do not forget the debt that you owe to the past, yet discern the signs of the age in which you live and be in peace and harmony with it. Let not lack of thinking and blind traditionalism retard or arrest your progress.

Faith and Prayer

Prayer is the most direct path leading to Ahura Mazda. Prayer can be termed as the soaring of the soul to heaven on the wings of words. One should rise with the dawn. He or she should then wash the body with clean water and purify his or her soul with prayer. After the prayer, one should be ready to attend to the daily chores before the rising sun calls for duty.

Prayer is the most powerful and the most potent means of loving fellowship between the devotee and Ahura Mazda. The power of prayer is great indeed. It opens the gate of one's inner temple to let Ahura Mazda in.

Prayer is having noble and pure thoughts. Silent meditation is the best for attaining peace and spiritual enlightenment. In silent meditation, one can feel the presence of Ahura Mazda.

In audible prayer, righteous words are articulated by giving utterance to righteous thoughts in clear and impressive voice. One should dress one's thoughts and give expression to them in as perfect and inspiring language as possible.

Those who practice prayer with sincerity and devotion will realize its power and the sublime heights to which it can raise the mind.

Faith in Ahura Mazda gives meaning to existence, makes life colorful, and gives peace of mind and inner bliss that passes all understanding. Faith is the belief in the unknown as belief is faith in the known.

There is only one path and that is the path of righteousness. Righteousness will ultimately triumph over evil and wickedness. So one should never be dejected and never give way to the deadly emotions of anger, envy, fear, lust, greed and grief. One should always remain optimistic.

In cases of dispute and quarrel, patience and perseverance are our greatest friends. Time is the best judge. Ultimately, righteousness will prevail and right shall shine as right and wrong shall be branded as wrong.

All the trials and tribulations, sorrows and sufferings, defeats and disappointments are great disciplinarians. These will lead one to spiritual enlightenment.

One should have abundant faith. Faith gives meaning to life. Life loses its luster, when it loses faith. So never lose your faith.

Hope gives us confidence and enables us to endure and overcome all the hardships of life with courage confidence and contentment. One should not brood or mourn over the sorrows of yesterday, forgetful of the joys and happiness that tomorrow has in store for us. One should realize the unlimited latent possibilities that lie dormant within oneself.

CHAPTER 7

Hinduism

AN INTRODUCTION TO HINDUISM

Hinduism is one of the world's oldest religions, and it encompasses a wide variety of beliefs that originated in India. Hinduism is also known as Sanatana Dharma to Hindus. Sanatana in Sanskrit means "everlasting," and Dharma can be interpreted as "religion." Thus, Hinduism can be defined as an everlasting religion.

What is Hinduism? Is it a religion or culture? Hinduism is unique in the sense that it cannot be slotted into any particular belief system, and it is both a religion as well as a way of life. In fact, India gave the world the oldest and most profound philosophy. Many saints, sages, philosophers, and thinkers, ancestors of the present-day India, explored the Eternal Truth behind human existence, experienced the truth, and—based on their actual experience—propounded several theories and philosophies to define the Truth. They also evolved a set of rules and guidelines for leading a pure and spiritual life. The rules thus laid down for good and dharmic living constitute the Hindu religion.

Christianity or Islam or Buddhism each had a founder. Hinduism did not. There is no religious head like the Pope and no organization like the Vatican. The ancient seers and saints who shaped the Hindu religion simply emphasized the teachings of the Vedas, the Hindu scripture, which are believed to have no origin. There are two types of Hindu scripture, namely the heard (called Sruti) and the memorized (called Smriti).

Most Hindus believe that God takes many forms and is worshipped by many different names. Each person and every creature embodies a spark (called Atman) of the universal soul, equated with God. On death, the

Atman or soul is reborn in a new body. Thus, God is in every object in the universe, and everything that exists—human, animals, earth, water, fire—is part of God. This aspect is brought out in the Bhagavad Gita, where the Lord says, "I am pervading the universe. There is nothing else besides me."

Hinduism is basically monotheistic—the belief in one God, though there is a misconception that it is polytheistic. The Vedas categorically and clearly state that God is Infinite, and the Infinite can be represented in infinite ways and also manifests in infinite ways. In short, Hinduism believes not only in one God, but also in his infinite manifestations around us and within us. Since it is rather very difficult for mankind to visualize the infinite, Hinduism has presented mankind with his form to help visualize him. It is this aspect that often confused with polytheism. The concept that the Supreme or the Infinite can be worshipped in any form is unique to Hinduism.

Hindus believe that every action, whether good or bad, hurtful or compassionate, has an effect on this life and also on future life. This is called Karma in Hinduism. By accumulating positive Karma, Hindus can eventually break free from the cycle of birth and death and achieve liberation or freedom or moksha, which is complete union with God.

Hinduism believes in the transmigration of the soul. Such transmigration is what results in reincarnation. This is the basic theory of Karma in Hinduism.

In Hinduism, OM or AUM is of paramount importance. The symbol OM or AUM is a sacred syllable representing Brahman, the impersonal Absolute-omnipotent, omnipresent, and the source of all manifest existence. According to the Hindu scriptures, OM or AUM was the first sound, out of which the rest of the universe was created.

On Hinduism, Max Mueller, German scholar and philosopher, interested in religions of India and Sanskrit, said, "If I were asked under what sky the human mind has most deeply pondered over the great problems of life, and has found solutions to some of them, which well deserve attention even of those who have studied Plato and Kant, I should point to India. And if I were to ask myself from what literature we, who have been nurtured almost exclusively on the thoughts of Greeks and Romans and of one Semitic race, the Jewish, may draw the corrective which is most wanted in order to make our inner life more perfect, more comprehensive, more universal, in fact more truly human a life, again I should point to India."

Hinduism

Origins and Founder

Hinduism is a very ancient religion. According to historians and scholars, Hinduism was supposed to have been founded somewhere around 3200 B.C. According to the great Hindu epic, Mahabharata, the more approximate date is around 3102 B.C. The word Hindu is derived from the name of an Indian river called Indus. In ancient times, the river Indus was called Sindhu. Later the Persians, who migrated to India changed the name Sindhu to Hindu and the land as Hindustan. The inhabitants of Hindustan came to be called Hindus and the religion followed by them became Hindusim.

Chief Scriptures

The oldest Hindu sacred books date back to the time of the Aryans, more than three thousand years ago. These are the four collections of hymns and prayers called the Rig Veda, the Sama Veda, the Yajur Veda, and the Atharwa Veda. The oldest and the most sacred is the Rig Veda, or Song of Knowledge, and it contains over one thousand hymns.

The other most important Hindu sacred texts are the Upanishads and the two long epic poems, the Ramayana and the Mahabharata. The Vedas and Upanishads are called Shruti, or heard texts. The other texts are known as Smrithi, or remembered texts. The Upanishads are made up of spiritual teachings given by the saints and gurus (teachers) to their disciples (students), using parables and stories to convey a spiritual message. While the Vedas are about worshipping the Gods through fire, rituals, and sacrifices, the Upanishads concentrate on the relationship between an individual and Brahman (God).

Another important sacred text is the Bhagavad Gita, or the Song of the Blessed One, a philosophical part of the epic poem Mahabharata. The Bhagavad Gita is the jewel of India's spiritual wisdom. It is an exposition of Vedantic philosophy and can be termed as a gospel. Its essential message is timeless. In it God speaks to man, his friend, and it contains ecstatic mystical utterances about the nature and attributes of God, God's relation to man, and the ways and means to reach God.

Though Hinduism is one of the world's oldest religions, its beginning cannot be dated. Its roots go back more than four thousand years to the time of the great Indus Valley civilization, which thrived along the River Indus. Many clay figures have been found among the ruins of the Indus Valley cities. Some of these show gods and goddesses that are similar to those worshipped by the Hindus today. The Indus Valley civilization collapsed around 2000 BC. Around five hundred years later, a group of people called the Aryans began to arrive in India from the northwest. Their religion combined with the Indus Valley religion to form the basis of Hinduism.

The religion of the Indo-Aryans is generally known as Hinduism or Brahmanism. Both these words were coined by the foreigners. The River Sindhu flowing into the Arabian Sea and forming a part of the western boundary of India was known by the ancient Persians as the Hindu. The Greeks borrowed this name, changing it into Indos, which was later converted into the English word Indus.

The Greeks called the country east of the Indus by the name of India. Its inhabitants came to be known as Hindus and their religion as Hinduism. Hindus prefer to call their religion Sanatana Dharma, the eternal religion, because it is based upon the eternal principles and the teachings of the Vedas.

Beliefs

The doctrine of Karma and rebirth form an important part of the Upanishidic teachings and has exerted the greatest practical influence upon the Hindu society. It is one of the strong pillars on which Hindu Dharma rests. The doctrine was formulated in response to the question as to what becomes of a man after death. The essence of the doctrine of Karma is a belief in a moral foundation of the universe, in which virtue and good deeds are rewarded and evil punished. The doctrine of Karma and rebirth is certainly an original contribution of Hinduism to philosophical thought.

Karma means action. Action plays a vital part in molding a person's future not only here on earth, but after death as well. The law of Karma is the application of the law of cause and effect in the moral world. Hinduism teaches that the good and evil tendencies of this life and a man's happiness and sufferings are the inevitable consequences of the actions of his previous life, and actions performed in this life determine those of the next. Hinduism holds that Divinity or Atman is contained in all beings. Hinduism believes in many Gods and Goddesses. The three most important are called the Trimurty, a trinity or triad of gods known as Brahma, the creator, Vishnu, the preserver, and Siva, the destroyer.

Another important belief in Hinduism is reincarnation, which means that upon the death of the body, a person's soul is reborn in another body, human or animal. One may be born many times, in a cycle of death and rebirth called samsara. The aim of a Hindu life is to break free from the cycle of birth and death and attain liberation (called moksha) or salvation. Those seeking liberation are advised to undertake pilgrimage to holy places, bathe in sacred rivers like the Ganges, perform daily prayers, study the scriptures, and meditate daily. According to Hinduism, there are four paths leading to liberation, and one can choose the path best suited to him. The four paths are as follows:

1. The path of devotion—This path consists of sustained daily prayers, sincere worship, and devotion to a personal God.
2. The path of knowledge—In this path, the aspirant will study and learn under the guidance of a spiritual master or guru.
3. The path of action—In this path, all actions should be performed selflessly as an offering to God without any thought of reward for oneself.
4. The path of self-control—In this path, an aspirant undertakes yoga and meditation.

In Hinduism, certain basic concepts influence thinking and daily conduct, such as upholding Dharma, ahimsa or nonviolence, respecting one's parents and elders, leading a simple and spiritual life, and so on.

An important school of Hindu philosophy is called "yoga." Yoga means union. To the worker, it is a union between men and the whole of humanity. To the mystic, it is a union between his lower and higher self. To the lover, it is a union between himself and the God of love. And to the philosopher, it is the union of all existence.

There are four divisions of yoga. They are called Karma Yoga, Raja Yoga, Bhakti Yoga, and Jnana Yoga. A person who practices yoga is called a yogi.

Karma Yoga teaches attainment of good through selfless work. It teaches where and how to work, how to employ to the greatest advantage the largest part of one's energies in the work that is before him.

Raja Yoga teaches that the power of concentration is the key to knowledge. The more power of concentration, the greater the acquisition of knowledge. How to check and control the mind with its thousands of thoughts and bring it under control by concentration is the basis of Raja Yoga.

Bhakti Yoga is for the man of an emotional nature, the lover. It teaches that love itself is the highest recompense of love—that God himself is love.

Jnana Yoga is for the philosopher, the thinker who wants to go beyond the visible. To him, God is the life of his life, the soul of his soul. God is his own Self. Nothing else remains which is other than God.

Practice

Hindu devotion is largely an individual and family matter. Hindus do not congregate on any particular day for worship. Many Hindu homes have a shrine to honor a particular god or all gods and goddesses. Hindu temples are buildings dedicated to a particular god or group of gods and goddesses. Some of the famous temples are on the banks of sacred rivers like the Ganges.

Traditional Hinduism used to observe a caste system, the division of people into groups by occupation and social standards. Since India became independent in 1947, the government has tried to end this caste system.

Sri Sankara and Hinduism

No study of Hinduism will be complete without a study of the life and works of the great saint, poet, and philosopher Sri Sankaracharya, affectionately called Sankara. He is considered an incarnation of Lord Siva. The greatest philosopher and sage was praised by the great sage and philosopher Swami Vivekananda as follows: "He who declared, 'I will come whenever virtue subsides' came again and this time, manifestation was in the south, and up rose the young Brahmin, of whom it has been declared that at the age of sixteen, he had completed all his writings, the marvelous boy Sankaracharya arose." What a glorious tribute to a spiritual genius.

Sri Sankaracharya was born in Kaladi, a small village in South India, in AD 788. He was born in a Nambudiri Brahmin (a priestly class) family. Sankara attended a Vedic school from a very young age. With his brilliant mind, Sankara quickly mastered the philosophy of religion as well as the Sanskrit language. Sankara then renounced the world in search of the eternal truth. He found a guru in Govinda Bhagavadpada, who initiated Sankara into the order of sanyasa, which means hermit in Hinduism. In Hinduism, a person who gives up all the attachments to the world and devotes his or her life to God is called a sanyasi. Blessed by his guru, Sri Sankara went to Benaras in North India, to spread the message of Advaita philosophy, often described as a monoistic system of thought. He had discussions and debates with many learned leaders and philosophers of various religious schools, refuted their views, and firmly established the supremacy of non-dualistic Vedanta. Sankara spent all his energies in reforming the Sanatana Dharma, and he elevated the Hindu scriptures to the highest pinnacle. Sri Sankara visited many holy places in the country. He traveled the length and breadth of India, mostly on foot, and established four religious centers, called mutts: Sringeri Mutt, at Sringeri in the south; Sarada Mutt, at Dwaraka in the west; Jyotir Mutt, in the north; and Goverdhan Mutt, in Puri, in the east. These spiritual centers continue to propagate the teachings of Sankara.

The divine birth of Sankara is evident from the unusual combination of knowledge, devotion, and action that he possessed. In his short life of thirty-two years, Sri Sankara made Hinduism a vibrant and living faith. In the midst of all his ceaseless travels, Sri Sankara found time to write commentaries, philosophical treatises, and several devotional songs and hymns in praise of Hindu gods and goddesses. These helped guide young devotees and aspirants longing after a spiritual path. In Sri Sankara, one finds the rare combination of savant and sage, philosopher and poet, mystic and religious reformer, a brilliant debater and great thinker, and above all, a kind, loving, compassionate, and genial soul. Sri Sankara's great literary works are commentaries on the Upanishads, Bhagavad Gita, and the Brahmasutras. Others are devotional songs on all the Hindu deities.

Further, Sri Sankara was an ideal son to his mother. His great love and respect for his mother triumphed over rigid rules governing the order of sanyasa, and on her death, Sankara performed the funeral rite for his mother, against the protest of many.

Sri Sankara passed away in Kedarnath, at the foot of Himalayas, at the age of thirty-two. What Sri Sankara achieved in his life could have been possible only by a divine soul.

Motherhood

Hinduism and its scriptures give pride of place to the mother and motherhood. Some of the holy books state that there is no need for a person to visit temples and pray to God; it will suffice if the person worships his or her parents, since the parents are considered to be visible gods. The epics the Mahabharata and the Ramayana stress the great importance of motherhood again and again. The prince Rama and the Pandava princes all consulted their mother and followed her advice in all matters; they took no action without getting their mother's blessings and approval.

Sri Sankara's writings show his great respect and love for his mother. Sri Sankara composed "Sri Mathrupanchakam" as the only tribute to his mother. It is comprised of five slokas, or verses, which were handed down by word of mouth. These five slokas exalt the sacrifices of a mother for her child with absolutely no expectation of return or reward. Sri Sankara pours out his heart for his beloved mother, and the following verses glorify motherhood:

"The extreme mental stresses and strains coupled with unbearable physical labor pains at the time of child birth, the tiredness and weakness of the body and having to undergo acute physical discomforts and endure a soiled bed for a whole year are all well known. With all humility and respect, I bow to that mother of mine. Her son, however great and highly placed he may be, is unable to compensate her in full even one of the many troubles she has cheerfully undertaken for carrying the child in her womb and all the consequential sacrifices and sufferings."

"Seeing me in your dream in the garb of a sanyasi, you came to the gurukula (school) and wept very much. Seeing your copious tears of acute sorrow and grief, all the people in the gurukula also wept in your presence. In all humility and respect, I bow at the feet of that mother of mine"

"Oh beloved mother, at the time you were dying, I was not by your side and I could not even offer you water. On the day of your death, according to the normal procedure for the Sradha, I should not offer the Sradha homa. Further at the time of your death, I could not chant the 'Tharaka' mantra (prayer) for purifying the soul. Oh beloved mother, please take unlimited pity and compassion on me, who did not come at the proper time."

"You have said 'Oh son, you are my pearl, you are my eye, you are a king, you live long.' In that mouth of my beloved mother, I am now placing only dry rice."

"At the time of delivery, you cried loud, 'Oh mother, oh father, oh Siva.' For that mother's sake this prayer is made in humility and with folded hands. Oh Krishna, Oh Govinda, Oh Hari, Oh Mukunda so that they may bless and protect the departed soul."

"Oh Mother, let all my speech be your prayer, let all my crafts and technology be your worship and be the mystic gestures of my hands adoring you. May all my movements become your devotional circumambulation. May everything I eat and drink be oblations to you. Let my lying down in rest and sleep be prostrations to you, mother. Whatever I do may all that become a sacramental service and worship for you."

"I know no mantra, yantra or stotra. I know no invocation or contemplation. I know no stories in your praise. I simply know that to run to you. Mother destroys all distress. I do not ask of you, O Mother, riches, good fortune or salvation. I seek no happiness, no knowledge. This is my only prayer to you, that as the breath of life forsakes me, still I may chant Your holy name."

The Bhagavad Gita—The Song Celestial

Bhagavad Gita literally means the "song of the divine" or the "song of God." It is a brilliant exposition of Vedanta philosophy based on every aspect of human nature. The Bhagavad Gita is considered part of an epic poem, and it is the most popular and widely read book in Hindu religious literature. It is one of the greatest devotional and spiritual works that the world has ever seen. Like the Bible and the Qur'an, the Bhagavad Gita contains ecstatic philosophical and mystic utterances about the nature and attributes of God and explains how a devotee can attain God. It is a gospel and song celestial. The message conveyed to humanity in the Bhagavad Gita is timeless and eternal. The Bhagavad Gita describes the teachings of Krishna, the incarnation of God to humanity through his friend and disciple Arjuna, a Pandava prince. In simple words that belong to no particular race, the incarnate God speaks to man—his friend—the eternal truths.

The Bhagavad Gita is not regarded by Hindus as the scriptural teachings revealed by God to humanity but as the teaching of divine incarnations, saints, and philosophers, who further elaborated on the eternal God-given truths of the scriptures. The Bhagavad Gita has greatly influenced the spiritual, social, cultural, and political life of India and its teeming millions throughout the centuries, and it continues to influence the lives of millions even today.

A gist of the important teachings of the Bhagavad Gita are given below:

The soul is never born and never dies. The soul is unborn, eternal and everlasting. The soul is indestructible, can never be cut by any weapon, nor burned by fire or moistened by water. Like a person discarding old and worn out garments, the embodied souls casting off worn out bodies, enters new ones.

It is one's duty to work and one's right to perform his prescribed duty. One should not however, expect or desire for the fruits of the action. One should perform one's duty without any attachment or hope of reward.

One who has intense faith and devotion to God, and controls his senses, attains supreme and lasting peace.

A person whose actions are without any desire or motive and whose actions are burned up in the fire of knowledge, is called a sage.

The joy which is derived from the contact of the senses with their objects, though appearing like nectar in the beginning, proves to be like poison in the end.

Passion, anger and greed constitute the triple gate of hell, leading to the damnation of the soul. A devotee should be free of all these sentiments.

Even the most vile sinner should be considered a saint, if he worships God with exclusive devotion and sincerity, for he has rightly resolved.

Whoever offers with love and devotion, a leaf, a flower, a fruit or even water, God will appear in person before that devotee and cheerfully partake of that article so lovingly offered by the devotee.

Surrender all duties to God and seek refuge in Him. He shall absolve you of all sins. Endowed with knowledge and pure reason, partaking of pure food, living in a quiet and sacred place, renouncing all desires and objects of the senses, controlling the body and mind, freed of all passion, egoism, violence, arrogance, anger, lust and greed, constantly absorbed in prayer and meditation, such a person becomes qualified to be one with the Eternal.

Peace

Hinduism preaches peace, love for all human beings, service to elders, kindness to all living beings, and devotion to God. Peace finds a very prominent place in all the scriptures and sacred texts. In fact, the general practice is to invoke a prayer for peace before starting a holy text. Thus the religious hymns begin with the words, "May peace—physical, mental, and spiritual—be on us forever."

The key to a health and happy life is mental peace. Peace is a state of the mind wherein there is calm, repose, tranquility, and freedom from all disturbances. All beings love peace, because it is their original state. It is in peace alone that social progress, growth, and prosperity are possible. Peace is the criterion for mutual understanding and cordial relationships.

Elements in nature are normally at peace. Occasionally, they are in turmoil and press hard for readjustment. Beings resort to strife because of compulsion. Peacemakers among men are the salt of the earth. Jesus Christ said, "Blessed are the peacemakers, for they shall be called the children of God."

We should examine ourselves to see if we are agitated or nervous and then find out the reasons for the same. By careful self-analysis, we should be able to remove all the disintegrating emotions and negative thoughts. Once these negative thoughts are eliminated, we will experience mental peace.

We should remember that that the greatest healing of fear or nervousness takes place when we attune our lives to God. When we surrender completely to God and constantly pray and meditate, perfect peace will prevail in our mind. Happiness is rooted in godliness, and those that go against this universal law pay the heavy price of lack of inner peace.

Moral laws harmonize body and soul with the divine laws of nature, or creation, producing an inner as well as outer well-being, happiness, and strength. Those who are inwardly content and peaceful are living rightly. Happiness and peace come from right living. People should avoid undue excitement, restlessness, and sudden emotions, which cause mental worries and tensions. These result in mental agitations, which rob a person of peace and tranquility. An agitated mind causes mental distractions, resulting in shoddy performance. On the other hand, a person with a calm and peaceful mind can produce excellence in all his activities.

We must cast off all fear and nervousness. These are due to ignorance. If our heart is quiet and peaceful, we will be free from all fear and anxieties. We should make our home an abode of peace. Peace is a divine quality. A peaceful mind is like a lovely rose spreading its fragrance of tranquility and harmony.

Peace is essential for progress and prosperity. When the mind is peaceful and calm, it can produce excellent results. All the religions teach the importance of peace. In Hinduism, it is customary to invoke a prayer for peace before starting a scriptural book. Great importance is given to peace, since peace alone will ensure mental calmness, which in turn will enable an aspirant to acquire knowledge.

Benefits of Prayer

All the religions of the world glorify the power and the benefits of prayer. Prayer is the easiest way to reach God, since prayer purifies the mind. Only a purified mind devoid of all negative tendencies can make any progress on the spiritual path.

Prayer is a reverent and sincere petition made to a deity or other object of worship. It is any act of communion with God, such as a confession, praise, or thanksgiving. Prayer is often used to make a devout or earnest request for a particular aspiration. All religions emphasize the importance of prayers and the benefits that follow from sincere prayer.

Prayer is the deepest impulse of the human soul. Most of us are inclined or inspired to pray only when things that we plan go wrong, or when we experience failures and disappointments, or at moments of emotional upheaval. In such trying moments, something is stirred up within our hearts; a faith in a greater being or superpower or God is born, and prayer follows.

The most important argument in favor of prayer is that it relieves the mind of worry, fear, anxiety, and tension. Prayer ensures peace and calmness of the mind. It neutralizes all mental repressions and purifies the subconscious. Dedicated and sincere prayer will ensure hope, enthusiasm, mental peace, and energy, thereby enabling us to face life with confidence and faith. Life is not always a bed of roses, or sweetness, or happiness and success. Life can be full of sorrow, pain, misery, drudgery, suffering, disappointment, and failure. Worry, fear, anxiety, and tension eat into the vitals of a person's life. Prayer thus frees us from anxiety and fear and sustains us in moments of sufferings and sorrow. Prayer also helps us keep our spirits up in hopeless situations and difficult circumstances.

If prayer is practiced with sincerity, fervor, devotion, and regularity, we will experience the great benefits that prayer brings, and this will encourage us to further efforts and a deeper, greater faith.

The function of prayer is to create a mental condition that frees the mind from the deadweight of worldly life and worldly worries. Freed from all the daily trials and tribulations of life, the mind can hold communion with God.

Prayer is a companion to humility. Recognition of a higher power or a being who is full of grace and sympathy, love and kindness, caring and compassion can bring out our humility and self-surrender. Then we can unburden ourselves to God. This unburdening has the tremendous psychological benefit of freeing us from all the pulls and pressures of life. Once all our worries are unburdened to God, and once we surrender ourselves completely to God, there will be perfect peace and tranquility.

Adversity is the greatest teacher. In fact, many important lessons of life are learned only through sufferings and sorrows. When we have seen the happiness and suffering of life, we begin to ask if there is nothing beyond this apparent world. Then we pray. Only when we pray can our hearts open to the transcendental truth. Suffering is a door leading to God, and prayer unlocks the door. Prayer thus leads us nearer to God.

Many know prayer only as a form of request for a desired object, either for oneself or someone else. But prayer can also take other forms, such as adoration, an expression of love for God. Prayer is contemplation; union with divine.

> "One may attribute the various forms and aspects of God that are current in society to imagination, and may have no faith in them. Yet God will shower His grace on a person if he believes in a divine power that creates and directs the world, and prays with a distressed heart, 'O God, I do not know Thy real nature. Deign to reveal Thyself to me as Thou really art.'" —Sri Ramakrishna

Types of Prayer

All religions stress the importance of prayer. Some religions encourage prayer at a specified place, called mosque or synagogue or temple. However, Hinduism is very flexible regarding prayer and encourages prayer at any time and at any place, at one's convenience. The only stipulation is that one should be pure physically and mentally and one should focus one's mind on his favorite god or goddess.

There are different types of prayers. However, four distinct types of prayers are mentioned in the various scriptures of the world. The four types of prayers are petition, intercession, adoration, and contemplation. Christianity in particular has developed prayer as a discipline and made prayer the most important method of spiritual practice.

Petitionary prayer is the most common type of prayer for ordinary people beset with many problems and tossed by numerous desires. They pray for relief from these troubles and pray to God that they be given some peace and solace. In Hinduism, as in other religions, people resort to petitioning

God through prayers, sacrifices, and offerings for helping them through their difficulties.

Bhagavad Gita recognizes those who turn to God in distress as one type of devotee, and such devotees get recompense for their prayers in the ordinary course of events. God will answer prayers if they are made with sincerity, devotion, and with a pure mind. In this connection, the Lord says that whenever someone offers him, with devotion, a flower or fruit or even water, he will appear in person before that devotee to accept the devout offering.

Intercession is a prayer not for oneself, but for others. This type of prayer is the most unselfish in motive. Intercession, according to William Law, is the best arbitrator of all differences, the promoter of true friendship and understanding, the best cure and preservative against all unkind emotions, all angry and haughty passions. Advanced souls have the power to redress the suffering of others through such prayers.

Intercession is another type of prayer resorted to by many God-realized souls for the benefit of humanity. There are several anecdotes in the Hindu scriptures wherein saints and sages have prayed to God to alleviate the sufferings of others.

Adoration is the means to, and expression of, the love of God—a love that finds its consummation in the knowledge of the Godhead, which is the fruit of meditation and contemplation. Adoration is the act of loving God. In adoration, a devotee's mind is filled with great love for God, and there is no other thought except the devotee's overflowing love for God. In adoration, a devotee does not expect anything in return.

The fourth and the highest type of prayer is contemplation. Contemplation is the state of union with the Lord.. In this type of prayer, the devotee totally surrenders his self-interest and takes the attitude of "Thy will be done." Meditation is thus coupled with adoration and consecration. The devotee who desires nothing in life but God finds it natural to pray like this. When such an attitude matures, the devotee fully surrenders himself to God and becomes his instrument. Prayer then becomes continuous. A devotee's life itself becomes a continuous prayer. Whatever he does becomes an offering to God. Though this the purest form of prayer, the other types of prayers are not without merit. They improve one's conduct and character and purify the mind so that one can practice the highest form of prayer

Complete resignation to God is ideal prayer. Faith is recognition of a higher power and its loving-kindness; a prayer is resignation to that higher power and utter abandonment to its will. The higher power is intensely personal to a devotee. The more his conviction, the greater is the fervor and the more complete is the surrender.

Union with God

According to the scriptures, the purpose of human existence is to realize God and to achieve union with him. Unfortunately, most beings are so engrossed with securing material comforts that they have no time even to think of God. On the subject of union with God, the Lord says the following in the Bhagavad Gita:

"Endowed with pure reason, partaking of simple sattvic food, living in a sacred and lonely place, having renounced all the objects of the senses, having disciplined the mind and the senses, and controlled speech body and mind, dispassionate and eradicating passion and prejudice, constantly engaged in meditation having abandoned egoism, violence, arrogance, hatred lust, greed and anger, such a person becomes qualified to be one with the Eternal."

An aspirant seeking union with God should have the following basic qualifications:

First and foremost is discipline at the physical level. The negative aspect of the discipline is to prevent sensual dissipation, which will deflect an aspirant from the spiritual path. By exercising self-control and discipline, a person can avoid dissipation. The positive aspect is utilizing the conserved energy to lead a spiritual life, namely seeking God and aspiring to have union with him. Intelligent self-control will result in mental peace, harmony, and calmness, and these will ensure mental purity. For attaining union with God, it is essential to have a pure mind.

The second qualification is discipline at the mental level. The mind normally seeks material things and worldly pleasures. It runs after the sense objects of the world. The natural tendency of the mind is to dwell on past acts of passion and indulgence and to reflect upon the chances of securing of similar enjoyments in the future. These mental indulgences will result in serious agitations. When the mind is agitated, it will not be possible either to think dispassionately or to undertake meditation. When the mind is calm and peaceful, it can be turned towards higher values of life. It is then very easy for the aspirant to concentrate and focus his mind on God.

The third is to have discipline at the intellectual level. As long as the intellect yearns for desires, material comforts, and worldly pleasures, the mind will be agitated. By identifying with one's material equipment—the body, the mind, and the intellect—the mind becomes filled with desires and more desires. There is no limit to a person's desires. Desire is the greatest enemy that prevents an aspirant from God-realization. If one can stop identifying with these matter layers and assert one's supreme self, then one can attain perfect peace of mind and ultimately achieve union with God.

Fourth is passionate longing for liberation in this very life. All worldly desires should be given up, and the only desire should be to gain spiritual liberation and ultimate union with God. Unless and until an aspirant has the sincere determination and dedication to achieve spiritual liberation, he or she will be immersed in the eternal cycle of birth and death. For such a person, attaining liberation will be impossible.

An aspirant seeking union with God should have the following qualifications:

1. Discrimination between the real and the unreal;
2. Detachment from the unreal;
3. Six-fold wealth of qualifications: calmness, self-control, self-withdrawal, endurance, faith, and tranquility;
4. Desire for self-realization.

The above four qualifications will enable a person to achieve peace of mind, whereupon all sorrows and sufferings will come to an end. The intellect of such a person of tranquil mind, soon withdrawing from all sense objects of the world, becomes firmly established in God.

Regarding union with God, the Lord says in the Bhagavad Gita, "Fix your mind on Me, be devoted to Me worship Me, and bow to Me; so shall you without doubt reach me. This I truly promise you; for you are dear to Me. Surrendering all duties to Me, seek refuge in Me alone. I shall absolve you of all sins; grieve not."

> "First is discrimination between eternal and the non-eternal. Next comes renunciation of the enjoyment the fruits of action here and hereafter. Then come the six treasures of virtue beginning with tranquility. And last is the yearning for liberation." — The Vivekachudamani, by Sri Sankara

Sanatana Dharma and Hinduism

What is Sanatana Dharma? It can be safely said that it is the Hindu religion as we find it today. Sanatana Dharma is a Sanskrit phrase meaning "eternal teachings" or "eternal religion." It is the recognition of the spiritual essence of life and its infinite religious expressions. It is very important to understand that it was first in India that Sanatana Dharma was encountered. Hinduism is not confined to just a geographical location and certainly not simply to an ethnic group. Just as there are Christians, for example, who are not from the Middle East, are not Hebrew, and do not speak Arabic, there are Hindus of all races and nationalities. Just as anyone can become a Christian, anyone can become a Hindu. Sanatana Dharma is not circumscribed by the confines of a single country. It is a universal religion, which embraces all other religions, as it is eternal and everlasting.

Sanatana Dharma has no beginning, since nobody can say when it started. It is without a beginning and so without an end. Sanatana Dharma has no founder. All religions are known by their founders or prophets, but this is not the case with Sanatana Dharma. It has neither any prophet to begin it nor any book or authorized scriptures told by the prophet, who got a revelation from God.

Sanatana Dharma is not based on spiritual experience of any single individual or any such revelation. It is based on realizations and experiences of a large number of seers, sages, philosophers, thinkers and mystics, who realized the Infinite and were illuminated. It does not owe its origin to any single person or prophet nor does it adhere to any spiritual authority like the Pope It believes in scientific precision and experiments to arrive at Truth.

Sanatana Dharma is the oldest living religion of the world today. It can be termed as an eternal and everlasting humanitarian religion of all mankind. It is not limited to the teaching of any particular people or class of people or any particular form of worship. It absorbs all religions, faiths, forms of worship and even diverse kind of rituals and customs into its fold.

Sanatana Dharma believes that there is nothing that is not God. The Lord is enshrined in the hearts of all. God permeates everything and nothing permeates Him. There is peace invocation in the Isopanishad, which says, "All this is full/from fullness, fullness comes; When fullness is taken from fullness/fullness still remains." This belief is all comprehensive and all-absorbing. In fact, there is nothing that is not God. The central message of Sanatana Dharma is, "Truth is one, but the people describe it in different ways. Those on journey to Eternity may differ, but once reached there, all differences sink into oneness."

Sanatana Dharma is a cosmopolitan religion. It wishes the happiness of entire humanity. Man or woman is basically divine. There is divinity in every human being. He or she has to realize it. Sanatana Dharma says, "Let every one without distinction be happy. Let every one be without any ailment. Let every one be noble and righteous. Let there be no one to have any share of sorrow or grief." This is philosophy of Sanatana Dharma.

Self-Control

All the scriptures extol the virtue of self-control. An aspirant should develop self-control if he wants to progress in the spiritual path. By self-control, the devotee gets rid of all material thoughts and earthly desires. The mind becomes pure and calm when all the undesirable negative thoughts are driven away. Without a calm, serene, and pure mind, it will not be possible to practice meditation.

A Hindu saint said, "Self-control will place a man among the gods. A person devoid of self-control will be driven into the thickest darkness of hell. Let self-control be guarded as a treasure. There is no greater source of good for man than self-control."

Self-control is the bedrock of Vedantic discipline. Without self-control, it is not possible for an aspirant to progress in the spiritual path or achieve any success in meditation. Self-control enables a person to empty the mind of all material and worldly concerns, desires and passions, and then, through meditation, fill up the void with a spirit of Truth. To meditate without practicing self-control is futile.

Self-control is different from the practice of self-mortification, self-torture, and meaningless austerities. Self-control means development of willpower and strengthening of the determinative faculty, which controls all the sense organs.

A parable in the Upanishad known as the parable of the chariot fully illustrates the concept of self-control. In the parable, the body is compared to a chariot. Inside the chariot is seated the Self, the master. The determinative faculty, or buddhi, is the charioteer. The mind is the reins. The senses are the horses, and their objects are the roads along which the chariot moves. The chariot serves the purpose of carrying to the destination the master, who is the Supreme Self, temporarily identified, through ignorance with the body, the senses, and the mind. If the buddhi (the driver) is weak and the mind (the reins) are not held firmly, the senses (the horses) become uncontrollable, like the vicious horses of a bad charioteer. But if the buddhi functions properly and the mind is firmly held, the senses remain fully under control like the trained horses of a good charioteer.

Thus, without self-control, a person cannot reach the destination: self-realization. If a person is devoid of understanding, and impure, he can never reach the goal, and he enters into the cycle of births and deaths in the world of ignorance. But he who is gifted with understanding, purity, and a well-controlled mind will surely reach the goal and will be freed from the cycle of births. By strengthening the willpower and the determinative faculty, the mind and the senses can be kept under perfect control. This will prevent the aspirant from going astray through the enjoyment of objects that will hinder his spiritual progress. Thus, strengthening of the willpower and the buddhi is the very core of self-control.

On self-control, Swami Vivekananda said, "The man that has practiced control over himself cannot be acted upon by anything outside; His mind has become free; such a man alone is fit to live well in the world. The calmer we are and the less disturbed our nerves, the more shall we love and the better will our work be."

The Eternal Law of Karma (Or Causation)

The doctrine of Karma and rebirth is the most vital part of the Upanishadic teachings, and both concepts have exerted great practical influence upon the Hindu society. Karma is one of the strong pillars on which Hindu Dharma rests. The eternal laws of Karma and reincarnation are inseparably connected with the soul's state of bondage when it is associated with mind and matter. Karma, literally meaning action, denotes both action in general and the result-producing subtle impressions that remain with the doer even after an action is outwardly accomplished. It is in the latter sense that an action plays an important part in molding a man's future, not only here on earth, but after death as well.

The doctrine of Karma has nothing to do with fatalism or inactivity. Properly understood, it means that each act should bear its fruit, good or bad, according to its nature.

Hinduism teaches that the good and evil tendencies of this life, and a man's happiness and suffering in the present, are the inevitable consequence of the actions of his previous life, and the actions performed in this life determine those of the future. A person's future will be molded by his present activities. The law of karma is thus the greatest incentive for self-effort. It does not make man subject to the arbitrary decree of a whimsical god or goddess, but goads him to be the architect of his own destiny to the best of his capacity and invests him with the responsibility for all his actions.

It asks him to reconcile himself to his present lot, without unduly worrying himself with affairs over which he will have no control. It inspires him at the same time to put forth his fresh and best efforts for improving his future as much as possible. Whatever may be the mistaken notions about Karma among those who take shelter in a doctrine of parasitic salvation, avoiding moral and spiritual struggles, Karma in its true import includes both destiny as well as self-effort. Of these two, self-effort is the most important factor in life. Self-effort alone will enable a person to improve his future. The eternal law of Karma says that a person cannot escape the results of his acts, good and bad. However through penance certain bad acts may be counter-acted.

Hindu scriptures state, "Know that destiny is the result of one's own actions acquired in another bodily existence. Hence the wise person calls one's self effort as superior."

Concepts of God

There are many concepts of God in Hinduism, and the most common is that of a personal entity. God has a distinct identity, and all animate and inanimate beings are created, sustained, and destroyed by him. God is viewed as the all-merciful, all-loving, all-knowing, and all-powerful ruler of the universe. There is no discrimination in his blessings, and he gives liberation to the devotee who has unflinching devotion to him. The Bhagavad Gita mentions two concepts of a personal God: God with form and attributes, and God with attributes but without form.

The main concepts of God are as Creator, Sustainer, and Destroyer. In the concept of God as the Creator, God is seen as the creator of animate and inanimate things in the universe. God is the eternal seed of all beings. This aspect is clearly brought out in the Bhagavad Gita, where the Lord says, "My Prakriti or Nature in her primordial and undeveloped state is the womb of all creatures. In that, I place the seed of consciousness. The birth of all beings follow this combination of Matter and Spirit. Of all the bodies that take birth from different wombs, this Primordial Matter is the Mother and I am the procreating father."

The next concept is that of incarnation, or what is called the Avatara. This concept is a unique feature of Hinduism. In incarnation, God descends to this phenomenal world whenever there is an increase in unrighteousness, a decrease of Dharma and evil in the world. God then decides to intervene personally to set matters right and uphold Dharma by punishing the evildoers and protecting the righteous. This is explained in the Bhagavad Gita, where the Lord says, "Whenever there is decline of righteousness and unrighteousness is on the increase, then I body Myself forth." The wicked are punished and the righteous are protected. Holy books are full of such incarnations of God, where his devotees are saved and the wicked are destroyed. The epics Ramayana and Mahabharata fully illustrate this aspect of God reaching out to save his devotees from the wicked and evil-minded.

Another concept of God is the Viswarupa. In Viswarupa, God displays his universal form, power and glory. Thus, Sri Krishna, the incarnation of the Supreme Being, showed his universal form to Arjuna, his disciple. God also gave Arjuna the divine eyes to see his universal form, and Arjuna saw this entire universe and all the worlds, including the abode of Gods in the Lord's universal form.

Another concept of God is that of Enjoyer. God is the Indweller in the body, who enjoys through the body and the senses. God is the Enjoyer since he is the recipient of all offerings made during sacrificial rites and penances.

Another aspect of God is Adhidaiva and Adhiyajna. This aspect is fully brought out in the Bhagavad Gita, where the Lord says, "The Purusa (Brahma) is Adhidaiva and in this body I Myself dwelling as the Inner Witness am Adhiyajna." The term Adhidaiva refers to the Cosmic Being, who is said to reside in the solar sphere. All deities are part of him, who is the totality of all creatures in the universe. Adhiyajna means the presiding deity of all sacrificial rites.

Another concept of God is Vibhutirupa. Vibhuti means the divine glory of God, which is manifested in objects of exceptional eminence. God abides in the outstanding characteristics they exhibit, and whatever thing is found to be of preeminence is but a part of Divinity, or God.

Purushottama is another concept of God. God is the Ruler of the universe, and he is the source of all existence.

Lastly, God is omnipresent. Sri Ramakrishna says, "That seeing God everywhere forms the highest state of realization."

Types of Devotion (Bhakti)

Infinite love of the Lord of the universe is called devotion, or bhakti. Devotion to God is spontaneous and not motivated by any personal considerations. Expectation of any reward or benefit cannot coexist with the practice of devotion. Devotion to God expresses itself in the form of service, and no work done for God is felt tiresome. A person endowed with devotion or bhakti gives everything, including his very life, to God.

According to Vedanta, there are five principal objects or values within a human life. They include virtue or righteousness; wealth; love or desire of sensual enjoyments; final emancipation; and devotion or bhakti. Of these, devotion is considered the highest and the best. The unique feature of devotion at its highest level is that the Jiva, or individual soul, feels the Lord as his own and loses himself in the Lord's service.

Devotion is defined as a state of mind, where all the thoughts and actions of the devotee are focused exclusively on God.There are three basic types of devotion. These are:

1. Devotion through confrontation;
2. Devotion combined with true knowledge; and
3. Devotion that is devoid of knowledge.

Ravana, in the Hindu epic Ramayana, is a good example of devotion through confrontation. Ravana, the demon king, was a great devotee of

God. He however, indulged in evil deeds and died fighting with Rama, who is an incarnation of God.

The second type of devotion has been attained by many sages who achieved union with God through a combination of knowledge and devotion. The scriptures are full of anecdotes about such men and women. This is the ideal type of devotion or bhakti.

The third type is devotion to God devoid of knowledge. In the scriptures, it is said that whatever sentiment man entertains towards God—whether it is fear, anger, friendship, or sense of oneness—he will attain God through that emotion. Sri Ramakrishna said, "The world is a huge lunatic asylum where all men are mad, some after money, some after women, some after name or form and a few after God. Thinking of God, some weep, some sing, some dance, some say wonderful things, but all speak nothing but God."

The intense yearning of Gopis (the cowherd girls) for God is an example of the purest form of devotion. The love of Gopis is something very unique, pure, and noble. It is the very ideal of love, a love that wants nothing in return, a love that does not care for anything in this world or in the world to come. It is the purest and noblest form of love, which has nothing to do with the physical aspect of love of human beings.

The practice of devotion can be classified under the following heads:

1. Listening to the glory of God;
2. Singing the glory of God;
3. Constantly thinking of God;
4. Adoring the feet of God;
5. Worshiping God through Vedic hymns and prayers;
6. Performing salutations to pay obeisance to the Lord and singing his glory;
7. Practicing an attitude of being servant to God;
8. Cultivating loving intimacy with God.

Any one of the above types can be practiced by a devotee. What is required is constant remembrance of God, focusing all thoughts on God, and undertaking all actions for his sake.

Self, Atman, or Brahman

When studying Hindu scriptures, one frequently comes across words such as Self, Atman, Brahman, Consciousness, and the like. It is, therefore, essential for a student of Hindu scriptures to fully understand the meaning and significance of these words.

In the Bhagavad Gita, the Lord says, "Whatever being animate or inanimate is born, know that to be as emanated from the union of matter and spirit. Matter is said to be the cause of production of the body and senses, while the spirit is said to be the cause of pleasure and pain. The spirit dwelling within the body is really transcendent and has been declared as the Supreme Lord."

A human being is thus made up of matter and spirit. The spirit in a human being is the real Self. It is the godhead within a being. The matter is comprised of the physical body, the mind, and the intellect. These are the three pieces of equipment that enable a person to see, think, and act. The body, mind, and intellect by themselves are inert and insentient; it is the spirit or godhead within which enliven and activate them. This life energy is the real Self. This is called Atman in the Sanskrit language. In other words, the Self and Atman are one and the same.

Atman activates the equipment to produce perceptions, emotions, and thoughts, but the latter does not in any way affect Atman. Atman is pure consciousness, which helps the sense organs to see, the mind to feel, and the intellect to think. Atman can be compared to the electrical energy that enables equipment like fans, heaters, radios, etc. to function. But the functioning of the electrical equipment does not in any way affect electricity.

Atman is different and distinct from the material equipment of the body, mind, and intellect and their functions. Only in the presence of Atman does the physical body act, irrespective of whether the actions are good or evil. Similarly, it is the Atman that enables the sense organs to see the objects of the world. In the same way, it enables the mind to feel the emotions and the intellect to think. Atman always remains detached and independent of all activities. Atman is ever pure and without attributes and action. Atman is a mere witness and never gets involved in any of the activities. In its presence, however, everything gets activated. Thus, Atman can be compared to a king, who, sitting on the throne, activates his ministers, counselors, army, and all other staff. By himself, he remains a mere observer.

There is an aphorism in the Upanishads that says, "This Self is Brahman." "This" refers to the Self within, or Atman. This Self or Atman, which activates a human being, is the same as Brahman, which activates the entire universe. This Vedic statement—"This Self is Brahman"—enables an individual to practice and find out the identity between the Self or Atman and the all-pervading Reality or Brahman.

According to Vedanta, only the all-pervading Brahman is real, and the world of plurality is unreal. The Atman or Self in an individual is the same as Brahman. Further, Vedanta also states that the Self or Atman is Consciousness, which is by nature pure, eternal, and blissful and which is the Witness and illuminator of all illusory things.

On Atman, Sri Ramakrishna said, "That which is the Pure Atman is the Great Cause, the Cause of the cause. The gross, the subtle, the casual and the Great Cause. The five elements are gross. Mind, buddhi, and the ego are subtle. Prakriti, the Primal Energy is the cause of all these. Brahman, Pure Atman, is the Cause of the cause. This pure Atman alone is our real nature. What is Jnana? It is to know one's own Self and keep the mind on it. It is to know the Pure Atman."

Hindu View of Religion and Philosophy

What is religion? It is the expression of a person's belief in and reverence for the Supreme Being or Power that is recognized as the Creator and Governor of the universe. It is the spiritual and emotional attitude of one who recognizes the existence of a Supreme Power or Being.

What is philosophy? It can be described as the love and pursuit of wisdom by intellectual means and moral self-discipline. It is the investigation of the causes and laws underlining reality and inquiry into the true nature of things based on logical reasoning rather than empirical method.

In Hinduism, philosophy and religion are inseparable. Hinduism has witnessed many great thinkers, saints, sages, and philosophers, all of whom have enriched, enlivened, and ennobled Hinduism. The goal of Hindu religious leaders and philosophers has been the same: self-realization, which all spiritual aspirants should strive to attain in this very life. All the Hindu scriptures prove a healthy blend of religion and philosophy.

The purpose of religion is to seek the ultimate Reality, or God, while the purpose of philosophy is to enable an aspirant to seek Truth. Both religion and philosophy aim at the same intuitive vision of Truth and fulfill each other. According to Hindu spiritual leaders, philosophy is not an intellectual pursuit of any abstract idea but a sincere and dedicated striving for the realization of Truth. Consequently, Hinduism has maintained a very close and healthy alliance between religion and philosophy. Religion without philosophy tends to become meaningless and superstitious, whereas philosophy without religion becomes mere intellectualism.

According to Max Mueller, religion and philosophy have worked hand in hand and in perfect harmony in India. Religion derives its strength, vitality, and breadth of vision from philosophy, and philosophy gets its strength and spirituality from religion. Thus religion can be thought of as the practical form of philosophy, and philosophy can be thought of as the rational form of religion. The goal of philosophy is truth, while the goal of religion is God. In the final analysis, both God and Truth are one and the same: Reality. Religion is based on faith, and philosophy is based on sound and logical reasoning.

In Sanskrit, philosophy is called darshana, a word derived from the root dris, which means "sight" or "to see." In Hinduism, darshana literally means sight, but it is usually translated as philosophy, meaning a system which brings about direct vision, experience, and realization of Truth. Hindu philosophers were men of great wisdom, vision, and faith, who had God-realization. Consequently, their system, based on their own transcendental experience, led to the same goal, namely God and Truth. Thus, the goal of both religion and philosophy is the same: God-realization.

Religion will become mere sentimentalism if it is not reinforced and strengthened by philosophy. Religion is the practical application of philosophy to one's daily life, and philosophy provides it with a strong foundation. Hindu saints and seers blended in Vedanta both religion and philosophy. According to Hindu religious leaders, a philosopher has the spirit of adoration and reverence cherished by a religious person, and a religious person has the insight and understanding of a philosopher.

It is not sufficient for aspirants to subscribe to doctrines and dogmas with great faith. They should also live up to a higher life and attain the divine experience of God-realization. Spiritual life is a continuous struggle between good and evil. Divine and demoniacal tendencies are found in all beings. The aspirant should constantly endeavor to eliminate evil and strengthen the good. One should be able to distinguish the divine attributes that lead one to Reality from the demoniacal qualities that cause ignorance and bondage.

Whenever religion has placed emphasis on mere forms and dogmas, thereby clouding the vision of aspirants regarding the ultimate Reality or God, philosophy has corrected the errors of religion. Thus, it is evident that religion without philosophy is incomplete, and vice versa.

OM, or AUM, in Hinduism

OM, or AUM, is the quintessence of the Vedas and is the most powerful and profound concept of the Hindu faith. It is a symbol of the Absolute. According to the Bhagavad Gita, there is peace, harmony, and bliss in the deeply philosophical and musical sound of OM. By vibrating the sacred syllable OM, if a person thinks of the Ultimate Personality of Godhead and quits his or her body, he or she will definitely reach the highest state of "stateless" eternity.

The Upanishads describe the power and importance of OM. According to the Mandukya Upanishad, OM is the one eternal syllable from which all that exists develops The past, the present, and the future are all included in this one philosophical sound, and all that exists beyond the three forms of time is also implied in it. OM, the symbol of the Absolute, is described as follows in the Katha Upanishad: "The goal which all the Vedas declare, which all austerities aim at, and which men desire when they lead the life of continence is OM. This syllable OM is indeed Brahman. Whosoever knows this syllable obtains all that he wants and desires. This is the best support; this is the highest support. Whosoever knows this support is adored in the world of Brahma."

OM is a sacred syllable representing Brahman, the impersonal Absolute, Omnipotent, Omnipresent, and the source of all manifest existence. The sacred symbol helps a person realize the Unknowable, since Brahman as such is incomprehensible. Thus, OM represents both the manifest and the unmanifest aspects of God. This also explains why OM has been termed "pranava," meaning that it pervades the entire life and runs through one's prana, or breath.

OM is a powerful and eternal syllable in Hinduism. It is not a word as such, but rather an intonation which, like music, transcends all the barriers of age, race, and culture. OM is made up of three Sanskrit letters, namely "aa," "au," and "ma," which, when combined, together make the sound OM. This is said to be the basic sound of the entire universe and to contain all other sounds. OM is a prayer or mantra in itself. By constant repetition of OM with the correct intonation, it can resonate throughout the body so that the sound penetrates to the center of one's Atman or the soul. As a prayer, OM ensures harmony, mental peace, and bliss.

The power of OM is great. When one chants OM, one creates within oneself a vibration that attunes sympathy with the cosmic vibration. One then starts thinking universally. There is a momentary silence between each chant and the mind moves between sound and silence till eventually the sound ceases. And in that total silence, there is no other thought. In such a state, where the mind and intellect are transcended, the individual self gets merged with the Infinite Self.

OM thus plays a very conspicuous and dominant role in the daily life of Hindus. The Hindus normally begin their day or start their daily work or undertake a journey by uttering OM. The symbol of the sacred syllable is found on letterhead, and many Hindus wear the sign of OM as a pendant. The sacred symbol is enshrined in all the Hindu temples, family shrines, and all places of worship. A newborn child is ushered into the world with the holy sign of OM. From birth, the syllable is initiated into the life of a Hindu, and it remains with him or her till death as a symbol of piety and purity.

OM provides a dualistic viewpoint. On the one hand it projects the mind beyond the immediate to what is abstract, and on the other hand, it makes the absolute tangible and comprehensive.

LOVE, THE WAY TO GOD

To reach God, one should take the path of love, the easiest and surest way. All the scriptures stress that God is love and love is God. All the Hindu scriptures state that God is an ocean of love, mercy, kindness, and compassion. The scriptures are full of anecdotes showing God's infinite love for all living beings. The epics the Ramayana and the Mahabharata illustrate this divine love of God. When anyone invokes God, God immediately rushes to respond to the call in order to render help. This aspect of God's infinite love for his devotees is fully illustrated in the Bhagavad Gita, where the Lord says, "Whosoever offers with love and devotion a fruit or flower or even water, He appears in person before that person to accept the gift of love offered by the devotes."

The easiest way to reach God is through love. A person should live in love, be loving to all other beings, do good to others, and see God in everyone and everything. This is the surest and easiest way to reach God. Love for God should manifest itself by way of service to other fellow beings, particularly to the poor, the sick, the elderly, and the downtrodden. Love in the form of service should take the form of food for the hungry, sympathy and consolation for the sick, help for the suffering, and solace for the forlorn. A heart full of love, kindness, and compassion is the temple of God. We should develop compassion and love, live in love, and base all our thoughts and deeds on love.

Love for God should fill our heart and overflow. We should not have thoughts of hatred, anger, jealousy, lust, and greed. We should develop love towards all. Negative thoughts such as hatred, anger, pride, and prejudice corrupt and poison the mind. Genuine and pure love destroys all such evil tendencies. When love is enthroned in our heart, there will be peace, contentment, harmony, and bliss.

To love God is to see God in every being. In the Bhagavad Gita, the Lord explains how a person can develop true love. He says, "He, who has no hatred or malice towards any creature, who is friendly, loving and compassionate towards all, who is freed from the bondage of 'I' and 'Mine,' who is not affected by the pairs of opposites like pleasure and pain, joy and sorrow, honor and dishonor, and who is patient and forbearing in spite of privation, in such a person true love will blossom."

God is all-powerful and all-knowing. He is the source of all love. God is an ocean of love. Through love, one can merge in the ocean of love. Love destroys all evil tendencies and binds all hearts with understanding, harmony, and happiness. God resides in a loving heart. When one looks through the eyes of love, everything appears beautiful, all thoughts and actions become love, and the whole world becomes a loving family. Such is the power of true love.

Love is the greatest and most powerful of all virtues. Where there is hatred, love brings peace, where there is sorrow, love brings joy, and where there is pain, love brings pleasure. Love purifies the heart and enables a person to reach God. The spark of love has to be cherished and nurtured so that it may reach God. Then every thought and action will become divine.

The aim of life should be to give happiness to all living beings. Love is the means to achieve this objective. We should start the day with love, fill the day with love, and end the day with love. A pure heart, full and overflowing with love, gravitates towards God, since God is love. Love helps one to see God everywhere and in everyone.

A heart devoid of love is dreary and dry as a desert. Love should fill one's heart, and it should grow with every moment of our life. Spiritual practices such as prayer, worship, reading of the scriptures, and meditation will fill the heart with divine love. Love should sweeten every word, every deed, and every thought. God will reside in such a loving heart.

Perseverance/Self-Effort

The Hindu scriptures stress the importance of perseverance and self-effort in all human activities, particularly in one's spiritual life. Even for success in our daily activities, it is essential for us to work sincerely and with dedication. Perseverance and self-effort will ensure success. The lives of all men and women who have achieved great distinction illustrate the power of perseverance and dedicated efforts. Whether the goal is material benefits such as wealth, fame, and power, or real knowledge in order to succeed on one's spiritual path, self-effort is a must.

The great epics the Ramayana and the Mahabharata are full of anecdotes demonstrating the power of perseverance and self-effort. To win a battle against the enemy or to govern a kingdom or to teach the youth about the values of life or to achieve liberation—all these require dedicated self-effort and perseverance. Success in any endeavor will depend on the intensity of these efforts. In the Bhagavad Gita, the Lord explains that to achieve anything in life, whether material or spiritual, one should practice self-effort, as the following passages illustrate.

"A person should lift himself by the Higher Self. He should not weaken the Self. The Higher Self is the friend and the lower Self is the enemy of oneself. That person, who has conquered the lower Self by means of the Higher Self, the Self is the friend of him. But to one whose lower nature is not conquered, it becomes an enemy."

"You are entitled to work only, but never to the fruits thereof. One should not work for the sake of fruit or allow himself to be inclined towards to inaction."

"Surrendering all actions to God, fixing the mind on the indwelling Self and casting away all desires and selfishness, one should fight the battle of life without any fear or excitement."

"Whatever you do, whatever you eat, whatever you offer in sacrifice, whatever you give away in gifts and charity and whatever disciplines you practice, do all these as an offering to God. Thus one will be freed from the bondage of all actions, which bring good or bad results with your mind firmly fixed on non-attachment, you will be freed from all bonds and will reach the Supreme Spirit, your true Self, the abode of supreme peace and bliss."

The above verses from the Bhagavad Gita highlight the importance of perseverance and self-effort in all actions. Further, they show that self-effort and total surrender to God should go hand in hand. Both these are to be considered as expressions of Divine Grace.

The importance of perseverance and self-effort are also given great importance in the Upanishads, which cite them as requirements for success in any field of human activity. The following passages from the Upanishads illustrate this.

"Success of all actions rests equally on one's effort and destiny. Of these two, destiny is the expression of the efforts made in a previous life."

"Men secure their desired objects by their self-effort. Those who lack in self-effort speak only of destiny. Neither the idle nor those who depend only on destiny ever reach their desired goal. It is, therefore, very essential that a person should by all means persist in his self-effort."

"The stream of tendencies that flow through good and bad choices should be controlled and directed along good path. When it has entered the evil path, it has to be directed towards the good path."

Self-Surrender

The scriptures state that self-surrender to God is the easiest and the surest road to spiritual success for an aspirant. According to the scriptures, placing oneself at the feet of the Lord in self-surrender marks the culmination of all spiritual endeavors. All the holy texts as well as the epics clearly point out the benefits that will accrue to the aspirant by his or her self-surrender to God. When devotees surrender to God, all their problems will be resolved, and they will feel lasting peace and happiness.

This aspect of total surrender to God is beautifully brought out in the

Bhagavad Gita, where the Lord says, "Surrender all duties to Me, seek refuge in Me, I shall absolve you from all sins." The Lord further advises his friend and disciple Arjuna as follows: "Therefore, mentally surrendering all actions to Me, and with Myself as your sole object, have your mind constantly fixed on Me, resorting to the 'Yoga' of equanimity. With your mind fixed on Me, you shall get over all difficulties by My Grace. And, if out of pride you will not listen to Me, you will be utterly destroyed."

The Lord assures aspirants supreme peace when they surrender to him by saying, "Seek refuge in Me with all your being. Through My Grace, you shall obtain supreme peace and the Eternal Abode."

When the faithful surrender to God, they will be freed from all pain, suffering, and sorrow. Through God's grace, they attain lasting peace and bliss. In this regard, the Lord says, "Fix your mind on Me, be devoted to Me, and bow to Me, so shall you without doubt reach Me. This, I truly promise to you; for you are dear to Me." The Lord assures devotees who surrender to him that he will absolve them of all sins and ensure peace and bliss and eventual liberation. Through self-surrender, aspirants can attain the highest pinnacle of spiritual advancement.

Self-surrender to God does not mean that persons should give up all their duties and responsibilities and remain idle. Self-surrender does not require inactivity or idleness. When devotees surrender to God, it is the Self or Atman that is offered to God first of all, and along with it the body, the mind, the ego, and the intellect. Once the devotees thus surrender to God, they will feel that it is the Lord who is functioning through their body, mind, and intellect. Prior to this, they believed that it was they who did everything, whereas now they understand that it is the Lord who is doing everything. The consciousness that they are the doer is merged in the Divine Consciousness, for the mind and intellect have been surrendered to the Lord. At this stage, the mind and the intellect cease to function independently. Thereafter, the Divine will be their will, Divine thought will be their thought, and Divine activity will be their activity. When devotees make a self-surrender to God, the Lord takes the whole responsibility in respect of such devotees. In this connection, the Lord says in the Bhagavad Gita, "With the mind and intellect dedicated to Me, you shall doubtless come to Me."

In self-surrender, the aspirants should dedicate to the Lord all that they hold as their own. Every resolve, every thought, every desire and every action proceeding from the body, the mind, the ego, and the intellect should be offered to the Lord. The mind and the senses, which run after all worldly enjoyments, should be reined in and turned towards God. And the devotees need only take refuge in God in order to free themselves from all fear, sorrow and pain.

As Prince Rama says in the epic the Ramayana, "Whoever takes refuge in Me only once and seeks My protection with the words 'I am Thine,' I grant him security against all creatures; such is my vow."

Total surrender to God will lead a person to liberation.

The Vedas, the Upanishads, and Vedanta

Any study and understanding of Hinduism will require some knowledge of the Vedas, the Upanishads, and the Vedanta, since these are the three pillars of Hinduism. As the Holy Bible and the Holy Qur'an are the core of their respective faiths, the Vedas, the Upanishads, and the Vedanta are the core of Hinduism and the very foundation of Hindu beliefs and practices. Let us now examine these one by one.

The Vedas are the sacred scriptures of Hinduism that embody the supersensuous experiences of the ancient Hindu sages, saints, seers, philosophers, and thinkers. The Vedas, which contain eternal truths regarding the soul, the universe, and the Ultimate Reality, are eternal. They are without beginning and are not connected to any human authorship. The teachings of the Vedas were handed down by word of mouth. The Hindus have utmost respect for every word of the Vedas, since they revealed great and eternal spiritual truths.

It was the sage Vyasa who arranged the Vedas into four books, called the Rig Veda, the Yajur Veda, the Sama Veda, and the Atharva Veda. The Vedas deal with two ideals: material happiness here and hereafter, and the Highest Good. Material happiness on earth or in heaven can be realized through observance of ethical laws, performance of one's Dharma, charity, prayers and worship of God.

The Vedas can be spilt into two parts, the Karmakanda and the Jnanakanda. The Karmakanda deals with rituals and sacrifices, whereas the Jnanakanda teaches philosophical wisdom. The Upanishads are located within the Jnanakanda.

The Upanishads teach the knowledge of Brahmans and the word Upanishad means wisdom. The actual word is derived from "upa" (a competent teacher), "ni" (completely), "shad" (loosens and destroys the pupil's attachment to the relative world). This enables the aspirant to attain Supreme Freedom or Liberation and Bliss. Since the teachings were transmitted orally from father to son and from teacher to disciple, over a period of time many sections of the Vedas and Upanishads, together with their various readings disappeared. One hundred and eight Upanishads remain, of which eleven are known as major Upanishads. The eleven major Upanishads are Aitareya, Taittiriya, Chhandogya, Brihadaranyaka, Mundaka, Mandukya, Isa, Kena, Katha, Prasna, and Svetasvatara.

All the Upanishads teach the knowledge of Brahman and is, therefore, called Brahmavidya. Brahman is derived form the Sanskrit word "brhma," which means to grow or increase. It is the Absolute, the Supreme Reality, the All-Pervading Consciousness, the Spirit behind the universe and the Godhead. Through a knowledge of the Brahman, the aspirant attains the Highest Good, Liberation, Immortality, and Abiding Peace. The wisdom contained in the Upanishads is also called Atmavidya, the Knowledge of the Atman, or the Self. Atman, which is the Immortal Spirit in man, is identical to Brahman, according to Non-dualists.

Lasting and Real Happiness through Vedanta

The wisdom of Vedanta shows humanity the path to real and lasting happiness. In this world of ours, there is both good and evil, joy and sorrow, pain and pleasure. They all exist side by side. As long as there is life on earth, there will be suffering and happiness. Suffering by its very nature is a major problem of life. So is the solution. If we examine carefully, we will see that we are ourselves responsible for our suffering, and, therefore, we have to find ways to overcome this.

In this connection, Sri Ramakrishna points out the example of the camel eating thorny bushes. Eating the thorny bushes results in the bleeding of the camel's mouth. The camel, however, continues to eat even then, since it is under the mistaken impression that the blood that it is tasting comes from the thorny bushes. It is the same case with human beings, who believe that happiness and unhappiness come from external objects, whereas they come from inside. Further, identification with the body and mind causes sorrow and suffering. We think that we will ever stay young and healthy and live forever. Groping in darkness, we are harassed by the trials and tribulations of life. Death suddenly snatches away our near and dear ones. This happens as a result of cause and effect, and we suffer due to our ignorance. The wisdom of the Vedas teaches us how to get rid of our ignorance, overcome all our sorrow and suffering, and achieve lasting and real happiness.

The wisdom of the Vedas will come to the rescue of human sorrow and suffering and will show the way to real happiness. Vedantic wisdom will destroy our ignorance, which is the root cause of all suffering and sorrow in this world. Vedanta says that it is ignorance that converts the kingdom of heaven into hell. One may employ all sorts of methods for overcoming suffering and unhappiness, but none of them will help except the knowledge of our Self within. Once we know our true Self, we can transcend all suffering and sorrow. The pain of body and mind does not belong to the Self that is beyond time and space.

Vedanta has a clear and precise knowledge of the different states of the mind. It recognizes the role of samskaras, or tendencies created in the previous births that cause our present condition. Further, Vedantic wisdom states that desire and fear are the main roots that result in the cycle of births and deaths. It regards the ego or the false notions of "I" and "mine" identified with the body as the sole cause of all human problems. Vedantic meditation will clear the mind of sorrow and suffering. This involves affirmation of one's true Self, which is beyond all desire, fear, birth, and death.

The Upanishads clearly show the way to get rid of all human suffering and sorrow and experience real and lasting bliss. The Shvetashvarata Upanishad says, "When men shall roll up space as if it were a piece of hide, then there will be an end of misery without one's cultivating knowledge of God. Since it is impossible to roll up the sky like a piece of hide, it will be impossible to remove suffering and sorrow without realizing God. It, therefore, means that by realizing God, one can overcome all suffering and achieve real happiness."

Vedantic wisdom teaches us to keep our thinking faculty clear and sharp so as to ensure tranquility of mind. According to Vedanta, our body of the soul undergoes several changes, such as childhood, youth, and old age. In each of these changes, the preceding stage dies, and the succeeding stage is born. Growth requires the decay and death of the previous state. Vedanta also tells us that countless desires keep a person continuously engaged in action, which causes acute stress and strain. For securing lasting happiness, a person should get rid of all desires. Attachment to desires will result in recurring birth and death.

Vedantic wisdom further tells us that by cultivating equanimity, we can remain calm and unshaken when misfortunes strike. Thought is another vital factor that can determine our happiness or unhappiness.

Chapter 8

Sikhism

Introduction to Sikhism

Sikhism is a progressive religion and dates back to 1500 A.D.. It is rooted in the teachings of the ten Gurus, the first of which was Guru Nanak Dev. The Sikh religion today has a following of over twenty million people worldwide, and is ranked as the world's fifth largest religion. Over 80 percent of the world's Sikh population live in the state of Punjab in India. Most Sikhs speak both Punjabi and English. Gurumukhi is the script of the Sikh scriptures, which is also used for writing the modern Punjabi language.

Sikhism is a comparatively new religion in India, and it was founded by Guru Nanak, its first Guru. After him, there were nine more Gurus. The Sikh scripture is a book called the Guru Granth Sahib. The tenth Guru decreed that after his death, the spiritual guide of the Sikhs would be the teachings contained in that book. The Sikhs show the book the respect that they would give a Guru.

Sikhs believe in one God, who is timeless and without form. The world and the universe are a reflection of God, who created them and directs them. The Sikh scriptures state, "God is the sole creator and judge. Keep him ever in mind. Nothing but God has any power." God cannot be found by human effort, but reveals himself to those who seek him through prayer and an unselfish life.

Sikh teachings emphasize equality, service, and protection of the weak, the sick, and the aged against all injustice. Sikhs follow the teachings of the ten Gurus, who lived in India from the fifteenth to seventeenth centuries AD, and the faithful now regard the book of their hymns and poems as the Guru for all the time to come.

Sikh teachings emphasize that everyone has equal rights, irrespective of caste, color, creed, race, or sex. Sikhism places great importance on service. Sikhs avoid superstitious behavior, pilgrimages, statues, and blind rituals. They think that religion should be practiced by living in the world and facing life's problems with sincerity and with hard and honest work.

The majority of Sikh customs are closely associated with the Khalsa, the body of initiated Sikhs to which most adult Sikhs belong. Sikhs who have been initiated into the Khalsa wear what is known as the 5 Ks—namely, uncut hair, a steel bracelet, a wooden comb, cotton underwear, and a sword. According to Sikhism, the Sikh who wears these things has dedicated himself to a life of dedication and submission to the Guru.

The central theme of Sikhism is that every Sikh should lead a good and noble life by keeping God in his or her heart at all times. One should live honestly and work hard. Everyone should be treated equally, and one should be generous to the less fortunate.

Sikhism

Founder

Guru Nanak, the founder of Sikhism, was born on April 15, 1469, in a humble village at Talwandi, in the district of Lahore (now in Pakistan). Those were turbulent times and the political, economic and social conditions were bad. People had to worry about their daily food and there was no time for religion. Further, very few cared either for religion or for spirituality. It was in such troubled times that Guru Nanak was born. From his childhood, Nanak was of a religious temperament and had a spiritual outlook. His teachers and schoolmates were surprised to see such deep and sincere devotion, such inborn knowledge of spiritual matters in Nanak at such a young age.

When his schooling was over, Nanak was entrusted with the task of looking after his family's cattle. While the cattle were grazing, young Nanak could be found sitting under a tree deeply absorbed in meditation. Consequently, Nanak was punished for neglecting his duty. But every time he was put to severe tests, he was miraculously saved by a divine hand. Once, Nanak's father gave him some money and told him to use it for something beneficial. Nanak used the money to buy food for some monks, an act that brought him great satisfaction. He felt that he had obeyed the true spirit of his father's orders.

Nanak displayed a lack of attachment to material things even at a tender age. Seeing this, people who came into contact with him were fully convinced that Nanak was born to fulfill a definite purpose in life. Some years later, Nanak started his mission: spreading a new gospel to propagate divine life. His generous heart was opened, and his arms outstretched to embrace the entire world. He was opposed by the emperor, pundits, and mullahs, but his honesty of purpose, spirituality, great devotion, and divine love silenced everyone. Those who criticized him were convinced of the sincerity of his purpose, and many of them later became his faithful followers.

Nanak traveled extensively throughout India. He also visited Persia, Kabul, Mecca, Medina, and other places. In all the places that he visited, Nanak spread his catholic and universal message of love and brotherhood, service to mankind, and equality of all human beings. His teachings were accepted with great respect by Hindus as well as Muslims. The main theme of Nanak's message was that God is one, God is love, and God is unity. According to Nanak, God resides in mosques as well as temples. All human beings are equal in the eyes of God. All are born, and all die. What matters is devotion to God and service to mankind, irrespective of caste, creed, and color.

Nanak was regarded as a spiritual teacher—or Sat Guru—by the time he was forty. His disciples came to be known as Sikhs. All the verses that he taught came to him from heaven through divine inspiration and communion with God. The collection of his teachings is called Japji Sahib, and the famous text Guru Granth Sahib also embodies them. For Sikhs, these are holy and very sacred, and they are worshipped with sincerity and devotion.

Another feature of Nanak's life was his universal message of love to the hearts of all people. He was adored and respected both by Hindus and Muslims. In fact, he was held in such high esteem that when he died, in 1539, both Hindus and Muslims claimed the right to dispose of his body according to their respective customs. Nanak' s body was covered with a piece of cloth, and when the cloth was removed the next morning, people who had gathered to pay homage to their great Guru were surprised to find beneath the cloth only a heap of choicest fresh flowers.

Nanak was full of love and he preached God's love for all. Being pure and humble, he preached purity and humility. Nanak was an apostle of peace and an embodiment of equality. His message to humanity is that God is the Lord of all.

Beliefs

The main theme of Guru Nanak's message is that God is one, God is love, and God is unity. God resides everywhere. In the eyes of God, all human beings are equal. Devotion to God, service to mankind—irrespective of caste, color, or creed—is the fundamental duty of everyone.

Chief Scripture

The collection of most of the teachings of Guru Nanak is called Japji Sahib, and the famous Guru Granth Sahib also embodies the teachings.

Guru Granth Sahib incorporates hymns of spiritually accomplished scholars. Sikhism being a relatively young religion was surrounded by a large Hindu community. Therefore, it has, to some extent, interacted with Hindusim and Hindu culture has socially influenced the Sikh community and vice versa. Sikhism is however, a distinct and separate religion.

Sikhism asserts its own unique cannons, prophets, places of worship, traditions, ceremonies and institutions. The Sikh Gurus devised unique and distinct ceremonies for birth, childhood, marriage and death. All these ceremonies reflect the Sikh devotion to one Supreme Being.

Guru Gobind Singh created Khalsa, the saint-soldier and gave Sikhs their unique baptism ceremony of Amrit and a unique code of conduct. Sikhism, with its unique concept of God, its scriptures, traditions and history, is a unique and distinctive religion.

No description of Sikhism will be complete without reference to the rise of Sikh militarism and the founding of the Khalsa. When Sikhism began to draw large followers, the then Muslim rulers of India began to consider them as a threat to their religion. Guru Arjan was imprisoned and tortured by the Moghul governor and his death gave a strong impetus to Sikhs to unite in self-defense. Arjan's son Hargobind succeeded as Guru and he appeared dressed as a warrior. He put on two swords, which symbolized spiritual power of the Guru and earthly power. Together, the two swords came to symbolize the journey of the heavenly and earthly aspects of Sikhism. It was Guru Gobind Singh, who founded the Khalsa, meaning the "pure one." Members of the Khalsa were ready to die for their faith. They swore to fight fearlessly and to give their lives willingly for their faith.

Sikh Philosophy

Besides the absolute value of the Divine itself, the Sikh Value system comprises the following:

1. Physio-economic values—A Sikh treats his or her body as the sacred abode of the Spirit. There is no place for austerities and torturing of the body as a way of salvation.
2. Intellectual Values—Knowledge and wisdom are the key concepts. Reason plays the vital role and truth is the highest value to be cherished by everybody at all times.
3. Aesthetic Values—Loving devotion to the Lord, generating ecstatic

state of bliss leading to the enjoyment of the grandeur and beauty of His creation.

4. Ethical Values—Virtue as reflected in valor, purity of conduct, realization of the Divine presence in all human beings and service of the mankind.
5. Spiritual Values—Mukti and Nirvana in Sikhism is emancipation in life through Divine Grace.

The three pillars of the Sikh Way of Life are as follows:

1. Meditation on God—Sikhs should concentrate their minds on God. They should reflect on God's virtues, such as love, benevolence, and kindness and should practice to inculcate such virtues in their character. Meditate on the form of the Master and take his word as gospel truth. The Master is the Infinite, bow unto Him. He, who is saturated in the true Master, the Word personified, gains a seat of honor in His presence.
2. Earning with hard labor—Every Sikh should earn his or her livelihood by honest means. They should not be parasites on society and should not be idle. All Sikhs should work hard and utilize their earnings for the betterment of the family and those who are needy.
3. Sharing earning with the needy—The recitation of Nam helps the faithful to realize that they are a member of the human brotherhood. This creates feelings of kindness and love for those who need help. It is essential that people share their earnings with the less fortunate. According to the teachings of the Guru, it is one's duty to help the old, sick, and the poor. Whatever one shares with others must be done out of a sense of responsibility and not out of pride or arrogance.

Worshipping the Eternal God

Guru Nanak advised all his followers to worship only the one almighty God, by thinking of Him and by believing in the brotherhood of mankind. According to Nanak, there is no place where God does not exist. Worship of God is accomplished by reading the scriptures, prayers and meditation.

Understanding Gurbani

Sikhs are required to regularly read and understand the Gurbani (any composition of the Gurus) written within the Guru Grant. The daily recitation of hymns makes the mind pure and free of anger, lust, and greed. The hymn encourages the reader to develop good character. The Sikhs accept the word of the Guru as their guide.

Working and Wishing Well for All of Humanity

The importance that Sikhs attach to working and wishing well for others can be seen in the prayer: "O God, in Your name, shower Your blessings on everyone." In other words, Sikhs pray not only for themselves alone but also for all of humanity.

Maintaining Ethical Behavior

For Sikhs, lying, cheating, drinking alcohol, stealing, etc. are forbidden. They should not commit adultery, and everyone should show respect for women.

Accepting the Will of God

Sikhs believe that all good things are gifts from God. God has given life, an expression of His Will. Sikhs believe that everything happens according to God's will. Sikhism upholds war against oppression and aggression

God

God is one. God is love. God is unity. Though God is one, He has innumerable forms. He is the Creator of everything in this world, and He Himself takes the human form. He is without any kind of fear. Since God is love, He has no enemy. He is beyond death, and he is free from rebirths.

There is only One Being, who is the Creator and the uncaused Cause of all. He has created the whole universe through His ever-active will, which is diffused throughout. You are beyond finiteness. Being finite, we praise You in finite terms. We can never know or understand how great You are.

Whoever knows the mystery expressed by the numeral One, he becomes one with Him. In order to achieve Him, one must make His will as his own. The Absolute is wordless, imageless and nameless. When it came into being, it was called Word or Sabad, which is the cause of all creation

He who can give himself up to His supreme will definitely achieve his goal. No other action counts in achieving this objective. The Divine will is revealed unto man by communion with the Holy Sabad—the Divine Word. Whosoever searches for joy eternal, he should seek that in the all-pervading spirit.

The creation and the ultimate dissolution of the universe is caused through the Word. Further, through the Word, it takes its existence anew. The whole world is stuck deep in misery and pleasure. All actions are directed by assertion of egoism. Superstition cannot be removed or egoism ended, unless and until one is in communion with the Word or Sabad.

One cannot fully understand Him through reason, even if he reasoned for ages. One cannot achieve inner peace by outward silence, even if one sat dumb for ages. One can neither attain contentment with all the riches of the world, nor reach Him with all mental ability and skill. One should know that all things are manifestations of His will. His will is beyond description and by His will is matter quickened into life.

Teachings of Sikhism

The most distinctive character and the fundamental concept of Sikhism is its doctrine of the Guru-disciple relationship. In Hinduism, a spiritual seeker who wishes to attain liberation has to seek a Guru for proper instructions and guidance. The Guru is one who has a personal sense of enlightenment and a conviction that he has been commissioned by God to guide aspirants to liberation. The Sikh concept of a Guru is far richer. The Primal Guru is God himself and is named in Sikh writings as Sat Guru, or True Preceptor.

The essence of God is beyond human comprehension, but God graciously communicates himself to humanity. He does this through his Word or his message of enlightenment. Thus, he manifests himself as a divine teacher or Sat Guru.

The ten Gurus of Sikhism were emphatic that God was the Guru and they were faithful messengers through whom his Word was revealed. Guru Nanak and his successors believed that Sabda, or Sound, was the manifestation of Brahman, which became coherent in the words that they uttered. The tenth Guru installed the Adi Granth as Guru, which affirmed the original doctrine that Guruship belonged to the divine author.

The central theme of Guru Nanak's teachings is that God is a personal God, the divine Guru and the spiritual teacher. Anyone, who becomes aware of the inner activity of God as Guru and responds to that voice by living in accordance with the teachings of Guru Granth Sahib, attains spiritual liberation in this very life.

Corporate worship as well as individual meditation are the means of achieving God-realization. Sikhism places great importance upon its followers becoming god-oriented. In serving one's fellow men, one obeys God. One should lead a pure spiritual life untainted by lust, covetousness, attachment, anger, and pride. The duties of a Sikh have been summed up in three phases: The first is to keep God's name in the mind all the time. The second is to earn a living by honest means. The third is to give to charity. Service on behalf of the community is another highly praised virtue.

His Will

By His will is greatness obtained. By His will only are some born high and some others low. By His will are the joys and sorrows of mankind ordained. By His will and grace do the devoted and the pious obtain salvation. By His will, the impious undergo endless transmigration. Everything exists under His will only.

If one is attuned with His will, he will be completely freed from egoism. Some sing His greatness, but according to the power bestowed upon them. Some sing of His bounties, taking them as His signs. Some others sing of Him as incomprehensible.

Some sing of Him as transmuting dust unto life and life unto dust again. Some others sing of Him as the Creator and Destroyer and the Giver of life and the Withdrawer of life. Some sing of Him as at once being the nearest and the most distant. There is no end to His description. Innumerable have tried in vain to describe Him. He stands beyond all description.

The recipient of His bounty may tire of His bounty, which is untiring. Mankind has fed upon it ages upon ages. His will directs the entire world and yet, He dwells beyond concern or care.

True is the Lord and true is His holy Word or sabad. His love is boundless and infinite. Men and women who pray for His gifts are readily granted their wishes untiringly by Him. When everything in this universe belongs to Him, what can we offer at His feet and what can we say to win His love?

In the early hour of the dawn, when everything is calm and quiet, be in communion with the Divine Word. It is also the right time to meditate on His glory.

Our present birth is the fruit of our past actions. Liberation or salvation can come only with His grace. The Lord can never be established nor created. The formless One is limitlessly complete in Himself.

Those who worship Him are honored. Let us sing of the treasure house of all virtues. With a heart overflowing with pure love and devotion, let us sing of Him and hold communion with the Word. All our sorrows and sufferings will then come to an end and our hearts will be filled with bliss.

The Master is the song eternal or Word personified. He is the Vedas and scriptures. He is Divinity. He is Siva. He is Vishnu. He is Brahma and He is their consorts Parvati, Lakshmi, and Saraswati.

The greatness of the Master can never be described by oral eloquence.

My Master has taught me that He is the Lord of everything in the universe. I can never forget Him. No one can get salvation without His grace, regardless of karmas.

Glory of God

One can discover untold spiritual wealth within oneself, if one abides by the teachings of one's Master. Following the teachings of the Master and leading a pure life will unfold spiritual riches within oneself.

If a man could extend his life by eight or ten times, if he were known throughout the planes of creation and everyone followed him and if everyone praised him to the skies; all these will have no real value at all, if God's eye does not look kindly upon him.

Without God's goodwill, he will be reckoned as the meanest worm among worms and sinners will charge him with sins. God bestows virtues on those who lack them and adds to the store of the virtuous. But there is no one that can bestow anything upon Him. He, the Lord, is the only doer and there is no one other than He.

May my ignorant mind always dwell on Him, by whose grace only all your works are accomplished. Always and ever keep His presence in your mind. Only through His grace can you find the Truth. You must attune yourself to Him.

One should remember Him at all times, whether day or night. By His grace, you are cast among the noble kind. By His grace, you are enabled to keep your honor. Let us sing of His glory with a heart full of loving devotion.

All your attempts to describe His glory will be in vain. He alone knows His greatness. He alone knows Himself. His devotees praise Him, yet they never get full knowledge of the Infinite. Like rivers flowing into the ocean, they know not the depths therein. Even great kings and emperors with untold wealth and vast empire, cannot compare with an ant filled with the love of God.

Endless are His praises, His works, His gifts, His vision and His inspiration. Endless and beyond understanding is His purpose. His benevolence is manifold and no one can record it. He is the giver of all, expecting nothing in return.

Many are the warriors who are beggars at His door. Many are those, who decry Him after receiving and misusing His gifts. Many are the fools, who eat and enjoy without thinking of Him, who is the giver of all.

His generosity and mercy are peerless. His devotees singing His praise have sunk in silence. And so have the Vedas, the scriptures and the learned. Countless speak of Him and countless arc about to make an attempt. Countless have departed while singing of Him. Still He remains indescribable.

He is the supreme Master and does what He wishes. He is the King of Kings and the Almighty Lord. He is Truth and Reality. In the past, He was Truth and Reality. At present, He is still Truth and Reality. In future also, He will be Truth and Reality.

Sabad or Word

One can attain the status of a saint or a man of supernatural powers or a Muslim divine or a Yogi or a God, by communion with the Word or Sabad. By communion with the Word, one can understand the mysteries of the earth and the heavens, as well as the earthly regions, the heavenly pleasures and the netherworlds.

By communion with the Word, one can escape unscathed through the portals of death. One can attain the divine powers of Siva, Brahma and Indra by communion with the Word. One can win respect and esteem from all irrespective of one's past.

The Word washes away all sins, sorrows and sufferings and one lives in perpetual peace and ecstasy. The Word will guide one in the spiritual path and help him to safely cross the ocean of matter. By communion with the Word, one can develop yogic insight. With the mysteries of life and self, all revealed, one can then acquire the true import of the scriptures and the Vedas.

By communion with the Word, one becomes the abode of truth, contentment and true knowledge. He will also get the fruit of ablution at sixty places of pilgrimage. He becomes the abode of all virtues and a true spiritual king.

By communion with the Word, the spiritually blind or the ignorant find their way to realization and cross beyond the limitless ocean of illusory matter. By constant practice of the Word, one gets into universal consciousness. He then develops clear vision, understanding, clairvoyance and trans-vision of the entire creation.

By constant practice of the Word, one is freed from all the pain, sorrow and suffering and he does not enter the abode of the God of death. Such is the great power of Word, but only few know about it.

By communion with the Word, one not only saves oneself, but saves all his kith and kin and leads them to freedom. Having saved himself, he can guide many others to freedom. Thus the Word will save anyone, who can practice it.

By communion with the Word, one is freed from all desires and temptations of the world. He escapes from the wheel of transmigration and finally attains salvation.

Word or sabad is the proverbial bull that is harmoniously sustaining the creation. Whoever knows and realizes this verily understands the Truth. It is only the Word that is carrying the crushing burden of the entire creation. No other power can carry such a heavy load. Only the power of the divine Word can support it.

Guru

Guru or Spiritual Master occupies a very unique, exalted and important place in Sikhism. Guru is the most dominant theme in Sikhism. All the Gurus of Sikhism were emphatic that God was guru and Gurus were faithful messengers through whom His Word was revealed.

Everyone chants the name of the Lord. But merely uttering God's name without any sincerity and devotion will not enable them to realize Him. But, when through the Guru's grace the Lord gets enshrined in the heart, one gathers fruit.

Within your home is the treasure. By the Guru's grace, you can attain it and the door opens unto you. Guru was the only one in the beginning and Guru will be in the end. The sublime, the transcendent, the yonder of the yond God, that Guru has Nanak met.

O my friend, my Guru, illumine my heart with the Lord's name. It is your light that lights all hearts, through the Guru's wisdom. The gems, the jewels, the rubies are in the mind. If one were to find and listen to the Guru's call, "it is He who gives to each. On Him, on Him, let me call. Life wears out each day and each night. So go and call on the Guru and fulfill your destiny.

He is a true preceptor who shows the real home within the temple of the body, where five different sound currents are reverberating, and gives a clue to the Holy name. Serve the true Guru with single-minded devotion, infinite love and dedication. You should know that the true Guru is the Holiest of the Holies. He will fulfill all the desires of your heart and you gather that blessings, the fruits that your heart longs for.

Let us all recite the name of God in the company of the holy men. The Lord's name is the ocean of peace. Through the grace of the Guru only can one attain Him. Dwell on Him day and night, so that you merge imperceptibly in His name.

All repeat the name of god monotonously. They cannot fully understand or fathom the mystery of it. If through the favor of a Guru, it gets engrained in the mind, then and then only one reaps the fruit thereof.

Prayers

Prayers play a very important part in the lives of Sikhs. Sikhism lays great stress on prayers. In all the gurudwaras (places of worship) around the world, one can see devout Sikhs offering prayers. There are five prayers, five times for prayers and five names of them. The first should be truth. The teaching of all Gurus revolve around the need for each Sikh to find out the eternal Truth. The second is what is right. The third is charity in God's name. The fourth is good intention and the fifth is the praise and glory of God.

Like the black bee, I crave day and night for the honey of the Lotus feet. Grant Nanak, the nectar of Your mercy, Lord, that he may merge in Your name. I am powerless to describe what Your excellence is. Sacrificed am I, a myriad times to You and that which pleases You is the only good done.

I beseech You, O true Guru, the true being, God's own to take pity and awaken the name in us. We, the humble and the lowly have sought refuge Your refuge and we request your blessing in the form of awakening the name in us.

I am an ignorant wretch. I have neither chastity nor truth nor wisdom in life. Nanak, therefore seeks humbly the refuge of those who forget You not. I have impurities attached to my name. But I surrender to you, O Lord and may You cover my shame.

We, the meek and humble and the lowly belong to You only, O Lord. Please save us, You highest of the high. Your name is our only mainstay and in Your name lies our peace and happiness.

O Lord, You are the true Master. The entire universe overflows with Your creation. The lowliest of the low born, Nanak, seeks their company. The friendship of the great is in vain, for where the weak are cared for, there your mercy literally rains.

Keep me Lord, as You will, for I have no one else to go but You. I seek to meditate on You, my Lord, every moment of my life. And the more You the Lord come unto us, the more the Guru's Word tastes nectar-sweet. Yours is the mind. Yours is the body. You are my Master. Please rid me of my ego and merge me in You.

I stand on the wayside and ask the travelers and wayfarers to show me the way to my Lord. I follow the footsteps of those, who have enjoyed the love of my God. I beseech them and pray to them. I seek to meet my love, O brothers, take me to my Master.

Nanak says that fortune smiles on them to whom the light of the Word is revealed. Save them all, my Lord in Your mercy. For without You, there is no one to protect them from the tyranny of the God of death. Let Nanak not forsake Your name. Have Your mercy on him, O Lord.

Meet me, O life of my life, so that I may sing Your praises in the society of saints. O the Master of Nanak, take pity and permeate his body and mind. O Lord, give me the mind that will never forget You. Give me the wisdom, O Lord, so that I can meditate on You all the time and praise You with every breath.

Spiritual Gems

Day by day, your life is getting shorter and shorter. So earn here and now the profit of God's name. You will then abide in happiness in the next world. And find an eternal home. Then there will be no more return to this world.

Just as fragrance abides in the flower and reflection is within the mirror, so does Your Lord abide within you. Having known this why do you go on searching for Him without?

The ray has merged in the sun and the wave has merged in the sea. The light has merged in the Light and man is fulfilled. That which you practice day and night has been writ on your forehead. You cannot hide your shame from Him, when He the seer sees all within.

If compassion is your mosque, faith your prayer mat, honest living your Koran and contentment your fast, then you are verily a true Muslim. Let good deeds be your kaaba, truth your Prophet and your prayer be for God's grace. Let the rosary be His will and God will keep your honor.

The path of one who believes is full of honor. He lives with honor and leaves with honor. He walks straight on the highways and does not wander in the by-ways. He is duty bound to Dharma. When the hands and feet are dirty and soiled, water washes them clean and pure. When the clothes are dirty and spoiled, soap renders them clean. When the mind is polluted by sin and shame, it is made clean and pure by the love of Your name.

With great difficulty, you have obtained this precious human birth from God. Now is the time for you to attain to your Lord. No other work is more important than attaining your God. Join the society of the holy men and utter the divine Lord's name. Dedicate yourself to swim across the ocean of life. Life is fast ebbing away and you have not assembled yourself nor taken to meditation. You do not know what it is to serve the holy and your King, the Lord God.

We cannot escape the inner fire of desire, lust, attachment etc by resorting to countless outward rites and rituals. He, who wants to seek and attain joy eternal, he should seek that in the all-pervading spirit. The house that you have to attain after death, reach there by withdrawing your spirit from the body in your lifetime.

Live uncontaminated in the world like a lotus flower with its head well above the muddy pool or like a sea fowl that springs into air with the wind, unaffected by water. A man of realization alone can know a realized soul.

The air is master, the water the father and the earth the mother. Day and night are the two nurses in whose lap the whole world is at play. Our actions, whether good or evil, will be brought before his court. Only by our deeds shall we move higher or be cast into the depths.

The enjoyment of that food is evil, if it gives pain to the body and produces evil thoughts in the mind. The wearing of that dress is evil, if it gives pain to the body and produces evil thoughts in the mind. They are not called pure, who only wash their bodies. They are pure, who enshrine the Lord in their hearts.

The impurity of the heart is greed and impurity of the tongue is falsehood. The impurity of the eyes is gazing on another's wealth and the beauty of another's wife. The impurity of the ear is listening to scandal and slander.

If I read through millions of pages and know their mysterious intent and even if I write with an ocean of ink with the speed of winds, still it will be impossible for me to value You and Your name and glory.

The Guru Granth

The Guru Granth is the holiest of the holy Sikh scriptures. It plays an important part in the daily life of a Sikh. Sikh historians have recorded the passing of the holy authority of Guru from Gobind Singh to the Guru Granth. When Guru Gobind Singh lay dying, he called for the Guru Granth. When his disciples brought the holy book, the Guru placed a coin and a coconut before it. He then commanded all his disciples and others who were gathered to acknowledge the Guru Granth as the Guru in his place. Thus, the Guru Granth became the eternal Guru for the Sikh people. From then on, Sikhs revered the Guru Granth as the Divine Word and as the physical representative of the Guru. Thus the Guru Granth is acknowledged as the visible manifestation of the body of the Gurus.

The Guru Granth opens with the numeral One. It is the first word of the first statement of Guru Nanak: *Ikk Oan Kar,* which literally means "one reality is" or "there is one Being." *Ikk Oan Kar* (IKK) is both a verbal and a visual statement. IKK, the concept of Oneness, was central to Nanak's vision and the focus of his message. Further, instead of writing the word IKK to express Oneness, Nanak used the numeral One to express the Ultimate Reality. The numeral One transcended barriers of language and was visible to all, besides being simple and universal.

The second word, OAN, or Reality, is equivalent to the Sanskrit OM. The symbol for the third word, KAR, symbolizes the eternal nature of the One that is without beginning or end. These first three words, *Ikk Oan Kar*, are the fundamental affirmation of Sikhism. The Guru Granth describes the Reality, its relation to the world and to the people of the world. The Guru Granth does not contain historical narratives or biographical details like the Christian Bible. It is without dogmas and does not stipulate a code of behavior or list any obligations. Guru Granth is composed mainly of spiritually exalted poetry, and its central theme is the individual longing for the Divine or Ultimate Reality.

The Guru Granth is an invitation to all the followers of Sikhism to participate in its offerings of the "three delicacies" of truth, contentment, and contemplation. Through these three delicacies, Sikhs may understand the essence of the universe, satisfy their spiritual appetite, and calm their restless minds and spirit in contemplation. Guru Granth is the spiritual authority for all Sikhs, and it is treated with the highest respect and veneration. Sikhs open the Guru Granth at dawn, and after dusk it is closed. It is read in times of uncertainty and unrest, or in times of celebrations and hope.

Sikh Thought

The Holy Guru Granth begins with a short passage called the Mul Mantra..The Mul Mantra is a portion of a special prayer of extraordinary beauty and power. It is rhythmic and brief. In short, the Mul Mantra expresses the Sikh belief in the nature of being and reality and the relationship of the individual to the world. This passage states the fundamental and essential creed as well as the basic belief of Sikhism

The first three words of the Mul Mantra represent the most fundamental belief of Sikhism. These three words, *Ikk Oan Kar* , mean "there is One Being." The first word of the Mul Mantra is written as the numeral One. It proclaims the existence and total Oneness of the Ultimate Reality. This Ultimate Reality is defined in the Mul Mantra as without form or gender and not limited by space or time. Further, it has no shape, no color, and no beginning or end. It fears nothing and is at odds with nothing. In this respect, Sikhism differs from Hinduism, since it rejects the theory of divine incarnation. Further, in focusing on the One, Sikhism rejects the many gods and goddesses of Hinduism.

Sikh scripture accepts and affirms the various ways of reaching the Ultimate Reality or the One. Nanak advised the Hindus and Muslims that they should be authentic Hindus and Muslims. The One is common to all people of all faiths and cultures. Arjan Singh, the fifth Guru, declared that, underneath, all true religions are the same, and some call it Rama, some call it Khuda, some worship it as Vishnu, and some as Allah. By stressing the basic similarity of the Hindu and Islamic traditions, Sikh Gurus tried to create understanding and goodwill their divided society. According to the Sikh Gurus, the Ultimate Reality is the same for all people.

The Oneness of Reality is the bedrock of Sikhism. Consequently, scholars term Sikhism as a monotheistic religion. Yet to call Sikhism monotheistic misses a basic aspect of Nanak's vision. Sikhism does not subscribe to a belief in a personal God. The Sikh Reality is indeed One, but it has no image or form. For Nanak, the One is the experience of the One Being or the Ultimate Reality.

The second line of the Mul Mantra, namely, *Sat Nam*, means "truth is the name." The first stanza of the Guru Granth's first hymn explains as follows: "Truth, it has been from timeless eternity. Truth, it has been in the present and Truth, it shall be forever. Truth to the Sikhs is a way of living. In Sikh thought, grace refers to the divine glance of favor. Everyone and everything exist within the orbit of divine vision. Sikhs believe that after death, they will be reborn into the world and the good deeds in the present life will enable them to achieve a better future life."

Sikh Ethics

Guru Nanak defined Sikh ethics as a code of behavior: "Truth is higher than all, but higher still is true living." The infinite One is termed as Truth in the Mul Mantra. Truth is regarded as the highest Reality. It is not enough to know the Truth; one should live Truth as well. Sikhism places great importance on human life. In Sikhism, every human life is considered precious, and all forms of life deserve utmost respect. All human beings have emanated from the One, and consequently, all have within them a spark of the Divine. The main objective of the Sikh moral code is to reach out to others and help them experience for themselves that divine spark.

According to Sikhism, egotism is the root cause of all human suffering, sorrow, and misery. The ego in a person causes him to view everything as "I," "mine," and "me." It is the ego in a person that results in pride, anger, and arrogance. Constant focus and concentration on I, mine, and me separates an individual from others as well as from the Universal One. An egotistical person is selfish; he lives only for himself. His life is marked by malice, hatred, and ill feeling towards others and a mad craving for pomp and power. Such a person cannot experience the joy of the divine spark within him.

How can an egotistical person be enabled to experience the divine spark within? A simple formula—having faith and being full of love—can break the walls of ego. By listening to the Divine Word, a person can gain knowledge and wisdom, which will cause all suffering and sorrow to disappear. The sound of the Divine Name leads one to the ultimate goal of immortality.

The first step is having faith, which takes one to the spiritual path. According to Nanak, strong and sincere faith is the pathway to freedom. Having faith in the Divine Word frees one from the cycle of birth and death.

The next step is to be full of love. Love dissolves the individual ego and enables one to experience the joy of the divine spark within. Love purifies the soul. Love is an essential ingredient in Sikh ethics. It is the pathway to the Infinite One.

According to Nanak, there are five stages by which a person can attain the Ultimate Reality. These are the realms of duty, knowledge, art, grace, and truth.

Khalsa and the Five K's

The Khalsa was founded by Guru Gobind Singh to create a community of those who undertook to uphold the Sikh religion, its scriptures, and its values and to defend all those in need, irrespective of their caste, creed, or religion.

The Sikhs suffered severe persecution for many years. In order to face and overcome all these, Guru Gobind Singh, the last human Guru, gathered all the Sikhs at Anandpur, a town in Northern India. At this meeting, the Guru called for a man who was willing to die for his faith. One man came forward and went into a tent with the Guru. Then the Guru reappeared with his sword covered in blood. The Guru then called for another volunteer, and another man came forward and went into the tent with the Guru. Once again, the Guru came out with a bloody sword. One by one, five willing men came forward and met with their deaths in the tent. Finally, the Guru opened the tent for all those assembled to see, and all the five men were inside, alive.

This was the beginning of the Khalsa, the community of committed Sikhs who were willing to die to uphold the Sikh religion and defend the weak. The Guru also gave all male Sikhs the name Singh, meaning lion, and the name Kaur for women, meaning princess, thus abolishing all traces of a caste system.

The ritual of joining Khalsa is a private matter and is undertaken in the Gurudwara, a temple of the Sikhs, in the presence of close family members. The initiation ceremony is called Amrit Sanskar or Pahul. Five members of the Khalsa should be present, and each of them hands to the new member one of the five K's. The person joining the Khalsa vows to defend the faith; to serve others; to abstain from alcohol, tobacco, and drugs; and to pray regularly, morning and evening. He is then given sugar crystals and water, called Amrit, to drink, and then he says, "The Khalsa is of God, and the victory is to God." The Amrit is then sprinkled on his hair and eyes five times. Then the Mool Mantra is recited and prayers chanted.

The five K's, signs of faith, signify that the wearer is a full member of the Khalsa

1. Kesh—Uncut hair. Devout Sikhs do not cut their hair or beard at any time.
2. Kanga—A comb to keep the hair tidy.
3. Kara—A circular steel bangle symbolizing one God and one truth without beginning or end. The steel is a symbol of strength.
4. Kirpan—A small sword or dagger. This is to fight all injustice and oppression and to defend the weak and all those who are in need.
5. Kacchera—A short trouser or breeches dating from the times when men wore robes. The breeches signify readiness to ride into battle for the faith.

Khalsa is thus a very important aspect of Sikhism. It creates strong bonds of affinity among all the followers of Sikhism. Khalsa is unique and sets apart all Sikhs from others. Further, it creates a sense of pride and honor, as well as a joy in defending their faith and helping all the weak. To become a Khalsa is the aim of many followers of the faith.

Guru Nanak—Miracles

Guru Nanak came to the world with a message of peace, unity, love, and devotion to God at a time when there were fights between followers of different faiths. This great saint began to spend his time in meditation and spiritual practices and he preached the gospel of peace, brotherhood, unity of humanity, love, and sacrifice. Of Guru Nanak, Swami Vivekananda said, "Here it was that in later times the gentle Nanak preached his marvelous love for the world. Here it was that his broad heart was opened, and his arms stretched to embrace the whole world, not only of Hindus, but of Mohammedans too."

When one looks into the life and teachings of Guru Nanak, two miracles show the greatness and glory of the saint. There is a remarkable incident in connection with Guru Nanak's visit to the holy Muslim city of Mecca. At Mecca, Nanak was found sleeping with his feet towards the Kaaba. Now, Kaaba was a very sacred place for the Muslims, who prostrated themselves before it when performing their prayers, so Nanak's act was considered an outrage and sacrilege. A Muslim cleric, Rukan-ud-din, who observed this, was angry and annoyed, and he remarked, "Infidel! How dare you dishonor God's holy place by turning your feet towards him?" In his anger, he even kicked Nanak. To this, Guru Nanak gently replied, "I am tired. Please turn my feet in any direction where the place of God is not." On hearing this, Rukan-ud-din took hold of Nanak's feet angrily and moved them towards the opposite direction. Then a strange thing happened. The mosque also began to move. Rukan-ud-din was struck with wonder and disbelief. It was then his eyes were opened to a great truth: he recognized the glory and greatness of the great saint Guru Nanak.

Another miracle occurred when Guru Nanak visited Hassan Abdal in the Attock district in the North Western Frontier in 1520 A.D. When local Muslim saints became jealous of Guru Nanak's popularity and forbade him from getting water from the local spring on the top of the mountain, that spring is said to have dried up and a new spring arose at the bottom of the hill where Guru Nanak was staying. This further enraged one of the Muslim saints and he hurled a big rock from the top of the hill towards Guru Nanak; the rock stopped midstream and the impression of Guru Nanak's hand was etched on the rock. The impression of Nanak's hand on the rock exists even today. This is also the origin to the beautiful shrine by the side of the spring today, the "Punja Sahib".

The above two miracles of Gum Nanak show the spiritual greatness and glory of Guru Nanak. He was a reformer who attacked the corruption in society. He strongly protested against formalism and ritualism and carried the message of peace and love for everybody. He was very liberal in his views. He did not observe the rules of caste, and he tried his very best to remove the superstitions of the people. He preached purity, justice, goodness, and the love of God

Mystic Poems of Nanak

According to Guru Nanak, "The road to the abode of God is long and arduous and a spiritual aspirant should be dedicated and sincere in his efforts. There are no shortcuts and everyone must undergo the same discipline. Everyone should purify his or her mind through service to humanity and 'Nama Smarana'. Everyone must live according to the will of God without grumbling." How can we find God? According to Guru Nanak, there is one way, and that is to make God's will our own. Be in tune with the Infinite. There is no other way. The first stage in making the divine will our own is through prayer for divine grace. Guru Nanak said, "Approach God with perfect humility. Throw yourself on His Mercy. Give up pride, show and egoism. Beg for His kindness. Be prepared to die in the pursuit of His love and union with Him."

The beautiful composition of mystic poems uttered by Guru Nanak is contained in Japji (a collection of the teachings), which is sung by every Sikh at daybreak. The Sohila (a collection of hymns of Guru Nanak) contains the evening prayers. In the Japji, Guru Nanak gives a vivid and concise description of the stages through which everyone must pass in order to reach the final resting place or abode of eternal bliss. There are five stages, or Khandas. The first is called "Dharma Khand" or "Realm of Duty." Everyone must do this duty properly and tread the path of righteousness. Everyone will be judged according to his or her actions.

The next stage is "Gyan Khand" or "Realm of Knowledge," where the spirit of divine knowledge reigns. The aspirant does his duty with intense faith and sincerity. He has the knowledge now that only by doing his duty in a perfect manner, can he reach the abode of bliss or the goal of life.

The third stage is "Sharam Khand" or "Realm of Ecstasy." There is spiritual rapture here. There is beauty. The Dharma has become a part of one's own nature. It has become an ingrained habit. It is no more a mere matter of duty or knowledge.

The fourth stage is "Karam Khand" or 'The Realm of Power." The God of power rules over this realm. The aspirant acquires power. He becomes a mighty hero. He becomes invincible. The fear of death vanishes.

The fifth or the final stage is "Sach Khand" or "The Realm of Truth." The formless One reigns here. Here the aspirant becomes one with God. He has attained Godhead. He has transmuted himself into Divinity. He has attained the goal of his life. He has found his permanent resting place and now ends the arduous journey of the soul.

Guru Nanak again and again insists thus: " Realize your unity with all. Love God. Love God in man. Sing the love of God. Repeat God's Name. Sing His glory. Love God as the lotus loves water, as the Chatak loves rain, as the wife loves her husband. Make divine love thy pen and thy heart the writer. Open your heart to Him. Enter into communion with Him. Sink into His arms-and feel the divine embrace.

Guru Nanak gives a very beautiful summary of his teachings in one of his hymns as follows:

Love the saints of every faith,
Put away thy pride.
Remember the essence of religion
Is meekness and sympathy.
No fine clothes,
Not the yogi's garb and ashes,
Not the blowing of horns,
Not the shaven head,
Not long prayers,
Not recitations and torturing,
Not the acetic way,
But a life of goodness and purity
Amid the world's temptations.

Guru Nanak's Tapas, Meditation, and Wanderings

Guru Nanak practiced rigorous meditation in order to realize God. He was always in a deep meditative mood and, in fact, he was so much absorbed in meditation that he did not take care of his health. Nanak's parents thought that he was sick, so they sent for a doctor. Nanak said to the doctor,

> You have come to diagnose my ailment and prescribe medicine. You take my hand and feel the pulse. Poor ignorant doctor, you do not know that the pain is in my mind. O doctor! Go back to your house. I am under God-intoxication. Your medicine is of no use to me. Few know my disease. The Lord, who gave me this pain, will remove it. I feel the pain of separation from God. I feel the pain which death may inflict. O ignorant doctor! Do not give me any medicine. I feel the pain that my body will perish by disease. I forgot God and indulged in sensual pleasures. Then I had this pain. The wicked heart is punished. If a man repeats even a portion of the Name of the Lord, his body will become like gold and his soul will be rendered pure. All his pain and disease will be annihilated. Nanak will be saved by the true Name of the Lord. O physician! Go back to your house. Do not take my curse with you. Leave me alone now.

Nanak gave up food and drink for some time. He became wholly absorbed in divine contemplation. He observed perfect silence. He concealed himself in the forest for days at a time.

Nanak's Message of One Reality

Guru Nanak experienced the Ultimate Reality as being without any form and transcendent above all things. It has been recorded that, although Nanak did not actually see the Ultimate Reality in any concrete form, he heard the Divine Words. It was said that a cup of nectar appeared before Nanak, and he drank from it. Nanak's revelation was spectacular, but something that his followers can experience themselves.

According to what is known of Nanak's life history, when Nanak emerged from the river, where he had gone to take his bath, he pronounced the famous words that formed the strong pillars of the foundation of Sikhism. He said, "There is no Hindu, there is no Muslim." With these words, Nanak rejected all religious and sectarian distinctions among human beings. This statement, however, does not deny the variety and richness of different religious beliefs. In fact, it embraces them all and celebrates the shared values and beliefs of all humanity. The vision of the Ultimate Reality enabled Nanak to recognize the unity of society beyond the narrow concepts and categories such as Hindu, Christian, Muslim, Jew, or Buddhist. According to Guru Nanak, all the great religions of the world teach the one great truth: the devotion to the One Reality.

Guru Nanak taught this message of One Reality and the one fellowship of the entire humanity. Nanak traveled the length and breadth of India and to distant places such as the Middle East to spread the Divine Word. During his travels, Nanak met and discussed with the Hindus, Muslims, and Buddhists their scriptures and their religious philosophies, and he taught an inner way of reaching the Divine. Nanak advised people to discard all external rituals and ceremonies. According to Nanak, the most important thing was the firm belief in the One Reality.

The teachings of Guru Nanak attracted people from all sections of society, from different religions and different cultures. His love, compassion, liberal message, and advice, which he delivered simply and directly, captivated the hearts of one and all. Those who saw and heard his message of One Reality and later became his followers came to be known first as "sishyas," a Sanskrit word meaning disciples, and in the end came to be called Sikhs.

Nanak established three important elements of Sikh religious and social discipline. They are the Seva, the Langar, and the Sangat. These three elements were the most powerful factors that encouraged the Sikh values of equality, fellowship, and humility, and these in turn affirmed a sense of family hood. Seva meant giving voluntary labor in the service of the community. Seva is the highest ideal in Sikh ethics. By undertaking Seva, followers of Sikhism developed humility, overcame ego, and purified their body and mind. Langar is another vital element of Sikhism. It is concerned with community meals and the kitchen in which food is prepared. Community meals and the preparation of the meals ensured a spirit of service, understanding, and a sense of equality and family affinity. People sat in rows without any regard to caste, creed, race, or religion and ate the meals that they had all prepared. Such community meals communally prepared and eaten was a novel, bold, radical, and revolutionary thing in Nanak's time. Sangat is a mode of both spiritual and moral inspiration. According to Guru Nanak, through Sangat, one attains the rare treasure of the Divine Name.

Nanak traveled widely in India, visiting many holy places. He had debates with Hindu scholars and Muslim priests. Wherever he went, Nanak conveyed his message of love, unity and peace. He enjoined on all people to live righteously and with brotherly love. By interacting with Hindu and Muslim intellectuals and scholars, Nanak tried his best to unite Hindus and Muslims.

There is an interesting anecdote regarding Nanak's attempts to unite Hindus and Muslims. In one of his travels, Nanak halted at a place, which had many Muslim priests. On hearing about the arrival of Nanak, the Muslim priests sent Nanak a cup of milk filled to the brim. Nanak accepted the cup of milk and put inside some lumps of sugar and then placed a flower on the top and returned the cup of milk to the Muslim priest. When Nanak was questioned by one of his disciples as to why he did so, Nanak told him the significance of his action. He said that by sending him a cup of milk filled to the brim, the Muslim priests wanted to convey their message that the place was full of priests and there was no need or room for another religious leader like Nanak. By returning the cup of milk with the lumps of sugar and a flower on the top, Nanak wanted to tell the Muslim priests that he would mix with them like the lumps of sugar and predominate over them like the flower placed on the top of the cup. The Muslim priests then realized the greatness of Nanak and came to see him. They apologized for their action and sought his blessing. Nanak blessed them and gave them spiritual advice.

Chapter 9

Buddhism

An Introduction to Buddhism

Buddhism stands on three strong pillars, namely, on the founder Buddha, teachings of the Buddha and the Sangha, the order of Buddhist nuns and monks. Though Buddhism was born in India and cursorily known outside Asia, at the turn of the twentieth century, today, Buddhism is a great world religion. There are over four million Buddhists worldwide. Buddhism is the state religion of Thailand and Bhutan.

As prophesied, Siddhartha saw the three signs of suffering, namely, sickness, old age and death. These sufferings and sorrows touched his heart and he left his palace and all earthly possessions to seek mental peace and find a solution to the problems of suffering and sorrow. The Buddha spent several years to understand the cause of suffering and find the way to end it, before he reached enlightenment. He realized that wisdom could not be attained through self-mortification. At last, meditating under a tree near Gaya, in India, he attained illumination. Prince Siddhartha became the "Buddha," the fully awakened one, and the tree which sheltered him came to be known as the bodhi (enlightenment) tree.

Buddhists believe that we are tied to the cycle of births and deaths due to craving and desire and can be born again in many different forms. They believe that they can find a way to escape from this cycle, to be finally released from reincarnation to reach the highest peace and freedom, called Nirvana. The Buddha taught, "If you walk towards knowledge you will leave these rebirths behind. You do not go on becoming."

The Buddha's teachings are a guide for all his followers, who try to perfect the qualities of wisdom, kindness, compassion, and harmlessness. Eventually, they can be awakened to secure Nirvana.

The Buddha spoke of an Eightfold Path to enlightenment. This aspect is traditionally represented as an eight-spoked wheel. This Eightfold Path is a guide for all to live a life of love, kindness, compassion, and nonviolence. The Buddha decided to share his wisdom with others. His first sermon was preached in a deer park at Sarnath, near the ancient holy city of Varanasi.

Just before his death, when his favorite disciple, Anandaj, started weeping, the Buddha comforted him, saying, "All component things must dissolve. Buddha can only point the way. Become a lamp unto yourself, work out your own salvation diligently."

Besides being a great spiritual teacher and preacher, the Buddha was also a great social reformer. He revolted against oppressive social customs and laws and proclaimed his philosophy of liberty, equality, and fraternity for the common welfare of all. The Buddha can be credited as the creator of the virtues like liberty, tolerance, fellow-feeling, kindness, compassion, moral character, benevolence, service, and sacrifice.

The Buddha is not only the "Light of Asia" but the "Light of the world." His great contribution to the spiritual and cultural advancement is beyond measure. His life and teachings have greatly influenced the daily lives and aspirations of millions of people around the world.

Buddhism

Founder

Siddhartha Gautama (563–483 BC), who came to be known as Buddha, was the founder of Buddhism. Siddhartha was born to Queen Maya Devi and King Suddhodana at Lumbini, near Kapilavastu (present day Nepal) in India. He was named Siddhartha, meaning "he who has accomplished his purpose."

On Siddhartha's birth, Suddhodana invited a saint to see the royal child. When he saw Siddhartha, the saint said supernatural signs indicated that the child would bring deliverance to the whole world. The saint also warned the king that the child might renounce the world if he came across suffering, disease, the aged, or the dead. On hearing the prediction of his son's future, the king was very much worried. The prediction regarding Siddhartha's renunciation of the world alarmed the king so much that he got his son married at a young age and took all possible precautions to prevent his son from seeing any sick, aged, or dead person. Siddhartha was literally imprisoned in a pleasure garden with all kinds of enjoyments.

But the inevitable happened, and the saint's prophecy came true. Siddhartha was eager to see the city, and during one of his visits, he came across an old man, a diseased person, a dead body, and a sanyasin (a person who has renounced the world.) On seeing these, Siddhartha 's mind went into in turmoil. On enquiring, he was told that disease, old age, and death are the inevitable fate of all human beings. Siddhartha was very much perturbed, and he plunged into deep thoughts. On returning to the palace, he was told that his wife had given birth to a son, who was named Rahul. This news, however, made Siddhartha unhappy. He thought, it is bondage heaped on bondage, and he decided to renounce the palace, his family, and the world in order to discover the eternal truth.

Having taken a firm resolve, Siddhartha left his family behind one night and renounced everything. He became a recluse. He went to Uruvilva (Buddha-Gaya) and sat beneath a Bo tree. He started meditating and took a vow not to get up unless and until he attained enlightenment. After six years of introspection, meditation, and hard questioning, Siddhartha finally attained enlightenment, and he became Buddha, the Enlightened One. He then began preaching his new gospel.

Buddha delivered his first sermon at Saranath, near Benaras (Varanasi). He preached his great message for over forty-five years and established a well-organized order of Buddhist monks. He passed away at the age of eighty, on the day of the full moon, which came to be known as the thrice-blessed day, since on that day he had been born and he had also attained enlightenment.

Buddha had contributed greatly to the spiritual and cultural advancement of humanity. His life, his mission, and his teaching have influenced the daily lives and aspirations of millions around the world. The history of Buddhism extends over two and a half millennia and has exercised tremendous influence over most of Asia. No other religion has existed as a major influence in such a disparate culture for such a long time. More than half the world population lives in areas where Buddhism has at some time been a very dominant religious force.

Scriptures

The teachings of Buddha were passed on by word of mouth and were put down in writing several years after Buddha had passed away. The earliest Buddhist texts were written in Pali language. These are accepted by the Theravada School (the leading school of thought on Buddhism) as authentic. They comprise thirty one books organized into three collections called Tipitaka meaning three baskets or collections. These are:

1. The Vinayaka Pitaka, which deals with the rules and regulations for Buddhist monks and nuns.

2. The Sutta Pitaka, which contains the parables and sermons delivered by Buddha and his disciples
3. Abhidhamma Pitaka which consists of commentaries on Buddhist doctrine.

Beliefs

Buddhists share with Hinduism a belief in the cycle of reincarnation. When a person's body dies, the soul is reborn in another person or animal. Buddha believed there was a way out of this cycle of death and rebirth. He taught that a person should seek a state of detachment from worldly things and desires. Achieving this state, Nirvana, could bring about contentment and would be the end of the reincarnation cycle for the soul.

Buddha rejected extreme asceticism and extreme self-indulgence. He recommended a Middle Way. The Buddhist discipline is summarized in the Eightfold Path, which consists of right knowledge, right thought, right action, right livelihood, right effort, right mindfulness, right concentration, and right speech.

Origin

Buddhism dates from the time of prince Siddhartha, the Buddha, about 2500 years ago.

Practice

From early times, Buddhists established orders of monks. The monks withdrew from the everyday world and lived austere lives of meditation. They lived on alms contributed by lay Buddhists. Although many monks devoted their lives to their orders, others spent a year or two as monks before taking up responsibilities as layman. Early monks served as missionaries, carrying the message and tenets of Buddhism through all of Asia. Collective rituals play a smaller part in the life of a Buddhist, when compared to the rituals in the lives of Jews, Christians, or Muslims. Buddhist temples are primarily for individual meditation.

Schools and Sects

The most significant division in Buddhism is between the Theravada and Mahayana schools. Theravada Buddhism, which remains most influential in Sri Lanka, Burma, Thailand, and Cambodia, is most traditional in seeking to concentrate on the life and teachings of Buddha. Mahayana Buddhism, which became prominent in China and Japan, offers a more liberal interpretation of Buddhist teachings. It reveres other enlightened teachers, or Buddhas, and emphasizes the importance of each person's seeking to become a Bodhisattva, one who seeks Buddha hood through compassion and contemplation.

Another school of Buddhism is Tibetan Buddhism which emphasized the role and use of rituals, prayers, magic etc. With the aid of prayer beads and prayer wheels, Tibetan Buddhists repeat prayers thousands of times every day.

Truths and Precepts

The bedrock of Buddhism rests on the Four Noble Truths and Five Precepts. The Four Noble Truths explain the existence, cause, and ending of sorrow. The main emphasis of Buddhism is the removal of suffering and misery from this world. The Four Noble Truths are as follows:

1. Existence of sorrow;
2. Cause of sorrow;
3. Cessation of sorrow; and
4. Way that leads to the cessation of sorrow.

Next are the Five Precepts, which must be strictly followed by all Buddhists. They are as follows:

1. Abstain from killing.
2. Abstain from stealing.
3. Abstain from adultery.
4. Abstain from lying.
5. Abstain from liquor.

Besides the above important precepts, there are other precepts that Buddhists also strictly follow, below:

Do not kill.
Do not steal.
Do not commit adultery.
Do not tell lies.
Do not slander.
Do not speak harshly.
Do not engage in idle talk.
Do not covet others' property.

Do not show hatred.
Think righteously.
Open your mind to the eternal truth.
Practice righteousness at all times.

All Buddhists have to strictly observe and follow the above precepts in their day-to-day lives. They should also understand the significance of the Four Noble Truths. Once the aspirant understands the Four Nobel Truths, he will find eternal bliss.

Eightfold Path and Acts of Merit

Followers of Buddhism should walk in the noble Eightfold Path and practice the Acts of Merit. The Eightfold Path is made up of the following:

1. Right Understanding. This means we should be free from superstition, ignorance, and delusion. The mind should be filled with noble thoughts.
2. Right Thought. Our thoughts should be high, noble, and worthy of the intelligent.
3. Right Speech. The words uttered should be right and should generate love. The speech should be candid and truthful. Further, it should be full of kindness and compassion.
4. Right Actions. All our actions should be pure and honest. Right actions will ensure peace and harmony.
5. Right Livelihood. We should lead a clean and pure life. We should not cause any hurt or suffering to any living being. Further, our livelihood should not cause any harm or danger to any living being.
6. Right Effort. All our efforts should be correct. Right efforts can come only by practicing self-training and self-control.
7. Right Mindfulness. We should develop an active and watchful mind. By focusing the mind on the Four Noble Truths and Five Precepts, we can achieve right mindfulness.
8. Right Concentration. We should ensure that our mind does not wander after material things, which bring suffering and sorrow. By practicing daily meditation on the eternal truth, we can develop right concentration.

The Acts of Merit are as follows:

1. Give charity to all the deserving.
2. Strictly observe the precepts of morality.
3. Cultivate and develop good and noble thoughts.
4. Render service and reach out to others.
5. Honor and help your parents and elders.
6. Give a share of your merits to others.
7. Accept the merits that others give you.
8. Hear and practice the doctrine of righteousness.
9. Preach the doctrine of righteousness.
10. Learn from your faults and rectify them.

By practicing the above Eightfold Path and Acts of Merit, an aspirant can attain the bliss of spiritual life.

Setting the Wheel of Dharma in Motion

Buddha set the wheel of Dharma in motion at Sarnath, India, and he began to preach to the five Buddhist monks. A gist of the sermon given by the Buddha is given below:

He who has recognized the existence of suffering, the cause of suffering, the remedy of the suffering and the cessation of the suffering has really understood the Four Noble Truths. He will walk only in the right path.

Right views will be the torch that will light his way. Right aims will be his guide. Right words will be his dwelling place on the road of life. His gait will be straight, for it is the right behavior. His refreshments will be the right way of earning his honest livelihood. Right efforts will be his steps and right thought will be his very breath. Then peace will automatically follow in his footprints.

Whatsoever is originated will be dissolved again. All worry about the self is vain. The ego is like a mirage and all the trials and tribulations that touch it will pass away. They will disappear like a nightmare when the sleeper wakes up.

He who has awakened is freed from all pain and fear. He has then become Buddha. He knows the vanity of all his cares, his ambitions and his pains.

Happy is the man who has overcome all selfishness. Happy is the man who has attained peace and found the truth.

Truth is noble and sweet. It can free from evil. There is no savior in the world except truth. One should have confidence in truth, although he may not be able to comprehend it, although he may suppose its sweetness to be bitter and may be shrink from it at first. One should trust in truth.

Self is a fever. It is a transient vision and a dream. Truth is wholesome, sublime and ever lasting. There is no immortality except in truth. Truth alone abides forever.

A man who stands alone, having decided to obey the truth may be weak and slide back into his old ways. One should help each other and strengthen other's efforts. Be like brothers; in love, in holiness and in the zeal for the truth. Spread the truth and preach the doctrine in all quarters of the word, so that in the end all living creatures will be citizens of the kingdom of righteousness. Lead a holy life for emancipation from suffering and sorrow.

Compassion

The core of Buddhism is compassion. Buddha was compassion incarnate, and the teachings given below are based on kindness and compassion.

> "I look for no recompense—not even to be reborn in heaven—but I seek the welfare of men to bring back those who have strayed from the path of virtue, to enlighten those, that live in the night of error and to remove all the pain, misery and suffering from the world. I practice universal benevolence and compassion not for the sake of my own well-being but for my earnest desire to contribute to the happiness and well-being of all living beings. Do not harm or wound another being, whatsoever may be the cause of your suffering. Whoever hurts and harms living creatures and is devoid of sympathy and compassion for any living being, he will be known as an outcast. True religion consists in having goodwill towards all living beings. Cherish in your heart boundless goodwill to all living beings. The true signs of religion are love, goodwill, truthfulness, purity, nobility and kindness. All beings long for happiness. One must therefore extend compassion to all. Hatred never ceases by hatred. Only by love will hatred cease."

> "Patience is the highest form of asceticism. Buddha says that Nirvana is supreme. He is not a recluse who hurts or harms others. And he is not an ascetic who gives trouble to others. By inflicting pain on others, he who wishes his own happiness is not released from hatred. He gets himself entangled in hatred."

> "As the mother protects her child even at the risk of her life, so let him who has recognized the truth cultivate good-will among all beings. The charitable man is loved by everybody. His friendship is prized by all. In death, his heart is at perfect rest and full of happi-

ness, for he does not suffer from repentance. People do not generally understand that by giving away their food, they gain more strength. By bestowing clothing on others, they gain more beauty. By founding abode of purity and truth they acquire great treasures. A loving and compassionate man gives everything with reverence and his mind is free from hatred, envy and anger."

"A charitable man has found the path of liberation. He is like the person who plants a sapling which gives shade, flowers and fruits in future years. Even so is the result of charity, even so is the joy of him who helps the needy; even so is the great Nirvana."

"Immortality can be achieved only by continuous acts of kindness. Perfection is achieved by kindness, compassion and charity. What is necessary is a loving heart full of kindness and compassion."

Meditation

Meditation plays a very important part in the daily life of the Buddhist. For a Buddhist, the day begins with meditation on the realities of life and the search for the ultimate Truth. By practicing daily meditation, the aspirant attains awareness.

In Buddhism there are five types of meditation. The first and the most important is the meditation of love. In this meditation, you must adjust your heart to sincerely long for the happiness and welfare of all beings. You should also wish for the happiness of your enemies as well.

The second is the meditation of pity. In this, you should think of all living beings who are in pain and distress, vividly visualizing their sorrows and sufferings. This will ensure great compassion for them in your soul. This development of kindness and compassion leads to awareness.

The third meditation is the meditation of joy. In this, you think of the prosperity of all others and rejoice in their rejoicings. This purifies your mind and fills it with positive thoughts.

The fourth is the meditation on impurity. In this, you consider the evil consequences of corruption and the adverse effects of sin and diseases. You will then realize how trivial are the pleasures of the moment and how tragic are its consequences.

The fifth is the meditation on serenity. In this you rise above all earthly emotions such as love and hate, tyranny and oppression, poverty and wealth, anger and jealousy, and the like.

You then regard your own fate with impartial calmness and perfect equanimity. Developing a peaceful and tranquil mind is vital for a Buddhist.

There are four Dhyanas, or beatific visions. The first and foremost is seclusion. In seclusion, you must free your mind from all feelings of sensuality. The second is the development of a calm and serene mind full of joy and happiness. The third is to take delight in things that are spiritual—development of deep spiritualism is the first step for an aspirant. The fourth is the development of mind in perfect purity and peace. In such a state, the mind will be above all feelings of joy and sorrow. You should be sober and abandon all wrong practices, which will stultify your mind.

There are four means by which Riddhi, or domination of spirit over matter, is achieved These are:

1. Weeding away all the bad qualities that might arise in your mind;
2. Putting away all bad qualities that have arisen;
3. Producing goodness that has not yet come into existence; and
4. With sincerity and dedication searching for the truth till you find it.

Mind

Mind is a great powerhouse. It is the forerunner of all activities. Mind is the highest of all sensory powers. All relative concepts have their beginning in the mind. Development of a pure and peaceful mind is of utmost importance to a Buddhist.

Mind is the precursor of all perceptions. It is the most subtle of all the elements in the phenomenal world. All objectified consciousness has its origin in the mind. For one who speaks and acts with a pure mind, happiness will be with him all the time like a shadow.

Some people think that they are hated, mistrusted, misunderstood, and unappreciated. People who have such thoughts in their minds can never become free from the causes that inflict their destructiveness upon themselves.

He who has attained complete mastery over himself by self-control is the greatest conqueror. He is more powerful and greater than one who has defeated a thousand enemies.

One whose mind wanders in search of outward beauty and grandeur, who is unable to keep masterly control over his senses, who eats impure food, and who is by nature lazy and lacking in courage—ignorance, sorrow, and suffering will overtake him just as a storm will shatter and uproot a sapless tree.

Just as rainwater leaks into a house that is not protected with a perfect waterproof roof, attachment, hatred, and delusion will enter the mind that is averse to meditation.

He whose mind is totally freed from lust and hatred and who has discarded both good and evil, to such a vigilant one there is no fear. A heart that follows the path of ignorance does greater harm to man than his most hateful and dangerous enemy.

A wise man controls the flickering, fickle, and unsteady mind. The mind is hard to check and control, extremely subtle, swift. By self-control and discipline, one can control the mind. A controlled mind is conducive to peace and happiness. What neither a father, mother, nor any relative could do, a well-directed mind does, and this elevates one to great heights. For an awakened man, there is perfect peace and happiness.

Total abstention from evil, performance of good acts, and purification of the mind are the doctrine of the Buddha.

Sermon at Sarnath

Buddha gave his first sermon at Sarnath to five monks. A gist of is sermon is given below:

On should show respect to all elders. To show disrespect to one's father is wrong and to despise him is a sin.

Abstinence from food, going naked dressing in rough garment or other external acts will not cleanse a person, who is not free from delusion.

Reading the scriptures daily, making offerings to priests and sacrifices to God, acts of self-mortification will not cleanse a person, who is not free from delusion.

Anger, greed, drunkenness, bigotry, obstinacy, envy, deception, self-praise, abusing others and evil intentions constitute uncleanness. One should follow the middle path shown by Buddha.

A person who fills his lamp with water cannot dispel darkness. Similarly, a person who tries to light a fire with rotten and wet wood, will fail.

All mortifications are vain, painful and totally useless. All mortifications are in vain as long as the self continues to lust to worldly pleasures. But a person, in whom the self has become extinct, that person will be free from lust and worldly desires.

In a pond, water surrounds a lotus. The lotus floats on water, yet the petals of the lotus do not become wet.

Sensuality of all kinds is enervating and a sensual person is a slave to passion. Seeking pleasure is degrading.

To satisfy the basic necessities of life is not evil. It is one's duty to look after his body so as to remain healthy. Without a healthy body and a healthy mind, a person will not be able to trim the lamp of wisdom.

The Four Noble Truths

The Four Noble Truths are the core of Buddhism. They are as follows:

Noble Truth of Suffering—Birth is suffering. Decay is suffering. Death is suffering. Sorrow, pain, grief, and despair are suffering. Not getting one's desire is suffering. In fact, all aspects of life are suffering.

Noble Truth of the Origin of Suffering—It is desire or craving which gives rise to fresh rebirth. The craving rises and takes root wherever there are delightful and pleasurable things. The source for this craving is the eye, ear, nose, tongue, body and mind. Further visual objects such as sounds, smells, tastes, bodily impressions and mental objects being delightful and pleasurable also give rise to craving. Craving also takes place and take roots from consciousness, perceptions, thinking and reflections since these are delightful and pleasurable.

Noble Truth of the Extinction of Suffering—It is the total and complete renunciation of this craving, its sacrifice and abandonment; liberation and detachment from it. It is wiping away greed, lust, hate and extinction of delusion.

Noble Truth of the Path leading to the extinction of Suffering—It is the Noble Eightfold Path, the way in the way that leads to the extinction of suffering;

1. Right Understanding
2. Right Thought
3. Right Speech
4. Right Action
5. Right Livelihood
6. Right Effort
7. Right Mindfulness
8. Right Concentration

Understanding the above Four Noble Truths will lead to the extinction of all sorrow and sufferings. It will give the aspirant lasting peace of mind.

Permanent Treasure

Buddhism rests on spiritual values and the importance of understanding and strictly adhering to the Eightfold Path. Material wealth is transient and impermanent. The only things that will last forever are the good things we do in life, such as charity, service to other beings, practicing the doctrine of righteousness, and observing the precepts of morality.

For his future financial security, a man buries a treasure in a deep pit. He is happy and confident that his hidden treasure will be useful when he needs it most. It will be safe from robbers, and it will come in handy if he falls into debt. Further, the hidden treasure will be a boon in times of famine or if he meets with unexpected bad fortune.

But such a treasure hidden in anticipation of possible eventualities may not profit the owner of the treasure. First and foremost, there is every possibility of his forgetting where exactly he hid the treasure. His enemies may steal it. His own relatives may also take it when he is careless. So all material treasures, even if they are well hidden, are only transient.

But there is one treasure will last and never leave you. It is safe from robbery and will go on increasing in value all the time. Such a treasure is charity, goodness, restraint, self-control, and service to others. A man or woman can store up such a well-hidden treasure, which will remain with him or her at all times. Further, this treasure cannot be given to others or stolen by others. So a wise man should always do good and give charity. This real, permanent treasure will never leave him.

Spiritual Gems

For a spiritual aspirant, the Noble Eightfold Path will show the way. Anyone can attain the bliss of spiritual life by strictly following the Eightfold Path. We should not cling to wealth, as it will poison and erode the mind. He who does not cling to wealth but uses it for the good of others will be a blessing to his fellow beings

Whatever work we are doing, we should do it sincerely and diligently. It is not life or power that makes a man a slave, but the longing for and cleaving to life, wealth, and power. Buddha Dharma does not stipulate that a man should go to a forest or resign from the world unless he strongly feels he is called upon to do it. What is required is for us to free ourselves from the illusion of the self, to make our heart pure, give up the thirst for material comforts and pleasures and lead a life of righteousness. The good and evil deeds will follow us like a shadow.

When a tree is burning, birds cannot live on that tree. Similarly, where there is passion and lust, truth cannot dwell. Lust is a very grave danger to one and all. It is like a tidal wave that carries everyone away. No one can escape from it. But we can ride over it with the boat of wisdom, with reflection as the rudder. Since we cannot escape from the results of our deeds, we should practice only good and noble deeds.

We should lead a virtuous life and exercise reason. This life is transient, and we should, therefore, meditate deeply on the vanity and impermanence of all earthly things. Deep meditation leads to awareness.

It is a common for people to see the faults of others. They not only fail to see their own faults, but try to hide them. We should listen to everyone with patience. He who weighs both sides of any issue impartially is a sage. When there is any difference, both the parties should present their respective cases to the Sangha (Association of Buddhist monks). The Sangha will then study the case and work out a mutually acceptable agreement.

A word spoken in anger is a sharp sword. Coveting others' property is a deadly poison. Passion is like a fierce fire and it will burn everything. Ignorance is darkness. It is the cause of all suffering and pain. It causes ruin. Envy and selfishness destroys friendships. Hatred is a deadly disease, and Buddha is the best physician

No one should deceive or despise another. No one should cause harm to another due to anger or hatred or resentment. He who is free from pride, lust, and passion will have a peaceful and tranquil mind. Such a person will be perfectly happy, and he will wander in the right path.

He who is full of faith and virtue and possessed of honor, repute, and wealth will be respected and honored wherever he goes.

Just as a tree with firm roots, though cut down, takes root again and springs up, even so while craving is not completely rooted out, sorrows spring up again. Whoever overcomes craving will be freed from sorrow. We should make an honest effort to root out all craving. As the rust emanating from iron eats itself away, our bad deeds lead to sorrow.

Health is the greatest wealth. Contentment is the greatest treasure. It is the supreme bliss.

Success breeds hatred and envy. The defeated person lives in disappointment and pain. One who gives up success and failure will live happily and in peace.

There is no crime like hatred, and there is no fire like lust. There is no ill like the body, and there is no bliss greater than Nirvana.

Right Speech

Buddhism stresses right speech and gentleness, kindness, and compassion in speaking. Right speech means abstaining from lying, spreading gossip, bad manners, harsh language, and arrogant talk.

Some people avoid lying. They speak only the truth all the time, and they are wedded to the truth. They are reliable, trustworthy, honest, and worthy of confidence. Under no circumstance will they utter a falsehood, either for the sake of their own or another person's advantage. They will never resort to deception.

Some people consciously avoid spreading gossip, and abstain from it. They will never repeat what they have seen or heard, since doing so might lead to misunderstanding and enmity. In so doing, they try to unite those who are divided. They consciously avoid any gossip or scandal.

Some people avoid bad and harsh language. They speak only such words that are gentle, sweet, loving, and soothing to the ear. They utter kind and loving words that go to the very heart of a person. Such people are friendly, courteous, kind, compassionate, and agreeable to everyone.

Some people abstain from vain and arrogant talk. They speak at the right time, at the right place, and with the right words, in accordance with actual facts. They speak only what is good and useful; they speak of the laws and the discipline. Speech uttered at the right moment that is moderate and full of facts and sense is called the Right Speech.

While speaking to another, we should always utter kind and loving words in a sweet manner. We should be truthful, frank, gentle, and patient. The person spoken to should feel happy and relaxed in hearing our speech. Right Speech is one step in the Eightfold Path, and the person who understands this will have peace of mind and happiness.

Wisdom

Buddhism stresses the importance of wisdom. Buddha urged all his followers to use their wisdom, since it was the path that led to liberation.

Four actions are essential to developing wisdom: association with noble persons who have enlightenment; meditation; hearing Dharma; and practicing Dharma.

The four essential things that matter are suffering, the cause of suffering, liberation from suffering, and the way to attain liberation. Right understanding can help us to face and overcome all problems of life. To understand means to give up all longing for material things. Wisdom enables us to understand all problems clearly and take correct remedial action. With the cessation of suffering, we can experience total freedom. According to Buddha, this is the state of Nirvana.

The aim of a Buddhist is to know the enlightened way of being. Nothing in this world has the power to take away this enlightenment, and we can experience this enlightenment in this very life. Enlightenment liberates us from the problems of mundane existence and enables us to attain perfect wisdom. Enlightenment helps us to understand the cause of suffering and how to end it. The enlightened one respects and applies the ethics of meditation, service, wisdom, and not harming any living being.

Compassion and kindness for all living beings will overflow from the hearts of enlightened ones. Freed from anger, jealousy, and lust, their minds are pure. With pure minds, they experience much happiness and peace.

By following the teachings of Buddhism, Buddhists become wise. With wisdom guiding them in all their thoughts and actions, they display generosity of spirit, loving kindness and compassion for all living beings.

Loving-Kindness

Metta Sutta (loving-kindness in Pali, an ancient Indian language) is a quality attributed to Lord Buddha. It is a teaching about a fundamental aspect of Buddhism known as loving-kindness. All human beings have within them a latent wish for loving-kindness and the welfare of all beings. That is why we often find ourselves spontaneously reaching out to help others. The idea expressed in Metta Sutta with great dignity, simplicity, and beauty is that if we are humble and relinquish our own attachment, our natural loving-kindness will flow out to all beings without limitation.

The following teachings expound on the practice of loving-kindness: "May they be strong and upright, honest, of gentle speech and humility. May they be content and unburdened with self-control. May they be wise, not proud and devoid of attachment and desire for the possession of others. May they do nothing mean, vulgar or bad. May all beings be happy and may they live in joy, peace and safety. May all beings, whether strong or weak, tall or short, seen or unseen, near or far, born or yet to be born, live in happiness and peace. Let no one cheat another or despise any being and let no one cause any harm to another by anger, envy or hatred."

Just as the mother watches over her child with loving-kindness, willing to risk even her own life in order to protect her child, likewise should we all, with a boundless heart, cherish all living beings, suffusing the whole world with infinite, unobstructed loving-kindness. We should remain in such a mental state whether standing or walking, sitting or lying down, and during all our waking hours. This way of living in loving-kindness is the best in the world. Persons who achieve this state, unattached to speculations, views, and sexual desires, and with a clear vision, will attain Nirvana. He will never be reborn into the cycles of suffering.

The Enlightenment

The turning point in the life of Buddha came when he saw for the first time in his life a sick man, an old man, and a dead man. These sights caused him to agonize over the meaning of birth and death. He pondered over the question of why men were born only to suffer, become sick, grow old, and finally die. When he was deeply immersed in these thoughts, it was said that Buddha saw a holy man, or ascetic, who had renounced the world in pursuit of Truth. This made Gautama give up his family, his princely name and status, and all his earthly possessions and go in search of Truth. He sought answers from Hindu teachers and Gurus, but was not successful. He then pursued a course of meditation, fasting, and extreme self-denial. Still, spiritual peace or enlightenment eluded him. Finally, he came to the conclusion that his extreme course of self-denial was not helpful and he decided to follow the Middle Way, avoiding the extremes of lifestyles. Deciding that the answer to his question was to be found in his own consciousness, he sat in meditation under a Peepal tree. Resisting attacks and temptations by the devil Mara, he continued steadfast in his meditation until he transcended all knowledge and understanding and attained enlightenment.

In Buddhist terminology, Gautama became the Buddha—the Awakened or Enlightened. He had attained the ultimate goal, Nirvana, the state of perfect peace, inner bliss, and enlightenment, freed from all desire, sorrow, and suffering. He became known as Sakyamuni, and he often addressed himself as Tathagata (one who thus came to teach).

Different Buddhist sects hold different views on this matter. Some consider him strictly as a human being, who found the path to enlightenment for himself and who wanted to convey his experience to his followers. Some others consider him as the final one of a series of Buddhas to have come into the world to revive Dharma (Dhamma in Pali), the teaching or way of the Buddha. Still others view him as a bodhisattva, one who had attained enlightenment but postponed entering Nirvana in order to help others in their pursuit of enlightenment.

Having attained enlightenment, Buddha embarked to teach his newfound truth, his Dharma, to others. His first and the most important sermon was delivered in the city of Varanasi, in a deer park, to five monks, or bhikshus, or disciples. He taught them that to be saved, one should avoid both the course of sensual indulgence and that of asceticism and follow the

Middle Way. One should also understand and follow the Four Noble Truths, which can be summarized as follows;

1. All existence is suffering.
2. Suffering arises from desire or craving.
3. Cessation of desire means the end of suffering.
4. Cessation of desire is achieved by following the Eightfold Path and controlling one's conduct, thinking, and belief.

The sermon on the Middle Way and the Four Noble Truths embody the essence of the Enlightenment and is considered as the epitome of all the Buddha's teachings.

The Wheel of Dhamma

The Wheel of Dhamma was set in motion by Buddha at Sarnath. He began to preach to the five bhikshus, opening to them the gate of immortality and showing them the path and bliss to Nirvana. He said,

> "There are these two extremes, which are not to be indulged in by one who has gone forth. What are the two? That which is devoted to sensual pleasure with reference to sensual objects: base, vulgar, common, ignoble, unprofitable; and that which is devoted to self-affliction: painful, ignoble, unprofitable. Avoiding both of these extremes, the middle way realized by the Tathagata-producing vision, producing knowledge-leads to calm, to direct knowledge, to self-awakening, to unbinding"

> "And what is the middle way realized by the Tathagata, which producing vision, producing knowledge, leads to calm, to direct knowledge, to self-awakening, to unbinding? Precisely this Noble Eightfold path, namely, right view, right consideration, right speech, right undertaking, right livelihood, right effort, right mindfulness and right concentration. This is the middle way realized by the Tathagata—producing vision, producing knowledge leads to calm, to direct knowledge, to self-awakening, to unbinding."

> "Now this, bhikshus, is the absolute truth of stress: Birth is stressful, ageing is stressful, death is stressful; sorrow, lamentation, pain, grief and despair are all stressful; association with the un-beloved is stressful, separation from the loved is stressful, not getting what is

desired is stressful. In short, the five substances for sustenance are stressful."

"And this, monks, is the absolute truth of the origination of stress: the craving which makes for further becoming-accompanied by passion and delight, relishing now here and now there, i.e. craving for sensual pleasure, craving for becoming, craving for non-becoming. And this, monks, is the absolute truth of the stopping of stress: the remainder less fading and stopping, renunciation, relinquishment, release and letting go of that very craving."

"And this, monks, is the absolute truth of the way leading to the stopping of stress: precisely this Noble Eightfold Path, namely, right view, right consideration, right speech, right undertaking, right livelihood, right effort, right mindfulness and right concentration."

"Vision arose, insight arose, discernment arose, knowledge arose, illumination arose within me with regard to things never heard before" This is the absolute truth of stress'. This absolute truth of stress is to be comprehended'. 'This absolute truth of stress has been comprehended'. 'This is the absolute truth of the origination of stress. This absolute truth of the origination of stress is to be abandoned'. This absolute truth of the origination of stress has been abandoned. This is the absolute truth of the stopping of stress. This absolute truth of the stopping of stress is to be directly experienced'. This absolute truth of the stopping of stress has been directly experienced'. This is the absolute truth of the way leading to the stopping of stress. This absolute truth of the way leading to the stopping of stress is to be developed'. This absolute truth of the way leading to the stopping of stress has been developed"

"And, monks, as long as this knowledge and vision of mine, with its three rounds and twelve permutations concerning these four absolute truths as they actually are- was not pure. I did not claim to have directly awakened to the right self-awakening unexcelled in the cosmos with its deities, Mara and Gods, with its contemplatives and priests, its royalty and common folk. But as soon as this knowledge and vision of mine, with its three rounds and twelve permutations concerning these four absolute truths as they actually are-was truly pure, then I did claim to have directly awakened to the right self-awakening unexcelled in the cosmos with its deities, Maras and Gods, with its contemplatives and priests, its royalty and common folk. This knowledge and vision arose in me; "unprovoked is my release. This is the last birth. There is no further becoming"

These are what the Blessed One said to the five monks and a rapture thrilled through all the universe.

Tibetan Buddhism

Introduction to Tibetan Buddhism

Tibetan Buddhism is the body of Buddhist religious doctrine and institutions characteristic of Tibet and certain regions of the Himalayas. It is a brand of Buddhism, which spread from India to Tibet, sometime after Buddha had traveled to Eastern China from India. Buddhism became a major presence in Tibet towards the end of the eighth century CE. It was brought from India to Tibet at the invitation of the Tibetan King, Trisong Detsen, who invited two Buddhist masters to Tibet and had important Buddhist texts translated into Tibetan language.

The core of Tibetan Buddhism is tantric. Tantric systems transform the basic human passions for the purpose of spiritual development. It enables the aspirant to develop self control and self discipline.

Tibetan Buddhism

Tibetan Buddhism is a combination of Buddhism and the primitive beliefs and practices of the region. Tibetan Buddhism is also called Lamaism. This form of Buddhism is conspicuous by the prominent use of mantras, a series of syllables in long recitation. Tibetan Buddhism places great emphasis on the use of rituals, prayers, magic, and spirits in worship. Prayers are repeated thousands of times a day using prayer beads and prayer wheels. The complicated rituals and prayers of Tibetan Buddhism can be learned only under oral instructions by lamas or monastic leaders, among whom the most revered and respected are the Dalai Lama and the Panchan Lama. When a lama dies, a search is made for a child in whom the lama is said to have been reincarnated to be the next spiritual leader. It is estimated that about one-fifth of the Tibetan population are monks. In Tibet, lamas serve as teachers, doctors, land-owners, and political figures.

To fully understand the essence of Tibetan Buddhism, one should have good knowledge of Tibetan culture, belief, customs and traditions. Tibetans respect three Tibetan gurus or spiritual masters namely, Padma Sambhava, Atisha and Tsong Kapo as actual Buddhas. They are considered as Buddhas who propogated the teachings of Buddha in Tibet. Tibetan Buddhism is a culture that feels itself touched by the experience of real Buddhas living among them.

For Tibetans, Shakyamuni Buddha, the foremost Buddha of this world, is considered a divine being who is believed to have conquered death. Tibetans believe that Shakyamuni Buddha himself taught about the Universal Vehicle—which teaches that there are infinite number of Buddhas—as well as the Apocalyptic Vehicle and Monastic Vehicle. He believed that every human being can become a Buddha.

Padma Sambava was the earliest and most legendary Buddha in Tibet. It was said that he was born by miracle from a lotus blossom and was adopted as a Prince of Afghanistan. He visited Tibet by the end of the eighth century, and his impact in Tibet was tremendous and crucial. Without him, Buddhism would never have taken such deep and strong roots in Tibet. He conquered the minds of the kings and tribal chiefs through his great wisdom, and Buddhism spread far and wide in Tibet.

Another great Buddha was Atisha, who was born as a prince of the Zahar kingdom of the Pali dynasty. At the age of twenty-nine, after exhaustive Tantric studies, he renounced his throne and became a Buddhist monk. He later became a famous teacher of Buddhism in Tibet.

A later Buddha, Tsong Kappa, was born in AD 1357 in Tibet. He was a child prodigy and was recognized as the incarnation of the God of Wisdom. He spread teachings of wisdom by writing treatises. His life and teachings had a profound impact on Tibetan Buddhism.

Methods of Meditation

In Tibetan Buddhism, there are countless methods of meditation, but three are the most effective and easy to practice. The three methods are "watching" the breath, using an object, and reciting a prayer (or mantra).

Watching the breath is the most ancient and effective method, found in all schools of Tibetan Buddhism. In it, you concentrate and focus your attention lightly and mindfully on your breath. Breath is life, the fundamental expression of life. In Judaism, breath means the spirit of God. In Christianity, too, there is a link between the Holy Spirit and the breath. In Buddhism, breath is termed the "vehicle of the mind." This is because it is the breath that activates our mind. So, when you calm the mind by breath, you are taming and training the mind. When you meditate, breathe naturally and focus your awareness on the out-breath. When you breathe out, just flow out into the out-breath. Each time you breathe out, you are letting go and releasing all your grasping. Each time you breathe out and before you breathe in again, you will find a natural gap as the grasping dissolves. You must rest in that gap, in that open space. And when you breathe in, do not focus on the in-breath, but continue resting your mind in the gap that has opened up. Do not concentrate too much on the breath. Rather than watching the breath, identify with it as if you were becoming it. Thus, slowly the breath, the breather, and the breathing become one, and the duality and separation dissolve.

The method of using an object is to rest the mind lightly on an object. You can use an object of natural beauty or something that embodies the truth, such as the image of Buddha or Christ or your master. Just seeing such an object connects you to the inspiration and truth of your own nature.

Reciting a prayer is uniting the mind with the sound of a prayer. When you chant a prayer, you are charging your breath and energy with the energy of prayer and thereby working directly your mind and subtle body. There is an ancient Tibetan saying: "If the mind is not contrived, it is spontaneously blissful, just as water, when not agitated, is by nature crystal clear and transparent."

Understanding Death

Tibetan Buddhism stresses the importance of understanding death. To anyone born in this world, death is inevitable, a natural part of life. All of us will have to face death sooner or later; the only thing we cannot know is when, how, and where our death will take place.

There are two ways by which we can deal with death. We can choose to ignore it or to think of it clearly and dispassionately and try to reconcile to the inevitable, thereby minimizing the suffering and sorrow it can bring. But by no method can we overcome death. So long as we are alive, the prospect of death will always remain, staring us in the face. Since we cannot escape death, there is no point in unduly worrying about it. Death is like changing worn clothes for new ones. Since death is unpredictable, the only sensible thing to do is to understand it. The first and foremost thought for Buddhists is the desire to die a peaceful death.

The mind is full of thoughts, and if the thoughts are noble and spiritual, the mind automatically becomes tranquil. The state of our mind at the time of death can influence the quality of our next birth. Whatever object we are thinking of as we leave the body at the time of death, that and that alone we will attain. It is the predominant thought of our last moment that determines our future destiny. So if we can develop a virtuous state of mind fully absorbed in spiritualism, we can hope for a happy rebirth.

By helping others to die peacefully, we can prepare for our own death. Since the dying are helpless, we should endeavor to help them with tender, kind, loving words, removing their physical discomfort, and lessening their anxiety. We should assist them in every way to die in peace. A dying person, if he is spiritually minded, can be encouraged and inspired if we remind him of spiritual matters. Such kind and compassionate acts on our part will ensure a peaceful and relaxed attitude in the dying man's mind.

Commenting on death, a Tibetan monk said, "The birth of a man is the birth of his sorrow. The longer he lives, the more stupid he becomes, because his anxiety to avoid the unavoidable death becomes more and more acute. What bitterness. He lives for what is always out of reach. His thirst for survival in the future makes him incapable of living in the present."

Wisdom

According to Tibetan Buddhism, the three important tools of wisdom are listening and hearing, contemplation and reflection, and meditation and awareness. To discover the freedom of the wisdom of egolessness, we must listen to spiritual teachings constantly and repeatedly. Listening will keep reminding us of our hidden wisdom. Slowly but steadily, as we listen to the spiritual teachings, some passage, some words and insights in them will awaken some memories of our true nature.

Listening is rather a more difficult process than many people imagine. By listening in the manner outlined by the masters, many of our preconceived notions and prejudices will be washed and cleansed away. By listening with a clear and quiet mind, it will be possible for the truth of the teachings to enter our heart and for the meaning of life and death to become very clear. The more we listen, the more we will hear; the more we hear, the more we will know; and the more we know, the deeper and clearer will be our understanding.

The second tool of wisdom is contemplation and reflection. The deepening of our understanding can come only through contemplation of what we have heard. As we contemplate what we have heard, it gradually begins to penetrate, percolate, and permeate our mind-stream and saturate our inner experience of our lives. All the daily events begin to mirror more subtly and directly to confirm the truth of the teachings.

Gems from Tibetan Buddhism

Tibetan Buddhism stresses the need for individual pursuit of salvation or liberation and thus overcome the cycle of life, death and rebirth. It enables the aspirant to control and tame the mind through sitting meditation and by using prayer wheels. Some of the gems from Tibetan Buddhism are given below:

Planning for the future is like going fishing in a dry ravine. Nothing in this world works out the way you want. So give up all your plans, schemes and ambitions. If at all you have got to think about something, think about the uncertainty of the hour of your death.

Rest in natural great peace this exhausted mind. The mind, beaten helpless by karma and neurotic thought, like the relentless fury of the pounding waves in the infinite ocean of samsara, needs rest and peace.

With mind far off, not thinking of death's dancing and performing these meaningless activities and returning empty-handed now would be utter confusion. The need of the hour is recognition of the spiritual teachings. So begin practice the path of wisdom at this very moment.

From the blossoming lotus of devotion, at the center of my heart, rise up, O, Compassionate Master, my only refuge. I am plagued by my past actions and turbulent emotions. Please protect me in my misfortune and remain as the jewel ornament on the crown of my heart, the fountain of great bliss and arousing all my mindfulness and awareness.

In horror and fear, I took to the remote mountains. Again and again, I meditated on the uncertainty of the hour of death. Having captured the fortress of the deathless, unending nature of mind, all my fears and anxieties of death are gone once and for all.

The nature of everything in this world is illusory and ephemeral. Those with dualistic perceptions regard suffering as happiness. They are like those, who lick the honey from a razor's edge. How pitiful are those, who cling strongly to concrete reality. For correct understanding, please turn your attention within.

Whatever is born in this world will die. Whatever has been collected and stored will be dispersed. Whatever has been accumulated will be exhausted. Whatever has been built, will collapse. And what has been high and tall, will be brought down to low.

Whatever joy there is in this world, all comes from desiring others to be happy. Wishing others happiness will automatically fill your mind with perfect and lasting happiness. Whatever suffering there is in this world, all comes from desiring happiness to yourself.

One who is calm and tranquil, free from complexity and with a clear and pure mind is bound to succeed in all his endeavors.

Contemplation and reflection will unfold and enrich what we have begun to understand intellectually and will carry that understanding from our head to our heart.

The third tool of wisdom is meditation and awareness. Meditation will awaken in us the real nature of our mind and introduce us to our unchanging pure awareness, which underlies the whole of life and death.

If your mind is empty, it is always ready for anything; it is open to everything. In the beginner's mind, there are many possibilities; in the expert's mind, there are few.

Karma

According to Tibetan Buddhism, Karma doesn't mean that life is fatalistic or preordained. Tibetan masters consider Karma an ability to create and to change. Karma can be thought of as creativity, because we can all determine how and why we act. We can change.

Everything in this world is impermanent, fleeting, fluid, and interdependent. How we think and act can definitely change our future. There is no situation, however hopeless it may seem, which we cannot use to help us evolve. Similarly, there is no crime or cruelty that sincere regret and spiritual practice cannot purify. Tibetan masters have said that negative action is good in that it has one good quality about it. It can be purified. There is always hope. Even hardened criminals and murderers can change and overcome the nature that made them perform evil acts. By cleverly utilizing the present condition with wisdom, we can free ourselves from the bondage of suffering and sorrow.

Whatever is happening to us now, good or bad, is the result of our past Karma. Once we realize this eternal truth, we do not view or consider sufferings or troubles as failure or as tragedy. We do not then indulge in self-hatred or self-blame. We see the suffering and pain as the fruition or result of our past Karma. According to Tibetan Buddhism, suffering or pain is like a broom that sweeps away all our negative Karma. In fact, we can be grateful that one piece of our Karma is coming to an end and we will be free from it. We know that good fortune, a fruit of good Karma, may pass away if we do not utilize it to our best advantage. Similarly, misfortune, the result of bad Karma, may give us an opportunity to evolve.

In Tibetan Buddhism, Karma has an important place. For Tibetans, Karma has a practical meaning in their daily lives. The basis of Buddhist ethics is to live out the principle of karma, in the knowledge of its truth. One should understand Karma as a natural and just process. Karma should inspire a sense of personal responsibility for all our actions. In Tibet, even at a very young age, children are taught what is right, and this instills a sense of the importance and omnipresence of karma in their impressionable minds.

All of us can see Karma in operation. When we look back on our life, we can clearly see the consequences of our own actions. When we have caused harm to someone, it has invariably rebounded on us. When we have given trouble to someone, we have felt disgust and self-hatred. The memory of such thoughts teach us about Karma and how it influences our very lives. All our fears and doubts are due to Karma, the result of our own past actions.

When we have negative thoughts and act negatively, it will lead to pain, suffering, and sorrow. By the same token, if we have positive thoughts and positive action, we reap peace and happiness.

The Mind and the Nature of Mind

Tibetan masters consider that life and death are in the mind only and nowhere else. Mind is revealed as the universal basis of experience. It is the cause of happiness as well as suffering. Mind is the creator of life and death.

There are two very important aspects to the mind. The first is the ordinary mind. The ordinary mind is called Sem by the Tibetans. The Tibetan masters have defined Sem as that which possesses discriminating awareness and which possesses a sense of duality, which accepts or rejects something external. Basically, it is that which can associate with an "other," with any "something," that is seen as different from the perceiver. Sem is discursive, dualistic thinking mind which can only function in relation to a projected and falsely perceived external point.

Sem is the mind that plots, manipulates and desires. It is the mind that flares up in anger, indulges in negative thoughts and emotions. It goes on asserting and confirming its existence by fragmenting, conceptualizing and solidifying experience. The ordinary mind is constantly shifting and subject to external influences and habitual tendencies. Sem is unstable, grasping and minding others business. Its energy is consumed by projecting outward. Sem or ordinary mind has a false, dull stability and inertia. It is due to Sem or ordinary mind that we undergo change and death.

The second is the very nature of mind, which is absolutely untouched by change or death. The very nature of mind is hidden within our own mind, our Sem enveloped and obscured by our thoughts and emotions. Under certain special circumstances, some inspiration may give us glimpses of this nature of mind. These glimpses will bring some light of understanding, meaning and freedom. This is because the nature of mind is the very root of understanding. Tibetans call it Rigpa, a pure, pristine awareness that is intelligent, radiant and always awake. It is knowledge of knowledge itself. To realize the nature of mind is to realize the nature of all things.

Saints and mystics have given their realization different names and interpretations. But what they have experienced is the real nature of mind.

Hindus call it "Self," "Brahman," and "Atman." Christians call it God and Buddhist calls it Buddha nature. It is said that when Buddha attained enlightenment, all he wanted to show the world was the nature of mind and share what he has realized with humanity. Even though we have the same inner nature as Buddha, we have not recognized it. This is because it is enclosed and wrapped in our ordinary mind. Our Buddha mind is enclosed within the walls of our ordinary mind. But when we become enlightened, we can realize the nature of mind.

Facing Death

Life is uncertain and impermanent. We walk down a street thinking and planning many things, and a car suddenly races by and almost runs us over. Similarly, if we watch the television or read a newspaper, we see death everywhere. All of us take life for granted. We can be quite hale and healthy one day and suddenly fall sick and die the next day. We cannot be certain, when we go to sleep, that we will definitely wake up tomorrow. As a Tibetan saying goes, "Tomorrow or the next life, which comes first, we never know."

Some of the Tibetan masters, when they went to bed at night, would empty their cups and leave them upside down by the side of their bed. This was because they were not sure whether they would wake up and need them the next morning. They even put out their fire at night, since they were not sure of requiring it the next day. They lived from moment to moment with the possibility of imminent death. Some masters who realized the fragility of life advised their followers to reflect on their lives as a condemned prisoner taking his last walk from his cell or like an animal lining up for its end in an abattoir.

It is important to reflect calmly and dispassionately that death is real and that death will come suddenly, without any warning. Tibetan masters used to encourage their students to reflect and imagine their own death as a part of a calm contemplation: the emotion, pain, panic, utter helplessness, the grief of their dear and near ones. and the realization of what they had done and not done in their lives.

Since life is so fragile and impermanent, we should take life and death calmly. Taking life serenely is to find a middle way and not over-stretch our lives, but to simplify our lives. The key to find a happy balance in life is simplicity. Once we simplify our lives, peace of mind will automatically follow. With the attainment of peace of mind, we will have more time to pursue the things of the spirit and the knowledge that only spiritual truth can bring. This will enable us to face death.

The main reason why we have so much suffering and sorrow in facing death is because we do not realize or we ignore the eternal truth of life's impermanence. We want everything to continue as it is and believe that things will always remain the same. So we undergo shattering emotional crisis if someone very dear to us dies suddenly. Even Buddha died. This should awaken us to the eternal truth that everything in life is impermanent and death is inevitable and an inescapable fact of life. Once we understand this impermanence of life, we can face death calmly.

Healing in Tibetan Buddhism

In Tibetan Buddhism, healing means healing of both the body and the mind. To understand healing from the Tibetan Buddhism perspective, the starting point is to consider the Buddhist concept of mind. According to Buddhist teachings, the basic nature of the mind is pure. The mind is the creator of sickness and good health. In fact, the mind is considered to be the creator of all problems, physical and mental. Thus, the Tibetan Buddhist considers the cause of any disease to be internal and not external.

In Tibetan Buddhism, the concept of karma is closely linked o health and sickness in an individual. Karma means action and all actions of an individual are either positive or negative. The negative karmic actions cause sickness, while the positive ones result in happiness, health and success. According to Tibetan Buddhism, to heal sickness, one must engage in positive actions. Since karma is the creator of all happiness and suffering, one should strive not to have any negative karma.

According to Tibetan Buddhism, for lasting healing, it is necessary to heal not only the current disease with medicines and other forms of treatment, but also find out the cause of the disease, which originates from the mind. If one does not heal or purify the mind, the sickness and problems will recur again and again. In order to heal the mind and also the body, one should eliminate all negative thoughts and their imprints and replace them with positive thoughts and their imprints.

According to Tibetan Buddhism, the basic cause of sickness is selfishness, since selfishness causes one to engage in negative actions. These negative actions can be of the body, speech or mind, such as thoughts of anger, greed, jealousy etc. These feelings result in an unhappy mind. On the other hand, actions and thoughts directed for the welfare of others bring peace of mind as well as happiness.

Tibetan medicines are effective. It consists mainly of herbal medicines. The unique thing about Tibetan herbal medicine is that in the course of its preparation, it is blessed with prayers and mantras, thus giving the medicine great healing power, potency and effectiveness. Tibetans believe that by taking such medicines, they will have complete recovery from any disease. Further, many Tibetans believe that diseases are associated with spirits. In such cases, the Lamas (Tibetan monks) will recite certain prayers and mantras and perform some religious ceremonies to stop the harm from the spirit.

Zen Buddhism

An Introduction to Zen Buddhism

Zen Buddhism represents a sectarian movement within the Buddhist religion that stresses the practice of meditation as the means to enlightenment. Zen roots may be traced to India, but it was in East Asia that the movement became distinct and flourished. The word "Zen" derives from the Chinese "ch'an," which in turn derives from the Sanskrit word "dhyana," which means meditation. The most distinctive feature of Zen Buddhism is the great importance given to meditation or more specifically, "Zazen" or sitting meditation.

Traditionally, Zen has placed great importance on the master disciple relationship, and the significance of the teacher's role in the disciple's spiritual development. Zen puts emphasis on direct experience, flashes of insight that pierce through the concepts and thoughts that words embody.

According to Zen, it is possible for a person to attain enlightenment in this very life through the practice of meditation and development of mental and spiritual disciplines.

Zen was originally developed in China, but it was later stressed by Japanese Buddhists such as Eisai and Dogan. Zen meditation is a rigorous practice designed to reveal things to you about yourself, which are necessary for the purpose of attaining enlightenment.

By releasing conscious, directed thinking, you allow random, un-requested thoughts to arise to awareness—a torrent of ideas, which reveal a chaotic universe normally hidden from us. It requires courage to face such thoughts and it requires sustained efforts to become detached from it all, learning how our own thoughts are a source of our own suffering, which must be let go in order to achieve peace and harmony.

Zen talks of Buddha nature—which we are when we are truly awakened. Paradoxically, it is not something that can be discovered because it has never been lost—it exists and can be experienced through various disciplines and practices. Most significant among these is meditation. In Zen, this is a means of waking up to what we are by dealing the mind of attachments, concepts and habitual thought processes. The experience of awakening is known as "satori," which comes from the Japanese word "satoru," meaning to know. Other practice includes the consideration of what is known as "Koans"—Zen riddles that can only be understood by bypassing the rational mind.

In Zen, there is also a rich cultural tradition, which encompasses art, poetry, gardening and drinking of tea. There is no doubt that this form of Buddhism has distinctive approach, which is at once challenging and engaging.

Zen Buddhism has become very popular among non-Buddhists in the US as well as in Europe. Zen Buddhism seeks to transmit the spirit of Buddhism without demanding allegiance to all the teachings of Buddha. What is distinctive of Zen Buddhism is that it uses what is known as "Mondo," a question and answer technique to reveal truths from within the seeker, which will bring enlightenment.

Zen Buddhism

Zen Buddhism is a blend of the Chinese and Japanese school of Mahayana Buddhism that asserts that enlightenment can be attained through meditation, self-contemplation and intuition rather than by reading the scriptures or hearing the teachings of masters.

In the simplest terms, Zen can be described as a unique blend of Indian mysticism and Chinese naturalism sieved through the rather special mesh of Japanese characters.

Zen's main aim is none other than the aim of the Indian Buddha himself, the attainment of an absolute or ultimate knowledge lying behind all changes and the "sway of the opposites." The state of consciousness known in the Zen Buddhism as "Satori" is held to be comparable to that special level of insight attained by Buddha, while seated in deep meditation under the sacred Tree of Enlightenment in the sixth century before the birth of Christ. Zen is firmly grounded in specific exhortation of the Buddha, notably his trenchant suggestion, "Look within, thou art the Buddha" and his deathbed injunction to his disciples "Be a lamp unto yourself. Workout your own salvation with diligence."

In the centuries following Buddhism's first appearance in China - an event of imprecise date - there took place a vital exchange of ideas between the transplanted teachings of Buddhism and the two classic Chinese philosophies, namely, Taoism and Confucianism. Together in time, these three philosophies might be said to have created a fourth, a subtle blend of all; Indian metaphysical abstraction, Taoistic paradox and Confucian pragmatism.- Zen Buddhism.

Zen Buddhism cannot be strictly termed as a religion. The followers of the Zen do not worship any God as in other religions. All the philosophies of the east are contained in Zen Buddhism. The essence of Zen is the training of the mind and awakening.

What Is Zen?

What is Zen? It is not a religion in the strict sense of the term that is commonly understood. Zen has no God to worship. It has no dogmas, religious encumbrances, and practices. Zen has no ceremonial rites to be followed, no sacrifices to be made, and no future abode to which the dead are destined. Lastly in Zen, there is no question of looking after the welfare of the soul that is inherent in other systems of religious practices. Zen is against all religious conventionalism.

Though Zen has no God to worship, it does not automatically follow that Zen denies the existence of God. Zen neither denies nor affirms it. When a thing is denied, the very denial involves something not denied. The same applies in the case of affirmation. This is pure logic and Zen is above logic. In Zen, therefore, God is neither denied nor insisted upon, since in Zen there is no such God as conceived by the Hindu, Christian and Jewish minds. Thus it will be seen that Zen is neither a religion nor a philosophy. In simple terms, Zen can be described as a way of life.

In Zen, all the philosophies of the East have crystallized. But this does not mean that Zen is a philosophy. It is not a system based on logic and analysis. Zen is essentially of the whole mind and can be described as the spirit of a man.

It believes in inner purity and goodness. The central idea in Zen is disciplining of the mind and making it its own master through an insight into its real nature. This getting into the real nature of one's mind is the fundamental aim of the Zen Buddhism. Thus, Zen is more than meditation and prayer. The discipline consists in opening one's mental eye so as to look into the very reason of existence.

Normally, in meditation, one has to focus the mind on a particular object, a durable symbol like the sun or beautiful landscape or any other symbol relating to God. In Zen this is scrupulously avoided.

Zen emphasizes the attainment of freedom, namely freedom from all natural encumbrances. Meditation is not Zen. Zen reflects or perceives and does not meditate. What makes Zen unique is the systematic training of the mind. Zen reveals itself in the most uninteresting and uneventful life of an ordinary man, recognizing the fact of living in the midst of life as it is lived. Zen systematically trains the mind to see this. It opens the eyes of a man to the greatest mystery as it is daily performed. Zen enlarges the heart to embrace the eternity of time and infinity of space. It makes one live in the world as if walking in the Garden of Eden. One noteworthy aspect is that Zen accomplishes all the spiritual feats without resorting to any doctrine or dogma, but by simply asserting the truth that lies in our inner being.

Essence of Zen Buddhism

The essence of Zen Buddhism is trying to understand the real meaning of life. One should endeavor to find out the true meaning of life without being misled by logical thought or words and seeing into ones own nature. The central theme of Zen Buddhism is that all human beings are Buddha and all that one has to do, is to discover that truth by one's own efforts.

For painting a picture, a painter needs a canvas, paints, brushes, and other accessories. Similarly, a sculptor requires wood, stone, cutting tools, and other equipment. But for a person who has awakened to the nature of the Mind, the entire universe is the canvas, and the hands, feet, emotions, and intellect are the implements.

Each and every moment is happiness when one is freed from the enslaving notions of "This is my body, this is my mind." At the core of each individual, there is creativity. If the aim of an artist is to make the invisible visible, the purpose of Zen is to bring into consciousness the substrata of both the unconscious and conscious.

The objective of Zen training is awakening. It is the actual living of a creative and harmonious life. The essence of Zen Buddhism can be summarized as follows: Zen is a sect of Buddhism. Zen is Mind, and the Mind is the foundation of Zen Buddhism. Zen has no doctrine or dogmas, but leads to the ultimate source of all Buddhist teachings: the enlightenment experience of the Buddha. Zen is a discipline for the illumination of the Mind and freedom of action. Zen demands maturity as well as responsibility from its followers. It demands aspirants to stand on their own feet and not God's. One's freedom should not be limited and fettered by attachment to God.

Society and Responsibility

Zen Buddhism places great importance on responsibility and social activities. Responsibility in Zen Buddhism means ready responsiveness. Responsibility is reaching out promptly to others when they have problems or difficulties. A sense of responsibility comes when a person is fully aware. Compassion and service are the core of Buddhism. Those who are compassionate, kind, and loving exert tremendous positive influence on the lives of people. They inspire and motivate others to act in similar ways. In fact, the entire Sangha, or community, benefits by the acts of such persons.

By sitting and meditating, we can benefit society. By purifying our mind and transcending the ego, we can indirectly purify other minds. Further, this will have good effects on our family, friends, and other acquaintances. Everything depends on the state of our mind and what our conscience tells you. In Buddhism, compassion and wisdom are the two qualities that we develop through constant practice and meditation. We simply do what we feel needs to be done, without being attached to the result. The important thing to remember is how to act. When we get deeper and deeper into our practice, we give our very best and at the same time respond spontaneously to the needs of all situations.

We must remember that Karma is not a fixed thing, but always keeps changing, since the relation between cause and effect is dynamic. The more we practice, the more we become aware of these things. The more we are aware of these things, the more our past karma changes. Gradually, our future karma will be created from a basis of awareness.

In Zen Buddhism, social action is considered as a kind of meditation, which will lead to the development of compassion, equanimity, tolerance, and responsibility.

Peace and Enlightenment

Everyone in the world wants peace. The yearning for peace is very strong in the minds of all people, particularly among the young. This is because it is the young who join the army and get involved in war and its consequent suffering and sorrow. This powerful longing for peace has grown up with the young people, who have experienced the pain and misery of prisons and concentration camps with all their inhuman torture.

Buddhism is basically a religion of peace. Through the long history of Buddhism, it has never fought or become involved in a war of any kind. Buddha preached and practiced peace. Buddhist precepts emphasize total abstinence from killing, hatred, and causing harm to any living beings. Peace is the core and essence of Buddhism. According to Buddha, peace in the world is the result of a peaceful, kind, compassionate, and loving heart. Peace springs from right understanding and right selfless action. There can be no peace without inner harmony and understanding. Buddha symbolizes one's own potential for harmony, understanding, kindness, and compassion.

Enlightenment in Zen Buddhism means opening the mind's eye. This raises important questions, such as "Who am I and what am I? What is my real nature?" These questions arise in our mind, and it is difficult to find answers. We try to locate the answers from books, but we fail. Only the experience of self-awakening can help us find the correct answers. Personal experience is the ultimate testing of Truth. This is Zen discipline. We must be sincere and dedicated. Enlightenment comes only when we have achieved selfless purity.

In order to achieve this selfless purity, we must work hard. We should clear the mind of all prejudices, false notions, irrelevant ideas, and rigid opinions. In this connection, Zazen is a discipline to remove all the pollution of the mind so that the inherent purity, wholeness, and radiance that are obscured by the mental dirt can emerge, and then our inborn love and compassion will shine. Zazen is an expression of truth that all beings have been whole and complete. Our real nature is like a circle to which nothing can be added or subtracted. That is enlightenment.

Work and Awareness

It is universally known that many people look upon work as drudgery and boredom. Whether in the office, in a factory, or on a farm, the tendency is for people to wish to work as little as possible. This is because they do not find the work interesting, thought-provoking, or fulfilling.

In Zen, the concept of work is completely different. In Zen, in everything that we do becomes a potential opportunity for self-realization. For Zen Buddhists, every action and every movement done sincerely, with dedication and devotion, is an expression of Buddha. The greater the pure-mindedness with which the work is done, the closer we are to self-realization.

To enter into the awareness of Zen means to free the mind of its uncontrolled thoughts and make it pure and clear. It is believed that much power is created by practicing awareness in the midst of work. Thus, our daily work becomes our meditation, and the work on hand our practice. In Zen, it is termed "working for oneself." Total creativity is possible only when the mind is totally absorbed in the work. In this creativity, our intuitive wisdom and joy are released.

In Zen, everything is in the doing—a doing arising out of awareness. The violence, suffering, sorrow, and misery in the world are due to lack of awareness because the mind feels divorced from life and nature. The mind is dominated by feelings of "I" and "mine," which destroy mental peace due to craving earthly desires. Such a mind devoid of awareness is insensitive to people and things, for it can neither see nor understand the true value of things. The mind devoid of awareness sees things as objects to be used for fulfilling its desires. The person who is aware sees the complexity and interrelatedness of all lives. Out of this awareness, he develops a respect for the value of things. And from this respect comes the desire to see things used properly and not to be destructive.

The un-mindful acts of people without awareness reveal an indifference to the value of things. This indifference is due to the mind seeing itself as separated from a world of change. This indifference deprives a person of his harmony and happiness.

Perfection of Character

In Zen Buddhism, great importance is given to the perfection of character. Most people normally shy away from the idea of perfection. They know that nobody is perfect, so they neglect their own character by not taking steps to correct themselves. Others tend to be perfectionists. However, the aim of Zen practice is the perfection of character.

Yamade Roshi , a Zen Buddhist philosopher, shows us how to reveal the essence in ourselves and the world. He sums up the Six Perfections of classical Buddhism with the term "perfection of character." These Six Perfections are relinquishment, morality, equanimity, vigor, meditation, and realization.

Relinquishment is the total cutting off or letting go of the three poisons of greed, hatred, and ignorance. These three are the cause of all suffering, pain, and sorrow. One should, therefore, consciously and systematically get rid of them.

Morality means the moral quality or character of being in accord with the principles of right conduct. It is the observance of the precepts of not killing, not stealing, not lying, not misusing sex, not clouding the mind, and so on. Precepts are useful to the Zen student who seeks to internalize them to find their source in the mind and to make morality altogether familiar. In Zen Buddhism, moral behavior is considered the mark of the truly mature person.

Equanimity is the condition of not being upset or thrown off balance by any unexpected adverse happenings. It is not endurance, and, at the same time, it is not apathy. Equanimity is a matter of graciously accepting minor criticisms. Often, the so-called little things are more of a challenge than dramatic threats. Equanimity is the quality of the mind, wherein a person remains calm and unperturbed in the midst of all adversity.

Vigor is active or healthy mental force. It is acting with energy, strength, and vitality. Vigor is unfettered by any conceptual attachments. Vigor is not blind, nor is it mere spontaneity.

Meditation is rigorously focusing and quieting the human mind. The Sanskrit term is "dhyana paramita," and the model for dhyana is the figure of Buddha, seated erect, cross-legged, fully alert and completely at rest. Dhyana is the mindful spirit of the Zen student in daily life.

Realization is the acknowledgement of the interpenetration and intercontainment of all things, beginning with yourself, and of their empty infinity in the vast and fathomless universe.

Thus, it can be seen that the purpose and aim of Zen practice is the perfection of character.

Acquiring a New Viewpoint (Satori)

Satori is the spiritual goal of Zen Buddhism. It is a very important concept in Zen. The aim of Zen discipline is to acquire a view point called satori, which is imperative for focusing into the essence of things. All people live in the same world and most of their actions also appear alike. For example, when two people drink tea, this simple act of drinking may look similar. But according to Zen Buddhism, there is a wide subjective gap between the way each person drinks. The reason for this is that there may be no Zen in one person's drinking, while there is Zen in the other person's drinking. Thus, Satori expresses the Zen way of viewing the world.

Satori is the core of Zen Buddhism. Without Satori, there is no Zen. The life of Zen begins with the opening of Satori. Satori can, therefore, be defined as the unfolding of a new world, not properly seen before due to the confusion of a dualist mind. Satori is something that is not capable of any intellectual analysis. It is an experience, which a person has to undergo and such an experience cannot be communicated to another, unless the latter had a similar experience. If Satori is capable of analysis and by so doing it becomes clear to another who never had it, then Satori will cease to be a Satori. This is because for a Satori to be turned into a concept, it will cease to be itself.

The way of instruction in Zen is either to indicate or show the way so that one's attention can be directed to the goal. Attaining this goal must be done by one's own mind. Satori translates into individual enlightenment or a flash of sudden awareness. All the causes and conditions of Satori are thus in one's mind only. They are just waiting for the maturing. When the mind is ready for some reason or the other, such as a bird flying or a flower blooming or a bell ringing, one discovers one's new real self. There is nothing to teach or explain in Zen that will increase one's knowledge. No knowledge is really one's own, unless it grows out of oneself.

Dhyana (Zazen)

Zazen is at the heart of Zen Buddhist practice. "Za" in Japanese means "sitting". "Zen" is from the Chinese word "Ch'an", which is from the Sanskrit word "dhyana", which refers to a state of deep absorption in meditation. Thus, Zazen means sitting in absorption. The aim of Zazen is just sitting and opening the hand of thought.

Zen is a form of mysticism. As a product of the Eastern mind, it is unique in its methodical training of the mind so as to mature it in acquiring a new viewpoint, namely the state of Satori. Zazen is thus an important characteristic and aspect of Zen.

Zazen or Dhyana in Sanskrit means sitting cross-legged in perfect tranquility and in deep contemplation. This practice has its origin in India, where it is practiced by all seekers of Truth. From India, the practice spread all over the far East. Followers of Zen strictly observe Zazen, the prevailing practical method of spiritual discipline in the East.

Dhyana is derived from the root "dhi," which means to reflect upon or to perceive or to fix the mind upon. Thus, Dhyana literally means to fix the mind upon and reflect. It means to hold one's thoughts collected and not to allow them to dissipate and wander away from the correct path. In Dhyana, the mind is concentrated on a single object of thought. In order for conditions to be most favorable for this, one should control all external details, such as regulating eating, drinking, and sleeping. In addition, the body should be kept straight and erect, so that one is in a comfortable and relaxed posture. The next important factor is the choice of a suitable place to sit and practice. The place should be calm and quiet.

In Buddhism, Dhyana as practiced originally was one of its three branches of discipline: moral precepts, contemplation, and knowledge. Buddhism placed great emphasis on moral precepts, namely keeping one's passions under control. As practiced by Zen devotees, however, Zazen does not have the same objective in mind as in the case of Buddhism. Zen does not make Dhyana an end in itself, but an essential tool to the mastering of Zen.

Zen and the Eight Gates

The Buddha's teachings of the Noble Four Truths and the Noble Eightfold Path point the path towards the end of our suffering and sorrow. The Eight Gates of Zen are an expression of the Noble Eightfold Path through the traditional practices of Zen Buddhism. They enable us to reclaim our lives and to return to intimate contact with our inherent stillness and clarity. These Eight Gates are:

1. Zen Study;
2. Zazen;
3. Liturgy;
4. Art Practice;
5. Body Practice;
6. Buddhist Studies;
7. Work Practice; and
8. Right Action.

1. Zen Study is indispensable in helping us navigate the difficulties along the way, directly pointing to our inherent perfection. Zen Buddhism originates in the teachings of the Buddha. After achieving enlightenment, the Buddha realized that everything is subject to change and that suffering and sorrow are due to desire and attachment to things, which by their very nature are impermanent. By ridding oneself of these attachments, one can be free of suffering.

2. Zazen is a particular kind of meditation unique to Zen Buddhism. Zen Buddhists are generally called "meditation Buddhists." Basically, Zazen is the study of the self. It is The Buddha Way to study the self. The aim of Zazen is first to still the mind and later, through practice, to reach a state of pure wakefulness so that the mind can realize its own Buddha-nature. According to Dogen Zenji (noted Zen Buddhist philosopher),"Zazen is itself Enlightenment."

3. Liturgy makes the visible the invisible, bringing into awareness the shared experiences of the community. It is an expression of the underlying religious truths and beliefs within our lives.

4. Art Practice. In Zen Buddhism, art practice is a dynamic way of studying the self and expressing the understanding that we discover within ourselves.

5. Body Practice. In Zazen, the focus is on breath. The breath is life. The word "spirit" means breath. The words "ki" in Japanese and "chi" in Chinese, meaning power or energy, both derive from breath. Breath is the vital force and it is the central activity of our bodies. Mind and breath are one reality.

6. Buddhist Studies. A study of the Buddha's teachings, Buddhist texts and commentaries help us to establish sound religious practice.

7. Work Practice. Right Livelihood is one of the important aspects of the Noble Eightfold Path. Right Livelihood should not bring hurt or danger to any living being. It is about transforming every dimension of our lives into sacred activity. Our daily lives become fruitful opportunities to widen

our spiritual practices as well as to explore work that nourishes ourselves as well as others.

8. Right Action is one of the key aspects of the Noble Eightfold Path. All our actions should be peaceful, pure, sincere, and honest. It should bring peace, happiness, and harmony to the community.

Chapter 10

Jainism

Introduction to Jainism

Jainism, an ancient religion, has its origin in India. The followers of Jainism are called Jains. The belief in complete non-violence or "ahimsa" is central to the Jain belief and tradition. All Jains scrupulously avoid violence towards all living beings and consider it the individual's responsibility to act with wisdom, compassion and peace.

It has not been possible for historians to trace the origin of Jainism, but the historical evidence and many researchers have established the fact that Jainism is an ancient religion. The history of Jainism contains references to sixty-three Supreme personages (called Salakapurusas), who lived during each of the ancient periods of time. They guided and inspired the people to follow religion and ethics during the period of the advancement of human civilization. Among the Supreme personages, the Tirthankaras occupied the highest position. According to historians, twenty-four Tirthakaras were born. The first of them was Rsabhadeva, and the last of the Tirthankaras was Mahavir, who lived about 2500 years ago. Buddha Tataghata was his contemporary.

Jainism is one of the oldest religions. It covers many different periods of history.

The word "Jain" refers to the follower of the "Jinas," meaning "those who overcome." Altogether, there are twenty-four Jinas, who are also called Tirthankaras. They are regarded by the Jains as great spiritual teachers. The last of them was Mahavir. The Jinas continue to be regarded as great teachers, whose example helps others to escape from the cycle of birth and death and to achieve freedom from reincarnation. The belief in ahimsa or nonviolence is central to Jainism, and Jains try to avoid violence towards humans and towards life in any other form, including animals and plants.

Jains believe that all life is closely bound up in a web of interdependence and that all aspects of life belong together and support each other.

The symbol of Jainism is the upright hand. It represents nonviolence and reassurance and is a reminder of the responsibility of every person to act with peace, understanding, and wisdom. The word "ahimsa" appears on the palm of the hand.

More than 98 percent of jams in the world live in India. The two other largest Jain communities are in the United States and the United Kingdom.

Jainism

Founder

Lord Mahavir was born near the beginning of the sixth century BC and lived through the great part of that century. When Lao Tze was teaching his disciples the mystery of the Tao in China, Mahavir was founding the religion known as Jainism. Lord Mahavir, the prophet of the Jain religion, was the twenty-fourth Tirthankara (name given to Jain spiritual leaders and saints). He was born in 599 BC at a place called Kundagrama, in the kingdom of Vaishali, in the Indian state of Bihar. His father was Siddhartha, a chieftain of Kundagrama, and his mother was Trishala. When Mahavir was born, there were great celebrations befitting the birth of a royal prince. It was said that the Queen Trishala had fourteen auspicious dreams when the child was in her womb. The prince was named Vardhamana, meaning one who brings prosperity. He was, however, popularly called Mahavir, the great hero, who subdued and conquered his passions.

Even as a young boy, Mahavir was brave, fearless, and handsome. He was very much loved by everyone. Once, during his childhood, Mahavir was playing with some children in the garden when a huge snake curled itself round the trunk of a nearby tree. Seeing the snake, all the children fled in terror, but Mahavir boldly held the snake by its hood and flung it away like a piece of rope.

From his very childhood Mahavir was extremely quiet, resolute, and totally indifferent to worldly matters. To change this attitude, Mahavir's parents arranged for his marriage. Mahavir married Yasoda and had a daughter. However, the new family ties did not make any change to Mahavir. Although he was surrounded by all the luxuries of the palace, he had a strong sense of detachment. This detached way of life made Mahavir renounce the world after the death of his parents. At the age of thirty, with the consent of his elder brother, Mahavir became a wandering monk. He gave away all his wealth and worldly possessions and decided to devote himself to a spiritual life. He subjected himself to rigorous austerities, including prolonged fasts, for more than twelve years, until he achieved omniscience. He neglected his body and spent most of his time meditating on his self. Finally, in the thirteenth year, Mahavir attained Nirvana. He was now a Jain, or a conqueror. From then on he devoted himself to teaching and the creation of a monastic order.

Mahavir faced great hardships and many indignities during his long spiritual practice, but he proved to be an embodiment of forbearance and forgiveness. After attaining omniscience, Lord Mahavir began to preach. During the remaining thirty years of his life, he traveled widely in promoting his order. People from far and wide came to hear his teachings. On one occasion, upon hearing Lord Mahavir's teachings, eleven prominent Brahmin scholars became his chief disciples. They founded the nucleus of the religious order of Jainism, which transmitted the teachings to others. Lord Mahavir established a four-fold congregation of monks, nuns, and layperson devotees. In the Sangha so established, there was no distinction between men and women; both were regarded equally. The women were initiated as nuns, a great revolutionary act in those days.

For more than thirty long years, Lord Mahavir went about with a missionary zeal, preaching the religion of nonviolence, non-absolutism, and non-possession. At the age of seventy-two, Lord Mahavir gave up his body at Pavapuri, in Bihar, India.

Beliefs

The aim of Jainism is total and complete conquest of attachment and realization. The basic teaching of Jainism is that right knowledge should be acquired by looking at mundane things with an eye of right faith and that the same should be translated into right conduct in life. The pivotal point of entire conduct and thought is the attainment of conquest over all attachments.

Nonviolence, non injury, and nonpossession are the foundation of Jainism. According to Jainism, commission of violence or nonviolence is dependent upon the mental condition of the doer and not in the act. He who conducts himself with the utmost caution is nonviolent in his thought and, hence, he is nonviolent. He who does not observe caution in his active daily life has violence in his mental state. So even if no violence is actually committed by him, he would be ethically violent. Hence, a person who possesses an attitude of many points of view is regarded as being possessed of right faith, and it is a person possessed of right faith that can acquire right knowledge and thus become capable of right conduct. Hence righteousness or right faith has special significance in Jainism. That is the foundation stone to the path of liberation.

Dharma (Religion)

Dharma is the essential nature of any substance. Right faith, right knowledge, and right conduct—called the three jewels—constitute the Dharma. Non injury to all living beings and giving protection to them are another important aspect of Dharma.

The ten characteristics of Dharma are supreme forgiveness, supreme humility, supreme straightforwardness, supreme truthfulness, supreme purity, supreme self-restraint, supreme austerity, supreme renunciation, supreme detachment, and supreme continence. Followers of Jainism should follow these ten characteristics of Dharma in their daily lives.

One should have perfect forbearance. One should not get excited or annoyed when provoked by others and should remain calm under all circumstances. Patience is a great virtue and every one should cultivate it.

One should uphold right conduct at all times. If at any time one makes an inappropriate speech or indulges in an ungrateful act, one should readily apologize for his fault.

One must practice humility in whatever he does. A monk who does not flaunt even slightly his family lineage, his looks, his caste, his learning, austerity, knowledge of the scriptures and character is the one that practices supreme humility.

In all speech and action, one should display humility. Even a monk, who has given up all worldly attachments, should not flaunt his learning, knowledge of the scriptures and his looks.

A person who does not insult or cause injury to others commands respect from others. On the other hand, a person who boasts all the time and does not possess any virtue or character is disliked by one and all.

A person who does not think, act and speak in a crooked manner and does not hide his weaknesses, observes the virtue of supreme straight forwardness.

A monk should avoid all speech that is likely to cause hurt to others. He should speak only what is true and good. At all times, a monk should observe the virtue of supreme truthfulness.

Precepts on the Three Jewels

Right faith, right knowledge, and right conduct, called the three jewels, are strong pillars of Jainism. To have deep and abiding faith in the existence of Dharma is right faith. To have correct understanding of the nature of substances is right knowledge. To sincerely persevere in the performance of penance is right conduct. These three jewels constitute the pathway to emancipation.

We understand by our right knowledge the nature of substances, develop belief in them by our right faith, and control ourselves by right conduct. We purify our soul by austerities and penance.

Knowledge without right conduct, acceptance of asceticism without right faith, and observance of austerities without self-control are futile, since they do not lead to emancipation.

Without right faith, there cannot be right knowledge; without right knowledge, there cannot be right conduct; and without right conduct, there cannot be release from karma. Unless we are released from our karma, there cannot be nirvana or salvation.

Right knowledge is of no use in the absence of right conduct. Action is of no use in the absence of right knowledge. In the case of a conflagration, the lame man gets burned down even if he is capable of seeing, while the blind man gets burned down even if he is capable of running away.

The desired result is best attained when there is a harmony between right knowledge and right conduct, for a chariot does not move on one wheel. This is like a lame man and a blind man coming together in a forest and managing to reach the town with the help of one another.

Right faith means a soul engrossed in itself. Right knowledge is knowledge of the real nature of the soul. Right conduct consists in faithful pursuit of that path.

It will thus be seen that right faith, right knowledge, and right conduct together constitute the path to Nirvana or liberation. The saints have averred that if this faith is followed in the right way, it will lead one to liberation. If not, it will only lead to eternal bondage.

Just as a fetter, even if it is made of gold binds a person, so also karma, whether auspicious or inauspicious, binds the soul.

It will be better to go to heaven by observing vows and austerity than to suffer much in hell by committing forbidden actions. There is so much difference between a person who stands in the shade and another standing in the hot sun.

He who desires no honor, no worship, and not even salutation, how will he desire praise? He who has self-control, strictly observes the vows, practices penance and sincerely seeks to know and understand the true nature of the soul is the real monk.

With scriptural knowledge, an aspirant becomes firm in his faith, meditation, observance of vows, and self-restraint. Such a person lives a life of purity throughout his lifetime without any doubt or wavering.

The World

This world is full of suffering and sorrow. It is impermanent and fast changing, and there is much instability. How can we escape from such a world so full of misery?

All sensuous enjoyments in this world only give momentary pleasures. They may give us an impression of sweetness in the beginning, but they end in prolonged misery and pain. By their very nature, these joys of the senses cause maximum sorrow and suffering and minimum happiness. These are veritable mines of evils. They are obstacles to the aspirant to emancipation. In fact, the luxuries and pleasures enjoyed by kings and emperors as well as the celestials are painful. They are only fleeting and are agonizing in the end. We should, therefore, avoid such things. A person who is suffering from an itch finds immediate relief and pleasure by scratching his body, but it results in immense pain later on. In the same way, an infatuated person foolishly considers the sensuous enjoyments as a source of happiness.

He who is immersed in the pleasures of the flesh and other material things becomes perverted. His soul gets impure and tarnished. He does not understand what is good and beneficial, and this takes him away from the spiritual path. He not only becomes dull, ignorant, and infatuated, but he fully entangles himself in his own karma, like a fly caught in phlegm. For such a person, there is no hope of emancipation.

The embodied soul knows and reflects upon the afflictions caused by birth, growth, old age, sickness, and ultimate death. Still, the soul does not abstain or refrain from pursuing the sensual pleasures, which cause so much misery and suffering. Such is the power of delusion.

A person who is worldly-minded gets attached to pain and pleasure, joy and sorrow, and consequently his karmas binds his soul. This bondage of karma results in the cycle of birth and death. As a result of birth, he gets a body, the body the senses, and the senses lead to their respective enjoyments, which in turn cause attachment and aversion. Thus, the soul gets bogged down in the endless cycle of births and deaths.

A person has to bear his sorrow all by himself. Neither his family members nor his friends can share his sufferings, since the karma follows only the doer. Just as a person feels free while climbing a tree but becomes helpless when he falls down, so also the soul is free while accumulating karma but is helpless when it ripens.

A person's faith becomes perverted due to wrong faith. He develops a dislike for religion like a person who dislikes sweets due to illness. Attachment and aversion are the root causes of karma and karma originates from delusion. Karma is again the root cause of birth and death. Not even the most powerful enemy inflicts so much harm and misery as uncontrolled attachment and aversion.

Basic Teachings

The basic teaching of Jainism is that a human being can conquer the limitations of physical existence and by dedicated, sincere, and rigorous spiritual discipline attain immortality. The fundamental belief in Jainism is that all existing beings fall into two categories: the jiva, or soul, and the ajiva, which is nonsentient. Due to its association with the non-sentient ajiva, the jiva, or soul, is unable to realize its true nature, which is immortality and omniscience. Further, the Jains also hold the view that each jiva has been externally associated with ajiva. This unique association of the jiva and ajiva, according to Jains, is due to karma. The only way by which the jiva or soul can be freed from this karmic bondage is by ascetic life and ascetic discipline. The goal of ascetic discipline enables the jiva to be liberated completely from all karmic association, rising to the uppermost reaches of the universe to abide there in perfection, knowledge, and self-containment.

Jains infer the existence of the jiva or soul from its function as knower and agent of activity in living things. They also hold the view that jiva's innate nature must be whole and complete. Thus, the jiva is held to be eternal and omniscient.

Another key element in Jainism is the nature of ajiva and the working of karma. All insentient entities fall under the category of ajiva, particularly space, time, and matter, the latter conceived as atoms. Jains do not deny the actual existence of ajiva, and consequently matter is real and eternal. Karma, as a subtle form of matter, is real and must be dealt with in a physical way. To detach jiva's association with karma requires cultivation of extreme detachment from all that is not jiva.

The third key element is ahimsa, or non-injury. Ahimsa is a main component of detachment from ajiva, from the material world of karma. Ahimsa embodies one's willingness to totally separate oneself from all acts of injury or violence. Ahimsa to the Jains means total separation from the mechanism of aggression, possession, and consumption. Thus, ahimsa can be said to be the hallmark of Jain's commitment to total and complete detachment. The emphasis on ahimsa has resulted in the insistence on consuming only pure vegetarian food, opposition to animal slaughter, and complete rejection of all types of violence. Jain laypersons are enjoined to engage only in occupations that minimize the possible destruction of living beings.

The achievement of total detachment is a very difficult task and involves rigorous spiritual and mental practice in day-to-day life.

Prayer

May the river of friendship eternally flow from my heart. My cherished desire is to see the entire universe in prosperity, happiness, and peace.

May my heart throb and sing with rapture on seeing virtue, and may my entire life be offered at the feet of the virtuous.

May my heart bleed on seeing cruelty, suffering, sorrow, wretchedness, and the irreligious. Let the tears of kindness, love, and compassion ever flow from my eyes.

May I be always there to guide and show the right path to the pathless wanderers of life.

Let me have plenty of patience if they do not listen to me.

May the spirit of kindly feelings and love enter all our hearts. Let us all sing in chorus the immortal song of human harmony.

May I never harm or hurt or cause injuries to any living being. May I never utter a falsehood.

May I never be greedy of wealth, jealous, or lustful for another's wife.

May I have always the company of learned saints and ascetics, and may I always remember them. May I always follow the rules of conduct and discipline that they observe.

May I always act in a simple and straightforward manner, and may my thoughts, feelings, and actions always be noble and pure.

May I always strive to help and do good to others, and may I always have a friendly feeling for all human beings.

May my heart overflow with love, kindness, and compassion towards all distressed and afflicted human beings.

May I never become angry, excited, annoyed, or irritated towards bad, cruel, and wicked persons. May I develop understanding, tolerance, and patience towards them.

May I never be ungrateful towards anybody, and may I never revolt against anybody.

May I always appreciate the good qualities of other persons, and may I overlook all their faults and foibles.

May my mind always remain calm, firm, steady, unswerving, and unshaken. May I bear and endure with patience the deprivations of dear ones.

May I bow down to all those who have achieved self-realization of their souls through meditation, self-control, and self-sacrifice.

Salutations to the liberated souls. Salutations to the preceptors. Salutations to the religious instructors. Salutations to all the saints of the world.

Self-Control and Vigilance

Jainism gives great importance to self control and vigilance as these two factors are the vital keys to a peaceful and happy life. The teachings of Mahavir stress the importance of self control and vigilance for developing a pure mind, which alone can ensure good thoughts and good deeds. For a person who has self control and vigilance, there is no fear or sorrow or suffering.

One should conquer his own self, although it is very difficult. One who can successfully conquer his own self will be blessed in this world and also in the next. One who conquers his self by his own self alone will experience supreme bliss.

When suppressed, emotions and passions can bring about the spiritual downfall of even the most virtuous monk, then what can we speak of the monks who are under the sway of attachment and desires.

Anger will destroy good relations and understanding. Pride will destroy humility and cause a person's downfall. Deceit will destroy amity, and greed will destroy everything else. One should conquer anger by forgiveness, pride by humility, deceit by straightforwardness, and greed by contentment.

When we commit an evil deed, intentionally or unintentionally, we should immediately desist from it with a firm resolve not to repeat it.

It is due to greed that a person commits theft. It is on account of attachment that one longs for hoarding. A person who hoards even the slightest amount of any object or gives consent to some one for hoarding will not escape from sorrow and suffering.

There is no fear for a person who is ever vigilant. There is, however, fear from every direction for a person who is non-vigilant. An indolent person can never be happy, and a lethargic person will never acquire knowledge. One who is full of attachment and desires can never attain renunciation. A person who is violent by nature can never be compassionate.

Pride, anger, carelessness, illness, and laziness are the five main obstacles in the path of acquiring knowledge. The eight characteristics of a person able to learn are nonindulgence in frivolity, self-control, not disclosing the secret of others, not lacking in good manners, not exhibiting bad manners, not being greedy, not getting angry, and being honest.

A person should meditate on his soul after controlling his diet, posture, and sleep and gaining knowledge by the grace of the preceptor. Service to the preceptor and elders, avoiding the company of ignorant people, study of the scripture, solitude, contemplation, and patience lead to emancipation.

Jain Practice

Monastic practice is a very important aspect of Jainism, a faith that gives great significance to the ascetic ideal. Jain religious practices are of two types. The first type includes those practices that are most informed by the ascetic ideal. The second type are those practices that are less directly linked to asceticism. The more ascetic model is framed by a vision of the complete path to liberation as consisting of further stages, called Gunasthanas. These stages relate to the gradual progress of the jiva, or soul, from a state of total karmic bondage to its final release or emancipation. At the fourth stage, the jiva is freed from karmic bondage to enable one to live as a pious layperson. The monastic path begins at the sixth stage.

On entering the stage of Gunasthana, a person takes the monastic vows. There are specific guidelines and a basic set of practices that should be strictly and scrupulously followed by the aspirant monks. Those aspiring for monastic orders should be physically strong and morally straight. The aspirants should study under a chosen preceptor, and when they are ready, a formal ceremony of initiation is performed. The new ascetics should then take five great vows, called Mahavrata. These five great vows should be strictly followed in the monks' day-to-day life. These vows call for the monks to strictly observe nonviolence or ahimsa, to avoid lying, to abstain from stealing, to avoid sexual acts, and to avoid acquiring any personal possessions. The aspirants will then be given a new name. The new initiates are expected to lead a life of very severe and rigorous discipline. In some Jain orders, the ascetics are to beg for their food and are not to accept any material possessions other than those given to them during the initiation.

During their day-to-day life, the Jain monks and nuns engage in study of the scriptures, meditation, and other spiritual disciplines so as to further the jiva's continuing disassociation from the karmic bondage and to progress quickly towards the ultimate liberation.

As Jain ascetics or nuns reach old age, they may make choose death voluntarily. They undertake a ritual death by undertaking fasting. This process of fasting for voluntary death is called Sallekhanda, and it is performed under the careful supervision of a preceptor. This sort of passionless death ensures that the ascetics will not void their spiritual progress by longing for material existence at the end of their lifetime. This is a very powerful sign of the dedication of Jains to conquer material existence by renunciation.

Precepts on Nonviolence

A wise person understands two basic principles: nonviolence and equality of all the living beings. Not to kill any living being is the quintessence of all knowledge and wisdom. One should understand that equanimity based on nonviolence is the essence of Dharma. This is the philosophy of nonviolence.

Just as pain is not agreeable to anyone, it is so with others. Knowing this principle of equanimity, treat others with care, love, respect, and compassion, as one treats oneself. All living beings wish to live and do not want to die. This is why personages devoid of attachment prohibit the killing of the living beings. Killing a living being is killing one's own self. Showing compassion to a living being is showing compassion to oneself. He who desires his own good should avoid causing any harm or injury to any living being.

It is said by Mahavir, that absence of all attachment is nonviolence, while the presence of any attachment is violence. Even the intention of killing is a cause of the bondage of karma, whether you actually do it or not; from the real point of view, this is the nature of the bondage of karma. A wise person is one who always tries to eradicate his karma and is not engaged in violence. A person who firmly endeavors to remain nonviolent at all times is verily a non-killer.

The scriptures say that the self is both violent and nonviolent. He who is careful is nonviolent, and he who is careless is violent.

No mountain is higher than the Meru mountain. Nothing is more expansive and broad than the sky. Similarly, there is no religion equal to the religion of nonviolence in this world.

Oh mortal being, be free from fear and let others be free from fear. In this world of impermanence, why should one indulge in violence and cause so much pain, suffering, and sorrow? One should sincerely practice nonviolence at all times in thoughts and actions.

The being whom you want to kill is none other than you. The being whom you wish to govern and enslave is none other than you. Thus, killing any living being is like killing your own self.

The objective of one's life should be to practice nonviolence towards all living beings. Lord Jina has said that no one should cause any violence or injury to any living being and one should practice nonviolence, non-injury, and equality to all living beings.

Precepts on Carefulness and Self-Control

Vigilance in walking, vigilance in speech, vigilance in begging for alms, vigilance in receiving and keeping down things and excreting are five acts of carefulness. Control of the mind, control of speech, and control of the body are the three acts of self-control. Together, these eight are called the mother precepts. Just as a diligent mother protects her child, these eight protect the right knowledge, right faith, and right conduct of the monk, the five types of vigilances are meant for the practice of religious life. The three types of self-controls are meant for the prevention of everything sinful.

If a tiny living creature is accidentally crushed to death under the foot of a monk who is normally very careful in respect to all his physical movements, the scriptures state that the monk will not attract even the slightest of karmic bondage. This is because the monk is not responsible for that violence. Just as possessiveness consists in a sense of attachment, so the violence consists in the intention of killing.

Just as a lotus leaf possessing the property of smoothness is not affected by water, similarly a monk practicing acts of carefulness is not touched by karmic bondage in the course of moving around in the midst of living beings.

Carefulness is the mother of religion. It is the protector of religion. It helps the growth of religion, and it begets perfect happiness and peace.

An attentive monk should prevent his mind from indulging in sinful or evil thoughts. He should be very careful that his mind does not indulge in thoughts of collection of implements, which cause harm to others. He should also ensure that his mind does not indulge in thoughts of evil actions. He should always control his speech. He should bring under control his body as soon as it is inclined towards a mental plan for causing harm or hurt or pain to others. Once the mind is kept under control, there is no possibility of any harm or hurt to anyone. Control of the mind is very essential for a monk in his pursuit of spiritual progress and ultimate liberation.

As a fence protects a field from animals and a ditch or rampart protects a city from the enemy, so the control of the mind, speech, and body protects a monk from sin.

Service to the preceptor and elders; avoiding the company of bad and ignorant people; regular study of the scripture; contemplating the meaning of the scriptural texts; patience and self-control—by all these things can an austere monk attain liberation.

One should practice Dharma before old age creeps up, since in old age the senses become feeble, and one falls a prey to all kinds of illness. It will not be possible to practice Dharma later with a feeble and incompetent body.

Knowing the worldly objects as bonds of the soul, the aspirant should proceed in his life with extreme caution and self-control. As long as the body remains strong, he should use it to practice self-restraint and self-control. When the body is devoid of its strength completely, a person should renounce it without any attachment, as if it were a lump of clay.

Precepts on Right Knowledge

The practice of right knowledge enables one to understand the eternal truth. It enables one to achieve self-control and self-restraint and thereby ensure purification of the soul.

After listening to scriptures, a person comes to know what is good and what is not good and sinful. And having thus known through listening, one ought to perform what leads to welfare.

Under the influence of his or her scriptural knowledge, he becomes firm in his or her faith, meditation, observance of vows, self-control, and self-restraint. From then on, he lives a life of complete purity throughout his or her lifetime, without any wavering or doubt. A needle with a thread attached to it does not get lost even if it falls in a heap of rubbish. In the same way, a person endowed with scriptural knowledge does not lose his self, even if involved in a cycle of birth and death.

According to the teachings of Jina, knowledge is that which helps one to understand the eternal truth, to have self-control, and to purify the soul. Knowledge with faith and conduct constitute the path of liberation. It is only through knowledge that ties of attachments and desires are severed, attraction towards auspiciousness is developed, and the feelings of friendship are strengthened.

He who knows that the self is wholly different from an impure body knows the entire body of scriptures. One who knows the soul as pure attains a pure self. But he who contemplates the soul as having an impure nature becomes himself impure.

He who knows the internal knows the external, and he who knows the external knows the internal. He who knows the self knows everything else. He who knows all things knows the self.

Be you always engrossed in pure knowledge; be you ever satisfied in it; be ever contented with it. You will then achieve supreme happiness.

Just as one getting hold of a treasure consumes it in a gentlemanly fashion, a wise man getting hold of the treasure of knowledge enjoys it, ignoring all pleasures derived from anything else.

Precepts on Right Faith

Right faith is the core of Jainism. Right faith is a part of the three gems of right knowledge, right conduct, and right faith. Right faith is the root of the great tree of liberation. It has to be understood from two points of view: the real point of view and the empirical point of view.

Without right faith, there cannot be right knowledge, and without right knowledge there will not be virtuous conduct. Without virtues, one's karma cannot be annihilated, and without annihilation of one's karma, there will be no liberation.

Lord Jina said that from the empirical point of view, right faith is faith in the existence of the soul and the other principles. From the real point of view, the soul itself is right faith.

From the real point of view, true monkhood constitutes righteousness, and righteousness constitutes real monkhood. But from the practical point of view, the causes of righteousness are called right faith itself.

Those persons who are devoid of right faith will not attain right knowledge, even if they practice severe penance for millions of years. Those who have renounced right faith are deprived persons. There is no liberation for a person devoid of right faith. Those who have renounced right conduct may attain liberation, but those who have renounced right faith will never attain liberation

He who has right faith is certainly pure. He who is possessed of right faith is certain to attain liberation. Belief in the existence of Dharma is right faith.

It is due to the magnanimity of right faith the great personage and those worthy of attaining emancipation have attained liberation in the past and will continue to do so in the future.

Just as it is on account of its very nature that a lotus leaf remains unaffected and untouched by water, similarly a righteous person remains unaffected by passions and prejudices and by the objects of sensuous enjoyments.

The practice of right faith leads to knowledge. By attaining knowledge, one understands the true nature of things; by faith, one believes in them; by conduct, one puts an end to the flow of karma; and by austerity, one attains purity and, ultimately, liberation.

Thus, right faith is a powerful tool in the hands of a person desirous of attaining liberation. Right faith will enable one to be released from the bondage of karma.

Knowledge without right conduct, asceticism without right faith, and austerities without self-control are all futile.

Precepts on Right Conduct

Jainism values the practice of right conduct. Right conduct from the practical viewpoint is to practice austerities.

Know that right conduct consists in desisting from inauspicious activity and instead engaging in auspicious activity. A person who possesses scriptural knowledge will not attain emancipation if he is not able to observe strictly the activities of austerity and self-control.

Though a person knows the right path, he fails to reach his destination due to inaction or absence of favorable wind for his boat. Similarly, knowledge will not achieve the desired fruit in the absence of virtuous deeds.

Just as a hundred-thousand millions of lamps kept burning are of no use to a blind person, of what use is the study of numerous scriptures to a person who has no character or integrity?

A person of right conduct triumphs over a learned person, even if his scriptural knowledge is very little. What is the use of wide study of scriptures for a person without right conduct?

He who is blissfully absorbed in his own soul to know his soul with the help of his soul becomes a person of right conduct; that ascetic attains emancipation.

Right conduct is really what constitutes religion. It is said that religion is equanimity. Equanimity is that state of the soul that is free from delusion, agitation, and excitement.

Equanimity, tolerance, pure thought, freedom from attachment and hatred, right conduct, religion, devotion to one's self; all these are said to be one and the same.

Purity of faith and knowledge constitute pure asceticism. Such pure souls are bound to attain liberation.

Knowledge without right conduct, asceticism without right faith, and austerities without self-control are all futile. Without right faith, there is no right knowledge, without right knowledge there is no right conduct. Without right conduct, there is no elimination of karmas, and without elimination of karmas, there is no eternal bliss.

Non-indulgence in frivolity, self-control, keeping the secrets of others in confidence, good manners, absence of greed and anger, and strict adherence to truth—these are the traits of a person of right conduct.

MEDITATION IN JAINISM

In Jainism, great importance is given to meditation, prayers, and penance. Meditation is enjoined on all monks as the most important part of their religion.

Meditation is a steady state of mind, while an active mind may be engaged in either contemplation or deep reflection or thinking.

Just as salt dissolves when it comes into contact with water, so too the mind becomes absorbed in meditation, the fire of the soul shines brilliantly, burning the auspicious as well as inauspicious karmas. If a person is free of passions, he becomes filled with the fire of meditation that burns all karmas.

A person who is totally free of all passions, who is pure in thought and body, who concentrates his mind, becomes absorbed in perfect meditation.

In practicing meditation, a person should sit in a comfortable posture; stop all activities of the mind, speech, and body; fix the gaze of his eyes on the tip of his nose; and slow down his breath.

A person engaged in meditation should condemn all evil conduct, seek pardon from all living beings, renounce negligence, steady his mind, and become fully absorbed in perfect meditation until the thing meditated on appears to be standing in front of oneself.

In the case of a monk, who has steadied all his mental, vocal, and bodily activity and who has thoroughly concentrated his mind on meditation, it does not matter whether he stays in a village or in a forest.

A monk devoted to penance and who is desirous of practicing meditation should keep his mind pure. He should not entertain pleasant or unpleasant thoughts about material things and objects of the senses.

A monk becomes steady in perfect meditation if he has understood thoroughly the nature of mundane existence, is free of all desire and attachment, is fearless, and has developed an attitude of complete indifference to the world.

A monk who meditates upon the soul with supreme faith and knowledge can be termed a "yogi." He puts an end to all his sins and becomes free from the conflicting feelings of pain and pleasure. He is a liberated soul.

A monk who sees that soul is different from the body as well as all other internal and external possessions becomes free from all desires and attachments and undertakes an absolute renunciation of body and also of all external implements.

If a monk fails to attain the knowledge of his real nature or soul while undertaking meditation, he cannot secure purity. He will be unlucky, like a person who fails to secure a precious stone.

Nirvana or Emancipation

Nirvana is the state of being free from both suffering and the cycle of rebirth. The concept of Nirvana is the foundation on which Jainism rests. The word "Nirvana" is derived from the Pali word "Nibbana", which means blowing out the fires of greed, hatred and delusion.

Nirvana is Jainism means emancipation or final release from the bondage of karma. It is freedom from sorrow, suffering, old age and death. Buddha described Nirvana as the perfect state of mind that is completely free from craving, anger and suffering. According to Mahavir, Nirvana means peace with the world, compassion and love for all and giving up all worldly things and desires. In Nirvana, the root causes of craving and aversion are extinguished, so that one is no longer subject to human sorrow and suffering as well as further state of rebirth.

It is very difficult to attain the state of Nirvana. It requires tremendous self control and self discipline as well as development of right faith, right knowledge and virtuous conduct. A person should meditate on his soul, control his diet and sit in meditation in accordance with the precepts of Mahavir. Having become enlightened through knowledge, having given up ignorance and delusion, and abandoned all attachments and aversion, one attains Nirvana or empancipation, which is supreme bliss. Dedicated and devoted service bestowed on the preceptor and the elders, keeping company with enlightened persons and daily study of the scriptures – all these constitute the path to Nirvana.

It is difficult to describe the state of Nirvana, since it transcends any verbal description. There is no pride, since Nirvana is devoid of all the blemishes of the mind. Where there is neither pain nor pleasure, neither joy nor sorrow, neither suffering nor obstacle, neither birth nor death, there is Nirvana. Where there are neither sense organs nor any obstruction caused by others, neither infatuation nor surprise, neither sleep nor thirst and hunger, there is emancipation.

In emancipated souls, there are attributes like absolute knowledge, absolute bliss, absolute vision, formlessness, existence and extension. Nirvana or emancipation is achieved only by great and illumined souls.

Chapter 11

Taoism, Confucianism, and Shintoism

Taoism

An Introduction to Taoism

Taoism in its early stages was more a philosophy than a religion. Its founder, Lao-tzu was dissatisfied with the chaos and turmoil of the times and sought relief by shunning society and returning to nature. Many details are not known about Lao-tzu, who is said to have lived in the sixth century B.C.E.

Taoism takes its name from the Chinese word "Tao," which means the "Way" or "Path," and refers to the Way of the Universe. The Tao is a natural force that guides all life throughout the universe. In Tao Te Ching, the Tao scripture, Lao-tzu expounded on Tao, the ultimate way of nature and applied it to every aspect and level of human activity. To Taoists, Tao is some mysterious cosmic force that is responsible for the material universe. The objective of Taoism is to search out the Tao, leave behind the world, and become one with nature.

Taoism is basically a school of philosophy. Reacting to the injustices, sufferings, misery, devastation, and futility that resulted from the harsh rule of the then feudal system, Taoists believed that the way to find peace and harmony was to go back to the tradition of the ancients before there were kings and ministers, who controlled and dominated the common people. Their ideal was to live the tranquil, rural life, in union with nature.

Taoists believe that distress and suffering arise when people struggle against the Way of Nature, but if they travel with the Tao, then their lives will be in peace and harmony with the order of the universe.

This order is kept in balance by the two opposing forces of "Yin" and "Yang." These are the forces that are continually changing and interacting with each other, giving order to all life. Many Taoists believe that if they withdrew from the world to remote mountains or other solitary secluded places, they are very much closer to nature and thereby discover the true meaning of the Tao.

The view of the Taoist is that there is no point in anyone doing anything to interfere with what nature has set in motion. Sooner or later, everything will return to its opposite. No matter how unbearable a situation is, it will soon become better. No matter how pleasant a situation is, it will soon fade away.

The symbol of Taoism is a circle of black and white with a dot in each, representing the interaction and balance of yin and yang. Yin is represented in dark shade. Yin is a cool dark force that is seen in rain, clouds, winter and snow. Yang is a hot bright force that is seen in thunder, the earth, summer and the sun.

There are about 15 to 20,000 Taoist priests, both male and female, in China. Taoist traditions are followed by Chinese communities all over the world and Taoist thoughts and literature are becoming increasingly popular with non-Chinese followers.

There are many temples and shrines in China that are centers of local pilgrimage. The major pilgrimage sites are, however, the five Taoist mountains.

There are hundreds of sacred Taoist texts.

Taoism

Founder

Lao-tzu, the founder of Taoism, was a Chinese philosopher who lived in the days of the prophet Jeremiah. He was born in the year 640 BC. The earliest Chinese history, written around the second century BC, includes a biographical sketch of Lao-tzu. According to Chinese historical records, his birth name was Li Her, and he was a contemporary of the Chinese scholar and philosopher Confucius. Very little is known about the life of Lau-tzu. The historical records indicate that he worked as an archivist in the royal palace in Luoyang, the capital of the Zhou dynasty. There he came to be known as Laozi (Lao-tzu). Lao-tzu was more of a title than a name, and it means "the old one" or "the master." He was also sometimes called "the old big ear."

According to tradition, Lao-tzu grew up in great wisdom during his lifetime. Since he was considered a very wise man, people came to him to consult on social, religious, and political matters. Lao-tzu was known for his virtue, erudition, and wise teachings. He was a bit rough, outspoken, and impartial in addition to being sharp tongued.

He worked in the royal archives of the Zhou court till he was almost ninety years old. By that time, the Zhou dynasty was on the decline. Lao-tzu became tired of the government work and he decided to leave the province. According to tradition, after many years of service in the government, Lao-tzu rode into the mountains on a water buffalo. On his way, Lao-tzu stopped to write the famous Tao Te Ching, which is the foundation of Taoist scripture.

Chief Scripture

The book Tao Te Ching—generally translated "the classic of the Way and the Power"—is considered a principal scripture of Taoism. In Tao Te Ching, the founder expounded on Tao, the ultimate way of nature, and applied it to every level of human activity. Quoting from a modern translation, it explains the concept of Tao as follows: "There was something mysteriously formed, born before heaven and earth. Perhaps it is the mother of ten thousand things. I do not know its name. Call it Tao."

This example shows that Taoism was basically a school of philosophy. Reacting to the adverse effects of the feudal system of the times which resulted in injustice, suffering and destruction, Taoists believed that the way to find peace and harmony was to go back to nature. Their ideal was to live in peace and harmony in unison with nature.

The Tao Te Ching is a collection of eighty-one short points, which are called chapters. Some scholars believe that Tao Te Ching may not be the work of one single person, but rather the collection of many. However, Tao Te Ching is traditionally attributed to Lao-tzu. Many of the poems are addressed to rulers and give valuable advice on just and good governance. Lao-tzu teaches the unimportance of importance. For example, water takes the unimportant part as it seeps into the ground. Unnoticed, it is the nourishing force that sustains life of all beings. The lower it seems, the more truly important it is. Like water, Tao gives birth to and nourishes everything but makes no claim to importance. Like water, a wise person will work without calling attention to himself, will do what is right and fair, and will become attuned to the nature of things. Such a person will understand Tao.

Beliefs

Tao in Chinese means "path," and the basis of early Taoism is the allowance of the affairs of men to take the part of nature. Taoism as a religion stresses peace, quietism, contemplation, and the elimination of all striving and strong passions. The main belief in Taoism is that there is a natural and correct way to do everything and that everything and everyone has its proper place and its proper function. The Taoists believe that if the ruler ruled justly and looked after the sacrificial rituals relating to heaven, there would be peace, prosperity, and plenty in the land. Similarly, if people are willing to seek out the "Way," or Tao, and follow it, everything will become peaceful, effective, and harmonious. If they are to go against the Way or resist it, there will be chaos and disaster.

Later, Taoism took on aspects of Confucianism and Buddhism, and Taoist monasteries were established throughout China. Taoism also developed beliefs on the afterlife which included the heaven and hell.

Beliefs of Taoism

The Tao is a mystical thing. It is beyond knowing, beyond identification, and it defies all description. In the scripture of Taoism, called Tao Te Ching, an attempt has been made to describe the Tao. It defines Tao as something which existed before heaven and earth, which though undifferentiated was yet complete. Soundless, formless, and changeless, it operates everywhere and can be termed the mother of the universe. It has no name, and it is called Tao.

The Tao is an impersonal force of existence. All beings in the world came from being, and being came from non-being. Further, being and non-being produce each other. Also out of non-being and being came the rest of the world. The Tao is not only the face of existence from which the world flows, but is also the "way" within the world. The Tao is the force that flows through nature, and it guides and motivates all objects in the world. The "way" in which the Tao flows ensures health, harmony, happiness, and peace.

The Te is the pattern within every object and that makes it what it is. Thus, Te is one's individuality and the inner connection to the universal Tao. According to Taoism, we should accept the Te both in ourselves and in all other things.

According to Taoism, force was inevitably responded to with force. Violent people do not die a natural death. This principle was true not only in cases involving violence, but also in the case of persons imposing their will on others. When someone imposes her or his will on a person or object, the pattern-Te in the object or person resisted. Therefore, the way to achieve one's purpose is to work with the pattern or the Te within the thing or person

Taoism is thus a system of ideas, many of which seem rather paradoxical. It is naturalistic in that nature is the basis and measure of everything. Taoism maintains a sense of the mystical and the unattainable, since the true "way" can only be approached. We can never fully comprehend it. The Tao is not personal. It cannot know us, and we cannot know it. Thus, the Taoist scripture only talks about the Tao and never to the Tao.

> "It may be considered the mother of the universe. I do not know its name; I call it Tao." —Tao Te Ching

Gems from Taoism

> "Can you control your animal nature enough to be pure in heart, never distracted from the one Way? Are you capable of the personal disciplines that can enable you to love unselfishly, wield virtue and understand all, while denying yourself."

> "Put life into your people without trying to own them. Depend on no one. Be their king but never the tyrant. This is what our mysticism requires of you."

> "Deep in all there is a stillness, where the root of life is and the root is God, from whom destiny proceeds, and without knowledge of that root, the eternal root, a man is blind and will, therefore, work evil. Let the king take note. When he knows that root, he will be of great stature as a man and king, whose righteousness will endow him with kingdom and makes him divine, because the way is at work in him. Thus the king may die, but he will not perish."

> "There was a time, when men shared with all other creatures the balance of nature, its spontaneity and change. Then the process of civilization came with its inevitable constituents namely, kindness, morality, wisdom and intelligence. Their opposites came with them namely, unkindness, immorality, foolishness and stupidity. Then there was trouble everywhere. The world is not to be owned and tinkered by any man. It belongs to God and those who try to usurp his right will definitely fail."

> "Things generally have their own individual characteristics and cannot be made to submit to the whims of one person. The king will,

therefore, avoid the temptation to try and make everything in the world conform to his plan and serve his vanity."

"The mean man pays the highest price because he trades virtue for gain. The hoarder takes the greatest loss because he accumulates pelf in preference to virtue. The man content has virtue and is self-restrained and so he is never in danger from shame or death."

Taoism and Life

Unlike Christians or Buddhists, Taoists do not believe in rebirth or reincarnation. In Taoism, there is no rebirth into a heavenly kingdom after death. Similarly, there is no reincarnation in another form. The Taoist simply focuses on life here and now in this world. According to a Taoist master, "A Taoist is one who starts out with this earthly life as it is." He wishes to live happily and peacefully as long as life lasts. He faces all trials and tribulations cheerfully. He has a keen appreciation of the beautiful and good in human life, wherever he finds them. He regards doing good as its own satisfactory reward.

Taoists wish and hope for a long life. They try to do everything possible so as to ensure that they have a long and happy life. To live according to the principles of Taoism requires self-discipline, self-awareness, and self-control. Taoists oppose all desires and excesses that threaten to rob them of a peaceful and happy life. By regular practice of many life-improving activities, such as exercise, meditation, and a balanced diet, they hope to live a very long life. They also firmly believe that by doing these things, they will achieve immortality in this very life.

Taoists believe that all human beings are part of the universe. If a person can bring his or her life into complete harmony with the natural laws of the universe, he or she could continue to exist as long as heaven and earth exist.

Taoism stresses the importance of preserving the three great treasures of human life: vitality, energy, and spirit. These three treasures are inseparable and interdependent. One cannot exist without the other. Vitality is associated with creativity and basic physical body functions, including procreation. Energy is associated with movement and strength. Spirit is associated with consciousness, intellect, and spirituality. These three treasures should be kept in perfect harmony and balance.

Harmony and Balance (Yin and Yang)

One cannot see the Tao, but one can experience it in the rhythmic cycles of nature: night and day, summer and winter, rain and sun, birth and death. These opposing forces convey the Chinese concept of Yin and Yang, central to Taoist understanding. The forces of Yin and Yang demonstrate Tao, which is in everything. Yang is the heavenly force and is the force of movement, of light, fire, warmth, and life. Yang literally means "the sunny side" of a hill. In Chinese, sun is tai yang, or great yang. Yin is the shadowy side of the hill. Yin is Yang's opposite.

But Yin cannot be separated from Yang. Just as there cannot exist any shadow without the sun, there cannot be Yin without Yang. The two operate together in the cycles that are a part of nature and of Tao. The concept of Yin and Yang sums up all the opposing forces in life, but the Taoists see these forces not as truly opposite, but as complementing each other, resolving their differences in the great circle that symbolizes the unity of Tao.

Yin and Yang, representing opposing forces, are not permanently fixed. A Taoist sees all things as relative to one another. A cloudy day is Yin and dark, when compared to a sunny day. Yang is bright, when compared to the dark night. In Taoism, good and bad, yes and no are not very much apart. So it is possible to accept all the problems and troubles of life with equanimity. The way of nature is neither right or wrong. It simply is. Taoists, therefore, endeavor to be like nature itself. Nature constantly changes from Yang to Yin and vice versa. The same is true of life. No can predict how things will turn out. What appears as good fortune may turn out to be a disaster. Success and failure, poverty and fortune have all equal drawbacks. All things are really the same in Tao. Taoists try to develop stillness within themselves through meditation and devotional activities that bring calm and peace.

Taoism and Harmony

The word Tao in Chinese means the "way." The Way is understood to mean the way of nature. Believers of Taoism see the cycles of nature and the constant change in the natural world as early signs of a great and universal force. This unseen force is called Tao. For the Taoist, Tao is the ultimate Reality, a presence that existed before the universe was formed and that continues to guide the world and all the things in the world. Tao is also identified as the mother and source of everything. That source is not a God or a Supreme Being. Unlike Islam or Judaism or Christianity, Taoism is not monotheistic. Taoists do not worship one God. They focus on coming into harmony with Tao.

While many world religions have a founder, Taoism has no one founder. It has no central figures like Buddha, Christ, or Mohammed. Taoism has, on the other hand, a number of great masters. The great masters taught and wrote about Tao, and Taoists read the works of these masters so as to find harmony and the Way. Finding the Way is rather difficult, because Tao cannot be taught. It can only be learned. Tao masters and writers guide the believers by pointing out the way, and each person must find his or her own Tao.

Taoism reaches into the intellectual, spiritual, and physical lives of its followers. According to Taoism, the physical body is a miniature model of the universe. A person cannot be in harmony with the universe if his or her body is not in harmony with itself.

Thus, in Taoism, the way a person treats his or her body is as vital as what that person thinks, believes, or does in relation to others.

A healthy body is the first step to achieving a spiritual state in life. Consequently, Taoism has been associated with many medicinal and nutritional products. Taoist masters have developed medicinal uses for thousands of plants, herbs, fruits, fungi, etc., and they have recommended a balanced diet to maintain good health. Exercise is another integral part of Taoist practice, as is control of breath. Another important aspect of Taoism is meditation. Taoists practice a form of meditation to help them to come into harmony with the ultimate Reality. Taoists believe that meditation prolongs life, and according to Taoism, a person has greater chances of achieving perfect harmony with Tao if he or she has a long life.

The objective of a Taoist is to achieve perfect harmony with Tao.

Scriptures and Beliefs

Taoism places great importance on meditation as a means of finding Tao. In the past, some Taoist masters concentrated on recording rituals and spells, alchemical formulas, and ways to attain immortality. Taoist beliefs had a profound effect on Chinese thoughts as well as their way of lives. The Taoist philosophy spread to workers and peasants in addition to the Imperial courts. Taoist beliefs were distinct and different from Chinese folk religion and traditions.

In the year AD 471, Taoist monks brought together the first Taoist canon, which drew from all of the main traditions of Taoism. The first Taoist canon contained twelve hundred scrolls. Besides the interpretation of the Tao Te Ching, it includes writings on alchemy, immortality, lives of immortals and good works and longevity. It had also philosophical essays and folk tales, magic words and meditation, rituals and liturgy and many aspects of Taoist thoughts.

The Tao Te Ching begins with the fundamental question of what is Tao. According to the Taoist masters, Tao is deeper than the deepest mystery that the mind can conceive. It cannot be explained because it is too vast for human understanding. Tao existed before anything existed, and Tao will continue to exist when nothing exists any longer. Tao cannot be seen or touched or experienced by the senses. It is expressed by the natural forces of the universe. Like the universe, it is without beginning and end. Tao is invisible and mysterious. Tao is the beginning of all things.

In the Tao Te Ching it is stated that the Tao gave birth to one, the one gave birth to two, and the two gave birth to three, and the three gave birth to all things. Taoists interpret this to mean the formless and vast Tao existed before anything else. From it came the origin of One. From this One came the balance of opposing forces, Yin and Yang, which are opposites but inseparable. Yin and Yang are expressed as the three forces of heaven, earth, and humanity. Thus, Tao is the ultimate Reality or force behind everything. The main belief of Taoism is to focus on finding a way to get into harmony with this ultimate force or reality and to go with the flow of Tao and the universe.

The Tao from which all beings came is called the Great Void or Emptiness. Taoists seek union with this emptiness, which is seen as a higher state than consciousness. Wisdom and serenity come from conforming one's life to the natural laws of the universe. Taoist meditations require emptying of the mind so that creative forces of Tao can flow in.

Humility

Just as the Tao pervades all things and all are dependent upon it, yet it claims no credit and exerts no authority; so the sage is able to accomplish great things by not making himself great. Heaven and earth endure because they do not live for themselves; so the sage puts himself last. Rivers and streams receive tribute from the valley streams by being lower than they are; so the sage is above others because he puts himself below them. One must overcome ones self. He who overcomes others is strong. He who overcomes himself is mighty. One must empty oneself. The use of a wheel depends on the hole for the axle; the use of vessels of clay depends upon the hollow space inside them; so is it with doors and windows and the space inside a room. The man who has forgotten himself is he of whom it is said that he has become identified with heaven.

Humility is the quality or state of being humble, free from arrogance and haughtiness. With humility goes gentleness, goodness, and unfailing kindness. Recompense injury with kindness and compassion. To those who are good to me, I am good. To those who are not good to me, I am also good. And thus all get to be good.

A good man who is humble is self-effacing. He is all humility. Consequently, his objective is peace, and the picture of peace consists of families secure on their land and the people thoughtful, kind, peaceful, and honest.

The highest goodness, like water, is characterized by humility. A good man or a good king is self-effacing like the Way.

An Introduction to Confucianism

Confucius was China's great sage, statesman, scholar, teacher, and philosopher, and of all Chinese sages, Confucius is undoubtedly the best known outside China. The word "Confucius" is a Latin transliteration of the Chinese "K'ungfu-tzu," meaning, "King the Master." In fact, the Jesuit priests who came to China in the sixteenth century coined the Latinized name when they recommended to the Pope that Confucius be canonized as a saint of the Roman Catholic Church.

In Confucianism, this concept is known as "Li," which means propriety, courtesy, the order of things, ritual, ceremony, and reverence. Regarding "Li," Confucius said,

> Of all things that people live by, Li is the greatest. Without Li, we do not know how to conduct a proper worship of the spirits of the universe or how to establish the proper status of the king and the ministers, the ruler and the ruled, and the elders and the juniors, or how to establish the moral relationship between the sexes, between parents and children and between brothers or how to distinguish the different degrees of relationships in the family. That is why a gentleman holds Li in high regard.

Because Confucius made few comments about God, many people view Confucianism as only a philosophy and not as a religion. Yet what he said and did showed that he was religious. This can be seen in two respects. First, Confucius had a reverent fear of a supreme cosmic power that the Chinese call "T'ien," or heaven. Confucius regarded T'ien as a source of all virtue and moral goodness whose will directs all things. Second, he placed great emphasis on meticulous observance of rites and ceremonies relating to the worship of heaven and the spirits of departed ancestors. Although Confucius never advocated these views as a form of religion, to generations of Chinese they have become what religion is all about.

Confucianism is found wherever traditional Chinese culture survives.

Confucianism

Founder

Founder Confucius was born in 551 BC in the city of Lu and died in 479 BC. He was a tutor to the son of the aristocracy. He taught the wisdom of the ancients, taking as his texts the Book of Documents and the Book of Songs, which described mainly Chinese life during that period. This period, in particular its founder kings Wen and Wu, provide for Confucius a golden age and model kings.

Chief Scripture

Confucian Four Books and Five Classics. The Four Books include the following:

1. The Analects (Lun Yu)—This book is a collection of sayings of Confucius and is
2. considered the primary and most important source of Confucian thought. The
3. Analects is more or less viewed as the chief scripture of Confucianism.
4. The Great Learning (Ta Hsueh)—This book is the basis of a gentleman's education and the first text studied by schoolchildren in old China.
5. The Doctrine of the Mean (Chung Yung)—This book is a treatise on the
6. development of human nature through moderation.
7. The Book of Mencius—This book is a collection of the writings and sayings of
8. Meng-tzu, or Mencius, who was the greatest disciple of Confucius.

The Five Classics include the following:

1. The Book of Poetry (Shih Ching)—This classic is a collection of 305 poems
2. providing a picture of daily life in early China of Chou dynastic times.
3. The Book of History (Shu Ching)—This book covers seventeen centuries of Chinese history, beginning with the Shang Dynasty.
4. The Book of Changes (I Ching)—This is a book of divination, based on

5. interpretations of the sixty-four possible combinations of six whole or broken lines.
6. The Book of Rites (Li Chi)—This is a collection of rules and procedures on
7. ceremonies and rituals.
8. Annals of Spring and Autumn (Chun Chiu)—This book is a history of Confucius'
9. native state of Lu.

Dates from

The time of Confucius, about 2500 years ago.

Confucius looked to the past era as a golden age, and he served as a creative transmitter of the ancient wisdom and culture. His teachings, based on his study of Chinese traditions, greatly influenced China, from the past to the present times. Confucius taught a moral code and a way of life based on love, humanity, integrity, harmony, peace, and understanding. Though he lived at a time when China was in deep turmoil and disorder, his teachings placed great importance on order, peace, and harmony. He emphasized the need for people to develop healthy neighborly relationships as well as a stable government.

According to Confucius, a good government could be created only by those who could reach the high standard of a gentleman. In his opinion, government service was the highest possible calling. Confucius withdrew attention from the spirit world and directed it towards man in society. Thus, the traditional Chinese duty to serve ancestors became a duty to serve them while they are living. Filial piety became directed not so much towards the dead father but toward parents during their lifetime. Thus was born the system of familial obligations and duties, the five relationships that characterized Confucian teachings. Kingship became model parenthood, and the sovereign acts as the father and mother of his people. Citizenship is conceived as an extension of familial duty. The genius of Confucianism consisted in converting society from the domination of magic to the supremacy of morals. In the religious sphere, the propitiation of ancestors became reverence for ancestors and was extended to reverence for parents, and to a rigid set of obligations among members of the family.

Confucius emphasized the important part played by family in society. Confucius taught that an individual developed his or her full potential within the family. He also stressed the obligations and responsibilities of each member of a family. The strongest of family relationships was that between a father and son. A father should provide for the family and the son should pay greatest honor to his father, even after his father's death. The five essential and important virtues were courtesy, magnanimity, good faith, earnestness, and kindness. All people who came to Confucius to learn were advised that education was the only way by which they could become good citizens and good gentlemen.

Confucianism later became a state religion, which formed the basis of the Chinese educational system, way of life, and good government.

Because Confucius made no comments about God, many people consider Confucianism only a philosophy rather than a religion. However, what Confucius said, taught, and did showed that he was religious. The fact that Confucius was religious can be seen from the following two aspects. First, he had reverence and fear for a supreme cosmic spiritual power or heaven, which Confucius regarded as the source of all virtue and moral goodness. Secondly, Confucius placed great emphasis on observing ceremonies relating to the worship of heaven and the spirits of departed ancestors. For the generations of Chinese and followers of Confucius, this is what religion is about.

There is another interesting story of Confucius that sets an example of filial piety. When Confucius was in his twenties, his mother died. Since Confucius was a strict and meticulous observer of ancient traditions, he retired from public life and mourned his mother at her grave for twenty-seven months, thus providing the Chinese with a classic example of filial piety.

Confucianism—Major Aspects

Confucianism cannot be called a formal religion in the conventional sense. Rather, it can be described as a religious belief system that forms the values that are implicit to most people in China, Japan, and Korea. The Confucian work ethic spurred rapid economic growth in Asia. This work ethic involves a strong commitment to the family. Loyalties in the family are established not only during this lifetime but continue even after death. Further, the Confucian work ethic is founded on a strong moral ethic of practicing virtues, giving good advice and words of wisdom, engaging in good work, and developing attitudes of loyalty, trust, and respect. It is the continuation of an individual's ethical system on the thoughts and values of his or her descendents.

What is the foundation of virtue and goodness in an age of confusion? In searching for an answer, Confucius went to the moral aspect of human nature. He asked each person to reflect seriously on his or her moral decisions and to act in a responsible manner when faced with adversity. Confucius found that the foundation for such a moral responsibility existed in the moral consciousness of the person, specifically in the Jen, which means humanity. Jen refers to the goodness or good nature residing in each person. All virtues emanate from this good nature. Through Jen, every person can realize his or her good nature and reach an ideal state of life. Jen is the goal of humanity and is the basic human quality that is good. Jen is the true nature residing inside each person. A person can achieve his or her goal through Jen. The harmonious and healthy way of living must be based on one's realizing of Jen.

Confucius spoke of Ultimate Reality as Tien. For harmony and peace, humanity must abide by the moral order. The main theme of Confucianism is to confirm humanity's natural goodness and find a way to actualize it. Human nature is basically good. Evil comes when we are compelled to act in an evil way and when our mind tends towards evil. Goodness is achieved through education, self-analysis, introspection, and good behavior.

Teachings of Confucius

The main thrust of Confucius's teachings was to make his students perfect gentlemen and good citizens. With this in mind, he took great pains to train talented and capable young men. It was Confucius's firm conviction that, after proper training, his students could become useful members of society by serving as officials in the local government. Confucius gave his disciples practical training in the six arts of writing, rituals, music, archery, chariot driving, and mathematics. His main concern was to make the students men of sterling and sound character who could set an example to others by their actions and thus change society.

Confucius did not look at family background and other considerations in accepting students. The only condition stipulated was that a student should demonstrate proper spirit, diligence, eagerness to learn, and ability. Correct behavior was imperative, since Confucius felt that good character and personal behavior were essential for changing and improving society. Mere outward signs of good behavior were not enough. Confucius wanted all his students to reflect sincerity, honesty, harmony, understanding, and love through their words and deeds. In the philosophy of Confucius, the basic ideals were based on five important virtues: integrity, knowledge, honesty, faithfulness, and uprightness.

The sum and substance of Confucian teachings is that society in general and the country at large will work harmoniously and justly when each person understands his or her proper role and acts accordingly. According to Confucius, "Let the ruler be a ruler, the subject be a subject, father be a father, and let the son be a son." In this manner, there will be peace and harmony, which in turn will bring prosperity and happiness to people.

Since family is the basic unit of society, Confucius stressed the importance of showing respect for fathers by sons, elder brothers by younger brothers, and husbands by wives. According to Confucius, a happy and contented family will ensure peace and harmony in society.

Confucian Beliefs

Confucius identified in human society five types of human relationships: the relationship between the ruler and the ruled, father and son, husband and wife, the eldest member of a family and his brother, and, finally, the relationship between the elders and juniors or friends. Confucius maintained that if within these relationships, every person lived by courtesy, understanding, and reverence and cared for social and religious harmony, then there would be peace and harmony within every family, society, and nation. Further, there would be social and political harmony in the entire world.

Confucius was an ideal teacher and great scholar who devoted his entire life to the study of all aspects of ancient wisdom. He further believed that he had found those principles of virtue that motivated the lives and actions of holy and wise men in ancient times. Confucius also believed that if these virtues were to be inculcated and followed in his own day, it would result in true nobility of character and integrity, happiness, well-being, and peace of the family, society, and the state. Being an ideal teacher, Confucius taught others what he learned by setting an example himself.

The five great Confucian classics are the Book of Odes, The Historical Documents, The Book of Rites, A Book of Divination, and lastly, The Annals of the States, which was popularly known as the Spring and Autumn classic. In using these documents, Confucius was very selective by using them to prove his belief that individual life, the social life, and all good governments should be founded on morality. According to Confucius, true nobility is nobility of character and integrity, which did not depend on royal birth and privilege. A truly noble character should be true to his innermost self. He should be loyal, faithful, kind, and considerate to others. He should be moderate in all his words and deeds, cultured in manner, and meticulous in observing those rites and ceremonies that pertain to human behavior and human relationships. He also emphasized the necessity of cultivating wisdom and sincerity in speech and actions.

Confucius was known in China as a great teacher—in fact, the first teacher—and his name was closely associated with Chinese culture. He never assumed that he was a sage and presented himself to his students as their fellow student. He never compromised on principles, and he expected the very best from his students. Power and pelf would easily have been his for the asking, if only he had been willing to compromise his principles, but Confucius preferred his integrity and character above everything in the world. He said, "With coarse food to eat, water to drink, and my arms for a pillow, I still have joy in the midst of these things. Riches and honors acquired by unrighteousness means no more to me than the floating clouds."

As a teacher, Confucius's aim was to produce men and women of noble and sterling character. For him, the supreme virtue from which all other virtues stem was Ren, meaning goodness, love, compassion, benevolence, and humanity.

The glorification of Confucius started after his death, when his disciples began to spread his ideals. The teachings of Confucius influenced the Chinese government to a great extent, and the officials were required to acquire knowledge of Confucian classics. There was even an attempt to elevate the status of Confucius to divinity.

Confucius, the Great Teacher

Confucius can be described as the Socrates of China. Chinese people respect, revere, and adore him as their greatest teacher. If there is any personality with which Chinese culture has been intimately connected, it is Confucius. His fame spread beyond the shores of China, until he was considered as a teacher of the world. Until this century, all schoolchildren in China for over two thousand years have raised their hands every morning towards a plaque bearing the name of their greatest teacher, Confucius. Further, all Chinese students have studied his teachings and pondered over them for hours. Consequently, these teachings have become part and parcel of the Chinese mind and have percolated to the illiterate in spoken proverb. Even the Chinese government has been greatly influenced by the teachings of Confucius, and a large number of government officials have been required to acquire a working knowledge of the Confucian classics. In fact, there were even attempts by some of the officials to elevate Confucius to the stature of divinity.

What is the reason the Chinese consider Confucius the greatest single teacher and the most powerful intellectual force? It could not have been his personality. It was his great love and dedication to teaching. He taught history, poetry, mathematics, music, propriety, government, sports, and manners. He was a Socrates and literally a one-man university. His method of teaching was also similar to that of Socrates. If we analyze his teachings, though, we feel rather puzzled. He taught his students how to be perfect gentlemen, how to cultivate good manners, and how to become good citizens. The fact that his sayings, so didactic and often commonplace, could have molded a civilization and culture appear to be one of history's enigmas. Some of his sayings appear below.

> "Is he not a true philosopher who, though unrecognized, cherishes no resentment"?
>
> "Do not do to others, what you do not wish to do to yourself."
>
> "Do not wish for quick results, or look for small benefits. If you wish quick results, you will fail to attain the ultimate goal. If you are led astray by small benefits, you will never achieve great things."
>
> "Noble people must practice what they preach and later practice what they preach. If you do not find anything wrong in your heart, there is nothing to worry about."
>
> "When you see someone worthy of honor, think how you can emulate and when you see someone not worthy, you must examine your own character."
>
> "I will not grieve if others do not know me, but I will grieve that I do not know them."

Confucius was an ideal teacher. Instead of lecturing, he discussed with his students their problems, he encouraged them to ask questions, and he patiently answered their questions. Another remarkable feature of his teaching was the total frankness with which he interacted with his students. At the same time, Confucius was uncompromising, and he expected much from his students. He was always ready to admit when he was wrong. All his students reported that their master's manner was informal and always cheerful. As a teacher, Confucius was kind, affectionate, considerate, and helpful. He took many pains to mold his students as good gentlemen and good citizens. He took every opportunity to correct his students. His great ambition and desire was that all his students would become good citizens of the future.

The glorification of Confucius began after his death. He was described as the greatest teacher ever.

Famous Sayings of Confucius

> "They must often change, who would be constant in happiness or wisdom. It is not possible for one to teach others, who cannot teach his own family.'
>
> 'Virtue is not left to stand-alone. He who practices it will have."

"When you see someone worthy of honor, think how you can emulate him, and when you see someone not worthy, you must examine your own character."

"The superior man is modest in his speech, but exceeds in his actions. He who merely knows right principle is not equal to him who loves them."

"To be able under all circumstances to practice five things constitute perfect virtue. These five things are gravity, generosity of soul, sincerity, earnestness, and kindness."

"Nobler people must practice what they preach and later practice what they preach. If you do not find anything wrong in your heart, then there is nothing to worry about."

"We do not know yet about life, how can we know about death."

"Mankind differs from the animals only by a little and most people throw it away."

"If you enjoy what you do, you will never work another day in your life."

"The master said, 'The good man does not grieve that other people do not recognize his merits. His only anxiety is lest he should fail to recognize them.'"

"It is by poetry that one's mind is aroused; it is by ceremony that one's character is regulated. It is by music that one becomes accomplished."

"A man should practice what he preaches, but a man should also preach what he practices."

"Do not wish for quick results or look for small benefits. If you wish quick results, you will fail to attain the ultimate goal. If you are led astray by small benefits, you will never achieve great things."

"If you govern your province well and treat your people kindly, your kingdom shall never lose any war. If you govern selfishly to your people, your kingdom will not only lose a war, but your people will break away from your kingdom."

"I will not grieve if others do not know me, but I will grieve that I do not know them. To rule by moral example instead of by force and violence. A ruler who had to resort to force had already failed as a ruler."

"Look at nothing in defiance of ritual, listen to nothing in defiance of ritual, speak of nothing in defiance of ritual, never stir hand or foot in defiance of ritual."

An Introduction to Shintoism

Shintoism is predominantly a Japanese religion and is synonymous with Japanese culture. Although Shintoism claims a membership of about three-quarters of Japanese population, a survey reveals that only three percent of the adult population actually profess to believe in Shintoism. Shintoism is so inextricably woven into the fabric of Japanese daily life that people are seldom aware of its existence.

The name Shinto means "the way of Gods." Shinto religion is closely involved with the landscape of Japan, and with ancestors of believers. Shinto ceremonies appeal to "Kami," the mysterious powers of nature, for protection and benevolent treatment. Kami are associated with natural features such as caves, streams, trees, and particularly mountains.

Shinto emerged with the advent of the wetland cultivation of rice. Wetland agriculture necessitated well-organized and stable communities and agricultural rites and which later played a vital role in Shinto, led people to conceive of and revere numerous Gods of nature. In addition to this reverence, fear of departed souls led to rites for appeasing them. This later developed into a worship of ancestral spirits. According to Shinto belief, a "departed" soul still has its personality and is stained with death pollution immediately after death. When the bereaved perform memorial rites, the soul is purified to the point of removing all malice, and it takes on a peaceful and benevolent character. In the course of time, ancestral spirit rises to the position of an ancestral, or guardian deity.

At fixed times during the year, believers gather to celebrate community ceremonies in Shinto shrines, but individuals often visit shrines to mark important stages or events in their lives. Some shrines are linked to particular Kami; for example, there are fox shrines, horse shrines and wolf shrines. There are also certain Kami, which are associated with areas, groups of people, or with different aspects of life such as youth or old age.

All Shinto shrines have a large gate called "torii," which consists of two upright bars and two crossbars. The "torii' can be seen alone in lakes, mountains or trees and other places associated with these mysterious powers in nature.

Shinto worship is found only among the Japanese. Many Japanese follow both Buddhist and Shinto beliefs.

The whole Japanese landscape is central to Shintoism, but Mount Fuji is regarded as the supreme home of the Gods. Pilgrims usually ascend this snow-capped mountain on foot.

Shintoism

Founder
None

Scripture
None

Dates
Shinto dates from antiquity and originated with the beginning of the Japanese culture. There is no chief scripture in Shintoism. Shintoism describes the religious life that flourished in Japan before the arrival of Buddhism, Confucianism, and Christianity.

Major Writings
The main written sources describing Shinto are documents called Kojiki, Nihongi and Yengishiki. Shinto does not have a known founder or a scripture like the Bible. It is without definite doctrines and without detailed theology. Since Shinto has no formal doctrines or teachings, its way of promoting the harmony of the community is through rituals and festivals. Feasting together at festivals around ancestral Gods contributes to peace, harmony, and a cooperative spirit among the people. According to Shintoism, to be in union with the Gods, one has to be cleansed and purified of all moral impurity and sin.

Shintoism is a set of rituals and customs involving pilgrimages, festivals, and worship of a great host of Gods. It is more or less a folk religion limited strictly to Japanese people, and thus it has no universal prophetic message. The word “Shinto” means the way to Gods.

Anyone who comes across and faces Japanese culture will experience the universe of Shinto. Shinto can be described as the very national air breathed by all the Japanese. While in Christianity, the followers of Jesus try to live out their faith every day, Shinto is more of background belief and practice than a lifestyle.

The highest deity is the Sun Goddess, known as the Ruler of Heaven.

Gods are generally worshipped through the sacrifice of rice and rice wine. Shinto did not evolve any ethical systems of its own, but gradually borrowed ethical principles from Buddhism and Confucianism.

From about AD 500, the emperor of Japan was considered the chief of Shinto and had immortal status of a god. In 1880, a state form of Shinto was organized in coordination with the Japanese newly awakened imperialism. In the years leading up to World War II, Shinto played a powerful and dominant role in the national life of Japan. The constitution of 1889 officially declared a non-religious Shinto. The militaristic form of Shinto disappeared after World War II, when Shinto was dis-established and the emperor officially disavowed his divinity. Today, many Shinto sects stress world peace and brotherhood.

Essence of Shintoism

Essentially, the formation of Shintoism occurred simultaneously with the Japanese ethnic culture, and it is a religious culture that was never practiced outside from this ethnic society. Shinto is so inextricably woven into the fabric of Japanese daily life that people are barely aware of its existence. To the Japanese, Shinto is less a religion than the air they breathe

It is rather difficult to know when exactly Shinto emerged. With the advent of the wetland cultivation of rice, wetland agriculture resulted in formation of organized and stable communities and many agricultural rites. These agricultural rites played an important role in Shintoism. Those early people conceived and revered many Gods of nature.

Besides this reverence, fear of departed souls led to rites for appeasing them. Later, this developed into a worship of ancestral spirits. According to Shintoism, a departed soul has a personality and is impure due to a pollution that occurs immediately after death. When religious rites are properly performed, the soul is purified, and it becomes a peaceful and benevolent character. In the course of time, the ancestral spirit rises to the position of an ancestral or guardian deity.

Gods of nature and ancestral Gods were considered to be spirits floating in and filling the air. During festivals, people called upon the Gods to descend to the specific places sanctified for the event. Gods were said to take temporary residence in shintai, objects of worship such as trees, stones, mirrors, and swords. Gradually, the landing sites of the Gods, which were purified for festivals, took on a permanent form. Shrines were built for benevolent Gods. In the beginning, people did not carve images of the Gods but worshipped the shintai, in which spirits of Gods were said to live. Even an entire mountain like Fuji served as a shintai. In time, there came to be so many Gods that the Japanese developed the expression "Yaoyorozu-no-Kami," which means "million Gods."

Shinto is a religion of festivals, and the Japanese year is full of religious festivals. Some of the important festivals are the New Year festival, the doll festival for the girls, the mid autumn full moon festival, etc. Many Buddhist festivals are also celebrated, including the Buddha's birthday.

Followers of Shinto consider acts that promote peace, harmony, and livelihood of a small community as good and those acts that hinder such things as bad. Harmony with Gods, nature, and the community was considered to be of very good value. Anything that disrupted the peaceful harmony was regarded as extremely bad.

Shinto as a State Religion

Emperor Meiji established Shinto as Japan's official religion in 1869. A Shinto ceremony was conducted for all the national leaders, and after the ceremony, the emperor read the imperial charter oath that made Shinto the official Japanese religion. The government then created a special and separate ministry to coordinate and oversee propagation and practices of Shinto. This department was armed with great authority. It could name priests, who until that time inherited their position as priest through their families. Priests who spoke against any government policy or who acted against any government program were summarily dismissed.

With a view to increase his power among the people and to encourage and invigorate Shinto worship, the emperor decreed that all citizens, including schoolchildren, should express their solidarity and loyalty to the state and the emperor through Shinto ceremonies and rituals. Children were indoctrinated with total and absolute loyalty to the emperor, who was also the chief Shinto priest. They were taught unwavering patriotism to Japan as a land created by the Kami.

During times of war, the government misused the Shinto belief that the divine sun goddess had given the Japanese the power above all others to justify the country's aggressive move to war. With the nation on a war footing, Shinto was expanded to increase political, social, and economic control over Japanese citizens.

The government gave increased financial assistance to the Shinto priest. The priest in turn taught the people patriotism with great enthusiasm and fervor. Further, the Shinto priest also supported unilaterally Japan's aggressive and expansive militaristic policies. During the Japanese war with Russia, there was glorification of the dead as war heroes at Shinto shrines, and the observance of shrine rites became universal throughout Japan. Further, through local shrine administration, the government ensured that all citizens supported their local shrines by offering their services and money. Thus, the Shinto enabled Japan to become a great economic power in Asia.

Shinto as a state religion ended in 1945, when Japan was defeated in World War II.

Shinto Religious Beliefs

Some of the religious beliefs practiced by the followers of Shintoism are explained below:

Animism—According to the essentials of Shintoism, there is life and divinity in all the phenomena of nature. All aspects of nature, such as mountains, rivers, winds, rain, lightning, stars, et cetera, displayed divinity. The ancient Japanese gave them names and called them Kami. The ancient Japanese belief was that the ancestral spirits resided in the nearby mountains. These spirits came down during springtime to assist the community through harvest and returned to the mountains after the fall.

Nature Worship—Closely related to animism, Japanese had great reverence for nature and engaged in nature worship. Japanese worship of nature resulted in the building of shrines in places of great natural beauty. Beautiful, clean, and quiet natural surroundings were selected for building shrines.

Ancestral Reverence—This is central to Japanese life and belief, and venerating the dead is an integral part of the Shinto religion. There are three separate categories of dead ancestors that are revered by Japanese. They are the recently dead, the nameless ancestors who have faded from living memory, and the outsiders.

Agricultural Rites—These appear in references to the Kami of the stars breaking down divisions / boundaries between rice fields. The major shrine festivals coincide with sowing, harvesting, and the cycle of rice cultivation. These prove how profoundly Shinto is related to agriculture.

Ritual Bathing—Ritual bathing in rivers, in order to cleanse oneself of pollution is a central religious concept. Purification is a distinct feature of Shinto belief, and the oceans, lakes, rivers, and waterfalls are all used for such purification.

Shinto Way of Life

Shinto stresses the moral values of loyalty, duty, and responsibility to one's family members, friends, clans, groups, community, and the nation. Many aspects of Japanese life and culture prove this aspect. In the Shinto way of life, to be human is to be together with other persons. Japanese society encourages and emphasizes community over individuality. The Japanese language has conventions on correctness in speaking to those above and below one in social status, and the oral communication strengthens a hierarchically structured system of human relations.

The principle of duty is the feudal notion of indebtedness, and this exerts tremendous pressure as well as influence on social relationships in Japan. For example, if one saves another man's life, such an act establishes a unique relationship between the saved and the saver.

Similarly, when a landlord makes a gift of land to his vassal, the vassal in return gives his loyalty and service to the landlord, thereby establishing a special relationship. The relation between a child and parents in a family is another example. Parents should take good care of their children and make them good citizens and of good character. Children should take care of their parents in their old age, look after them, and venerate them when they are dead. Such an understanding of mutual relationship of obligations is also evident between a superior and inferior in other walks of life.

In addition to such group and family loyalty, the Japanese people greatly value aesthetic sensitivity and refinement. This aesthetic sensitivity is relevant to the Japanese understanding of religious faith. Shinto stresses the importance of living in the purity of the present moment.

Japanese are very gracious and well-mannered people. They show extreme deference and courtesy. However, in business dealings and negotiations, Japanese are very tough and demanding.

Another important feature of the Shinto way of life is its emotional depth and purity. Shinto is greatly concerned with preserving and restoring a ritual purity of an unbiased mind and un-debased soul, since this forms the very basis of correct and proper action. Traditional Shinto still continues as an aspect of Japanese life and culture.

Chapter 12

African Religions, North American Indian Religions, The New Age Movement, Secularism, Animism, and Humanism

An Introduction to Traditional African Religion

Because of its great size, Africa is a land of many contrasts. Over many centuries, African people lived in close harmony with the land. Some were nomads who followed the animals they hunted. They established camps where the animals could graze and where water was available. Others were farmers who lived off the land. Thus, living in isolation, they developed their own language, customs, and religious practices. Their religious practices were tuned to serve their requirements and lives.

Traditional African religion teaches that people consist of social, physical, and spiritual parts. These parts are in harmony. If any part is out of balance, the person may become sick or suffer spiritually. Traditional African religion is the only religion that claims to have originated in Africa. Later, other religions like Christianity and Islam made their presence known.

Traditional African religion is unique; it differs from other religions such as Judaism, Buddhism, Islam, and Christianity. Although African people have legendary figures in their history, African religion has no single religious founder or central historical personalities like Moses, Jesus, Buddha, or Muhammad. Like Native American religions and Asian religions such as Shinto and Taoism, African religion originated with the people themselves. It is an expression of thousands of years of living close to the land and trying to find answers to the mysteries of life. African religion has no specific places of worship such as temples, synagogues, churches, or mosques.

Among African people, religion, culture, and beliefs are intimately bound together. The world is viewed as part of a communal group. People believed in sharing their property and services with other members of the community. In such communal spirit, they found security.

Traditional African Religion

Traditional African religion can be described as a religion of salvation that promises peace, wholeness, and well-being. It is a religion that affirms life and calls for joyous celebrations that include drums, music, and dancing. Africans firmly believe that the life in this world is a complex web of relationships that may either enhance and preserve life or may destroy life altogether. The objective of the indigenous African religion is to maintain those relationships in such a manner that life is fully protected and preserved. Africans believe that the harmony and peace provided by these relationships, both material and spiritual, provide the conditions for salvation, peace, happiness, and well-being of all.

Traditional African religion clearly defines the relationship between God, creation, and the cosmic life. Thus, God in Africa is a purely a rational being who can be known through various levels of relationship with creation. In relation to humanity, God is considered the great ancestor of the entire human race. Consequently, all over Africa, God is depicted in terms of parent rather than as a sovereign. In relation to the world, God is a husband who stands behind the creative fertility of the world that sustains human life. In relation to creation, God is the creator from whom life flows and who protects and sustains life.

The expressions of African traditional religion are many, and they have shaped and molded the lives of African people from time immemorial. The name of God varies across traditions, as do the names of the divinities and the spiritual practices. For example, in East Africa, people believe that prayer can be made at any time, since they would like to speak to God when they are happy, in African traditional religion, there is a daily reciprocity between the living and the dead, the ancestral spirit. The interaction with these realities is through prayers, rites, incantations, and libations.

From time immemorial, the people of Africa gathered in groups that were related by family ties and similar needs. These communities developed their own distinct, individual languages, cultures, practices, and religions. Although waves of exploration and modernization have had an impact on the traditional African way of life, it has been estimated that there are approximately six thousand different peoples in Africa today. Many of these peoples still continue to live by the spiritual influence of their ancestral way of live. Even though the pressures of modern life and civilization have forced many people to move from their native villages and to cities for their livelihood, most Africans still identify themselves according to the heritage of their ancestors.

Statistics on religion available from thirty-five African nations show that traditional African religion is very much vibrant and alive. Even though countries on the West African coast have a sizeable Christian population, many people still adhere to the African religion. Of the total population of religious adherents in Africa, more than 30 percent of the population practice African religion.

To fully understand and appreciate traditional African religion, one must look at Africa clearly and deeply. Africa is the second largest continent on earth. Because of its vast size, Africa is a land of contrasts. It has the world's greatest desert, the Sahara. This desert stretches across the north-central part of the continent, dividing north from the south. North of the Sahara lie countries that are rich with ancient traditions. Below the Sahara is a land of enormous variety. Virtually cut off from known civilization by the huge, empty Sahara, these lands remained nearly untouched by outside exploration for centuries. But they were not uninhabited. Recent scientific studies in Africa strongly suggest that Africa may be the birth place of human race.

African people below the Sahara lived in close harmony with the land. Some were nomads. As nomads, they wandered, following the animals they hunted. These people established camps where their herds could graze. Others farmed or lived off the land, gathering native plants for their food. Often, they were separated from their neighbors. Since for all practical purposes they lived in isolation, they developed their own language and customs. Traditional African religion teaches that people are made up of moral, social, spiritual, and physical parts. These parts function together in harmony. If any part is out of balance, the person may become physically ill or suffer spiritually. This explained why a conflict with another person made someone sick or a moral misdeed brought about misfortune.

Traditional African religion is not the only religion found in Africa today. It is, however, the only religion that can claim to have originated in Africa. The other religions in Africa include Islam and Christianity, but they originated in other parts of the world and were brought to Africa by foreign religious missionaries.

Another unique feature of traditional African religion is that is has no churches, mosques, or synagogues as do Christianity, Islam, and Judaism. African religion has shrines constructed according to the traditions of the particular geographical area. People also turn to a geographical or natural feature such as a mountain or a large tree for worship.

Unlike other religions, indigenous African religion has no single official ordained priest. There is no organized priesthood in African religion. Religious duties are carried out by a variety of religious leaders. There are healers, diviners, mediums, rainmakers, and elders, each with a special role in the maintaining of spiritual life of the people and the community.

To sum up, traditional African religion is a vital part of the rich African heritage.

The Supreme Being

Like other religions, there is a Supreme Being or God in African religion. African people believe in the existence of a power above which there was no other power. They called it the "Supreme Being." This Supreme Being was understood as the one and only God. When a postage stamp in Ghana was brought out with a pattern called "Gye Nyame," meaning "Except God," it was said how apt it was that an African country should be the first to remind the world of God's power.

Religious systems are usually classified as either monotheistic, meaning believing in one God or polytheistic, meaning believing in many Gods. African religion is rather unique in as much as both monotheism and polytheism exist side by side. Long before Judaism, Christianity and Islam appeared on the scene, African people believed in the Supreme Being. The African concept of monotheism is one of a hierarchy with the Supreme Being at its head. In this system, the Supreme Being rules over large number divinities. These divinities are treated as associates of God. This divine hierarchy in African religion makes it possible to consider it as both monotheistic and polytheistic.

In traditional African religious tradition, people associate the Supreme Being or God with certain basic attitudes. These attributes of God can be summed up as follows;

1. God is the creator of all things on earth.
2. God is the absolute controller as well as provider and sustainer of the universe.
3. God provides for what he has created.
4. God possesses all that he created.

All Africans believe that the power of creation is the most important attribute of God. African myths of creation support the idea that all Africans at all times have recognized the Supreme Being as the creator of all things. In African tradition and thought, God has absolute control of the entire universe and all that it contains. All other beings exist because of him. As the originator of the universe, the Supreme Being or God is the ultimate fountainhead of all powers of all natural rules for orderly and disciplined existence.

Peoples of the different regions of Africa express God as controlling and sustaining the creation in various ways. Through myths, legends, and proverbs, African people show that they are aware that God is the provider and sustainer. In African thought, the Supreme Being or God is not only the giver of life, but he is also the possessor of whatever has been created. In some African countries, God is described as the "Owner of everything" and the "Owner of all power."

Although they may pray and sacrifice to lesser Gods, African people hold the Supreme Being in special regard and respect as the great creator, provider, and sustainer of life. The Supreme Being alone is the originator of the world and all that is in it, and to him all people owe their existence.

The Spirit World

The spirit world is the central theme in African religion. In African religion, the Supreme Being reigns as God in heaven. He is not concerned with the day-to-day affairs of human beings, which he has delegated to the less important Gods who occupy the spirit world. This spirit world is made up of superhuman beings, beings of God's creation that occupy the spiritual universe between God and humanity and the space between heaven and earth. They tread the earth invisibly, so that they are present all the time in all places. It is to the spirits that human beings turn for guidance as well as help in times of distress, joy, or sorrow. People make requests to them regarding their requirements as well as wants. To them, they make offering and sacrifice for good health and happiness, for ensuring a good harvest, for the birth of children and protection from all dangers and evils. Spirits thus occupy a prominent position in the daily lives of Africans.

Superhuman beings exist in a hierarchy. They are ranked according to their nearness and importance to the Supreme Being. The most important superhuman beings are called the associates of God. These are lesser Gods, who rank below the Supreme Being and work in concert with him. Other influential spirits of the community are intermediates, guardians and ancestors. Intermediates are spirit agents and their main function is to act as go between divinities and human beings. Spiritual guardians and ancestors are protectors and they are spiritually positioned between superhuman beings and human beings.

African people consider spirits to be elements of power, authority, strength, and vital energy underlying all existence. Though this power is not visible, Africans perceive it directly. People have great faith and firm belief in these spirits, and they hold the view that the spirits are around them and everywhere. They point to the various events and developments in their daily lives, which go to prove the existence of spirits. They are also aware of the fact that these spirits should be handled with extreme caution and understanding. This explains the variety of rituals, practices, and taboos that confirm the existence of spirits.

According to African traditions, spirits are everywhere, and people feel their presence. Africans believe that spirits inhabit all places and that there are no objects or creatures, no corner of the earth that is not inhabited by the spirits. This conviction of the presence of spirits everywhere makes the African people very careful in handling them. There are spirits designated as spiritual guardians, and among the spiritual guardians, there are ancestors and spirits of departed heroes.

The spirits of the dead are part of the spirit world. Some are ancestors and others are the spirits of the ordinary dead. By and large, Africans do not worship their dead ancestors, but they venerate and respect them. Dead ancestors are held in great respect in all African homes. The ordinary dead are also respected with ritual observations by all the members of the community.

According to African belief, when a person dies, his or her soul gets separated from the body and changes from a soul to a spirit. Becoming a spirit is considered a social elevation, and the human becomes superhuman. This is considered an event of great importance by the family members as well as the community. People consider ancestors as guardians of the living, and consequently, ancestors are held in great respect in all African homes.

African Religion—Basic Beliefs

Followers of African religion make no distinction among religious and other aspects of their lives. Their beliefs are so closely bound to their culture that religion and culture are one. For Africans, religion is not something people do at certain times and certain places, but it is part of the fabric of living. Although the Supreme God is above the living, lesser Gods, spirits, and ancestors watch and guide the living. The spirits are sometimes displeased and annoyed by those who do not heed their advice and guidance. People and Gods are constantly interacting through ritual, prayer, and sacrifice, but mostly through the business of living.

Although traditional African religion varies widely from region to region and from people to people, there are a number of things that they have all in common. These are:

All things in the universe are part of a whole. There is no distinction between the sacred and the non-sacred.

There is a Supreme Being or God. This Supreme Being is the creator, sustainer, provider, and controller of all creatures. Serving with the creator are many lesser Gods and intermediary Gods as well as guardian spirits, who are involved in all human affairs. People communicate with these lesser Gods and spirits through rituals, prayers, and sacrifices.

Human life is imperfect, and sickness, suffering, and death are all parts of life. According to African belief, suffering and sickness are caused by sins and evil deeds. The sins and evil deeds result in the Gods and ancestors getting angry. Another belief is that suffering and sickness are also the result of people being out of harmony with nature and society.

Rituals and prayers may end suffering. Ritual actions may lessen and relieve the problems and sufferings of human life, either by satisfying the offended Gods or by resolving social conflicts. Rituals help to restore people to the traditional values and renew their commitment to a spiritual life.

Human society is communal. Ancestors, the living, the living dead, and those yet to be born are all an important part of the community. The relationship between the worldly and the otherworldly helps to guide and balance the lives of the community. Humans need to interact with the spirit world, which is all around them.

Among African people, religion, culture, and religious beliefs are tightly woven together. The African view of the world is fundamentally one of being part of a communal group. People believe in sharing their property and services, and they expect the other members of the community to share with them. The Africa people are of the conviction that whatever happens to the individual happens to the whole group, and vice versa.

Africans believe that their safety and well-being lie in this communal spirit. According to them, the world is but a part of the community.

Rites and Rituals

African religion is replete with rites and rituals. To African people, belief without rituals and rites will have no meaning whatsoever. Rituals cover so many aspects of African religious life that it is not possible to separate them from their daily lives. Religion has a profound influence on the thoughts, actions, and lives of people. Rites of passage and various other communal rites demonstrate how religion permeates all aspects of the lives of African people.

Rites of passage are the rites that relate to the human life cycle. These are the practices, customs and ceremonies that people perform to mark the different stages of human life, from birth to death and even beyond death. These stages include birth, childhood, puberty and initiation, marriage and family life, old age and death.

The early stages of life cover birth and childhood. These specifically include the stages of conception, the period of pregnancy, the actual birth of the child, the naming of the child, and its period of childhood. The rites of birth begin with the pregnancy of the mother. The conception of a child is considered a religious mystery and wonder in African tradition. Most Africans view conception as a cooperative venture between the parents-to-be and the associate Gods. Pregnancy is given great importance as well as respect. African people regard pregnancy as a sacred calling to motherhood.

Next in importance comes the event of naming the child. According to African tradition and belief, the name of a child expresses the very essence of the person who bears it. In other words, the name will reveal the personality of the person. Parents, therefore, take great care in selecting the most suitable name. All African names convey specific meaning. Mostly, African personal names have religious overtones and indirectly reflect their religious belief.

Puberty rites are ceremonies that mark the stage when a child moves from childhood to adolescence. The young ones are initiated into the adult world, marking the physical changes that signal the transition from childhood to the sexual world of adulthood. The young people are usually initiated either by physical initiation or through educational retreats. Initiation rites convey much religious significance and religious meaning.

The next important stage is marriage. African people consider marriage as a religious obligation. This is because without marriage, there can be no assurance of having descendents. The person, who has no descendent disrupts the chain of reincarnation. The African belief is that the departed count on being taken cares of by descendents and are assured of being incarnated through their descendents.

The last two stages are death and the ultimate funeral rites. According to African beliefs, in death the soul leaves the body and becomes a spirit. Although African people, by and large, accept death as part of life cycle, death calls for a ritual disposal of the body of the dead. There are funeral rites, and these mark the end of the time of mourning. Later, the designated heir is officially declared and installed for inheritance.

Magic, Witchcraft, and Sorcery

No study of African religion will be complete without examining the part played by magic, witchcraft, and sorcery. African people believe in the power and energy of the spirit world around them, in the influence of mystical forces in their lives. They experience the actions of Gods and ancestors and are closely attuned to the mystical and mysterious powers in their lives. Such mystical forces include magic, witchcraft, and sorcery, which affect people's lives as well as the lives of the community.

Magic as a mystical force plays a vital part in the lives of African people. Magic is the practice of manipulating mysterious forces for practical purposes. People who practice magic, are called magicians. African magic does not have anything to do with trickery or illusion, but it is a true religious element. African people believe that magic can be used for good as well as for evil. African religion is concerned with asking the cooperation of God and superhuman beings for the welfare of the people. Since the ritual leaders call upon higher powers, they are more or less practicing magicians. African people believe that ritual acts and talismans ensure magical protection from all dangers.

Witchcraft is another important aspect of African belief. Most African people believe in witchcraft and think that witchcraft is responsible for many of their misfortunes, such as infertility, disease, crop failure, personal failure, and death. Witchcraft is very much feared in African society. People believe that witches possess extra human powers that can cause much harm and evil. At the same time, people understand witchcraft as part of the religious forces that surround them. Some tribes in Africa believe that in the context of creation, God has also put the power of witchcraft in the world.

Witchcraft and magic are related, but they are different from each other. Africans believe that some people are born witches. There are also cases of hereditary witchcraft in which a person may be a witch without his knowing it. Witchcraft causes evil, harm, and unrest among people. People also seek protection from witchcraft for their community through prayers.

Next in importance comes sorcery. Sorcery is another mystical force practiced by Africans. It means use of magic or enchantment, the practice of magical arts. African people consider sorcery as the use of magic so as to cause or inflict harm on others, particularly to those whom they hate or seek revenge. While witchcraft may be termed as a mystical power, which can be used to harm other people, sorcery is considered as evil magic against others.

Sorcery is the use of supernatural power over others through the assistance of evil spirits, witchcraft, black magic, and the like. Sorcery is viewed as a greater danger and more evil than witchcraft or magic. While witchcraft casts spells or calls on mystical forces to do mischief and harm, sorcery resorts to artificial means such as the use of poison to cause much evil and great personal harm. For practicing such a thing, some African societies call those who practice sorcery as 'poisoners'. Sorcery is clearly evil magic, aimed at causing maximum harm to people as well as the community.

At present, the practice of sorcery has by and large disappeared from most African societies with the spread of education and modern civilization.

The Oral Tradition

African people have wonderful anecdotes to tell about the beginning of time and the creation of the world and humanity. The elders of the village ask all the children to gather in a central place, where they would tell them stories regarding the times when the world was young, when even animals could talk, and when God made the earth and created everything in it. Traditionally, the village elders normally tell the children the absorbing stories of their various heroes, religion and religious practices as well as various myths and the culture of their community.

Since Africans lived close to nature, they have always observed and studied nature and the world around them, especially the vast sky above them and the lakes, rivers, seas, and oceans that surrounded them. Similarly, they observed the forests, the animals, birds, and various other marvels of creation. And closely observing nature and studying it, they pondered deeply various aspects of humanity, such as how and when the world came into existence and what power fashioned their lives and what it meant to be alive. Over centuries, people found answers to these questions in the form of stories, myths, anecdotes, and proverbs. They passed down their answers by word of mouth from one generation to the next generation. Thus are oral traditions, which address questions regarding existence from the beginning of time, established.

The oral traditions constitute the method of transmitting history, culture, religious traditions, religious beliefs and practices by spoken rather than by written means. In most African traditional communities, it was mainly part of home education to memorize those traditions with great accuracy. Oral tradition has thus fulfilled the very important need of educating the young minds.

Oral traditions are transmitted in a variety of forms such as myths, legends, stories, anecdotes, and proverbs. Stories are mainly for educating and entertaining the community about life. Similarly, the myths deal with the divine and spiritual. They have religious subjects such as the origin of the universe, from where and how humankind originated, the destiny of the human race, and other related matters. Legends are stories of great heroes, families, and people. These legends are told and retold innumerable times until they become part of the lore of the community as a whole.

Regarding proverbs, they convey in a nutshell the wisdom about creation as well as experience. From very early times, African people have asked questions regarding their existence. Their deep study gave rise to the rich and varied creation myths of African people. Myths of creation tell of the sacred beginning of the people. They usually center on a Supreme Being, who according to African oral traditions is the creator of the world. They recognize the special status the creator has given to mankind.

The oral traditions in Africa have a close parallel to Hindu traditions, where spiritual lessons were transmitted orally to students by great spiritual masters and then passed down by word of mouth from one generation to the next generation.

North American Indian Religions

The Arctic Eskimos

The Arctic Eskimos view their world of wilderness, barren coast, ice and sea as people with spirits. Depending for their daily lives on land and sea animals, Eskimos believe in a soul specific to all beings. Thus when animals are killed, the killer or hunter bears responsibility for releasing the soul of living beings and rites are performed in relation to all aspects of hunting.

Eskimo society is not highly organized. In fact, organization in their society was almost non-existent. The family is the prime source of structure in Eskimo society. Kinship usually involved three generations from both the mother and father's side. These extended families were considered as one and consequently the action of a member was the responsibility of the entire group.

The Eskimos believe that their very existence depends on their taking the lives of other living beings. They also believe that animals will not present themselves willingly to the hunter as a sacrificial offering, when behavior codes are not followed or broken. Such traditions are supported by their beliefs in an all-powerful Goddess called Sedna. According to North American indigenous tradition, Goddess Sedna will release or withhold animals based on the degree to which the hunters observe the taboos. In addition to Sedna, there are the Masters or Keepers of the various types of animals. These Masters or Keepers will release or withhold the animals according to the behavior of the hunter. Thus the Eskimos are expected to strictly observe the behavior codes and attitudes towards the game.

Religious practitioners called shamans play a very important part of the daily lives of the Eskimos. By his knowledge of the spirit world, the shaman is able to know who has broken the taboos. Further it is believed by the Eskimos that the shaman can placate Goddess Sedna and predict weather conditions.

Southwest—Pueblos and Navajos

The two dominant groups of the American Southwest are the Pueblos and the Navajos. The cosmos of the Pueblos is portrayed in myths as incorporating a number of spheres pierced through by a hollow vertical axis. There are seven of these spheres. Commencing with the realm of a supreme life-giving bisexual power, the second and third sphere are identified with the Sun father, giver of light and warmth, and the Moon Mother, who gives light at night, divides the year into months, and expresses the life cycle of living beings. The central terrestrial fourth realm of the Earth Mother is the provider of all vegetation. The fifth sub-terrestrial realm is associated with the Gods of war. The Gods of the sixth realm are represented by persons wearing masks, who appear in seasonal dance-dramas and the seventh realm is identified with animal Gods.

The most sacred place of the Pueblo is the Kiva. It is an underground ceremonial chamber at the bottom of which is a hollow shaft, the Sipapu, leading underground and understood to be the very place of emergence, the Center of Centers. Access to the Kiva is by a ladder- so that descent leads back to the sacred realm and ascent recapitulates the mystic process of emergence.

Within the Kivas in each Pueblo settlement, preparations take place for rites and for the dance-drama of masked deities, which are enacted according to a seasonal calendar. The strict observance of the ceremonial cycle is controlled by a priest of a specific clan, who observes the annual movements of the sun. The dance-dramas are performed in open village plazas. This seasonal return of the sacred deities re-establish contact with sacred realms. Without the rites, it is believed that the recycling of life-sustaining power would end, whereupon the world and its people would perish.

The other prominent group of the American Southwest is the Navajo. Central to the Navajo view of reality is the understanding that the human personality is a whole, with every facet interrelated both within itself and with the totality of the phenomena. In this totality, everything exists in two parts, namely the good and the bad, the positive and the negative and the elements of male and female. They complement one another and belong together.. These elements are present in a manner that is balanced, harmonious, ordered and thus of beauty. This ideal equilibrium is precarious and can be put out of balance by violating the taboos, contamination by contact with ghosts, harboring evil thoughts or showing disrespect or carelessness in one's relations

The Navajos believe that symptoms of any illness indicate that the normal balance has been upset and must be restored. Such restoration of health for the Navajo necessitates participation in one of the several ceremonial 'chantways' of two to fourteen days duration. The chantway, specific to an illness is determined by a specialist. Sacred ceremonies must be made within a traditional Navajo circular dwelling.

Another Navajo practice is the use of plumed prayer wands, set to the four directions outside the ceremonial Navajo dwelling to compel the Gods to be present with their curative spiritual powers. Central to the complex ceremonies is the chanting of myths of creation. These chants must be made without any error. The patient is seated in the center of these, so that the powers of the Gods and other beings can work for the restoration of harmony, balance and thus remove the illness and restore back the health.

Native American Religions—Background

There are different religions among the Native Americans, depending on the particular group or tribe. A study of their religions is intimately connected and linked to their language, beliefs, culture, and other factors.

Before westerners reached North American shores, the land was inhabited by thousands of different groups of Native Americans. The natives lived mainly in villages. Their means of livelihood depended mainly on hunting, fishing, and farming. It is estimated that before the European explorers landed, more than one million Native Americans were living in North America.

Among the natives, there were many tribes and groups. Each native tribe was different from the others and had its own language. In exceptional cases, some tribes had languages that were more or less similar to that of neighboring tribes, and the people were able to understand each other. By and large, however, Native American languages were quite distinct from one another. According to historical records, there were more than a thousand different Native American languages.

In spite of different languages among different tribes, Native Americans managed to communicate. When tribes with very different languages met, they developed a sign language that enabled them to more or less communicate with one another. Besides having different languages, each tribe was conspicuous by its own distinct culture and customs. Further, each tribe had its own special methods of building homes and making articles for daily life such as clothing, tools, cooking utensils, hunting weapons, and farming implements.

There is no single Native American religion. Some semblance of similarity can be found among native religions in the same way some sort of similarity can be found between Buddhism and Taoism or between Islam and Christianity.

Native American religions differ from organized religions in as much as they are not systematic and do not have a worship building or priestly order or organizational structure. Further, most Native American religions do not rely on a central figure or have a founder such as Moses, Jesus, Muhammad, or Buddha.

The traditional Native American culture has been oral. There is no written set of beliefs or code of ethics or principles and rules. There are no holy books like the Bible or the Qur'an. Though there was no written creed, strict rules for living a decent and ethical life governed all Native American cultures. Tribe members were taught by examples, and those guiding principles were taught to children early on and became part of their daily lives. In Native American religions, life was considered a path and a spiritual journey.

The Path of Life

In Native American religions, this path of life has no beginning and no end. It always leads back to the starting path. The natives consider the path of life to be a spiritual journey.

The natives believed in Spirits. People get closer to the Great Spirit, when they are old. This is because they considered that people attain maturity when they get old. Each person may travel the path of life only once in his or her lifetime. For the tribe, however, life is a continuous cycle of births, childhood, adolescence, marriage, old age, and death. There is a conviction that the first person on earth traveled in the same path.

Ceremonies marking life's passage vary widely from tribe to tribe. All the tribes value each stage of life and celebrate it with rituals. In fact, there are rituals for all aspects of life. In Native American culture, each new birth is viewed as great happiness, and all new arrivals are greatly prized. All the persons in the village join in the celebrations marking the birth of a new baby.

Pregnant women strictly observe taboos and rituals to ensure that the children to be born are healthy and have long lives. When a baby receives a name, it becomes a full member of the tribe. In some tribes, the ritual for a new baby occurs on the eight day. The baby is washed and taken outside the home to witness the rising sun. The sighting of the sun by the baby is considered important for the health of the child. Cornmeal is sprinkled, and prayers are made for the well-being, good health, and longevity of the baby.

Naming the baby is another major ritual. Native Americans believed that names have the power to mold an individual's life. Selecting a name is the next important event. Names are chosen very carefully by the eldest member of the family or by the tribe. While the girls keep their birth names throughout their lives, boys get new names at different stages in their lives. Thus, a boy gets a name at the time of his birth, which is kept throughout his childhood. As he matures, new names are given to him by the tribal leaders.

Among Native Americans, there are many childhood rituals. These vary from tribe to tribe. Another noteworthy feature is that ceremonies for children reveal the likely roles that they will undertake when they reach adulthood. For some others, the ceremonies mark the qualities that the parents wish their children to have. Many parents wish their children to possess specific qualities, such as strength, health, industry, determination, or courage, and to ensure this, they have special ceremonies.

For girls, there are puberty rites. These rites vary from tribe to tribe. Among some tribes, the puberty ceremony is conducted by a special person called a shaman.

Native Americans expect their young men and women to marry and have a large family. Having many children is to ensure that the tribe grows stronger and more prosperous. Families take part in choosing mates for their children. Marriages are events of great rejoicing for the tribe. Death is accepted as a natural and inevitable part of life. Funeral and mourning practices also vary from tribe to tribe. The dead are buried, as people expect their bodies to return to Mother Earth.

Health and Healing

The world of spirit played a vital part in the lives of the Native Americans. The spirit world dominated every aspect of the Native American's life. Native Americans placed great emphasis on the health, welfare, and well-being of the tribe. It was their firm belief that human health for the individual as well as the group depended mainly on the proper action and interaction with the spirit world. The natives believed that wholeness and wellness depended on living in complete harmony with the forces of nature and the universe. All sickness and other physical discomforts were caused by living in disharmony with the forces of nature. For them, the cure for such illness was through rituals, which could restore a sick person to harmony and balance.

Most of the Native American celebrations have a healing and curing component. One of the popular celebrations connected with healing sickness is the sun dance. The sun dance of the Lakota tribe includes a time when persons who are sick can join the sacred circle of the dancers and secure the power of healing. Normally in the sun dance, the dancers dedicate their dances to their own healing as well as the healing of others.

Some tribes believe that illness is caused by supernatural forces. Various types of sickness are attributed to spirits. Some people believe that animal spirits cause illness in hunters who are not properly respectful to the animals they hunt and kill. Other groups attribute illness to bad actions, such as ignoring taboos.

Some tribes believe that illness is caused by unfulfilled desires. Dreams are also considered one of the reasons for illness. Some dreams are considered bad omens. Contact with evil spirits is another reason for sickness. It is believed that an evil spirit may come due to a spell cast by a witch or sorcerer.

In addition to the various spirits causing illness, some consider that serious illness may be due to soul loss. In soul loss, evil spirits, particularly those of the dead, capture the sick person's soul during sleep. In such cases, the patient may suffer from a wasting disease and become delirious and unconscious.

Healing is considered a sacred and holy calling by Native Americans. There are specialized native healers who use special healing rituals and natural means to heal and cure the people who are sick. It is believed that the power to heal comes from natural forces of the earth brought forth through prayer.

There are people who specialize in healing people, called Shaman. It is believed that Shamans received their power to heal from their relation to the world of spirits. This relation to the world of spirits is achieved through dreams and visions. Besides these, some Shamans secure their powers through studies. All share the ability to see visions and receive instructions from the spirits. Others enter into a trance to receive instructions from the spirits. After diagnosing an illness, the Shamans perform the proper ritual for curing the illness.

Ceremonies and Rituals

Ceremonies and rituals are major components of Native American religions. Most of the ceremonies revolve around dance and drama, which are used as a means of communication with the high powers. Native Americans consider dance as a kind of payer through which they can reach the high powers. Prayer is thus considered as a religious rite. Sacred dance and drama reflect the beliefs of the tribes and represent the actions of spirits. They dramatize the relationship between people, the world of nature, and the world of spirits. There are different types of dances for achieving specific purposes. Thus, there are dances that are meant, for example, for bringing rains. Since the tribes depended on agriculture for their food, rain was of great importance.

Similarly, there are dances to grow essential foods such as corn. There are also dances for successful hunting, a major activity of all the tribes. In addition, there are dances for the health, welfare, and well-being of the tribe.

Each tribe has its own particular style and form of dance. In some tribes, people came to dance as a group, and usually the dancers moved in a circle counterclockwise. In other tribes, the dancers moved in lines, and there were also solo dances. Both men and women dance. Usually, they dance separately and at different times. By performing these dances, the dancers bring the power of the spirit world to all.

The type and style of dance that a tribe has developed reflect the tribal character, their beliefs, and their views of the world. Thus, the tribes depending mainly on hunting for their existence developed dances that called on the spirits of their game, such as buffalos or bears. Tribes depending on agriculture and farming performed rites celebrating the agricultural cycle of sowing seeds, growth of the plants, and harvest.. In other words, for each specific purpose, the tribes developed appropriate dances to achieve their objective. Dance is usually performed in the open. The spiritual power of the dancer is very strong. It is believed that the dancer does not perform the role of a spirit but impersonates the spirit.

Among the Native American dancing, the dancers wear masks as well as costumes representing the spirit world. Each part of the costume has a significance and symbolic meaning. It is believed that through mask and costume, the spirit is supposed to enter into the body of the dancer, thus linking the human and the supernatural world.

Among some tribes, dancers wear large wooden masks that represent and depict the raven and other creatures of the area, such as whales, bears, and the like. All tribes also pay homage to animal spirits with dances that resemble animal movement. Hunting dances were made to honor the animals and to call upon the spirits to increase the animal population, which was essential for the survival of the tribe. Further, such dancing for successful hunting was also meant to enlist the cooperation of the animal spirits, so that the hunters are assured of a successful hunt.

Native American ritual and prayer are rich, varied, and diverse. All the ceremonies, rituals, and prayers are performed to enable them to communicate with the Great Spirit

The World of Spirits

Native Americans believe in a great sacred power or force from which all things emanate and which helps to keep the universe in motion. This sacred power is called the Great Spirit or Power that underlies all creation. The Great Spirit cannot be seen or touched. Native Americans believe that the Great Spirit is present in all aspects of nature, such as the change of seasons, day and night, growth and decay, birth and death, and in the movement of the sun, moon, and stars.

People learned about the Great Spirit mainly through oral tradition, important events, and ancestors. The Great Spirit is also experienced through dreams and visions, and children are taught at a very young age to pay great attention to their dreams and to examine their meaning.

The spirit world dominates all aspects of Native American life. In fact, there is nothing that is not touched by the spirit world in some way. A central concept of Native American religion is that everything in the world that can be seen or touched is alive with spirit.

According to the beliefs of Native Americans, several different kinds of spirits inhabit the world. They are classified as follows:

1. The sky beings, such as the sun, moon, and stars;
2. Spirits of the atmosphere, such as winds, rains, and a huge bird called the thunderbird. It is the flapping of the thunderbird's wings that causes thunder and lightning.
3. The rulers of animals and plants, such as buffalo spirit, bear spirit, or corn spirit, and places such as seas, rivers, mountains, waterfalls, etc.;
4. The powers of the underworld, such as snakes and other reptiles, cougars, and the rulers of the dead.

The spirits of the dead live as ghosts on earth and may be reborn as animals. Many Native Americans believed in sky spirits. They considered the Milky Way as a path of souls to which people went after death. Some hold the sun to be a great supernatural power who carries the torch that warms and illumines the world.

Animals such as bear, deer, and mice are considered as having distinct spirits. The bear spirit is held as the strongest and wisest of the animal spirits. Consequently, some tribes consider the bear spirit a powerful healing force. Many animal spirits, such as raven and buffalo, have the ability to change from animal to human and back to animal.

Native hunters prayed to the spirit of the game they killed for food. They thanked the deer and buffalo for giving up its life so as to sustain the members of the tribe. These tribes think that illness and other bodily discomforts came to hunters who failed to honor the animals that he hunted.

Some Native Americans believe that plants and trees also have spirits. Plants and trees that are not properly cared for or treated with respect and honor will not survive. Many tribes considered some food plants, such as maize, corn, beans, and squash, as gifts provided by the Great Spirit.

Summary of Native American Religions

The history of Native American religions was changed drastically with the arrival of European settlers and Christianity. The desire and need for land resulted in the European settlers stripping the Native American civilizations of all their land besides nearly wiping out their culture. Much of the history and culture of many Native American civilizations were thus lost. Consequently, it is difficult to locate data regarding the religious beliefs and rituals of many native American civilizations that flourished before the arrival of European settlers.

The three major tribes among the native American religions were the Iroquois nation of the Eastern woodlands, the Dakota or Sioux tribes of the central plains and the Apache tribes of the southwestern desert region.

The Iroquois

Among the native American tribes in North America, the Iroquois nation was the most highly organized civilization. The Iroquois tribe depended mainly on agriculture besides hunting. Their land was fertile with plentiful game and streams full of fish. This enabled the tribe to provide food for the people.

The Iroquois tribes believed in a powerful creator known as the Great Spirit. The Iroquois believed that the Great Spirit looked after their welfare. The ritual ceremonies practiced by the Iroquois tribes were systematic worship services in accordance with certain seasonal periods throughout the year. During the harvest time, they organized festivals and thanked the Great Spirit for his protection and their survival.

The Dakotas or Sioux

The Dakotas or Sioux as they are known inhabited the great plains and prairies. Their society depended entirely on hunting the buffalo, which provided them with all their needs. Thus the buffalo played a very vital part in the daily lives of the tribe. It is not possible to separate the Dakota people from the buffalo and consequently the buffalo played a significant role in the Dakota religious system.

The Apache

The Apache tribes lived in the southwestern desert region. Since they lived on a land devoid of fertile soli and water, all their time and energy were spent on survival. The hard life of the Apache tribes left little time for any religious ritual. The Apaches did not celebrate ceremonies for marriage and death. As regards religion, the Apaches were encouraged to establish individual relationships with the supernatural powers that surrounded them.

Native American Spirituality

It is rather difficult to trace the origin of Native American religions. According to details available, the origin can be traced back to fifty-sixty thousand years with the arrival of the first batch of people from northeast Asia. The religions of Native Americans developed from hunting taboos and beliefs in spirits. Since these people settled in America in slow stages and in small groups over several thousand years, it is difficult to know about the pattern of their immigration.

Apart from the traditional Native American spirituality, there were others who embraced Christianity. The Native American Church founded in 1918 had a membership of over several thousands and this constituted the largest Native American religious organization. The Native American Church incorporated Christianity, while gradually shifting away from the traditional Native American spirituality.

The major beliefs of Native American spirituality are given below:

To ensure individual and community prosperity, ceremonial rites were conducted involving supernatural objects. The original hunting knowledge brought by the first North American immigrants got replaced by new horticultural religious influence. The tenets of hunting pattern religion comprised animal ceremonialism, the quest for spiritual power, shamanism and life after death. The new horticultural religion, on the other hand, consisted of rain and fertility ceremonies, fertility rites, permanent shrines and temples, medicine and life after death.

Ceremony played a vital part in North American religions. Native American religious were adopted locally, employing both traditional and borrowed elements so as to suit local needs. The medicine men, called shamans and priests were very important members of the society and were held in great respect.

Another important religious practice was divination. Divination was an important stage in the celebration of rituals. It was divination that decided which ritual was appropriate and almost all religious ceremonies began with divination.

New Religion—The New Age Movement

The New Age Movement is a new religion. It is a set of beliefs and not an organization. The name "New Age" is from astrology, which predicts in advance a coming age of peace and harmony. The New Age refers to the process of changing and replacing the old or Pisces age and ushering in an Aquarian age. The New Age movement is a heterogeneous mixture for spirituality, since it allows a person to pick and select from among a wide variety of groups, teachers, and practices. There are absolutely no class restrictions. Followers of the New Age movement may be Hindus or Buddhists or followers of any other faith, and they can choose a path according to whatever draws them spiritually.

In the New Age movement, the God is impersonal and without moral distinctions. The basic belief came from Hinduism and Buddhism. The most important thing is that behind all the groups and practices, there is a unifying philosophy that binds the New Age movement together.

The New Age movement is not only the result of the teachings, philosophies, and practices of several historical movements, but it serves as the supporting and strengthening influence behind the teachings, practices, and trends in medicine, education, politics, science, business, arts, music, psychology, and other disciplines.

One of the new and important rising trends in New Age spirituality is the religion of witchcraft. Followers believe that spiritual knowledge and spiritual power can be secured through the manipulation of natural forces. Originally, witchcraft mainly attracted older men and women. Now it has become a major attraction for the younger generation, since it promises them power, mystery, as well as self-gratification.

Followers of the New Age movement believe that God loves everyone unconditionally. According to them, no one will be judged. New Age followers also believe that there are various paths to reach God. Sin is not an issue with God, but it can be dealt with on the level of human mind. A unique feature of the New Age movement is that salvation is based on the efforts of the individual. One should chalk out his or her path to reach God, and the greater the dedicated efforts, the greater is the possibility of attaining salvation.

Another belief of the New Age movement is the importance of developing a clean and pure mind. New Age believes in positive thinking. Positive and good thoughts are possible only when the mind is pure. Positive thoughts are conducive to good health. Further, positive thinking leads to harmony and peace, the two vital aspects for success and happiness on life.

As the name itself indicates, the New Age, according to followers, means a new way of thinking. The movement, therefore, places great importance on one's way of thinking. One should develop only positive thinking, which alone leads to good health, success, and peace. Positive thoughts ensure harmony within oneself as well as in the community. This will also eliminate all social strife and misunderstanding and create a climate of peace and goodwill.

Beliefs in New Age Movement

The major unifying belief of the New Age movement is one of perception. Humanity is suffering from a severe ignorance, since it has forgotten its true nature. We have forgotten that we are unconditionally connected to God and emanate from God, which is Universal Mind.

A new way of thinking is essential for the followers of the New Age movement. Great strides in science and information technology have radically changed the way of thinking and the way of life in this world. Scientific and technological developments have resulted in tremendous imbalance.. Economic power is in the hands of few, and this has resulted in exploitation. The world is sharply divided between the haves and the have-nots, which has caused deep divisions in society, social strife, unrest, disaster, and social disharmony. Materialism has dominated Western culture. Followers of New Age consider that it is not possible to find the sacred in the religions of the West. They believe that spirituality and sacredness can be found in the religions of the East.

The New Age view of God is that everything is divine, since it flows from the divine Oneness that is the essential Reality. The New Age concept of God is impersonal and can be described as monism and pantheism. Monism is the belief that God is one and that Reality is one unitary organic whole without duality or differentiation. Pantheism equates God with the forces and laws of the universe. Experiencing the divine Oneness by yoga, meditation, and the like will change our lives, and we will then view and value everything as a manifestation of the divine.

Love is another important belief of the New Age movement. The New Age followers believe that humanity's objective should be the perfection of our ability to love. Loving fellow beings will ensure better understanding and harmony.

For the followers of the New Age Movement, the goal of enlightenment is to release ourselves from attachment to all actions, good or bad. In this connection, there is close resemblance to Hinduism, which advocates all actions without expecting results or attachment. As we experience such a release, we will escape the cycle of birth and death or undergo reincarnation lifetime after lifetime.

Followers of the New Age movement encourage people to get in touch with their spiritual guides, who can assist them along the path of spiritual evolution and transformation.

According to the New Age movement, the ultimate goal for each individual is to relinquish all attachments and identification with his or her ego and become identified with and merged into the Universal Self.

Another belief of the New Age movement is the practice of witchcraft. The followers of the New Age movement believe that we can secure spiritual powers through manipulation of the forces of nature. Witchcraft has become a major source of attraction to the young as well as the old. All the followers of the New Age movement believe that by practicing witchcraft, they can find power, mystery, excitement, thrill, self-gratification, as well as a sort of rebellion against beliefs of some other religions.

SECULARISM

Secularism as a religion is something unique. It is total indifference or rejection or exclusion of religion and all religious considerations. Secularism means that consideration of the present well-being of mankind should predominate over religious considerations in civil affairs or public education. Thus, secularism is a combination of atheism, agnosticism, and functional atheism.

Atheism is disbelief in or denial of the existence of God, and an atheist is a person who denies the very existence of God. According to him, there is sufficient evidence to support his claim that God does not exist. An agnostic is a person who holds the view that any ultimate reality as God is unknown and unknowable. According to him, there is insufficient evidence to know whether or not God exists. The so-called functional atheist is one who is totally indifferent and has very little or no interest concerning the existence of God.

The fundamental tenet of secularism is the complete and total denial of the existence of God or, for that matter, the supernatural. Secularists assert that only matter in one form or another has existed for eternity and only matter will continue to exist. Secularism is thus a total negation of the existence of God.

Secularists view religion as inhibitive. According to them, humanity can survive only by facing all problems and can resolve them by reason and by scientific approach. Religion as such cannot solve our problems. According to secularists, humanity represents the process of evolution, and the personality and mind are nothing but the products of evolutionary process. Humanity is monistic or oneness, and a person consists of only one substance, namely matter.

Secularists consider that religion is an escape route for humanity in as much as humanity depends on the promises of liberation or freedom or happiness made by religion. Only by rational enquiry and a scientific approach to all aspects of life can humanity create a world in which there will be peace and justice. According to secularists, what is required for humanity to progress in life is not religion or God or some supernatural powers. For humanity to progress and prosper, there should be sincere and dedicated efforts to discover the truth and knowledge by scientific method of enquiry.

To discover truth and gain knowledge, it is necessary for a person to have an open mind, free from all preconceived notions and prejudices. Further, one should have a scientific mental approach. All humanity's problems are due to ignorance. The remedy lies in developing scientific enquiry into all aspects of life. For humanity to survive and progress, it is imperative that people face all problems rationally and resolve them through reason and scientific approach.

Secularists do not believe in any supernatural powers or miracles. According to them, these are only figments of imagination. Since they deny the very existence of God, it follows that miracles are not possible. Such things are created by people to fool the ignorant and the illiterate. In fact, religion exploits and feeds on the ignorance of people. Instead of believing on miracles, people should endeavor to solve all problems of life by their own efforts.

It is the firm conviction of secularists that by one's own efforts, one can discover truth and gain real knowledge.

Beliefs of Secularism

Secularism asserts that God is just a figment of the imagination or a projection of a person's thoughts, desires, and aspirations. God did not create man in his own image, but man made God in his image. Further, only matter existed in one form or other all the time, and only matter will continue to exist.

Having denied the existence of God, the next fundamental tenet of secularism is the rejection and denial of miracles and things caused by supernatural forces. In many religions, miracles play an important role, and the miracles are part of the religious beliefs. In secularism, miracles are created by people, with a view to propagate their religious beliefs. According to the beliefs of secularism, miracles and other incredible acts attributed to God and other supernatural forces mentioned in the scriptures of Hinduism, Christianity, and other religions are nothing but the handiwork of authors who are keen to propagate their religious views.

All the problems as well as complexities of the world are not due to God. These have nothing to do with God and can be rationally explained by the theory of evolution. Secularism considers religion as a convenient diversion from the realities of life. It is of the firm conviction that religion is restrictive, diversionary, and escapist in nature. Religion feeds on susceptibilities of human beings and exploits their ignorance. Religion does nothing more than pacify and lessen their fears and worries.

According to secularism, religion or God cannot help humanity in solving their problems. If humanity is to survive and make progress, people should face all problems squarely and resolve them by their own efforts through reason, intelligent study, and scientific approach. Humanity should be freed from the fetters and handicaps of religion and made to reject the inhibitions of religious dogmas. Religions as such cannot solve any problems of humanity.

Religions are restrictive in as much as they create closed minds. To discover truth and knowledge, one must have an open mind with a scientific method of enquiry. Only by reason, logic, scientific approach, and honest enquiry can one find out truth and attain knowledge. According to secularism, there is great antagonism between reason and faith as well as between science and religion.

The answer to humanity's problems is not by religion and religious dogmas, but by developing scientific method of enquiry into all aspects of life and having a sense of compassion, patience, love, and understanding for the individual.

According to secular views, humanity represents the process of evolution, and the personality and mind are nothing but the products of the evolutionary process.

Animism

Animism is any of various primitive beliefs wherein natural phenomena and things animate and inanimate are held to possess an innate soul. It is any theory of psychic concepts or of spiritual beings generally. Pythagoras and Plato first advanced the hypothesis of an immaterial force animating the universe. It is a doctrine that views the soul as the vital principle and source of both the normal and the abnormal phenomena of life.

The word animism is derived from the Latin word anima, meaning soul or breath. Animism as a religion refers to that which gives life or power to something.

All the world religions have concept of a Supreme Being or God. That God, for an ordinary human being, is distant, abstract, unseen, and unknowable. Further, it is beyond an individual's capacity or ability to visualize God or to have communion with him. The animist comes from the standpoint that God is far away and does not care about humans' daily concerns and problems. Even if God cares, he acts only through the spirits. Consequently, the animist takes everyday concerns and problems to a spirit to solve or relies on rituals or amulets to fulfill his or her needs. Thus, placing one's faith in a thing like a locket is animism.

Animism offers great attractions for people. First, it is popular since it infuses something sacred into a reality that has become devoid of anything spiritual because of science and the theory of evolution. Second, it gives people a way to face daily needs and problems. For example, if there is an accident or if someone is sick, there are spiritual reasons behind these that must be taken into consideration. If we do not take into consideration the spiritual reasons, we can neither comprehend the cause behind the accident nor remedy the illness.

Animism attracts people because it shows the way to cope with daily problems, concerns, and needs. Suppose a person gets cancer or some other deadly disease or loses his job or experience the death of a loved one. He gets the feeling that God, who is far away, remains silent. This feeling of God's distance and lack of caring make a person feel utterly helpless. Feelings of despair creep in. At such times, we see something that works—anything that will give us the power to set matters right.

Animism teaches that there is an impersonal spiritual energy that infuses some objects, words, and rituals, and such energy gives these objects the power that people long for fulfill their desires and needs.

Animism—Beliefs and Practices

Although the animist view is that God exists, it is beyond anyone's ability to see him, to know him, or to communicate with him. God is, in their view, too distant, too abstract, and too difficult to visualize.

All other religions are mainly concerned with moral issues, such as sin, evil, goodness, salvation, or liberation. Animism, on the other hand, gives the power to an individual to face his or her daily needs and problems, cope with them, and overcome them.

Similarly, in animism, the spirits are seen as either the connecting link between God and humans or as representatives of God. The animists firmly believe that the spirits have the power to do harm to others or bring good to them. An animist takes all his daily problems and worries to a spirit to help solve them.

Animism teaches that there is one Supreme Being or God, who is either an impersonal One or a personal Being. This God, however, is far away from his creations and too abstract and difficult to understand. He is also too distant for any communication with him. Further, God uses the intermediate spirits to carry out his will, and he cannot be approached by us or, for that matter, known by us.

The animist considers other formal religions like Christianity, Islam, Buddhism, and Judaism as being stuck on issues such as who is God, what is sin and salvation, and what is life and death. They consider other formal religions irrelevant, since they cannot help persons to cope up with their immediate problems and needs of their daily lives.

Animists believe in two different kinds of spirit-beings, namely those that had been embodied, such as our dead ancestors, and those not embodied, such as spirits and gods. The spirits are intermediates between God and us. Spirit-beings have great powers. Animists believe that the spirit-beings are localized geographically. Some spirits exert their powers over human endeavors such as business enterprise, marriage, personal relationships, community relations, conflicts, or war. Other spirits exert their pressure over other aspects of nature, such as earthquakes, storms, wildfires, oceans, or fields.

Animism as a religion also teaches that there is an impersonal spiritual energy that infuses some objects, words, and rituals, and such energy gives these objects the power that people want to fulfill their desires.

Humanism

Humanism as a religion is of very recent origin. One might not accept or classify humanism among the religions and spiritual traditions because it finds no proof or evidence of supernatural or transcendent realities. Humanism can be called the religion of the future, and all indications point to this. The concept of humanism as a religion of the future is catching up the imagination of many people around the world and there are many humanists who declare themselves to be religious humanists.

A humanist manifesto defines humanism as a "living and growing faith." Some people consider humanism as a philosophical movement. Humanism thus reflects clearly major significant and important attitudes and inclinations found in many modern societies.

According to humanism, traditional religions cannot help develop the full potential of men and women. What is required is an understanding of the needs of modern society, followed by the evolution of a system that will improve the quality of life and give meaning to life.

Humanism will be a major force in the next century, which is going to be a humanistic century. Scientific developments and information technology have revolutionized our way of life. Each and every aspect of modern life is affected by these developments. According to humanists, by careful use of all the modern technology, we can remove the poverty that prevails in many parts of the world. We can also find new medicines for many diseases and thus provide relief for those who are suffering. Further, we can improve the quality of life and provide humanity with great and new opportunities for achieving a meaningful and purposeful life. The many traditional moral codes and irrational cults will not meet the pressing needs of the future generation.

For humanity to survive and progress, bold and dynamic measures are required. By a judicious use of science and technology and understanding with love and compassion, new constructive social and moral values can be evolved. The ultimate goal of humanism should be the development of the individual to his or her full potential, the fulfillment of the potential for growth in each human being and not for a favored few.

A humanistic outlook will tap the creativity of each and every human being and ensure the vision and courage for a meaningful life. The years ahead will require dedicated men and women with a missionary zeal and enthusiasm, intelligence and courage, motivation and commitment, as well as the necessary skills for shaping a desirable future full of hope and faith.

Humanism is thus going to be the religion of the future. It will provide the purpose, enthusiasm, hope, understanding, and inspiration that so many seek. Humanism can thus give meaning, purpose, and significance to human life. In fact, many within religious groups believe in the future of humanism.

Humanism is thus an ethical process by which we move beyond the divisive dogmas, creeds, rituals, and customs of many religions. Humanism can usher in a secular society on a world scale, free from all ideological and moral codes that suppress freedom and ensure peace and harmony.

Humanism—Aims and Objectives

The latest manifesto on humanism has declared the aims and objectives of humanism. Some of the important aims and objectives are given below.

Humanists believe that traditional religions should be reinterpreted and reinvested with meanings consistent with the current social political and economic conditions. What are required are radically new human purposes and goals. While all of us must preserve the best ethical teachings in the religious traditions of humanity, we must reject outright all those features of traditional religious morality that prevent men and women from fully appreciating their potentialities and responsibilities.

Promises of salvation and damnation are demoralizing. They cause distraction and create tensions, social problems, and injustices. Traditional religions put obstacles in the way of human progress, understanding, and peace. Humanism ensures development of the individual to his or her full potential and the fulfillment of the potential for growth in every human being.

Moral values have their source from human experience. Ethics is autonomous, requiring no theological or ideological sanction since it stems from human need and interest. Happiness and realization of human needs and desires are continuous themes of humanism. The main objective of humanism is to strive for the good life now and pursue enrichment of life. Unlike traditional religions, which put up many restrictions and hurdles, humanism wants to provide men and women the purpose, enthusiasm, and inspiration to enable them to find fulfillment and happiness.

According to humanism, reason and intelligence are the most effective tools mankind possesses. Reason should be balanced with compassion and empathy. The dignity of the individual is the top priority in humanist values. All religious, ideological, and moral codes that denigrate and demoralize an individual and suppress his or her freedom should be totally rejected.

Another noteworthy objective of humanism is the right to birth control, abortion, and divorce. To develop intelligent awareness and understanding of sexual maturity, children should be given moral education. This will enable children to avoid all pitfalls and grow into healthy citizens.

Similarly, an individual should have a full range of civil liberties. This will ensure freedom and dignity for the individual. To achieve this objective, we must have an open, democratic society.

Another important aim is the separation of church and state. Similarly, the separation of ideology and state is imperative. To further the principle of moral equality, all discrimination based on religion, race, color, age, sex, or nationality should be eliminated

The world community should renounce violence and use of force as a method of resolving international disputes. The world community should engage in meaningful discussions and planning regarding the use of scarce natural resources. Humanists attach great importance to technology, and they consider that technology is vital for human progress and prosperity.

Chapter 13

John Paul II: An Apostle of Peace, Love, and Compassion & Unifier of World Religions

No study of world religions or global spirituality will be complete without studying the life, work, and achievements of a divine human being, a great leader of a great religion, a unifier of world religions, and a man of God—Pope John Paul II.

Never before in the history of mankind has a leader of a great religion united all of humanity into one loving family, proved that the essence of all the religions of the world is love and that all the nations of the world and its people could live in peace and harmony by practicing his message of peace, love, compassion, tolerance, and understanding. John Paul was a phenomenon. To him, all the religions of the world were the same. He made no distinction among the followers of different faiths. Throughout his life, John Paul preached the message of peace, love, and universal brotherhood. He stressed that the essence of all the religions of the world is love and that all the religions wanted their followers to practice love, peace, compassion, tolerance, and understanding. According to John Paul, all the religions of the world speak the same truth.

For people all over the world, John Paul was more than the spiritual leader of the world's Roman Catholics. To the Hindus, Sikhs, Buddhists, Zoroastrians, and Jains in India; Muslims in the Middle East; Jews in Israel; and followers of other faiths, John Paul was a symbol of peace, love, and compassion. Throughout Asia, Hindus, Muslims, Buddhists, Sikhs, Zoroastrians, and Jains joined Roman Catholics in church services and prayers to honor a great pontiff and a great human being.

John Paul brought people together by his message of peace, love, and compassion. In the early years of his pontificate, still young and strong, John Paul went to the very ends of the earth, guided by the message of Christ. As the world ambassador of peace and love, John Paul visited several countries in Asia, Africa, and Europe, reached out to people of different faiths, and conveyed the message of peace, love, and universal brotherhood.

None can ever forget how, on the last Easter Sunday of his life, John Paul, marked by weakness and suffering, came once more to the window of the Apostolic Palace, and one last time gave his blessings to the whole world.

The pope visited 129 countries during his lifetime. While taking papal diplomacy to great heights, he also reached out in unprecedented ways to leaders of other world religions. He was a great unifier who bridged the differences among world religions and brought peace, love, harmony, and compassion to a world torn apart by strife, hatred, and prejudice. John Paul was the very embodiment of the goodness of all religions.

In his death, as in his life, John Paul brought the entire world to the Vatican to witness a funeral that was unique, with the most extensive participation in the history of the world. Never before in history had there ever been a greater, more spectacular, and more grand funeral than the one for John Paul, with the participation of millions from all parts of the globe. An estimated two million people of various faiths stood in line for as many as fifteen to eighteen hours for the chance to walk by the pope's body as it lay in state.

The funeral of John Paul demonstrated something unique. It showed the greatness of the pope and how he was revered and cherished by all the people of the world, irrespective of their religious faiths. Further, it demonstrated that he was a unifier of world religions, proving that the essence of all religions is love. Finally, it showed how he tried to bridge the differences among world religions.

The funeral of John Paul was attended by seventeen reigning kings and queen, fifty-seven heads of state, thirteen representatives of international organizations, twenty-four ambassadors, and 142 non-Roman Catholic religious leaders, in addition to leaders from world religions and various religious organizations.

The funeral of Pope John Paul II was shown live on television in all parts of the world. In India, where most of the one billion people are Hindus, people wept for the pontiff. Many political and religious leaders praised the pope and urged the people to follow the path of peace and love shown by the pope. In Tokyo, the Dalai Lama, the spiritual leader of Buddhists, urged people to continue the pontiff's legacy of peace and love. He said, "Firstly, we have lost a great human being, a leader of a great religion. Now it is important that all of us should carry all his message and guidance with us. We must make every effort to fulfill his wishes." In the overwhelming Buddhist Sri Lanka, which the pope visited in 1995, people watched the funeral of a great world leader and wept for him. In the Middle East, people watched the funeral of a great man who tried to unite people of different faiths.

The funeral of John Paul brought about some miracles, proving the pontiff's message of peace and love will ultimately prevail. In death, as well as in life, the powerful message of universal peace, love, and brotherhood preached by the pope triumphed. Thus, during the funeral, the Israeli president shook hands and chatted with the leaders of Syria and Iran, who are the deadly enemies of the Jewish state. The French president, Jacques Chirac, who was a bitter critic of the U.S.-led war in Iraq, shook hands with the president of the United States. Britain's Prince Charles took the outstretched hand of Robert Mugabe, the president of Zimbabwe, who was criticized for human rights abuses. Such gestures of reconciliation during the funeral of John Paul showed once again how the message of peace and love propounded by John Paul changed the hearts of some of the world leaders.

As the people of all the world religions gathered in the early morning light near St. Peter's Square, some pilgrims, young, old, and sick, spoke about how all of them and millions of others felt about John Paul and why they were driven by a powerful force to attend the funeral.

A twenty-year-old Polish student, who traveled thirty hours by bus to attend the funeral, said, "I was touched by John Paul's humility, love, and compassion. John Paul changed my life. Now I want to live to share and help others. The pope is a person, who gave us love and showed us how to give love to other people. I feel love in the air. His great love for us."

A seventy-year-old priest from France who attended the funeral said, "This is the greatest saint of all two thousand years of the church. John Paul was the greatest pope that we ever had."

A Nigerian immigrant to Italy, who camped on the sidewalk for more than eighteen hours, said, "John Paul was very gentle, kind, and loving to us. He treated everyone as equal. His humbleness was what I admired most." A twelve year-old girl from Spain who attended the funeral said, "John Paul loved everyone. I love him."

Teeming millions came from all parts of the world, traveling days and nights, unmindful of the stresses and strains and driven by the one great desire of attending the funeral of a pope who was the embodiment of peace, love, harmony, and compassion. The millions who attended the funeral wanted to pay homage to a great leader, his character, his leadership, his ability to reach out and relate to people, his deep compassion, his great love for humanity. and his message of peace.

Pope John Paul II leaves behind a clear and rich legacy of peace, love, harmony, and compassion.

Creation of a New World Based on Love, Peace, Compassion, Tolerance, and Understanding

All of us live in a fast-changing, complex world with many cultures and religions. We live in a relative world. It is, therefore, imperative that we renew and review our approach to the Reality. We need to have more interaction, more exchange of ideas, more friendly discussions and debates in a spirit of trust, goodwill, and understanding in order to keep pace with the fast-changing circumstances of time.

The most striking and unique phenomenon of the modern age is the mingling of people, races, customs, cultures, and religions. Thanks to the wonderful great strides in modern science and information technology, time and distance have been bridged, and we are closer to each other than ever before. No person, culture, or religion can get away from the modern high technology and remain in isolation.

Another interesting feature is that the modern generation is appreciative of the various faiths. One need not give up one's own faith, but accept the spirit of others and assimilate those ideas. In other words, unity in diversity is the law of nature. It is also the imperative need of the hour.

Harmony of all faiths is a positive force that generates power to grow in one's own faith as well as to accept and understand the spirit of other faiths. No religion can claim the perfect channel into the ocean of divine wisdom, but religions are and should be complementary. The religions of the world are not contradictory or antagonistic to each other. They are but phases of one eternal religion, which existed all through eternity and will continue to exist forever. Therefore, it is the duty of every man and woman to accept all religions and try to accept them in a spirit of understanding, love, and goodwill. We must show by our lives that religion does not mean mere empty and high-sounding words, but spiritual realization and self-knowledge. In other words, the objective and purpose of religion is to enable a Christian to become a better Christian, a Muslim to become a better Muslim, a Hindu to become a better Hindu, a Jew to become a better Jew, and so on.

We have seen how all the religions of the world stress the importance of peace, love, compassion, tolerance, and understanding. According to the teachings of all the prophets, saints, and scriptures, these are the vital elements essential for the peaceful coexistence of people of different faiths and the progress of humanity, universal peace, harmony, and goodwill. Since all the religions are unanimous in expounding these vital elements, it is up to each one of us to strive by our personal example to build a society free from fear, fanaticism, hatred, and prejudice. By our thoughts and deeds, we should build a peaceful society based on trust, love, understanding, and cooperation.

How can we build such a society? This is a big question that stares us in the face. We are living in a world terrorized by religious fanatics and fundamentalists. In the name of religion, unthinkable atrocities are committed and continue to be committed on innocent men, women, and children, causing untold suffering, sorrow, pain, and misery to millions of innocent people all around the world. Look at any part of the world. What we see is so much manmade tragedy, suffering, and sorrow in the name of religion.

The holy city of Jerusalem is a standing monument of religious bigotry, prejudice, and hatred. The battle for the control of Jerusalem and its holy places has always provided passionate and often belligerent emotions from Jews, Christians, and Muslims. In the words of a historian, "Once an issue like Jerusalem is elevated beyond the reach of compromise, the more extreme and immoral actions become not only possible, but 'holy' to a disaffected minority." Lack of leaders of vision and humanity has resulted in death and destruction of a colossal scale for so many years in this Holy Land. In the words of late Pope, John Paul II, "It is the duty of believers—Jews, Christians, and Muslims—to seek every means to promote understanding and mutual trust in favor of peace for a land that God wanted holy." Unless and until Jewish, Christian, and Muslim leaders wedded to peace, goodwill, and love come together in a spirit of compromise, trust, and understanding, the holy land of Jerusalem will continue to be a source of perpetual friction, murder, mayhem, and misery. In the words of a research associate, "If Israel and Palestine are to begin to solve their conflict, then the recognition of a shared religious legacy is an imperative starting point. Judaism and Islam had a much greater chance of finding common ground than do Zionism and Palestine nationalism."

Thoughtless acts by a few misguided religious fanatics can ignite global passions and cause genocide. Like Jerusalem, there is a holy city in India called Ayodhya. This city is very holy to Hindus, since it is considered as the birthplace of Rama, the hero of the Hindu epic Ramayana, and whom Hindus worship as God. Ayodhya had also a historical mosque called Babri mosque, which was sacred to Muslims. Now, some Hindu extremists were of the view that a temple existed at the site where the mosque stood and that the temple was destroyed by the Mughul invaders long ago and a mosque was built in its place. So they pulled down the mosque and wanted to build a temple there, dedicated to Lord Rama. The destruction of the mosque resulted in a major Hindu-Muslim conflict all over India, resulting in senseless killings of innocents and causing destruction of property. The Ayodhya issue has not still been solved, and there is great mistrust, hatred, and misunderstanding between the followers of the world's two great religions. The fact that such a thing could happen in a secular country like India wedded to Gandhian ideals of nonviolence and respect for all religions is a reminder of how prejudice and lack of understanding and trust can cause so much suffering by the thoughtless acts of some misguided elements.

Then there are cases of state-sponsored persecution of religious minorities. The persecution of Zoroastrians, the followers of Zoroastrianism in Persia (now Iran), is an example. The Arab conquest in the seventh century resulted in the persecution of Zoroastrians and destruction of their scriptures and sacred books. Fearing death, many Zoroastrians took refuge in India, where they could peacefully practice their religion. Zoroastrianism took deep and strong roots in India, and the community flourished beyond all expectations.

Another glaring example is the persecution of Baha'is, followers of Bahaism and a peaceful law-abiding minority, by the Islamic Republic of Iran. Leading Baha'i leaders were put to death, and thousands have felt compelled to flee from their homeland.

Tibet is another example of state persecution. When Tibet was an independent state, Buddhism flourished in that country. Tibet was a land of Lamas, and almost the entire population followed and practiced Tibetan Buddhism. When Tibet became a part of China, the Communist government came down heavily on Buddhists and wanted to replace the Tibetan Buddhist culture with their own culture and way of living. The persecution by the Chinese forced the Dalai Lama, the spiritual leader, to flee to India with many of his followers.

It will be seen that instead of uniting people in peace, love, compassion, and understanding, religion has caused much havoc, suffering, and sorrow. This has been mainly due to the narrow and selfish vision of self-centered religious leaders who wanted power to promote their own interests. This is also due to ignorance of faiths other than one's own, resulting in suspicion, mistrust, misunderstanding, and prejudice. If religion is to bind people with unbreakable bonds, then the following steps have to be taken in slow and gradual stages.

The first and foremost step should be to combat terrorism and religious fanaticism. The wild fire of terrorism is raging unabated in various parts of the world. Before the fire consumes the entire world and causes further misery, sorrow and suffering, it is the duty of each one of us to put out this fire. If religion is to bind people with strong, unbreakable bonds of love, peace, compassion and goodwill, then the following steps should be taken:

1. Acts of terrorism committed by misguided religious fanatics are due to lack of understanding of the faiths other than their own. Ignorance breeds prejudice, hatred and violence. If in schools and colleges, students are taught about the existence of other religions and

the basic teachings of various religions, then they will not have any narrow mindset. Education broadens ones vision. If students are encouraged to read books on the leading religions of the world, they will know that the same truth is said in the Bible, the Quran, the Bhagavad-Gita, the Torah, Zoroastrianism, Buddhism, etc. Once the young minds realize that all the religions of the world speak the same truth, it will broaden their vision and create a sense of understanding and belonging with everybody.

2. Religion is peace and peace is religion. Without peace, there will not be any progress. All religious organizations, religious leaders and all religious clerics have their moral and social obligations to make sincere, dedicated and concerted efforts to spread their message of peace, love and harmony enshrined in all the religions. They should teach their followers to respect the faiths of others and practice tolerance, understanding and harmony.
3. The next important factor is the acute poverty prevailing in many countries. Poverty breeds violence and hatred. It is the recruiting ground for potential terrorists. Eradication of poverty should be the number one priority of all the developed and rich nations. Food, drinking water, shelter, etc should be provided to people who lack food and other basic amenities. Similarly, whenever there is natural calamity like an earthquake, flood or wild fire, steps should be taken immediately to rush aid to all the victims of such natural disasters.
4. Since many countries are a pluralistic society with great diversity in ethnicities, cultures and religions with various sects, the top priority should be to ensure communal harmony at all times. This can be achieved by cultivating the concept of interfaith, which will make everyone understand and respect other religions and their religious practices and coexist with tolerance, understanding, compassion, cooperation and love. When a peaceful and healthy environment of understanding and respect for other religions and some degree of tolerance is created, it will facilitate diverse social groups to work together for common good and thereby eliminate prejudice, hatred and violence. This will lead to peace and harmony among the various communities, irrespective of their individual faith, religious practice, customs and tradition. Once communal harmony is established, it will remove all the undesirable social ills such as fanaticism, extremism and terrorism. Communal harmony will ensure love, peace, understanding and harmony among the followers of different faiths. This will in turn bring prosperity, peace and progress. Every

country should, therefore give top priority for creating communal harmony, which alone will create a peaceful world.

5. Steps should be taken for separation of states from religion. In other words, politics should be divorced from religion. In a secular state, people of different faiths can all live in peace and follow their respective faiths without fear. In a secular country like India there are Hindus, Muslims, Christians, Jews, Sikhs, Buddhists, Jains, Zoroastrians, Baha'is and others, each following their respective faiths and practicing their religious practices peacefully. There are Hindu temples, Muslim mosques, Christian churches, Jewish synagogues, Sikh, Jain and Buddhist temples and in many cases these places of worship exist side by side. Such secularism promotes peace, love, compassion, goodwill and understanding among followers of different faiths. There have been instances of religious riots and fights between majority and minority communities. But by and large the secularism followed by India has stood the test of time and ensured religious tolerance, peace and harmony among people.

   On the other hand, in a theocratic state, the Government is run on a basis of particular religion. This will create two distinctive types of citizens, namely the favorite majority who follow the state religion and the minority faiths. Since the theocratic sate enforces the customs and practices of the state religion, the followers of other faiths feel insecure and this leads to mistrust, fear, and a sense of a helplessness and feeling of being second-class citizens. For ensuring peace and harmony the state should reach out to the minorities and make them feel secure. They should also provide educational and job opportunities for the minorities. The state, while following the state religion, should at the same time create a climate of peace, trust and goodwill among all sections of the population irrespective of their faiths.

6. The next important step is to teach the essentials of all the great world religions in all the schools throughout the world. Thus, in India with a predominant Hindu population, the children should be taught the beliefs and practices of Christianity, Islam, Buddhism, Judaism, etc. Similarly, in the Middle East, where children are mostly Muslims, they should be taught the basic knowledge of other religions. Likewise, in the western countries with a predominant Christian community, the school curriculum should include the basic teachings of all the other major religions. This will open the hearts of young, innocent minds to the concept of existence of religions other than their own. The child of today will be the citizen of tomorrow and some knowledge of religions other than his or her own

will enable creation of a climate of peace, trust and cooperation. This will be a major breakthrough and tremendous advancement in the context of the prevailing mistrust, prejudice, misunderstanding and hatred among the followers of different religions.

7. As a follow-up of education in schools and colleges of the great religions of the world, the next logical step should be to educate everyone of the importance and significance of religious festivals of all religions. Thus, all men, women and children should be briefed about the main religious festivals such as Christmas, Ramadan, Hanukah, Diwali, Buddha Jayanti, etc. In this connection, it is pertinent to point out the spirit of cooperation, spontaneous help and enthusiasm displayed by people of different faiths in India in celebrating the religious festivals of all faiths. This has created a feeling of brotherhood and goodwill among the followers of different faiths in India.
8. The next vital step is to strengthen the bonds of affinity and love and create a climate of peace, understanding and mutual trust through interfaith service. Interfaith service will bring about tremendous unity, trust, understanding and goodwill between followers of different religions. In this connection, I give below the views of some of the participants of an interfaith service, recently held in New Jersey, as reported by local newspapers: "About 70/80 people of Central Jersey's believers gathered at St. Paul's Church to weave a tapestry of faith, a blanket of hope created with hymns and prayers from world's major religions. They came to the annual Thanksgiving interfaith service with their arms outstretched and their hearts open to hear the words of faiths spoken and sung in several different languages. Christians, Hindus, Muslims, Jews, Sikhs and others shared the pulpit, offering prayers of conciliation and thanksgiving. Reading and hymns from the Christian and Hebrew scriptures, Hindu prayers, and Sikh hymns highlighted the evening. It was a great experience for all the participants, listening to so many different religions."
9. Another step to bring people of different faiths together is by encouraging interfaith marriages. Fortunately, the present generation of young men and women have broader visions of life. They are not shackled by the old religious dogmas and traditions. Exposed to different cultures in the work place and in the neighborhood, they have a modern and progressive outlook on life. This has resulted in considerable interfaith marriages all around the world.
10. Lastly, all the world leaders should unite and join together in creating world peace by preventing any religious wars in any part of the

> world. We have seen as to how prompt action by the world powers saved Bosnia. Wherever and whenever communal riots and religious killings take place, the world leaders should step in and nip them in the bud. It will be interesting to note how some of the recommendations made by the great spiritual leader Baha U'llah, founder of Bahaism, for universal peace and brotherhood are so very prophetic and relevant today. Baha U'llah said, "The principal reason of unrest among so many nations is the misrepresentation of religion by the religious leaders and teachers. They teach their followers to believe that their own form of religion is the only one pleasing to God and that flowers of any other persuasion are condemned by the All-Loving Father and deprived of His Mercy and Grace. Hence, arise among people disappointment, contempt, disputes and hatred. If these religious prejudices could be swept away, the nations should soon enjoy peace, harmony, and concord."

"Religion and science are like two wings upon which man's intelligence can soar into the heights, with which the human soul can progress. It is not possible to fly only with one wing. Should man try to fly with the wings of religion alone, he would quickly fall into the quagmire of superstition, while on the other hand, with the wing of science alone, he would also make no progress, but fall into the despairing slough of materialism."

"The community should strive with utmost zeal and endeavor to accomplish the education of men and women to cause them to progress and to increase in science and knowledge, to acquire virtue, to gain good morals and to avoid vices. If the community would endeavor to educate the masses, the understanding would be broadened, the sensibilities developed, customs would become good and morals normal. Thus, in all these classes of perfection, there would be progress and there would be fewer crimes."

Bibliography of Some Major Works Consulted

World Religions by Huston Smith. Founders of Great Religions by Burrows. Great Religions of the World by Severy. Wisdom of life by Codd Holy Bible by Zondervan Publishing House. Lessons from the Bible by David Peterson. Guide to the Bible by Stephen. Christianity by Issac. Crucible of Christianity by A.Toynbee. Christian Doctrine by Hausan. Catholic Faith by Johnson. Miracles of Saints by Bert Ghezzi.

Essence of Hinduism by Ravi Varma Hinduism by Ramdas. The Bhagavad Gita by Jayadalal. Bhagavad Gita by Suri. Gems form the Upanishads by Philip. Eastern Religions by Elizabeth Seiger. Essence of Hindu Philosophy by Sai Ram. Sayings of Hindu Mystics by Andrew Harvey Thirukkural by Teachers Publishing House. "Bhaja Govindam" by Purushotham Thirtha.

Islam by John Eposito. Islam by Calsan E.farah. Symbols of Islam by Wendal. History of Arabs by Philips K.H. Words of Faith by Rehman. Study of Islam by John Talbot. Islam by Mathew S.Gordon. Jewish Spirituality by Rabbi Laurence. Jewish Prayer by Hoffman. Story of Civilization by A.Durrant. Sufism by Mark.J.Sedgwict. Heart of Sufism by Hazrat Inayat Khan. The Wisdom of Islam by Robert Frazer. Buddhism by Richard.

World Religions by Dean Halvesse. Jewish Spiritual Guidance by Carol Kerry & Oiltzky. Sikhism by K.Singh. The Sikhs by Mcleod. Teachings of Guru Nanak by Avtar Singh. The Bahai Faith by Douglas Martin. Bahaism by Robert. The Bahai Faith by William S. Halahen. Baha' Ullah & New Era by J.E. Esslemal.

Tibetan Yoga by W.Y.Evens. Wisdom of Confucius by Lin Yutang. Sayings of Mahavir by Neal Robinson. Saman Suttam by Jitendra Varni. Essentials of Jainism by Atma Ram. Everyday Zen by Charlotte John Beck. Tibetan Book of Living & Dead by Sogyal Rinpoche. Phiosophy of Confucius by J.Legge. Manual of Buddhism by Narada Thera. Buddhism by H.Tsuji.

Mythology byJ.J.Williams. Buddhism by Richard. Great Asian Religions by George Fry. The Heart of Being by John Daido Zoon. South American Mythology by H.Osborne. Inner Peace by Joshi. Native American Religion by Paula R.Hartz Meditation by Anand. Spiritual Awakening by Duggal. Eastern Religions by Vincent. The Joy of Living by Mother Theresa.

Judaism by Arthur Hertzberg. Mixture of Shintoism & Buddhism by Hidenori Tsuji. Taoism and Lao Tsu by Gia-Fu feng &J. English. World Religions by G. Parrinder Hindu Gods and Rituals by Sekhar. Basics of Yoga by Purushotham. The Power of Prayer by Chinmayananda